Krause Publications

ORIENTAL
ANTI&QUES
ART *An Identification and Value Guide*

Sandra Andacht

Cover design: Anthony Jacobson
Interior layout: Anthony Jacobson
Editor: Tammie Taylor

Library of Congress Catalog Card Number 87-50296

ISBN 0-87069-485-5

10 9 8

Published by
Krause Publications
Iola, Wisconsin

Contents

Part II

Appendices

About the Author

Foreword

I feel greatly honored to be able to write this introduction. I have been privileged to be a collaborator and co-worker with Mrs. Andacht on *The Orientalia Journal* for the last five years. In this capacity, I continue to be impressed and often amazed at the breadth of her knowledge and her boundless enthusiasm. There have been rare occasions when she has been baffled by some item or other. However, like a tenacious bulldog, and with the aid of a large reference library and a circle of devoted friends and associates, she has persisted until the mystery was clarified. Aiding her in her monumental task are a fabulous memory and a natural gift of observation, so that the smallest details of various works of art are noted and entered into her mental computer.

The pricing (concluding values) of antiques is painfully difficult, being subject to the whims and vagaries of the marketplace. Reliance on the "prices realized" reports of reliable auction houses is one essential method of obtaining valid figures. Still, the wise reader will make allowances for psychological and economic variables when trying to judge the personal value of any item being considered for a collection.

Mrs. Andacht has still another virtue that enables her to render fair judgment in the task facing her. She can, at will, overcome the temptation to let personal likes and dislikes influence her judgments. Thus, insofar as it is humanly possible, Mrs. Andacht has been able to render impartial evaluations on all the pieces under consideration.

The amount of work entailed in constructing such a compendium of Orientalia and values has been truly beyond belief. The resulting effort is destined to become, and remain, for a long while, the gospel for collectors and aficionados worldwide.

Bernard Rosett

Acknowledgments

Articles
All of the articles contained in this volume have been reprinted with permission from the *Orientalia Journal*.

Line Art (Including Marks) and Art Direction
Carl Andacht

Photography
Daniel Stone Studios, Floral Park, NY, and Tom Edson (photographs of the Edson and Luhn collections)

A *special thanks* to the following for their contributions and support: Leon and Toni Andors, Richard A. Bowser, Lee Chinalai, Leonard Davenport, Tom and Kay Edson, Arthur Field, Liz Fletcher, Mark Fogel, Paul Fogelberg, Richard and Karen Goodman, Harold Jaffe, Howard and Florence Kastriner, Charles Kelly, Virginia Keresey, Larry Kiss, Dr. Michael B. Krassner, Richard Lambert, Steve Leonard, Ina Levy, David Migden, Carol Mohlenhoff, Raymond Nickel, Gardner Pond, Dr. and Mrs. Bernard Rosett, Mrs. Florence Simon, and Dr. and Mrs. Sam Sokolov.

The *author's appreciation* is also expressed to the Press and Oriental departments of Christie's and Christie's East, New York City.

Part I.

1

Apparel and Textiles

Chinese Apparel

Early Chinese apparel was characterized by upturned slippers, flowing robes, full sleeves, unshaped shoulders, and a center front opening. With the beginning of the Manchu dynasty, many fashion changes took effect: the shaved head and queue (long, hanging braid worn at the back of the head) replaced the Chinese topknot, for instance. The Manchu also redefined the style of clothing worn by both government and court officials, introducing slim belted trousers, boots, tight sleeves, close-fitting bodices (which overlapped on the front from left to right), horseshoe cuffs, and slits in the robes. The dragon robe, a semiformal court coat, was reserved for members of the Imperial family and for other nobles and officials. The five-clawed dragon was worn exclusively by the Emperor and his family.

Mandarin Square Insignia (Listed by Rank)

Rank	Civil Officials	Military Officials
First Order	Phoenix	Kylin
Second	Gold Bird (unidentified type)	Lion
Third	Peacock	Panther
Fourth	Crane	Tiger
Fifth	Pheasant	Bear
Sixth	Stork	Small Tiger
Seventh	Mandarin Duck	Rhinoceros
Eighth	Quail	Stork
Ninth	Paradise Flycatcher (similar to a sparrow)	Seahorse

The Manchu adopted the use of *mandarin squares*, badges worn to indicate rank. Civil officials wore various bird insignia, and animal insignia designated military officials (see above table). A solid square was used for the back of an outer jacket, and a split square (two halves) was worn across the open front. The badges were appliquéd in place and could be easily removed or changed as the wearer's rank was upgraded.

During the nineteenth century, wives of officials also wore mandarin squares. Their badges were mirror images of the ones worn by their spouses. For example, if an illustration shows a red sun disc on the upper right side of a mandarin square, then the square was worn by the wife of an official, since the husband's badge would show the disc at upper left.

Japanese Apparel

During the sixteenth through nineteenth centuries, Japan's economic growth stimulated the rise of urban centers, a wealthy merchant class, and a sophisticated bourgeois culture. The decorative and applied arts flourished, and textile design was among the supreme arts. Clothes featuring dazzling designs and made with fabric that demonstrated innovative weaving techniques indicated status and wealth for the men and women of the shogunal and imperial courts, as well as those of the wealthy merchant class.

In recent times, one particular Japanese garment that has become well known is the kimono. Originally a kosode (ladies' inner robe), it has evolved into a beautiful, elaborately decorated outer garment. This is how modern usage defines *kimono*, although the word is actually Japanese for *clothing*. Old kimonos make elegant hostess and lounging robes.

Obi (the cummerbund and back tie of the Japanese kimono) are just as collectible as the kimono. Today, there are a dozen or so uses for the obi. Often made of luxurious silk brocades with intricate patterns, they are ideal as wall hangings (panels) or converted into pillow covers.

Apparel and Textile Values

Altar frontal, red silk ground worked in shades of blue, green, and white with gold couching and peacock feather filaments; writhing dragon amidst clouds and secondary dragons above a wave band; cloud and lishui stripe; pleated short blue silk panels with peony roundels at the bottom; Chinese, late 19th century, 72" × 42", **$800–$1,200.**

Altar frontal; blue silk brocade, woven-in gilt braid; primarily pale oranges, greens, and blues; four-toed dragon above waves; narrow border of meandering lotus (below a fringe) woven with a pair of dragons; Chinese, late 18th century, 36" × 33", **$1,500–$2,200.**

Apron, green silk, front and back panels with couched gold dragons between phoenix and dragons on narrow pleats, Chinese, c1900, 36½" long, **$600–800.**

Banner, silk worked in colors; phoenix, cranes, lions, rock-work, flowers, fruit, and foliage on a red ground with green peacock feather filaments, all with a foliate gold-trimmed border; Chinese, c1900, 134" × 40", **$1,000–$1,500.**

Coat, pink brocade (Benares), long flaring form with gold meandering flowers on a ground of pink floral sprigs, quilted lining, Indian, c1920, 54" long, **$500–$600.**

Coat, blue broadcloth (Ainu) with lighter blue stitched pattern on the edges, Japanese, late 19th century, **$2,000–$3,000.**

*Appliqué picture, framed, hand-painted silk, the kites with real feathers, Japanese, Meiji period, frame size 11" × 15¾", **$550–$750.***

Dragon robe, silk, burgundy with gold couched dragons and Shou medallions; frayed cuffs, Chinese, c1900, 53" long, **$600–$900.**

Dragon robe, silk; couched gold dragons amidst clouds, bats, 100 Antiques, peaches; hem with rolling waves satin-stitched over the lishui in blue, peach, white, and yellow; Chinese, late 18th/early 19th century, 56" long, **$1,000–$1,500.**

Dragon robe, silk; light blue with couched gold dragons and clouds, bats, and peonies detailed in Peking knots; wide lishui stripe with waves, Chinese, late 19th century, 52" long, **$500–$700.**

5

Dragon robe, silk, sienna with Peking knotted motif of 100 Antiques and gold couched dragons with blue, satin-stitch clouds; Chinese, c1900, 50" long, **$700–$900.**

Elbow cushion covers, silk brocade worked in peach, yellow, and red-orange stylized lotus on a gray ground; Chinese, early 20th century, 8½" × 9", **pair, $600–$800.**

Jacket, silk, pink with red and white painted flowers, Japanese, early 20th century, 42" long, **$100–$125.**

Jacket, silk, ivory with autumnal painted flowers and embroidered leaves, Japanese, early 20th century, 38" long, **$185–$225.**

Jacket, silk, black with red lining and a white mon, Japanese, early 20th century, 40" long, **$200–$250.**

Jacket, silk, blue ground embroidered with gold couched floral medallions above couched gold and silver waves and lishui stripe, Chinese, 19th century, 39" long, **$1,000–$1,500.**

Jacket, silk, black with gold and silver couched double gourds and Shou medallions, Chinese, late 19th/early 20th century, 44" long, **$1,000–$1,300.**

Jacket, summer gauze, yellow with white sleeve bands and cloud collar embroidered with figures and flowers, Chinese, mid-to-late 19th century, 39" long, **$1,700–$2,000.**

Kimono, silk, pale purple with irises, early 20th century, **$350–$450.**

Kimono, silk crêpe, black with red lining, white chrysanthemums overall, early 20th century, **$150–$250.**

Kimono (wedding), silk, white with embroidered silver and gold cranes with prunus flowers, 20th century, 6'4" long, **$1,500–$2,500.**

Kimono, silk crêpe, pink chrysanthemums embroidered on a light blue ground, fringe on sleeves, early 20th century, **$400–$600.**

Kimono, silk, embroidered gold dragon and clouds overall, silk lining, black ground, early 20th century, **$700–$900.**

Kimono, silk, burgundy with embroidered wisterias and foliage, early 20th century, **$500–$700.**

Mandarin square, gold satin stitches and Peking knots, quail on rock-work, Chinese, late 19th century, 12" × 12", **$275–$325.**

Mandarin square, gold couching and Peking knots with satin stitches in colors, peacock, Chinese, c1900, 11" × 12", **$225–$275.**

Mandarin square, Peking knots and gold couching on a black ground, lion, Chinese, late 19th century, framed size 15" × 15", **$250–$300.**

Mandarin square, satin stitches and couching in white and gold, crane, framed within a carved rosewood-handled tray, Chinese, late 19th century, tray size 12" × 16", **$300–$375.**

Obi, silk, gold needlework with phoenix and pines in colors on a green ground, early 20th century, **$200–$300.**

Obi, silk, fans (all forms, including single stick) in colors on a gold ground, early 20th century, **$250–$375.**

Obi, silk, cranes and flowers in colors on a white ground, early 20th century, **$300–$400.**

Obi, silk brocade, gold and silver threads, floral motif with baskets of flowers, gold ground, c1900, **$450–$600.**

Obi, silk brocade, Three Friends (pine, plum, and bamboo) motif in greens, blues, and browns on an ecru ground, Meiji period, **$700–$900.**

Obi, silk brocade, black ground, cranes and fans in gold and colors, c1900, **$350–$450.**

Obi, silk brocade, riverscape in colors and gold, late 19th century, **$350–$450.**

Panel embroidered in silk threads, figures playing blind man's bluff, Japanese, c1910, framed size 9" × 12", **$300–$400.**

Panel embroidered in metallic silver and gold threads, peony blossoms and foliage on a tan ground, Japanese Edo period, early 19th century, framed size 36" × 36", poor condition, **$300–$400.**

Panel, silk-stitched tapestry (colors), 100 Children motif, red ground, Chinese, late 19th century, framed size 90" × 56", **$1,500–$2,200.**

Panel, silk kesi worked with figures in a scenic motif including a garden and pavilion on a blue ground, frayed borders, Chinese, 19th century, framed size 25" × 70", **$2,000–$3,000.**

Panel, silk kesi, the Immortals wandering about the Hills of Longevity; red, green, pale peach, and blue; Chinese, first half of the 19th century, framed size 72" × 45", **$5,000–$7,000.**

Panel, silk kesi woven with phoenix, flowers, streams, attendants, and four guardian patches with flowers and phoenix on a red-orange ground; frayed, new backing, Japanese, late Meiji period, framed size 72" × 40", **$1,200–$1,700.**

Panel, silk kesi, figures and pavilion in a garden on a blue ground, frayed borders, Chinese, 19th century, framed size 26" × 78", **$2,500–$3,500.**

Panel (door), silk squares with figures of the Immortals, 100 Antiques in black satin borders, Chinese, 19th century, 82" × 80", **$2,800–$3,300.**

Panel, silk with embroidered standing cranes in shades of gray, white, ivory, and silver in a marsh scene, Japanese, Meiji period, framed size 72" × 86", **$3,500–$4,500.**

Panel, cotton, gold leaf appliqué, central panel with applied flowering plants in gold leaf on a navy ground, border with profuse meandering floral designs, cotton lining, Indian, late 18th/early 19th century, 50" × 60", **$1,500–$2,000.**

Pillow, silk brocade, Imperial yellow, metallic gold dragon in center with a floral diapered ground worked in peach, blue, and green; Ch'ien Lung (Qianlong), 18th century, 26" high, **$2,000–$3,000.**

Priest's robe woven with motifs of phoenix, Shishi, and peony blossoms with dragons, Japanese, late Edo period, c1800, 45" × 78", **$1,200–$1,800.**

Priest's robe, floral pattern with applied brocade, Japanese, late 18th/early 19th century, 45" × 80", **$2,000–$3,000.**

Scenic picture, framed, embroidery on silk, satin-stitched in autumnal hues, Japanese, c1910, framed size 20" × 16", **$550–$775.**

Priest's robe, silk brocade, gilt thread with Buddhist wheels and trellis pattern, six applied square patches woven with floral roundels, Japanese, late 18th/early 19th century, 82" × 46", **$1,200–$1,600.**

Priest's robe, silk brocade, gilt and colors with bird and flower motif, Japanese, early 19th century, 51" × 52", **$1,000–$1,600.**

Robe, silk, blue with stitched irises, skirt tapering outward, cuffed sleeves, Chinese, late 19th century, 54" long, **$1,200–$1,500.**

Robe, silk, dark blue with satin-stitched motif of circular medallions featuring a pair of dragons, sleeves and hem embroidered with peony and plum blossoms, Chinese, late 19th/early 20th century, 54" long, **$1,200–$1,500.**

Robe, silk, embroidered with couched gold and knotted motifs of stylized flowers on a patterned red ground filled with satin-stitched butterflies, Chinese, c1900, 41" long, **$700–$900.**

Robe, silk, fur lining; red ground with pale blue, lavender, and salmon butterflies with black borders; separate collar piece, Chinese, late 19th century, 50" long, **$1,000–$1,500.**

Embroidered silk scissors case embellished with glass beads, Chinese, c1910, $100–$125.

Robe, silk, informal, satin-stitched with flowers in colors on a red ground, Chinese, late 19th century, 55" long, **$700–$1,000.**

Robe, silk, red with satin-stitched roundels of 1000 Flowers motif, sleeves embroidered with birds and butterflies, Chinese, c1920, 54" long, needs some work, **$800–$1,200.**

Robe, silk, couched dragons in gold on a pale orange ground (the dragons worked on deep blue medallions), Chinese, late 19th century, 55" long, some fading, **$1,000–$1,500.**

Robe, silk, informal, quilted red with scattered floral sprays and black borders embroidered with flowers, Chinese, late 19th century, 55" long, **$1,500–$2,100.**

Robe, silk gauze (summer garment) satin-stitched with large floral medallions on a red ground, wide sleeves in deep blue worked with floral roundels, Chinese, c1900, 53" long, **$1,500–$2,000.**

Robe, silk gauze, red couched gold dragons and clouds, Chinese, late 19th century, 55" long, **$900–$1,500.**

Robe, wool/felt, red ground worked with a pattern of white cranes in flight, wide cuffs worked in butterflies, Chinese, late 19th century, 52" long, **$900–$1,250.**

Embroidered silk brocade seat cover, gold ground with colors, the motif featuring five cranes and tortoise diapers, the tassels in the form of long-tailed tortoises, Japanese, early Meiji period, 24½" × 28", $1,800–$2,200.

Saddle cover, ivory ground with a pair of scalloped floral medallions and scattered floral sprays surrounded by an ivory primary border and two navy blue guard borders, Tibetan, late 19th / early 20th century, 4'7" × 2'7", **$800–$1,200.**

Scroll, satin ground embroidered with three laughing figures; orange, blue, and yellow; Chinese, 17th century, 58" × 24", **$1,750–$2,500.**

Silk hanging, red with multicolored embroidery in the satin stitch, trimmed, border not original, Chinese, c1900, 100" × 65½", **$1,200–$1,800.**

Scroll embroidered in satin stitches with a motif of peonies and rock-work in blues, ivory, and yellow; Chinese, late 17th / early 18th century, 30" × 15", **$1,700–$2,500.**

Seat cover embroidered on the front in gold and colored threads with three cranes and foliage, four gold kame tassels, Japanese, Meiji period, 20" × 21", **$1,200–$1,500.**

Seat cover, Imperial yellow, silk with satin-stitched lotus, Chinese, 18th century, Ch'ien Lung (Qianlong), 21" wide, **$1,200–$1,500.**

Shawl, rectangular, foliate boteh projecting from each corner, numerous stylized plants forming border, two rectangular panels of botehs flanking the red field, numerous floral motifs on grounds of green, blue, mustard and red, Indian, late 19th century, 11" × 4½', **$600–$800.**

Shawl, embroidered silk crêpe, rose with large peony at each corner, smaller flowers overall, some fringe remaining (but otherwise good condition), Chinese, c1925, 64" × 64", **$1,500–$1,800.**

Shawl, silk crêpe, black with embroidered flowers, butterflies, and Shou symbols overall, no fringe, Chinese, c1925, 60" × 60", **$700–$900.**

Shawl, silk, white with varied red roses overall, Chinese, c1930, 30" × 30", **$200–$300.**

Skirt, red silk, front and back panels decorated with foo dogs and Precious emblems, side pleats with dragon heads, Chinese, c1900, 36" long, **$700–$900.**

Theater costume, red silk, gold couching and satin-stitched florets, sleeves embroidered with lotus and lions, bats on waist, Chinese, 18th century, 50" long, **$3,500–$4,500.**

Wall hanging, blue cloth, dyed motif of Three Friends with mon, Japanese, 19th century, 60" long, **$300–$500.**

2

Armor, Weaponry, and Accoutrements of the Japanese

Beginning in 800 A.D. with the first sword of recorded date, there have been many thousands of swordsmiths who dedicated their lives just to the production of the blade. When the sword was several hundred years old, various schools began to concentrate on the production of decorative fittings (sword furniture). From this development, the sword has come to be considered an art form in which technical advances in metallurgy combined with great skill produce magnificent objects of beauty.

The following article, which addresses this aspect of the Japanese sword, should be of interest to both neophytes and long-term collectors/dealers. For detailed information about the terminology used, see the Glossary.

Connoisseurship of the Japanese Sword: How Not to Get Stuck

David Migden

The motive behind this article is an often-repeated one. Recently, I received a telephone call with regard to a Japanese sword. The glowing description, of course, inspired great interest on my part. I requested that the caller send photographs of the sword. When the photos finally arrived, I wondered if I was deaf or had been sent the wrong set of pictures! At least I hadn't driven 200 miles to check the sword.

Granted, definitive knowledge of any one facet of art or antiques is a worthy goal, but most of us don't have the time for such devoted study. For a dealer, collector, investor, or lucky inheritor, the best path is to develop an eye for the optimum. In whatever you choose to collect, buy, and/or sell, learn what is best. I am not saying one should reject anything lesser; just try to develop the perspective of artistic merit. The "eye" will keep you from that poke of embarrassment. I am not professing an "I don't know art, but I know what I like" attitude. This is a step above: developing the "eye" is "I know what I like and I know why." It is knowledge laid on intuition, and will prevent any collector from loading his or her cabinets with things that are loathed the day after purchase.

Definitive knowledge is an easy jump from the knowledge of form. Form is the main criteria for best of type. Form comes from manufacture (even a machine-made, twentieth-century object can be the best of its kind, if the designer's innovation was truly transmitted to the finished piece).

The Japanese sword blade is so esoteric an art object, it defies clear thinking. It is an object overlain with phallic significance; it is a killing machine, and its masters were copied and faked from the time they were made into the twentieth century. Forget about signatures! Signatures are the last consideration. The early-nineteenth-century swordsmith Suishinshi Masahide wrote that at one period he experimented with alloys and the blade he produced in that time is worthless. Masahide meant worthless as a weapon. I have owned one of those blades and it was truly ugly.

The Japanese sword expert should first hold the blade upright with his right arm extended. He must use light to integrate the qualities of forging and tempering as they enhance the overall form of the sword. Most collectors and dealers "ooh and aah" over a widely patterned temper-line or large, swirling grain. They miss the point. Temper and grain were controlled by the master smiths for the strength of form and spirit that made a great weapon. In Japan, the blades of the Hizen school are highly sought after. The forging of this school is a pearskin (no ripples to amaze the eye) and the tempering is straight. The Hizen blade is generally stout, robust, and immaculate.

It is best to have the "eye" in appraising a Japanese sword because most of the time you will find that it is out of condition. Then your eye looks beyond rust and grime to discern its worthiness. These swords were polished many times and a blade that is a mere shadow of its original self must also have a thinner value (no matter who signed it).

Values

Armor

Armor; a composite comprising 12 plates, black lacquered sujibako kabuto with kinen-jikoro, and a black lacquered hishiniui-do with kusari-kesan, kusari-goto, brown lacquered hambo, and a kusari-shitage; late 18th/early 19th century, **$1,500–$2,000.**

Kabuto, pear-shaped, leather, the bowl decorated with red and gilt lacquer motif of a flying dragon and waves, 18th century, **$300–$500.**

Swords

Aikuchi tanto; soft metal fittings; the wari-kogai and kozuka decorated with gilt bellflower mon; the hilt brass-covered and decorated in copper, sahari, and shakudo takazogan with gourds and vines; fitted with a 19th-century blade (kashira missing); unsigned; 15" long, **$600–$800.**

Aikuchi tanto; mumei blade; shallow sori; wide and narrow grooves each side; ko-itame jihada and kobushigata hamon; two mekugiana; kuroronuri saga decorated in aogai and togidashi with kiri leaves, flowers; the kojiri, kurikata, koiguchi, kozuka, and fuchi-kashira all of silver; the tsuba bound in whale fiber; finely carved dogan depicting phoenix and clouds; signed *Sanchiko*; late 19th century, 11½" long, **$6,000–$8,000.**

Katana blade inscribed *Misashi no Kami Morimichi*, in shrasaya, with koshirae and tsunagi; honzukuri and shallow torii-zori with mixed hada, gonome hamon, midare-komi boshi, and ubu nakago; 19th century, 64" long, **$1,050–$1,350.**

Katana with unsigned blade; honzukuri and torii-zori with short, wide and narrow grooves, the details obscured by scratching; kuroronuri scabbard decorated in hiramakie; copper fuchi-kashira with birds; cherry blossom menuki; and iron Mito tsuba with cherry blossom design; 17th century, 40½" long, **$700–$1,000.**

Tachi mounted in cloisonné, phoenix, and paulownia in colors on a black ground; bronze fittings engraved with phoenix and paulownia on ishime ground; the kabuto-gane of silver in the form of a phoenix head with sentoku eyes, unsigned, c1900; the blade, honzukuri, hagagissaki, and torii-zori with choji hamon (scratches obscure the forging details); ubu nakago inscribed *Bishu Osafune ju nin Yokoyama kozuki Daijo Fujiwara Sukesada*; 19th century, 33½" long, **$8,000–$12,000.**

Wakizashi inscribed *Satsuyo-shi Oku Motoyasu, hyowa sannen* (date: 1803), but made later; honzukuri, hagagissaki, and torii-zori with midare hamon of nie extending to ji and ara-nie clusters; in kiroronuri scabbard with soritsuno and unbound hilt with iron fuchi and tsuba (other mounts missing); 36¾" long, **$900–$1,200.**

Wakizashi blade, shallow torii-zori, one mekugiana, dated 1362, 15" long, **$500–$700.**

Sword Furniture

Fuchi-kashira; shakudo-shimeji; decorated with three dragonflies in gilt, copper, and silver; inlaid shell eyes; signed *Jochiku*; 18th century, **$700–$900.**

Fuchi-kashira, shakudo decorated with gilt dragons and waves, late 19th century **$300–500.**

Fuchi-kashira, shibuichi, decorated with shakudo and gilt phoenix, late 19th century, **$200–$300.**

Kozuka; shakudo-nanako ground; gilt, silver and shakudo takazogan of two ladies amidst flowers and foliage near a stream; late 18th/early 19th century, **$500–$600.**

Kozuka, shakudo-nanako ground, gilt and silver herons, 19th century, **$250–$350.**

Kozuka, shakudo-nanako ground, iro-e takazogan of warriors battling on a bridge; details in gilt, copper, silver, shakudo, and shibuichi; unsigned, 19th century, **$400–$600.**

Kozuka; shakudo-nanako ground; applied iro-e takazogan of grasses, kiku, and flowers in gilt, silver, and shibuichi; unsigned, 19th century Goto School, **$250–$500.**

Menuki, copper, in the form of vines and leaves with gilt details, **$100–$125.**

Menuki, gold, in the form of Fudo Mio holding a ken while standing on a rock before a flaming background, **$1,400–$1,800.**

Menuki, shakudo, the pair in the form of abalone shells, gilt details, **$200–$300.**

Menuki, shakudo, iro-e takazogan birds on ishime ground, **$400–$500.**

Tsuba, iron, circular, triple paulownia design with rounded chrysanthemum-shaped rim (Rakujie 1817–1884), 3¼" diameter, **$1,800–$2,500.**

Tsuba, iron, formed as a coiled serpent, eyes and tongue gilded, signed *Goto seiji*, mid-19th century, 3¾" diameter, **$1,200–$1,500.**

Tsuba, iron, circular, two cats and fish in a square rim, 18th century, 3½" diameter, **$600–$800.**

Tsuba, iron, square with rounded corners, decorated with two dragonflies—their eyes in silver and shibuichi, 19th century, 3½" diameter, **$600–$800.**

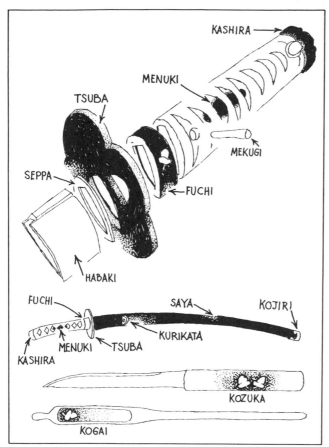

KASHIRA

MENUKI

TSUBA

MEKUGI

SEPPA

FUCHI

HABAKI

FUCHI — SAYA — KOJIRI

KURIKATA

MENUKI — TSUBA

KASHIRA

KOZUKA

KOGAI

Tsuba, iron, shaped like Hotei's treasure bag, the treasures rendered in cloisonné, Hirata school, 3" diameter, **$1,200–$1,500.**

Tsuba, sentoku, square with rounded corners, decorated with a kingfisher perched on a lotus stalk, fish swimming on the reverse, signed *Shoryusai Tsuneyuki*, late 19th century, 3½" diameter, **$1,200–$1,800.**

Tsuba, sentoku, oval, a hawk above a pine branch with two birds in flight, 19th century, 2¾" diameter, **$300–$400.**

Tsuba, shakudo, motif of frog in takazogan, late 19th century, 2¾" diameter, **$250–$350.**

Tsuba, shakudo, motif of Sennin, 19th century, 2½" diameter, **$200–$300.**

Tsuba, shakudo-nanako, insects and plants in Minbori with gilt dragons on the rim, 17th century, 3¾" diameter, **$800–$1,200.**

Tsuba, shibuichi, circular, Minamoto no Yoshire looking at a cherry tree at the Nakoso barrier, iro-e takazogan, signed *Soiken Masaharu kizamuk Kore*, 19th century, 2¾" diameter, **$1,500–$2,000.**

Other Weaponry and Accoutrements

Bow, bamboo and lacquer, signed *Masayoshi*, 88" long, **$800–$1,200.**

Left: Iron tsuba (sword guard) with inlaid motifs of a fisherman and pole, fish, grasses, and bird; silver and gold; 19th century, **$500–$700**. Right: Shibuichi tsuba (sword guard) with inlaid motif of a boy playing a flute while riding a water buffalo, 19th century, **$1,500–$1,800.**

Matchlock gun, octagonal barrel, garlic muzzle, sahari hirazogan motif of warriors, signed *Senshu ju Tsutsuzemon Shokichi saku*; wood stock, brass engraved with cloud motifs; 17th century, barrel length 96", **$1,500–$2,000.**

Matchlock pistol, iron barrel decorated with dragons in silver nunome-zogan, signed *Tamba no komi* (for decoration), signed *Ashu Todatatsu no Suke saku* (for barrel), oak stock, ramrod; brass match holder, pan cover, and lock plate; 17th century, 15" long, **$2,500–$3,500.**

Powder flask, lacquer on leather, copper mouth with gilt circular motif, 19th century, 6" high, **$250–$350.**

Powder flask, keyaki wood, circular with bone stopper, 19th century, 7½" high, **$400–$600.**

Powder flask, bamboo, staghorn stopper, 19th century, 6" high, **$200–$300.**

Powder horn, wood and staghorn, eggplant shape with wood and metal kagamibuta netsuke, mid-19th century, 6" long, **$600–$700.**

Stirrups (abumi), iron inlaid with silver and brass motifs of Shishi, first half of the 19th century, **$700–$900.**

Sword stand for daisho swords, gilt and black lacquer, scenic motif, 20" long, **$600–$800.**

3

Chinese Porcelain and Pottery

Chinese Export Porcelain

In the West, the introduction of wares known as *Chinese export porcelain* dates from the late seventeenth century, during the K'ang Hsi period. The Portuguese were the first to bring this porcelain to Europe, and Dutch traders successfully followed their example. In 1784, the China Empress landed in Macao near Canton (where the porcelain was decorated after its manufacture at Ching te chen). Shortly afterward, blue and white porcelain was shipped to America, where demand for these wares matched the high levels already reached in Europe.

Left: *Covered oval tureen, Chinese export blue and white, ribbed body, domed lid, applied leaf-and-peach handle, floral sprigs and key fret border at the cusped rim, the sides flanked by lion mask handles, a flaring foot, Ch'ien Lung, 18th century, 13" long (over handles). Realized price, Christie's East, New York City,* **$1,045.** Right: *Covered oval tureen, Chinese export famille rose, the domed cover with a pomegranate finial, the body enameled with peacocks perched on rock-work surrounded by leafy peonies within scrolling foliate border, the sides similarly decorated and flanked by iron red hare's head handles, 18th century, 11¾" long. Realized price (including the 10-percent buyer's premium), Christie's East, New York City,* **$1,760.**

Canton blue and white flourished during the eighteenth and nineteenth centuries, although there was no production from approximately 1839 to 1850 because of the Opium Wars.

The quality of this porcelain ware varies because of the way it was fired: The very coarse pieces were placed just beyond the door of the kiln so that they could screen or shield the better-quality ones against the intense heat. As a result, lesser-quality pieces have a residue—ash, for example—embedded in the porcelain. *Oatmeal* is the term used to describe these off-color wares. In addition, the varied intensities of heat within the kiln changed the blue pigment, causing some Canton blue and white to be pale blue, and some, almost black, with a number of hues in between.

The motifs found on these wares incorporate some or all of the following elements in various combinations: an island, a bridge or bridges, trees, birds, mountains, rocks, figures, clouds, boats, and a river.

Canton blue and white platter, 13½" diameter, **$300–$450.**

Nanking blue and white has motifs similar to those used in Canton blue and white; the difference between the two wares is found in the border. Canton blue and white has a blue lattice or network outer border, sometimes overworked with a primitive star pattern and an inner pattern of wavy lines. These wavy lines, called *clouds*, enclose a diagonal lined pattern called *rain*. Thus, the Canton border is referred to as *rain and clouds.*

Nanking flagon, Buddhistic lion finial, orange-peel glaze, 11½" high, **$900–$1,500.**

The Nanking border, on the other hand, is diapered on the outer edge, sometimes with a geometric, diamond-based pattern, and contains an inner border of spearheads.

Note, too, that the term *Nanking* was used by the English in the eighteenth century to denote better-quality Canton blue and white.

Fitzhugh is a pattern which may be found in red, sepia, blue, orange, green, and black, but basic Fitzhugh is blue and white, and was produced at the same time as Canton and Nanking, as well as in the same place. Sometimes its pattern elements are gilt-outlined or trimmed with gilt borders. A circular medallion adorns the center of the Fitzhugh pattern (from time to time, the medallion was replaced, by special order, with an eagle or monogram). While the border is generally post and spear, it can also be varied.

Other characteristics of this porcelain include four panels of floral designs, and a wide border broken in several areas and filled with diaper patterns. One Fitzhugh border contains a trellis with four split pomegranates showing fruit inside. Some of the diapered symbols are shaped like butterflies with their wings spread.

Armorial (or heraldry) pattern export wares date from the end of the K'ang Hsi period, c1695. Armorial designs were specially ordered: scenes replicated from European prints; ship motifs; figurines; animals; birds; and so on (border patterns also vary). The East India Company processed orders in Ching te chen and the porcelain blanks were sent to be decorated at Canton.

Famille Rose

Toward the end of the eighteenth century, export wares in the famille rose palette became increasingly popular in the West. The wares made for export were styled after the European mode of the times, with many of the patterns containing western or European figures. Other patterns contained Chinese and Mandarin figures; animals and fowl of all kinds were prominent in the designs. Shapes included animal-form tureens and garniture sets comprised of two beaker-shaped vases and three to five covered jars.

Most of the patterned wares date from the end of the Chia Ch'ing period and were developed in the early nineteenth century.

Punch bowl, Chinese export famille rose, gilt and painted in colors including puce and iron red with figures gathered at leisure by pavilions, late 18th century, Ch'ien Lung, 13¼" diameter, rim chips, **$1,500– $2,000.**

Left and right: A pair of famille rose models of the Hoho Erxian, each standing, dressed in a floral robe and holding a gilt and iron red ruyi sceptre in one hand, the other hand with fruit-laden peach spray, damages, late Ch'ien Lung, 8" high. Realized price (including the 10-percent buyer's premium), Christie's East, New York City, **$825.** Center: Covered oval sauce tureen; Tobacco Leaf; slightly domed lid with gilt-decorated, iron red finial; the oval bombe body with gilt, intertwined strap handles and decorated in bright colors with veined leaves and stylized flower heads; minor fritting to handle; late Ch'ien Lung; 5½" diameter. Realized price (including the 10-percent buyer's premium), Christie's East, New York City, **$1,760.**

Chinese export porcelain plaque of a standing Pu Tai, famille rose, orange-peel glaze, first half of the 19th century, set in its original hardwood frame, framed size 16" × 21", $1,000–$1,500.

Rose Medallion is a pattern which contains alternating reserves of birds and/or flowers and figures around a central floral medallion. Most pieces are decorated with four reserves. The space between the reserves is filled with pink peony blossoms and green tendrils on a gilt ground.

Rose Canton is the same as Rose Medallion, with the exception of the figures. Rose Canton contains absolutely no figures. The pattern has alternating panels or reserves of butterflies and flowers.

Additional patterns in the famille rose palette include the following:

Rose and Long Life
One large peony with a bird perched on a branch.

One of a pair of Rose Medallion baluster vases, mid-19th century, each decorated with panels of court ladies and alternating panels of figures in interiors with birds and fruiting, flowering boughs on a gilt and green ground, the neck flanked with Buddhistic lion-form handles, the shoulder with applied kylins, one heavily restored, chips to both, 35½" high. Realized price (including the 10-percent buyer's premium), Christie's East, New York City, $3,520.

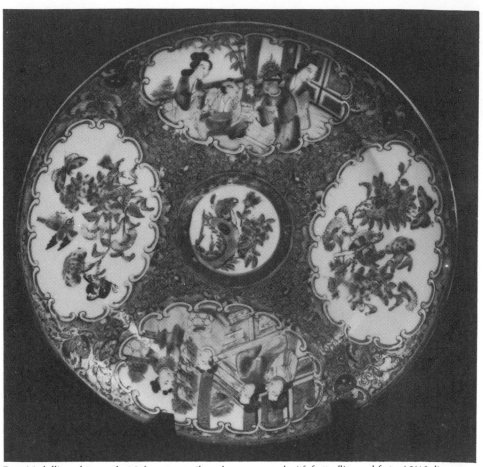

Rose Medallion plate, early 19th century, gilt and green ground with butterflies and bats, 10¼" diameter, **$225–$325.**

Rose Medallion soup bowl, c1885, 9" diameter, **$200–$275.**

Japanese Cloisonné
Left to right: Shallow rectangular tray with two finches on bamboo before the rising moon, the reverse with a design of cherry blossoms, silver mounts, signed Namikawa Sosuke, 12" × 10", sold at Christie's, New York City—realized price (including the 10-percent buyer's premium), **$8,800;** baluster vase with a bird perched on a leafy branch above flowering chrysanthemums, silver rims, signed Kyoto Namikawa, sold at Christie's, New York City—realized price (including the 10-percent buyer's premium), **$1,980;** globular-form covered jar with domed lid and brass bud finial, copper wire with birds flying among lilies, morning glories, daisies, and hydrangeas, signed Kyoto Namikawa, 4" high, sold at Christie's, New York City—realized price (including the 10-percent buyer's premium), **$1,045;** incense burner and cover, baluster form, five cabriole feet, pierced dome cover, 5¾" high, signed Kyoto Namikawa, sold at Christie's, New York City—realized price (including the 10-percent buyer's premium), **$12,100.**

Snuff Bottles

Front row, left to right: *Snowflake glass with red overlay motifs of 100 Antiques, 18th century,* **$1,200–$1,600;** *famille rose porcelain bottle with motifs in relief, late 18th / early 19th century,* **$900–$1,200;** *I Hsing cylindrical bottle, blue ground with flowers and birds, late 18th / early 19th century,* **$800–$1,200;** *porcelain bottle, a dragon on one side and a phoenix on the reverse, molded in high relief, Tao Kuang period,* **$1,800–$2,500.**

Second row, left to right: *Silver bottle with flower and bird motifs in low relief, Ch'ien Lung mark (and of the period),* **$2,000–$3,000;** *inside-painted crystal bottle signed Yeh Chen San, continuous motif of fish and aquatic plants, the exterior carved with sea animals, carved ears,* **$2,500–$3,500.**

Back row, left to right: *Amethyst bottle carved in high relief, early 20th century,* **$1,200–$1,800;** *lapis lazuli bottle in the form of a carp, 20th century,* **$700–$900;** *pear-shaped clear glass bottle with red overlay motifs of carp, waves, and bats, 18th century,* **$2,000–$2,800.**

Satsuma

Front row, left to right: *Censer with perforated silver wire cover, 17th century,* **$1,000–$1,500;** *tortoise-form sake kazu (wine pot) in bekko gusuri (tortoiseshell glaze), 18th century,* **$1,800–$2,500;** *bowl featuring panels of seasonal flowers, the interior with a diaper band and center motif of a phoenix in flight, late Edo period, 7" diameter,* **$900–$1,200;** *teapot with Shishi motif, blue mon on base, late Edo period,* **$1,000–$1,500.**

Back row, left to right: *Chaire, same gusuri (sharkskin glaze), 18th century,* **$2,500–$3,500;** *plate, the Masanobu mark on the back accompanied by a blue mon, c1810, 10" diameter,* **$3,500–$5,500;** *bottle, late 18th century, 7" high,* **$2,000–$3,000;** *censer in the form of Hotei (with sack) and child, designed so that the essence emits from his mouth and perforations on the sack, late 18th / early 19th century, restored,* **$1,200–$1,600.**

Kyoto Pottery

Front row, left to right: *Ash pot, gosu (blue) ground with flowers and scrolls, 18th century, 3½" high,* **$1,800–$2,200;** *blue-ground bowl with flowers and foliage, 18th century,* **$2,500–$3,500;** *box in the form of a drum with tomoe mon, 18th century,* **$2,000–$3,000;** *tea caddy with wood lid, impressed Ninsei mark,* **$2,800–$3,800;** *miniature cup with impressed Ninsei mark,* **$1,200–$1,600.**

Back row, left to right: *Sake pot with wire bail handle, the motif including mushrooms and foliage, the top with Tokugawa mon, 18th century, 6" high,* **$2,500–$3,500;** *three-piece censer—tray, bowl, and open-work cage—the bowl featuring a wheel motif, the cage with foliage and branches, marked Ninsei, 8" high,* **$3,000–$5,000;** *ewer in the form of a tree trunk with foliage and large peaches, 18th century,* **$2,700–$4,000;** *gourd-shaped bottle with open work and good luck and long life characters, 18th century,* **$3,500–$4,500;** *tea caddy with T-pattern motif, Ninsei mark,* **$4,000–$5,000.**

Japanese Imari
Left to right: Meiping bottle/vase, the reverse with an inscription which indicates that this piece was a gift at a Shinto wedding, c1880, 16" high, **$800–$1,200;** plate, a Sumo wrestler in low relief, c1870, 9" high, **$500–$700;** covered jar, hen-and-cock finial, early 18th century, **$2,500–$3,500;** charger (this piece has a box, not shown, which indicates the date of manufacture as March 1871), 24" diameter, **$4,500–$6,500.**

Nineteenth-Century Chinese Porcelain
Left to right: Yellow-ground bowl decorated with lotus and meandering scrolls and foliage, Tao Kuang mark (and of the period), 8" diameter, **$2,500–$3,500;** white-ground square-form bowl with high foot, the motif featuring beautiful Chinese women, Kuang Hsu mark (and of the period), 11" diameter, **$800–$1,200;** turquoise-ground bowl featuring a mother and many children in various poses, Chia Ch'ing mark (and of the period), 4½" diameter, **$1,000–$1,500.**

Japanese Studio Ceramics

Front row, left to right: Red-ground bowl with flambé glaze, signed Makuzu Kozan, c1900, 6" diameter, **$1,500–$2,200;** bowl with black ground, crackled interior, motif of Tokugawa mon, signed Tanzan, c1910, **$1,800–$2,800.**

Back row, left to right: Blue-ground vase with flowers (in low relief), birds, and trellis, signed Hansuke, late 19th century, 10" high, **$900–$1,200;** green-ground vase with wave motif at the base, applied gun metal–hued lizard around the rim, base signed Makuzu Kozan, c1900, **$3,000–$4,500;** blue and white vase, motif of puppies frolicking in the snow, signed Kawamoto Masakichi, c1882, 13" high, **$1,600–$2,500;** covered jar with chrysanthemums and waves, the base signed Ito Tozan, Meiji period, 7" high, **$3,000–$4,000.**

Blue and White Porcelain

Left to right: Japanese Hirado covered jar, 18th century, masked feet and ears, the reverse with dragon and clouds motif, **$2,000–$3,000;** Chinese blanc de chine, Shou Lao (with staff, gourd, castanets, and peach of long life), 18th century, 11" high, **$5,000–$7,000;** beaker-form vase, K'ang Hsi period, 14" high, **$1,800–$2,500;** Hirado carp-form vase, Meiji period, 12" high, restored, **$500–$650.**

Chinese Cloisonné
Candle holders, each formed as a standing crane, and well-grained, carved-wood, fitted stands, Ch'ien Lung period, 19" high, sold at Christie's, London—realized price (including the buyer's premium), **pair, $5,294;** vessels and covers in the form of standing Buddhistic lions, one looking to the left and the other looking to the right, 18½" high, sold at Christie's, London—realized price (including the buyer's premium), **pair, $2,647.**

Chinese Monochromes
Left to right: Cherry red bottle/vase (lang yao), 4½" high, Ch'ien Lung period, 18th century, **$3,000–$5,000;** blue water coupe, K'ang Hsi period, 3" diameter, **$2,500–$3,500;** lime green bowl with incised dragons and flaming pearl, Kuang Hsu mark (and of the period), 6½" diameter, **$1,200–$1,600;** liver red bowl, Yung Cheng mark (and of the period), **$3,000–$5,000.**

Famille Rose Export Porcelain

Front row, left to right: *Rose Mandarin two-handled bouillon, c1825, large size,* **$375–$600;** *Rose Mandarin punch bowl, c1830, 15" diameter,* **$3,000–$4,500;** *Rose Medallion barrel-form covered box, first half of the 19th century,* **$600–$900.**

Back row, left to right: *Rose Mandarin platter, c1820, 16" diameter,* **$1,200–$1,600;** *Rose Medallion spittoon, Tao Kuang period,* **$1,500–$2,200.**

Japanese Lacquer

Front row, left to right: *Tea caddy with a motif of maple leaves going upstream, late Edo period,* **$1,500–$2,500;** *kogo, c1915, 3¼" diameter,* **$1,000–$1,500;** *cloud-shaped tray, one of a set, late Meiji period,* **set of 5,** **$1,200–$1,500.**

Back row, left to right: *Writing box (suzuribako) with silver rims and silver water dropper, Meiji period,* **$2,000–$3,000;** *inro case (containing pullout drawers in which inro are housed), silver hardware, Shibayama-inlay motif, Meiji period,* **$3,500–$5,500;** *tiered box with nashiji inieriors, late 17th / early 18th century,* **$4,000–$6,000.**

Kutani

Front row, left to right: Kutani bowl in yellow and aubergine with dragon and flaming pearl motif, Yoshidaya revival, c1810, 5" diameter, **$2,000–$2,800;** fan-form okimono with rats, late 19th century, **$1,200–$1,500;** vases, late 19th century, 5" high, **$400–$600.**

Back row: Plate with Japanese lacquer repair, late 19th century, **$450–$700.**

Rose Canton candlestick, late 19th century, chipped, hairlines, **$125–$175.**

Rose Canton teapot, early 19th century, twisted handle, gilt acorn finial, 5" high, **$400–$600.**

Dragon and Chrysanthemum teapot, Kuang Hsü period with the mark of the Empress Dowager on a turquoise ground, late 19th century, 6" high, **$300–$500.**

Rose Mandarin bouillon, small size, twisted branch-and-leaf handles, first quarter of the 19th century, **$150–$200.**

100 *Butterflies*
As the name suggests. The butterflies can be found on a gilt or celadon ground. (This pattern dates from the last half of the nineteenth century.)

Butterfly and Cabbage
A butterfly lighting upon a cabbage leaf. The cabbage leaves radiate from a center medallion of the Shou symbol.

Tobacco Leaf
As the name suggests.

Garden
In the center, a segment of garden; there is also a great deal of open space.

Dragon and Chrysanthemum
This pattern, dating from the Kuang Hsu period, has become quite popular in the last few years. It contains orange dragons and white chrysanthemums on either a turquoise or yellow ground.

Auspicious Figures
Four figures alternate with clusters of symbols taken from the 100 Antiques pattern. This includes Buddhist and Taoist symbols and the attributes of the Eight Immortals. The symbols radiate like the spokes of a wheel around the center medallion—a figure.

Bouquet
A center motif of a floral bouquet with or without trailing ribbons and bows, surrounded by open space.

Rose Mandarin
This is the most expensive of all the rose palette export patterns. The pattern contains Mandarin figures in various poses (scenic landscapes and riverscapes are also included). The borders of the objects usually contain some combination of fruit, flowers, butterflies, and foliage (but all of those elements are not necessarily present).

Imari

The earliest Chinese Imari dates from the eighteenth century. For the most part, the glaze has a gray, greenish, or bluish green tint, and there is usually a brown or reddish brown foot rim (where the glaze stops). The red in Chinese Imari is a coral hue; the blue never runs, and it is always crisp and lighter than its Japanese counterparts.

This Imari bears no evidence of spur marks.

Chinese Imari plate decorated with a central panel of two flowers and rock-work surrounded by a blue diapered border divided with floral reserves, the rim with flowers and another diapered border, mid-18th century, 9" diameter, **$600–$900.** *Courtesy of the Luhn Collection.*

A large blanc de chine figure of Kuan Yin (Guanyin), standing in jeweled flowing robes, wearing a high diadem with a miniature figure of Amitabha, and holding a small pot, the right hand in vitarka mudra; on a lotus base, mounted as a lamp; 21" high. Realized price (including the 10-percent buyer's premium), Christie's East, New York City, **$2,860.**

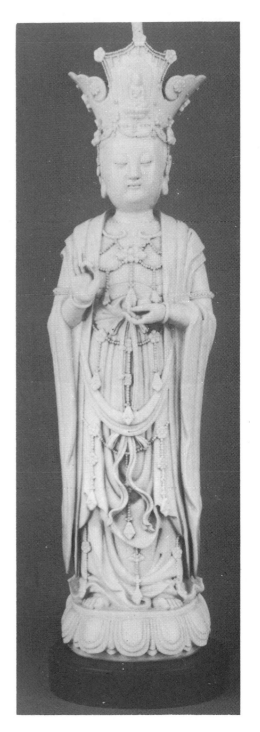

Blanc de Chine

Although *blanc de chine* (porcelain with a white glaze) was first produced during the Ming dynasty, wares of the eighteenth and early nineteenth centuries seem to appeal most to collectors, dealers, and other interested parties. The color of blanc de chine varies from stark white to a greenish white, with a range of shades in between.

Concensus suggests that the best pieces of blanc de chine are those which show a rose tint. To determine a rose tint, you need to shine a flashlight or penlight on the interior of the item in question. If there is a rose tint, it will show through the glaze and be visible on the exterior.

Values on Chinese Export Porcelain

Animal Tureens

Note: There are many contemporary reproductions of the following antique pieces currently being sold, often claimed as "authentic." Buyer beware!

Carp tureen, fin as the loop handle to the cover, iron red and gilt, repair to the tail, 19th century, 12" wide, **$2,000–$2,500.**

Crab tureen and cover, pincers curled to the front, eight legs around the sides, late 19th century, 7" wide, **$700–$900.**

Duck tureen; head, features, and tail in shades of brown, grisaille, and black; yellow webbed feet; repair to cover; 19th century, 11¼" wide, **$2,500–$3,700.**

Goose tureen, the cover formed as the upper part of the body, yellow beak, pink crest, puce head feathers, brown body feathers, feet tucked beneath a white breast, old restoration, Ch'ien Lung, 13½" long, **$18,000–$25,000.**

Armorial

Barber's bowl, famille verte, centrally painted shield-shaped coat of arms and coronets above a scroll with peony sprays, the upward-curving border reserved with animal cartouches on a blue cell-pattern ground, early 18th century, 9¼" diameter, **$2,500–$3,500.**

Barber's bowl, famille verte, centrally painted shield-shaped coat of arms and coronets above a scroll with peony sprays, the upward-curving border reserved with animal cartouches on a blue cell-pattern ground; rubbed—little of the pattern remains; early 18th century, 9¼" diameter, **$800–$1,200.**

Coffeepot and cover, famille rose, pear-shaped, large coats of arms and crests, shades of blue on a gilt foliage ground, puce landscapes, early 18th century, hairline in lid, crack in body, 8¾" high, **$800–$1,200.**

Meat dish, oval, a falcon crest in the center (below the motto *Vraye Foy* and above the molded tree-of-life strainer), c1800, 19½" wide, **$600–$900.**

Oval serving platter, Van Rensselear pattern, central butterfly medallion, gilt and puce floral bands, late 18th century, 20" diameter, **$600–$900.**

Plate painted with coat of arms and elaborate mantling below the crest within a scroll and dot band, the border decorated *en grisaille* with elaborate cartouches and figures, Ch'ien Lung, 14" diameter, **$1,675–$2,300.**

Plate, famille rose, central gilt shield-shaped coat of arms showing three nude female bust lengths below a larger crest, bamboo and flower-head borders, Ch'ien Lung, 15" diameter, **$1,500–$2,000.**

Plate, central shield-shaped coat of arms with leafy swags below coronet, all set on a rock-and-tree vignette below a red, blue, and gilt spearhead-and-scroll border, Ch'ien Lung, 9½" diameter, **$900–$1,200.**

Plate, coat of arms within feathery mantle beneath a seated lion crest, all within spearheads, four grisaille landscape scrolls at the border, Ch'ien Lung, two hairlines, 9½" diameter, **$500–$600.**

Plate, famille rose, molded and scalloped rim, centrally painted coat of arms and crest amongst floral sprays, the well with a gilt dentel band below with underglaze blue cell pattern, late 18th century, rim chips, 9½" diameter, **$300–$400.**

Punch bowl, plain interior, the exterior with two coats of arms, the shield supporting a gilt coronet and falcon crest, dividing a grisaille and peacock band, cracks, mid-18th century, 11½" diameter, **$500–$600.**

Soup plate, famille rose, central shield-shaped coat of arms beneath the crest and within floral mantling, the well with gilt scrolling band, the border with an underglaze blue band of prong and cell cartouches, a shaped rim, late Ch'ien Lung, 9½" diameter, **$350–$500.**

Tankard; famille rose; cylindrical; loop handles; shield-shaped coat of arms; blank scroll, crest, and mantling beneath a band of chain-link; restored crack; mid-18th century, 4½" high, **$375–$500.**

Teapot and cover, angular spout with foliate strap handle, small flower heads enclosing coat of arms, foliate finial, minor rim chips, Ch'ien Lung, 10" wide, **$400–$600.**

Tureen with hare-head handles, coats of arms on both sides and supporters beneath a floral swag, dentil band at rim, no cover, Ch'ien Lung, 12½" wide, **$500–$600.**

Tureen and cover, famille rose, coat of arms and lion mask pad feet, loop handles at ends, lotus bud finial dividing two stag crests at the rim, Ch'ien Lung, restored handles, 11½" diameter, **$1,800–$2,500.**

Auspicious Figures

Platter (oval) and strainer, early 19th century, 16" wide, **$2,000–$2,700.**

Tureen and cover with stand, puce key-pattern border, domed cover with fruit finial, early 19th century, stand—15" wide, **$4,000–$5,000.**

Blanc de Chine

Bodhisattva seated upon a Buddhistic lion, early 19th century, 16" high, **$3,500–$4,500.**

Box and cover, circular, molded peony blossom on lid, K'ang Hsi, 6" diameter, **$1,000–$1,350.**

Brush holder, cylindrical, reticulated with leaf and lotus motif, K'ang Hsi, 5" high, **$800–$1,200.**

Buddhistic lion seated with paw on brocade ball, mane braided down the back, taper sticks at the side, damage to taper sticks, early 18th century, 14" high, **$600–$900.**

Buddhistic lions seated on tall rectangular bases, each with brocade ball under one paw, bells on collars, damages, 18th century, 11½" high, **pair, $900–$1,200.**

Candle holder, column upon waves, two dragons encircling the column, chips and hairlines, 18th century, 6" high, **$800–$950.**

Censer, cylindrical with banded rim, three ruyi-shaped feet, incised geometric pattern, 17th century, 5" × 4", **$1,200–$1,500.**

Cup, branch handle, late 19th century, 3¼" wide, **$75–$100.**

Dish, Kuan Yin seated on rocky outcrop above a swirl of breaking waves and lotus plants, a small acolyte standing at the left, 18th century, restored, 10" high, **$500–$650.**

Kuan Yin seated on oval base; long, flowing robes and pendant jewelry; firing cracks; extremities chipped; impressed four-character mark, 18th century, 13" high, **$4,000–$6,000.**

Kuan Yin standing on domed base of molded waves; long robes, jeweled necklace and pendant, a long cowl across the high topknot; 19th century, 15" high, **$650–$950.**

Kuan Yin; long, flowing robes; a flower in one hand; marked *China*; 10" high, **$75–$100.**

Kuan Yin; long, flowing robes; a peach in one hand; marked *China*; 12" high, **$100–$125.**

Libation cup, oval form, three small feet, exterior with branches and prunus in relief, early 18th century, 3½" diameter, **$600–$900.**

Vase, flattened baluster form, hexafoil panels of branches and prunus with birds molded in relief, 19th century, 5½" high, **$200–$300.**

Vase, pear-shaped, long neck, flared rim, applied dragon, 19th century, 14" high, **$400–$600.**

Vase and cover, applied dragon's-head handles, Buddhistic lion finial, late 18th century, 7" high, **$900–$1,200.**

Water dropper, lotus leaf form, tripod foot, 18th century, 3" diameter, **$700–$900.**

Wine pot molded with prunus branches, upright handle, three bracket feet, flat cover, flower finial, early 18th century, rim chips, 8" high, **$3,000–$4,000.**

Canton Blue and White

Basket with under-plate, reticulated, 10" long, **$600–$800.**

Bidet with stand and wood cover, 15" long, **$1,800–$2,500.**

Bottle, water, 8½" high, **$450–$600.**

Bowl, cut corners, 10½" diameter, **$625–$825.**

Bowl, scalloped, 8½" diameter, **$400–$600.**

Box with cover, 5¾" square, 6½" high, **$700–$1,050.**

Cider pitcher and cover, Buddhistic lion finial, 8" wide, **$1,000–$1,500.**

Creamer, 3½" high, **$130–$165.**

Creamer, 3" high, **$125–$150.**

Dish, diamond shape, 9½" X 6", **$250–$400.**

Dish (vegetable), open, 9" X 7", **$225–$450.**

Dish, oval, 11" X 8¼", **$300–$425.**

Dish (shrimp), 10" X 9½", **$450–$700.**

Dish (vegetable), 11" long, **$300–$475.**

Ginger jar, 6" high, **$150–$200.**

Gravy boat, 5½" long, **$150–$300.**

Gravy boat, two-ended, with liner, 8" long, **$900–$1,200.**

Hot-water plate, 9½" diameter, **$300–$450.**

Hot-water plate; open, two-piece vegetable server with vented insert; 10½" long, **$450–$750.**

Jar, oil storage, 10" high, **$300–$450.**

Mug, twisted handle, 4" high, **$300–$450.**

Mug, twisted handle, 3½" high, **$300–$400.**

Platter, oval, 13" X 10", **$225–$400.**

Platter, 15" X 12", **$285–$450.**

Platter, well and tree, 18" X 15", **$600–$900.**

Rice bowl, cover and stand, 4½" diameter, **$100–$175.**

Soup bowl, 8½" diameter, **$75–$125.**

Sugar bowl, twisted handle, 4½" high, **$375–$500.**

Sweetmeat tray and cover, 6" long, **$600–$800.**

Syllabub and cover, **$125–$200.**

Teapot with cover, drum form, 5½" high, **$450–$600.**

Teapot with domed cover, **$600–$800.**

Tile, round, 6" diameter, **$300–$400.**

Tile, 6" square, **$300–$400.**

Trencher (salt), **$400–$500.**

Tureen, oval with strap handles, 8½" diameter, **$750–$1,000.**

Umbrella stand, 24" high, **$1,000–$1,500.**

Urn, baluster form, 13" high, **$650–$950.**

Washbowl and pitcher set: washbowl, 16" diameter; pitcher, 14½" high; **$2,500–$3,500.**

Dragon and Chrysanthemum

Dish, turquoise ground, orange dragons, white flowers, gilt border, late 19th century, 8" diameter, **$250–$350.**

Fishbowl, turquoise ground, orange dragons, white flowers, fitted wood stand, late 19th century, 8" X 16", **$2,500–$3,500.**

Garden seat, turquoise ground, orange dragons, white flowers, late 19th century, 19½" high, **$2,800–$3,600.**

Jardinière, yellow ground, dragons, white flowers, key-fret border, late 19th century, 9½" × 15", **$800–$1,200.**

Tile, turquoise ground, orange dragons, white flowers, key-pattern border, late 19th century, 25" square, **$1,200–$1,500.**

Vase and cover, yellow ground, two writhing orange dragons, white flowers, the cover with a gilt Buddhistic-lion finial, a turquoise floral band on the cover and at the foot, late 19th century, 28" high, **$2,200–$2,800.**

Figures

Actor (in role of warrior) pulling sword from scabbard, dragon robe, famille rose, late 19th century, 13½" high, **$450–$650.**

Boys, blue and white, mirror image, each on an oval base and holding a peach, early 19th century, 10" high, **pair, $1,000–$1,500.**

Boys, famille verte, mirror image, each holding a vase, their garb with tied emblems, aprons decorated with cranes; one restored; K'ang Hsi, 11" high, **pair, $1,000–$1,500.**

Buddhistic lion ewer, famille jaune, the lion clasping the side of a hexagonal ewer decorated with prunus and trellis patterns, late 19th century, 7½" high, **$250–$350.**

Buddhistic lions, famille jaune, looking to the left and to the right, each with forepaw on brocade ball, one with cub, yellow bodies, green manes, aubergine collars, reticulated eyes, 19th century, 14" high, **pair, $1,500–$2,200.**

Buddhistic lions, joss-stick holders on rectangular plinths, famille rose, early 19th century, 9" high, **pair, $850–$1,175.**

Buddhistic lions, Kuang Tung, flambé, glazed in red with blue and white streaks, late 19th century, 5" high, **$400–$500.**

Buffalos, each with a boy crawling on its back, the boys in yellow and blue attire, late 19th century, 8" wide, **pair, $350–$500.**

Cat night-light, white bisque, eyes pierced for illumination, incised marks to show fur, c1800, 7¾" wide, **$1,000–$2,000.**

Cat night-light, green and aubergine, crouching position, eyes pierced for illumination, early 19th century, 7¾" wide, **$1,700–$2,000.**

Dragon (coiled) with spiked fins on base of clouds, famille rose, late 19th century, 10" high, **$1,200–$1,500.**

Ducks, glazed turquoise, recumbent, c1900, 4½" long, **pair, $150–$250.**

Eight Immortals, each with an attribute, famille rose, rectangular plinth base, early 19th century, 9½" high, **$4,500–$5,500.**

Eight Immortals, each with an attribute, harlequin-pattern robes, famille rose, late 19th century, 9" high, **$2,500–$3,500.**

Elephants, heads lowered to the left and to the right, the saddles set with shallow candle holders, chipped tusks, famille rose, late 19th century, 9½" wide, **pair, $1,700–$2,400.**

Group of four children joined to form a pyramid, famille rose, Kuang Hsu, 6" wide, **$600–$800.**

Group of Immortals standing in three rows, each with an attribute; open, rock-work base; damaged; famille rose, early 19th century, **$300–$500.**

Goat, recumbent, horned and bearded, minor chipping, blue and white, 19th century, 4" wide, **$800–$1,200.**

Hawks looking to the left and to the right; standing on punched, rock-work bases; fine feather-work; glazed brown and white; 19th century, 8" high, **pair, $1,000–$1,500.**

Hawks standing on rock-work bases, glazed blue, late 19th century, 7½" high, **pair, $250–$350.**

Hound, seated and looking forward, belled collar, brown glaze, early 19th century, 6½" high, **$700–$900.**

Horse standing on four squares, looking forward; gray mane, yellow-glazed body with charcoal gray patches; turn of the century, 6" wide, **$250–$350.**

Kuan Yin, seated, hair piled high, long robes and cowl, three-color on biscuit, famille verte, K'ang Hsi, 8½" high, **$1,800–$2,500.**

Ladies standing and holding vases with ormolu-blossom candle holders, robes with circular floral patterns and waves around the hems, mounted as lamps, one head replaced, late 19th century, 15" high, **pair, $1,500–$2,250.**

Lovers seated on pierced rock-work, the man holding a goblet, damaged hands and chips at base, famille rose, early 19th century, 8" high, **$2,000–$3,000.**

Monkey, painted in sepia, seated beside a vase; the vase with a peony blossom and leaves; old repairs; famille rose, Ch'ien Lung, 5" high, **$2,000–$3,000.**

Parrots standing on rock-work bases, glazed turquoise, late 19th century, 12" high, **pair, $150–$200.**

Phoenixes on pierced rock-work bases, looking to the left and to the right; open beaks, red crests, plumage in bright colors, their tail feathers wrapped around circular bases; famille rose, late 19th century, 18" high, **pair, $2,000–$2,500.**

Pu Tai, elongated ear lobes, shaven head, key pattern on robes looped beneath a fat belly, a string of beads in one hand, rectangular plinth, fire crack on the front, Wan Li, 9" high, **$4,000–$6,000.**

Pu Tai seated and leaning on bag of happiness, red and puce garb, old repairs, Ch'ien Lung, 7" wide, **$1,200–$1,800.**

Pu Tai with children, famille rose, colors badly worn, Tao Kuang, 10" wide, **$300–$500.**

Quail, pair standing on ochre bases, incised feathers in green and brown, late 19th century, one beak chipped, **$300–$500.**

Shou Lao seated and holding a peach and sceptre, c1800, 9" high, **$1,500–$2,500.**

Shou Lao, open mouth, holding peach and staff, famille rose, 1900, 24" high, **$400–$600.**

Woman standing beside jardinière on rock-work column; she holds a lotus sceptre; minute chips; famille rose, early 19th century, **$375–$600.**

Young Immortal holding a flower blossom and ruyi sceptre, joyful facial expression, floral jacket, iron red and gilt pants, seated position, famille rose, late 19th century, **$250–$400.**

Fitzhugh

Oval sauce tureen and cover; brown; entwined, berried branch handles; gilt flower finial; early 19th century, 8" wide, **$1,200–$1,500.**

Oval serving dish, bright green over black, outlined pattern, gilt border, c1810, 18" wide, **$1,000–$1,500.**

Tazza, blue and white, shallow, quatrefoil bowl on waisted and domed foot, rectangular medallion of pomegranates surrounded by Fitzhugh-pattern bands, late 18th century, 12" wide, **$1,500–$2,200.**

Tea bowl and saucer, sepia and gilt with fruiting vine border, early 19th century, **$200–$300.**

Teapot; blue and white; short, grooved spout; intertwined, berried handle; oval floral medallion enclosing gilt monogram; Fitzhugh-pattern bands on the shoulder and cover; small crack in body; late 18th century, 6½" high, **$600–$800.**

Warming dish, green, circular, c1810, 9½" diameter, **$1,000–$1,500.**

Imari (Chinese)

Barber's bowl, peony sprays with cell pattern, foliage scrolls on border, reverse with peony sprays, fritting, early 18th century, 10¼" diameter, **$1,500–$1,800.**

Bowl, exterior motif of pavilions and willow, the interior border with trellis ground and floral cartouches, mid-18th century, 10½" diameter, **$500–$700.**

Dish, oval, motif of pagodas and riverscape, chips on rim, Ch'ien Lung, 15½" wide, **$500–$700.**

Chinese Imari bowl with scalloped rim, four panels of floral motifs and a central floral spray, late Ch'ien Lung, 18th century, 8½" diameter, **$600–$900.** *Courtesy of the Luhn Collection.*

Chinese Imari dinner plate with a central motif of a basket filled with flowers, the border highlighted with gilt, c1770, 9¼" diameter, **$700–$925.** *Courtesy of the Luhn Collection.*

Dish, central motif of flowers and basket, early 18th century, 8" diameter, **$600–$700.**

Jardinière, large clusters of scrolling lotus-head foliage and long fronds of curly leaves, a band of chevron at the rim, base drilled, 18th century, 16" diameter, **$2,500–$3,500.**

Jars, baluster form with domed covers, knop finials, pheasant on rock-work with dense floral patterns, the necks with a band of flowers, riverscapes on the covers, one jar restored, early 18th century, 24½" high, **pair, $3,500–$4,500.**

Jars, baluster form with domed covers and biscuit Buddhistic-lion finials, motif of birds on rock-work, peony lappets on shoulders and above foot, 18th century, 29" high, **pair, $9,000–$12,000.**

Plate, pagodas amongst peony and prunus, early 18th century, 9" diameter, **$400–$500.**

Pronk plate, attendant raising umbrella above a lady, the border with eight reserves of a single lady and birds within a cell-pattern ground, mid-18th century, 9½" diameter, **$800– $1,200.**

Tankard, cylindrical, scenic motif with dense florals, c1800, 3½" high, **$300–$500.**

Teapot and cover; globular; decorated with birds perched on branches, peony, and rock-work, late 18th century, 6" wide, **$350–$450.**

Tureen and cover, oval, floral handles, fruit finial, mid-18th century, 6½" wide, **$900–$1,200.**

Vases, beaker form, waisted, painted with pheasants on rock-work, cell-pattern lappets at the trumpet neck, riveted, early 18th century, 15" high, **pair, $1,500–$2,200.**

Chinese Imari, covered pot with handle, floral motif and trellis around the center with fighting cocks, mid-18th century, 4½" high, **$1,500–$2,000.** Courtesy of the Luhn Collection.

Left: *Chinese Imari tea caddy with floral motif and matching lid, early Ch'ien Lung, 18th century,* 4¾" high, **$1,000–$1,500.** Right: *Chinese Imari tea caddy and cover, panels decorated in floral motifs, mid-to-late 18th century, 4½" high,* **$700–$1,000.** Courtesy of the Luhn Collection.

Nanking Blue and White

Bowl, scalloped, 9" diameter, **$450–$600.**

Box and cover; 7" long, 3½" wide, 2½" diameter, **$1,000–$1,500.**

Dish, leaf-shaped, twig handle, 6" long, **$175–$275.**

Dish, leaf-shaped, no handle, 7½" long, **$200–$300.**

Dish (vegetable), oval, 11" long, **$400–$500.**

Flagon, Buddhistic-lion finial, orange-peel glaze, 11½" high, **$1,500–$2,500.**

Gravy boat, twisted handle, gilt trim, 7½" long, **$275–$300.**

Platter, 14" X 11", **$345–$500.**

Platter, oval, 19" X 16", **$450–$675.**

Pot (chocolate), pear-shaped, Buddhistic-lion finial, 9" high, **$750–$1,000.**

Saucer and cup, no handle, gilt trim, **$200–$300.**

Syllabub and cover, **$150–$250.**

Tea caddy, 5½" high, **$225–$350.**

Tea caddy, gilt trim, 5" high, **$600–$800.**

Trencher (salt), **$450–$600.**

Tureen with cover and under-plate, gilt-flower finial, twisted handles, 7½" diameter, **$600–$725.**

Umbrella stand, 24" high, **$1,200–$1,600.**

Rose Mandarin

Beaker vases, flaring neck, spreading foot, early 19th century, 15" high, **pair, $3,500–$4,500.**

Beaker vases, flaring neck, spreading foot, late 19th century, 15" high, **pair, $1,500–$2,200.**

Bough vases, octagonal, faceted sides, removable tops, first half of the 19th century, 10", **pair, $3,500–$5,000.**

Rose Mandarin barrel-form box with cover, c1875, damaged, 6" high, **$200–$300.**

Bowl; panels of figures, trees, and pavilions; gilt scroll ground; 19th century, 11" diameter, **$350–$500.**

Coffeepot and cover, ladies and pavilions, hairline, late 18th century, **$450–$600.**

Dish; oval; dignitaries, scholars, and ladies on a terrace with tables and awning; the border with butterflies and flowers; early 19th century, 16" wide, **$2,200–$3,100.**

Garden seat, hexagonal shape, a seated dignitary addressing an audience, double-pierced cash symbols on two sides; all between bands of fruit, foliage, and raised bosses; early 19th century, **$4,500–$6000.**

Garden seat, barrel form, a dignitary addressing an audience, pierced cash symbols, bands of fruit and flowers, upper and lower bands of raised bosses, early 19th century, 19½" high, **$3,500–$4,500.**

Rose Mandarin lid with gilt finial, early 19th century, **$200–$250.**

Jardinière, hexagonal (with stand), continuous scene of dignitaries, scholars, and ladies; flat rim with bird cartouches and floral ground; early 19th century, 9½" diameter, **$2,500–$3,500.**

Mug, cylindrical, Y-pattern ground in iron red, floral edge, panels of standing figures in landscapes, late 18th century, 4¾" high, **$450–$600.**

Punch bowl; butterflies, flowers, and foliage borders; key-pattern bands; early 19th century, 18" diameter, **$6,000–$8,000.**

Punch bowl; the border with flowers, butterflies, and foliage; early 19th century, 16½" diameter, **$4,500–$5,500.**

Punch bowl; flowers, foliage, and fruit borders; key-pattern band; early 19th century, 14" diameter, **$3,500–$4,500.**

45

Snuff box; gilt mounts; ladies, pavilions, and trees on lid and exterior; rubbed; 18th century, 3" diameter, **$1,500–$2,500.**

Teacup and saucer, puce landscapes, red and black cell patterns, 19th century, **$175–$225.**

Teapot and cover, landscapes with ladies and attendants, late 19th century, **$300–$400.**

Tureen and cover, dignitaries and children with seascape in the background, gilt scroll border, Buddhistic-lion finial, late 18th century, chips and crack, 15" wide, **$1,500–$2,000.**

Vase, baluster form, painted on both sides with panels of ladies and dignitaries, bands of fruit and flowers dividing the panels, gilt Buddhistic-lion cubs applied on either side of the neck, first half of the 19th century, 25" high, **$5,000–$6,000.**

Vases and covers; groups of ladies in two panels; the panels divided by two smaller panes of figures within gilt key-pattern borders edged with scattered fruit and floral sprays; early 19th century, 26" high, **$10,000–$12,000.**

Rose Medallion

Note: The values for Rose Canton are the same as those for Rose Medallion. Pieces dating from the late nineteenth century are approximately 25 to 50 percent less valuable than comparable pieces dating from the first half of the nineteenth century. Values depreciate for pieces which are rubbed (worn).

The objects listed are taken from a complete dinner service dating from the late nineteenth century. All the pieces are perfect unless noted otherwise.

Basin, 15" diameter, **$1,500–$2,000.**

Basket, reticulated, and under-plate, 10½" diameter, **$900–$1,200.**

Bowl, 4½" diameter, **$300–$600.**

Bowl, 8½" diameter, **$700–$950.**

Box with cover, 6" square, **$475–$600.**

Candlestick, 6" high, **$600–$800.**

Candlestick, 8" high, **$900–$1,200.**

Creamer, helmet shape, **$225–$400.**

Garden seat, hexagonal, with open-work cash symbols, 19" high, **$3,500–$4,500.**

Garden seat, barrel form, with double open-work cash symbols, 19½" high, **$2,500–$3,500.**

Pitcher, 6" long, **$300–$450.**

Plate, 8" diameter, **$200–$275.**

Plate, 12" diameter, **$285–$475.**

Plate, 14" diameter, **$450–$600.**

Platter, 16" diameter, **$700–$1,150.**

Platter, 9" × 12", **$600–$800.**

Punch bowl, 14" diameter, **$1,800–$2,200.**

Punch bowl, 15½" diameter, **$2,000–$2,800.**

Punch bowl, chips on rim, rubbing, 16" diameter, **$1,400–$1,600.**

Punch bowl, 16" diameter, **$2,500–$3,500.**

Punch bowl, 18" diameter, **$3,200–$4,500.**

Sugar bowl and cover, 6" long, **$300–$450.**

Teapot, helmet shape, **$475–$650.**

Vase, 6" high, **$125–$185.**

Vase, 8" high, **$275–$350.**

Vase, oviform, two fixed Buddhistic lion and ring handles, mid-to-late 19th century, 24" high, **$2,000–$2,500.**

Vase; oviform; panels of ladies divided by bands of flowers, foliage, and medallions; scalloped rim; c1885, 24" high, **$1,800–$2,400.**

Vases, pear-shaped, with cup-shaped rims and elephant-head handles, one damaged, late 19th century, **pair, $1,400–$2,500.**

Vases; oviform; applied gilt dragons around long neck; late 19th century, 26" high, **pair, $3,500–$4,500.**

Tobacco Leaf

Basin, late 18th century, 12" diameter, **$2,000–$3,000.**

Bowl, famille rose, flowers and large-veined leaves, two bamboo-form loop handles, rim in need of restoration, 18th century, 6" wide, **$475–$675.**

Dish, mid-18th century, 15" wide, **$2,500–$3,500.**

Dish, cushion-shaped, early 19th century, 7" diameter, **$900–$1,300.**

Plate, lobed, 18th century, 8½" diameter, **$800–$1,200.**

Salt (domed); famille rose; scalloped rim; the top painted with peony sprays; overlapping large serrated leaves in underglaze blue, turquoise, pink, and light green; 18th century, 4" wide, **$700–$900.**

Sauce tureen and cover with stand (red Tobacco Leaf), underglaze blue and red, hare-head handles, floral finial, exotic flowers and serrated leaves, floral roundels, 18th century, 8" wide, **$1,500–$1,800.**

Nanking Cargo Auctioned for More Than 15 Million Dollars

More than 20,000 people passed through the Christie's warehouse in Amsterdam during the weeks preceding the ten-session auction of the Nanking cargo salvaged from the wreck of the Dutch vessel *Geldermalsen*. Propelled by the romance and intrigue surrounding the shipwreck cargo that had lain under the South China Sea for more than 200 years, bidders pushed the final total for the auction, held April 28–May 2, 1986, to a staggering $15,192,581.

The sale—of over 100,000 pieces of blue and white Chinese export porcelain, 125 rare Chinese gold ingots, and two important dated Dutch V.O.C. bronze cannons—was watched by the salvager, Captain Michael Hatcher, and the divers who so brilliantly recovered the cargo from its 234-year resting place at the bottom of the sea.

It is debatable whether the gold ingots or the dinner services caused the most excitement during the sale. However, as the auctioneer brought the gavel down on the biggest service at $332,707, the audience in the auction applauded. Not surprisingly, the price was a world record for a porcelain dinner service sold at auction. The painted blue and white (with a lattice-fence pattern) dinner service, consisting of 140 place settings and associated table vessels and dishes, was sold to a private collector bidding by telephone. A similar service, this one comprising only 120 table settings, sold to a London dealer for $261,975.

Other exceptional prices realized were $42,787 for a blue and white deep dish painted with an exotic fantailed fish, and $47,541 for a pair of dishes of the same design. A single blue and white bowl-shaped jug brought $1,997; a pair of teapots fetched $3,566; a pair of hexagonal salt cellars realized $8,082; and a group of eight chamber pots sold for $10,459.

The whole world rallied to the sale with purchasers hailing from all corners of the globe. Packing the salesroom to capacity for all five days were collectors, dealers, and representatives of major establishments such as the Ritz Hotel in London, which bought a 24-piece-setting dinner service and 24 porcelain bowls to use in its Trafalgar Suite private dining room.

The following listing from this remarkable auction includes the 16-percent buyer's premium. The approximate rate of exchange was 2.5 DF = $1 US. All *the objects listed date c1750.*

Realized Prices

Bottle, blue and white, pear-shaped, continuous riverscape, garlic neck, flaring mouth, heavily encrusted, 10" high, **$3,016.**

Bowl, blue and white, painted around the exterior with a continuous band of chrysanthemum in a wide, leafy meander; 6¼" diameter, **$742.**

Bowls (12), blue and white, painted with the Scholar on Bridge pattern, 7¾" diameter, **$3,944.**

Bowls, Batvian, blue and white with brown exteriors, the interior with two large peony branches and a chrysanthemum branch above a central peony roundel below a trellis-pattern border, 7½" diameter, **$2,320.**

Children's chamber pots (2), underglaze blue and enameled, painted with tree peony on the exterior and a formal flower spray on the loop handle, 6¼" wide and 4¾" wide, **$1,392.**

Children's chamber pots (2); blue and white; painted with tree peony and bamboo on the exterior, three clusters of rose branches on the roundel everted rim, and a formal flower spray on the loop handle; 6¼" wide and 4¾" wide, **$1,578.**

Chamber pot, blue and white, painted with peony and bamboo issuing from rock-work on the exterior, a formal flower spray on the handle, and trellis pattern divided by four peony panels on the everted rim, 8¾" wide, **$1,948.**

Figure of a Dignitary, copper red and celadon, his head and hat reserved in the biscuit, the robe a flambé red on celadon with marine life adhering to the head and base, 7½" high, **$25,520.**

Figure of a lady in blue and celadon, a rose spray at her left shoulder reserved in the biscuit, rectangular plinth base, 7½" high, **$8,816.**

Figure of a seated boy, the apron glazed pale blue, smiling face, arms raised, fruit in right hand, legs bent at the knee, 4½" high, **$1,763.**

Figure of Shou Lao holding a fan, figure in biscuit, 7¾" high, **$2,552.**

Figure of a standing, saddled pony in blue and white; 3¾" wide, **$7,888.**

Figure of a white glazed pheasant on pierced rock-work base, the crested head turned to the left, 10½" high, **$2,227.**

Mug, underglaze blue and enameled, cylindrical form, loop-strap handle, painted with peony tree issuing from rock-work on a terrace below a border of trellis pattern, 5¼" high, **$1,578.**

Plates (12), blue and white, painted with the Peony and Pomegranate pattern within a band of trellis pattern, the border with three peony sprays, 9¼" diameter, **$6,496.**

Plates (12), Boatman and Six-Flower Border pattern, a fisherman punting his boat in a broad river landscape; a two-story pavilion beside pine, wutong, and rocks on the near bank (and a retreat on two); 9" diameter, **$6,960.**

Sauce dishes (12), provincial blue and white, freely painted with a central dragon and fire scrolls within a floral spray border, Swatow type, 8" diameter, **$1,624.**

Chinese porcelain vase with applied designs featuring a Chinese opera, beige and white, mid-19th century, 8" high, $200–$300.

Chinese pottery wine vessel in brown and green, the handle showing one animal devouring another (at the back), Yung Cheng (and of the period), 8" high (to top of handle), $1,800–$2,700.

Soup plates (12), blue and white, the Willow Terrace pattern in the well, three peony and chrysanthemum clusters descending from the rim, 9¼" diameter, **$6,496.**

Spittoons (2); blue and white; globular; painted with chrysanthemum issuing from rock-work and a band of petals around the broad, conical neck; its interior with a border of trellis pattern; 5¼" diameter, **$2,784.**

Teapots (2), blue and white, bullet-shaped, flat cover, straight spout, wide bracket handle, bud-shaped finial, painted with willow and peony issuing from a terrace on a rocky river bank, a scholar's retreat beside a pine on a distant bank, all below a trellis-pattern border, 8¾" wide, **$2,784.**

Teapots (2); blue and white; globular; shallow-domed covers, straight spout, loop handle, and bud-shaped finial; motif as above; 8¼" wide, **$2,784.**

Tureen and cover; blue and white; half-flower-head handles; chrysanthemum knop finial; painted on the side with peony, daisy, and orchid issuing from lattice-work fence; 8¾" diameter, **$1,856.**

Vases; blue and white; waisted; trumpet necks; painted with large cartouches of suspending tassels; 5¼" high, **pair, $789.**

Notes on Ch'ing (Qing) Dynasty Porcelains

The K'ang Hsi (Kangxi) Period: 1666–1723

Among the popular wares introduced during the K'ang Hsi period were those classified as *famille verte, famille noire,* and *famille jaune* (green, black, and yellow families, respectively). Famille verte can be found in combination with a powder blue (also known as *soufflé* blue), which was blown onto the porcelain through a tube—likely, one with a piece of gauze stretched over the end. Famille noire is marked by dark green over a black slip ground, while famille jaune has a yellow ground. The yellow enamels are always light and transparent; the transparency of the green hues is similar. Both yellow and green enamels produced toward the end of the period have varying shades.

Chinese porcelain footed box with cover; famille verte; motif of confronting dragons on two sides, the short sides having vases in various sizes and shapes (part of the 100 Antiques motif); a hardwood replacement lid with matching stand, both of which were produced in the late 19th / early 20th century (when it was fashionable to add lids and stands even if they were not needed); restoration to one leg; K'ang Hsi, 6" high, $1,200–$1,800.

Also during this period, the use of overglaze blue was instituted. Previously, porcelain had been subjected to the time-consuming process of double firing: once for overglaze enamels, and another time for underglaze blue. The new glaze, evident in five-color Chinese porcelain (wu ts'ai) and in famille verte wares, is thin with a lustered finish.

Three-color ware on biscuit—san ts'ai—is synonymous with the reign of Emperor K'ang Hsi. San ts'ai enamels were fired directly on the biscuit, mainly in hues of green and yellow with aubergine (eggplant purple).

From 1677, the use of the Imperial K'ang Hsi mark on porcelain was forbidden. This rule was not always observed, however, so there were pieces made toward the end of the period which in fact have reign marks.

Finally, it was during this reign that Canton and Nanking blue and white wares were introduced.

The Yung Cheng (Yongzheng) Period: 1723–1736

From 1723 the pink color palette referred to as *famille rose* was used to decorate Chinese porcelains, including the export wares. Famille rose pink is opaque, as are the accompanying greens and yellows, which are nevertheless similar to the shades of the preceding period. The use of bright turquoise, on the other hand, is similar to that of the Chia Ching period of the Ming Dynasty.

Designs from this period are less crowded than in previous wares, and are done in Chinese taste, incorporating an abundance of florals and birds. Individual pieces tend to have a less pronounced foot, but a sharper rim.

The paste of Yung Cheng porcelains is smooth, white, and quite fine. Enamels of the period have a shiny quality and are very clear, and the translucent glaze is whiter than that used during the K'ang Hsi period.

Marks include four or six characters, sometimes in a double square with canted corners. These marks were reproduced during the 1920s and 1930s on eggshell porcelains.

The Ch'ien Lung (Qianlong) Period: 1736–1796

It is often difficult to distinguish Yung Cheng wares from early Ch'ien Lung wares. The palette for this reign did, however, include several innovations such as the introduction of pale lime green, painting in sepia, and imitations in porcelain of wood grains (bamboo), lacquer, bronze, and silver.

An especially popular new color was European green, used throughout the remainder of the Ch'ing Dynasty. Look for this green (which may be a turquoise or blue-green hue) on the interior, inside rim, or foot of a piece.

Another innovation of the Ch'ien Lung period was the moving picture, which involved an outer section—a vase—rotating around a stationary, inner core. The inner core was painted with reserves of a continuous motif, visible through open panels in the outer vase. Thus, when the vase revolved around the core, it created the illusion that the picture inside was actually moving.

Ku Yüeh Hsüan (Ancient Moon Terrace), an opaque white porcelain resembling milk glass, is associated with the reign of Ch'ien Lung, even though it dates back to the reign of K'ang Hsi. Ku Yüeh Hsüan was made at

Partial dinner service, Chinese export, iron red and gilt, painted with peony cluster and entwined dotted bands within leafy foliage at the rims, some wear, late Ch'ien Lung:

Two large two-handled oval tureens and covers, one with stand, 15" wide

Small two-handled sauce tureen and cover, minor fritting, foot cracked, 8¼" wide

Two-handled vegetable tureen and cover, 13" wide

Four shallow shaped oval tureens and covers, one cracked and repaired, two chipped, fritting, 11½" long

One oval mazarine, 17½" long

Two deep, shaped square bowls, 10" wide

Pair of reticulated oval baskets and stands, handles removed and rims consequently over-painted, 10" wide

A similar pair of baskets and stands, handles removed, restored, 8½" wide

Sauce boat, 7¾" long

Twenty-three circular dinner plates, 18 cracked or repaired rim chips, one broken and repaired, 10" diameter

Fifteen circular soup plates, 10 chipped or cracked, 2 fritted, 9¾" diameter

Eleven oval platters of graduated size, four chipped, two cracked and one with repaired rim chip, 19" to 11" diameter

Eighteen circular side plates, 15 chipped or cracked, some with repaired rim chips, 7¾" diameter

Realized price, (including the 10-percent buyer's premium), Christie's, New York City, **$4,400.**

Chinese Kuangtung (Shekwan) figure of a Lohan, his garb in Kuan-type glaze, finely detailed, late 18th century, 6½" high, $500–$800.

Ching te chen and sent to the Imperial Palace Workshops in Peking (Beijing) for decoration.

Ch'ien Lung porcelain features a pure white paste with a smooth base rim. Colors are vivid and brilliant, not washed out. The glaze is translucent white. In the latter part of the period, orange-peel glaze (which has a rippled effect) came into use and was produced throughout the Ch'ing Dynasty.

Marks of the period consist of either four or six characters within a double square having canted corners. Like the marks of previous periods and dynasties, they have been copied extensively.

The Chia Ch'ing (Jiaqing) Period: 1796–1820

Among the distinguishing characteristics of this reign is the sand grit which is sometimes found embedded in the glaze (in and around the foot rim). In addition, the porcelain, for the most part, became more thick-walled. Copies of the preceding Ch'ing Dynasty reigns were also produced.

The Chia Ch'ing period initiated the production of Canton Rose patterned wares, which continued throughout the nineteenth and early twentieth centuries. These wares are currently made available in reproductions, as well.

Values on Chinese Porcelain and Pottery (Traditional)

Monochromes

Apple green bottle/vases, finely crackled, late 19th century, 6½" high, **$300–$500.**

Apple green bottle/vase, large crackle, brown foot, late 18th/early 19th century, 8½" high, **$500–$700.**

Apple green bottle/vase, crackled glaze, early 19th century, 5½" high, **$150–$225.**

Apple green bowl, incised chrysanthemum and leafy scroll, 18th century, 5½" diameter, **$600–$800.**

Apple green vase, body with dog-head handles, tall garlic neck, late 18th century, 8¼" high, **$1,000–$2,000.**

Blue bottle/vase; bulbous body; wide, long neck; white rim, base, and interior; Ch'ien Lung six-character mark (and of the period), 21" high, **$4,000–$6,000.**

Blue bowl, everted rim (chipped), white interior, Kuang Hsü six-character mark (and of the period), 4" diameter, **$200–$300.**

Blue bulb bowl, everted rim, white rim and interior, late 18th / early 19th century, 7½" diameter, **$350–$450.**

Blue jardinières, square, molded with bamboo borders, circular panels on sides, pierced, early 20th century, 11½" high, **pair, $375–$475.**

Blue kendi (powder blue), pear-shaped spout, traces of gilt decoration, flaring neck, Ch'ien Lung, 8½" high, **$700–$1,000.**

Blue kendi (powder blue), onion-shaped spout, traces of gilt floral decorations, landscape panel, 18th century, 9½" high, **$450–$700.**

Blue sauce dish incised with five-toed dragon and flaming pearl—the exterior, with lotus meander; Kuang Hsü six-character mark (and of the period), 13" diameter, **$400–$650.**

Blue sauce dish, plain interior, deep blue glaze stopping neatly around the foot, early 18th century, 8½" diameter, **$700–$900.**

Blue vase (powder blue), yen-yen shape, traces of gilt decoration, 18th century, 16" high, **$1,000–$1,500.**

Blue vases, slender necks, globular bodies, gilt dragons and flaming pearls, Kuang Hsü six-character mark (and of the period), 15" high, **pair, $1,200–$1,500.**

Blue vase (powder blue), square form, elephant head handles, gilt sprays of grasses, landscape panels, T'ung Chih six-character mark (and of the period), 11½" high, **$600–$800.**

Blue vase (powder blue); beaker form; four central, serrated vertical flanges; late 18th/early 19th century, 9" high, **$600–$800.**

Blue vases (powder blue), rouleau form, gilt-enriched landscape, pierced and mounted as lamps, late 18th/early 19th century, 18" high, **$800–$1,000.**

Blue vase (powder blue), baluster form, gilt chrysanthemums, late 18th century, 6½" high, **$300–$400.**

Blue vase (powder blue), even glaze, white interior, late 18th/early 19th century, 8" high, **$500–$750.**

Robin's egg blue brush washer, applied chih lung at rim, late 19th century, 3" diameter, **$350–$450.**

Robin's egg blue vase, flared foot, trumpet mouth, glaze shading to white on the interior; Ch'ien Lung mark, but late 19th century; 13" high, **$2,500–$3,500.**

Robin's egg blue vase, baluster form, late 19th century, pierced and mounted as a lamp, 15½" high, **$250–$350.**

Café au lait bottle/vase, pear-shaped, mask and ring handles, flared neck, 19th century, 9½" high, **$600–$800.**

Café au lait bowl, iridescent brown interior, pale brown exterior, white rim and base, K'ang Hsi six-character mark (and of the period), 4¾" diameter, **$2,000–$3,000.**

Café au lait bowl; everted rim; the exterior, a pale washed brown; plain interior; 18th century, 7" diameter, **$600–$800.**

Café au lait bowl, everted rim, molded with two thin ribs on the exterior, Ch'ien Lung six-character mark (and of the period), 7" diameter, **$2,000–$3,000.**

Celadon basin; stylized floral medallion and fretted border; flat, everted rim; brown foot rim; early Ming dynasty, 14" diameter, **$1,500–$2,000.**

Celadon bowl molded and carved on the exterior with sprays of lotus, tree peony, and fruits, with clouds and scrolls; plain interior; Yung Cheng six-character mark (and of the period), 13" diameter, **$10,000–$20,000.**

Celadon bowl, pale glaze with incised emblems and vases on the exterior, plain interior, late 19th century, 5½" diameter, **$200–$300.**

Celadon bottle/vase molded and carved with archaic dragons and tree peony between bands of lotus and stiff leaves; a key fret on the rim; Ch'ien Lung mark, but 19th century; 20½" high, **$1,200–$1,500.**

Celadon bowl; flat, everted rim; the interior with molded radiating petal flutes, the exterior with molded-in relief petals; recessed base; 18th century, 10" diameter, **$600–$900.**

Celadon bowl, square with canted corners, relief motif of phoenix outlined in gilt; Tao Kuang seal, but late 19th century; 5" square, **$300–$500.**

Celadon bulb bowl; tripod; bombe body; trellis pattern with clouds on the exterior; the interior—a burnt, reddish brown; Ming dynasty, 9" diameter, **$700–$900.**

Celadon bulb bowl (also called a *Narcissus* bowl), squat, three short feet, floral motif, flattened rim, Ming dynasty, 12" diameter, **$800–$1,000.**

Celadon dish, even glaze on exterior and interior, short foot, late 18th century, 6" diameter, **$200–$300.**

Celadon garden seat, barrel-shaped, molded lion mask and ring handles (four), Ming dynasty, 18" high, **$3,500–$4,500.**

Celadon garden seat, barrel form, plain exterior with two bands of bosses, early 20th century, 18½" high, **$350–$450.**

Celadon figure of Pu Tai seated on rock-work with one arm resting on bag of happiness; his hands, feet, face, and body all orange-fired gray biscuit; Ming dynasty, 17th century, 8" high, **$2,500–$3,500.**

Celadon figure of Pu Tai seated and leaning on bag of happiness; his face, feet, body, and hands glazed brown; early 20th century, 7" high, **$85–$125.**

Celadon figure of Shou Lao, early 20th century, 11" high, **$150–$200.**

Celadon jardinière, globular, everted rim, incised peony and foliage with cloud scrolls, plain interior, late 18th/early 19th century, 10½" high, **$800–$1,000.**

Celadon moon flask, each side with carved lotus sprays and leaves, long narrow neck, chih lung handles, Yung Cheng six-character mark (and of the period), chipped, 11½" high, **$4,500–$6,500.**

Celadon vase; pear-shaped; motif of scrolling foliage; loop and wide ring handles; pierced and mounted as a lamp; Ming dynasty, 12" high, **$1,000–$1,500.**

Celadon vase, two molded dragons around the neck and shoulder, mounted as a lamp, early 20th century, 16½" high, **$250–$325.**

Celadon vase, yen-yen form, trumpet neck, incised design of prunus and peony, crackled glaze, 16th century, 15" high, **$1,200–$1,500.**

Celadon vase; baluster form; molded with scrolling lotus and foliage; elephant-head fixed ring handles; Ch'ien Lung mark, but 19th century; 17" high, **$600–$900.**

Celadon vase; pear-shaped; molded with tassels of scrolls; pierced handles; Ch'eng Hua six-character mark, but late 19th century; 15" high, **$500–$700.**

Cherry red box and cover, turquoise interior and base, late 19th century, 4" diameter, **$175–$225.**

Cherry red (also termed Lang Yao) bottle/vase; even, rich red glaze pooling neatly around the foot; late 18th/early 19th century, 12¼" high, **$1,000–$1,500.**

Cherry red saucer dish, white interior, dark red glaze, Yung Cheng six-character mark (and of the period), rim chips, 8" diameter, **$500–$700.**

Cherry red vase, baluster, rib at the neck, 19th century, 14" high, **$700–$900.**

Cherry red vase, baluster form, one rib at neck, chips on the foot, 18th century, 13" high, **$2,000–$2,500.**

Claire de lune bottle; double gourd; even glaze stopping neatly around the foot; Ch'ien Lung six-character mark, but late 18th/early 19th century; 12" high, **$1,500–$2,200.**

Claire de lune brush washer, translucent glaze pooling at the foot, fret chips on interior, K'ang Hsi six-character mark (and of the period), 4¾" diameter, **$900–$1,200.**

Claire de lune bowl; incised motif of crane and clouds in a roundel on the interior, the exterior with a floral meander; 19th century, 9½" diameter, **$600–$900.**

Claire de lune vase, molded elephant head and ringed ears, pierced and mounted as a lamp, early 20th century, 14" high, **$200–$275.**

Claire de lune vase, square form, molded with Buddhist trigrams on the angles, short neck, spreading foot, crackled glaze, Ch'ien Lung six-character mark (and of the period), 11" high, **$9,000–$12,000.**

Copper red bowl; deep, rich, colored glaze thinning near the rim; white interior; Yung Cheng six-character mark (and of the period), 4¼" diameter, **$3,500–$4,500.**

Copper red bowl, plain interior, 18th century, 6" diameter, **$500–$700.**

Copper red jarlet, globular with wide mouth, white interior, glaze stopping neatly around the foot, K'ang Hsi six-character mark (and of the period), 3¼" diameter, **$1,050–$1,450.**

Copper red saucer dish, glaze thinning around the rim and darkening at the center, 18th century, 6½" diameter, **$700–$900.**

Chinese porcelain water container (brush washer) with a copper red glaze, fire crack in rim, 18th century, 4" diameter, **$200–$400.**

A large water container (brush washer for larger size brushes) with copper red glaze, 18th century, 8" diameter, **$800–$1,200.** (Note: The large-sized containers generally have nicks or chips to the rim because of the beating they received from the large-sized brushes.)

Left: *Chinese porcelain flambé-glazed globular vase; heavily potted with a thick, everted rim; the shoulders flanked by molded mask and ring handles; covered in a rich, streaked burgundy and lavender-purple glaze stopping short of the foot; the interior thinning to a grayish crackled glaze; 18th century; 9" high. Realized price (including the 10-percent buyer's premium), Christie's East, New York City,* **$1,540.** Right: *Chinese I Hsing (Yixing) teapot with a robin's egg glaze, faintly impressed mark on the base, 9½" high. Realized price (including the 10-percent buyer's premium), Christie's East, New York City,* **$1,100.**

Copper red stem bowl; ribbed foot; deep, rich glaze thinning at the ribs; plain interior; Yung Cheng six-character mark (and of the period), **$5,500–$7,500.**

Coral dish, the coral ground decorated with flowering chrysanthemums painted in a central roundel below a fluted well, damaged, 18th century, 7" diameter, **$600–$900.**

Coral vase, oviform body with tall slender neck, dragon applied at the neck, base and interior glazed in European green, early 19th century, 12" high, **$900–$1,200.**

Flambé bottle/vase, tapered cylindrical body, inverted trumpet–shaped neck, red glaze with lavender splashes, c1900, 9¾" high, **$250–$350.**

Flambé bottle/vase, globular, tall flaring neck, streaked glaze, violet blue in some areas around the foot and neck, late 19th century, 13" high, **$300–$500.**

Flambé bottle/vase, late 19th century, 5" high, **$75–$100.**

Flambé figures, Buddhistic lions glazed red with purple and white streaks, early 20th century, 10" high, **pair, $300–$400.**

Flambé jar, oviform, ribbed shoulder, animal mask handles, streaked olive and purple glaze stopping around a shallow-cut foot, glazed base, 18th century, 13½" high, **$650–$850.**

Flambé vase, pear-shaped, cup rim, rib at shoulder, streaked with cherry red and purple glazes, 19th century, 12½" high, **$400–$500.**

Flambé vases; rectangular with two molded, tubular handles; red glaze streaked with purple and gray; 10½" high, early 20th century, **pair, $300–$500.**

Gold bowl, short foot, exterior covered with an even gilt, Yung Cheng six-character mark (and of the period), 3½" diameter, **$1,500–$2,500.**

Iron rust bottle/vase; pear-shaped with a reddish/brown, mottled gray glaze; 18th century, 4" high, **$400–$600.**

Iron rust bottle/vase, gray-flecked reddish brown glaze, globular body, slender neck, concave base, 18th century, 4½" high, **$600–$700.**

Iron rust censer; tripod; globular body; short, everted rim; mottled glaze stopping around the neck of the interior; late 19th century, 6" wide, **$300–$450.**

Iron rust vase; mei ping form; pink-brown glaze with metallic gray, thinning to white around the rim; trimmed foot; concave base; 18th century, 3½" high, **$600–$800.**

Lavender vase, baluster form, short neck, rib halfway up the neck, large crackled glaze, K'ang Hsi, 8½" high, **$1,600–$2,200.**

Lavender vase; broad, ovoid body; tall neck; animal mask handles; Yung Lo mark, but late 19th/early 20th century, 5" high, **$200–$300.**

Lavender bowl, glaze thinning and pooling at the foot, plain interior, Hsien Feng six-character mark (and of the period), 6½" diameter, **$1,200–$1,800.**

Liver red saucer dish, white everted rim, even glaze, Tao Kuang six-character mark (and of the period), 8" diameter, **$700–$1,000.**

Liver red vase, mei ping form, tapered waist, pale glaze thinning to white around the lip and base, Ch'ien Lung seal mark (and of the period), rim fretting, 7½" high, **$1,200–$1,500.**

Mirror black bottle/vase, globular body, cylindrical neck, garlic mouth, 14" high, 19th century, **$500–$750.**

Mirror black teapot, globular with domed lid, traces of gilt birds and plants, 18th century, 5" high, **$500–$700.**

Mirror black vase, mallet shape, cylindrical neck, late 19th/early 20th century, 6" high, **$100–$175.**

Mirror black vases, ovoid bodies, open S-shaped handles, pierced and mounted as lamps, early 20th century, 12¾" high, **pair, $350–$500.**

Mirror black vase, rouleau form, traces of gilt floral motif, K'ang Hsi, old damages, 12½" high, **$600–$800.**

Mirror black vase, rib at the flaring neck, spreading foot, glaze thinning to brown at the rim, late 19th century, 18½" high, **$500–$750.**

Peach-bloom amphora, double white rib at the base of the neck, mottled copper red with greenish flecks; K'ang Hsi six-character mark, but 19th century; 8½" high, **$1,000–$1,500.**

Peach-bloom amphora, large patches of white and mushroom; K'ang Hsi six-character mark, but 19th century; 10" high, **$400–$700.**

Chinese porcelain vase with a mirror black glaze, six-character K'ang Hsi mark (and of the period), 7" high, $1,800–$2,500.

Peach-bloom amphora, soft mottled copper red with olive green flecks, late 19th/early 20th century, 6½" high, $600–$800.

Peach-bloom box and cover, a rich red glaze paling in some areas and having green spots, shallow concave foot, plain interior, K'ang Hsi six-character mark (and of the period), 2¾" diameter, $3,500–$4,500.

Peach-bloom box and cover, the glaze flecked with green, K'ang Hsi six-character mark (and of the period), 2¾" diameter, $6,000–$8,000.

Peach-bloom saucer dish, ashes of roses, 19th century, 12" diameter, $400–$600.

Peach-bloom vase, slender tapering form, narrow shoulder, tall flaring neck, mottled glaze with green flecks, glaze thickening around the base, deeply recessed base glazed in white; K'ang Hsi six-character mark, but late 19th century; 6½" high, $500–$700.

Peach-bloom water pot, three incised archaic dragons, roundels with clouds and scrolls, glaze in liver red to gray, K'ang Hsi six-character mark (and of the period), minor restoration at the foot, 5" wide, $1,500–$2,500.

Purple libation cup, oval shape, broad rim, angled strap handle, K'ang Hsi, 4" diameter, $1,500–$2,500.

Purple saucer dish; everted rim; interior incised with five-toed dragon, flaming pearl, and cloud scrolls; rim fretting; K'ang Hsi six-character mark (and of the period), 10" diameter, $2,000–$3,000.

Sang de boeuf bowl, shallow with raised rim, base and interior glaze pale blue; Hsüan Te mark, but 18th century; 10" diameter, $600–$900.

Sang de boeuf vase, baluster form, red glaze thinning at the bulbous neck and pooling in a double rib at the shoulder, late 19th century, 21" high, $600–$900.

Sang de boeuf vase, baluster form, slender body, trumpet mouth, glaze thinning to white at the rim, 19th century, 21" high, $800–$1,000.

Sang de boeuf vase, double gourd, the glaze with purple streaks at the neck, late 19th/early 20th century, 13" high, $600–$800.

Sang de boeuf vase, pear-shaped, spreading neck, band at shoulder, two elephant-head handles with fixed rings, early to mid-19th century, 8" high, **$600–$800.**

Sang de boeuf vase, pear-shaped, white interior and base, Ch'ien Lung six-character mark (and of the period), 10¾" high, **$900–$1,500.**

Sang de boeuf vase, pear-shaped, translucent red glaze with areas of flambé, first half of the 19th century, 10" high, **$300–$600.**

Tea-dust bottle/vase, even matte glaze, 19th century, 10" high, **$300–$500.**

Tea-dust censer, tripod, oval form with rounded sides, green-powdered brown glaze stopping short of the feet, 18th century, 4" long, **$600–$800.**

Turquoise bottle/vase, early 19th century, 4¾" high, **$200–$275.**

Turquoise bottle/vase, three ribs on the lower portion of the tall slender neck, evenly glazed, 18th century, 10¼" high, **$1,000–$1,500.**

Turquoise figures, the Eight Immortals, incised details, early 20th century, 6½" high, **$300–$400.**

Turquoise figures, Buddhistic lions, mirror image, rectangular bases, fierce expressions, early 20th century, 12" high, **pair, $300–$500.**

Turquoise figure, lady seated upon an elephant, crackled glaze, early 20th century, 10¾" high, **$250–$300.**

Turquoise figures; Pu Tai seated on flat, oval base; loosely draped robes open at the front revealing a large stomach; late 19th/early 20th century, 3" high, **pair, $250–$400.**

Turquoise garden seat, barrel-shaped, two rows of raised bosses, a center band of incised floral motifs, early 20th century, 19½" high, **$800–$1,000.**

Turquoise jar, speckled glaze, neck shaved, pierced-wood lid, 17th century, 5" high, **$400–$600.**

Turquoise water dropper, a Buddhistic lion, 18th century, 2" high, **$475–$550.**

Turquoise vase; globular; tall, cylindrical neck; four incised four-toed dragons; flaming pearls; flame scrolls; glaze partially covering the foot; biscuit base; late 19th century, 14½" high, **$400–$600.**

Yellow bottle/vase (lemon yellow), finely crackled, bulbous with long neck, early 19th century, 17½" high, **$1,050–$1,400.**

Yellow bowl (Imperial yellow), incised decoration—under the glaze—with two five-toed dragons pursuing flaming pearls amongst clouds and stylized waves, Ch'ien Lung six-character mark (and of the period), 5¾" diameter, **$3,000–$5,000.**

Yellow bowl incised on exterior with dragons, flames, rocks, and waves; white interior and base; damaged; Tao Kuang seal (and of the period), 4½" diameter, **$800–$1,200.**

Yellow dish, flared rim, glaze thinning at base, base glazed white, Ming dynasty, Chia Ching mark (and of the period), 6" diameter, **$15,000–$20,000.**

Yellow figures, the Eight Immortals, incised details, early 20th century, 5½" high, **$200–$300.**

Yellow moon flask, elephant-head ears, eight trigrams in relief, late 19th century, 9½" high, **$400–$600.**

Ming Dynasty Pottery and Porcelain Marks

Hung Wu
1368–1398

Hung Wu (seal form)
1368–1398

Yung Lo
1403–1424

Yung Lo (archaic form)
1403–1424

Hsüan Te
1426–1435

Hsüan Te (seal form)
1426–1435

Ch'eng Hua
1465–1487

Ch'eng Hua (seal form)
1465–1487

Hung Chih
1488–1505

Ch'eng Te
1506–1521

Chia Ching
1522–1566

Lung Ch'ing
1567–1572

Wan Li
1573–1619

Wan Li (archaic form)
1573–1619

T'ien Ch'i
1621–1627

Ch'ung Cheng
1628–1643

Yellow sauce dish, two five-toed dragons on interior, the exterior motif with cranes in flight, Kuang Hsü six-character mark (and of the period), 5" diameter, **$600–$800.**

Yellow sauce dish (Imperial yellow), mottled, restored, Ming dynasty, 6" diameter, **$1,000–$1,600.**

Yellow saucer dish (Imperial yellow/deep lemon), damaged, Ming dynasty, Hung Chih six-character mark (and of the period), 8½" diameter, **$1,500–$1,800.**

Yellow saucer dish (Imperial yellow), incised decorations of dragon and lotus meander over entire surface, plain interior, damaged, Ming dynasty, Chia Ching, 8" diameter, **$1,500–$2,200.**

Yellow vase; pear-shaped; high, hollow foot; applied elephant mask handles; flared, upturned mouth; the body carved with lotus and peony; 19th century, 8½" high, **$900–$1,200.**

Blue and White

Bottle, double gourd, motif of eight trigrams and fire scrolls, Ming dynasty, 16th century, fritting, 4" high, **$600–$900.**

Bottle, motif of arrow vases on tripod tables between borders of foliage, plantain leaves on neck, meandering lotus on flared rim, K'ang Hsi, 9" high, **$1,800–$2,400.**

Bottle, motif of alternating panels with ladies holding fans and seated beside tripod censers, lotus lappets around neck and hatched pattern on everted rim, K'ang Hsi, 9" high, **$2,000–$3,000.**

Bottle, pear-shaped, panels of riverscapes alternating with scholars, floral sprays at shoulder, body crack, K'ang Hsi, 10½" high, **$500–$700.**

Bottles painted with scrolling foliage between bands of lappets, the necks with applied dragons (mirror image), late 19th century, 14" high, **pair, $700–$900.**

Bowl, pheasant in flight, peony and bamboo on exterior, chips, Ming dynasty, early 17th century, 8" diameter, **$300–$400.**

Bowl, key-pattern panels on exterior with roundels of Arabic calligraphy, interior band of Arabic, made for the Islamic market, chipped, Ming dynasty, late 16th/early 17th century, 8" diameter, **$2,000–$3,000.**

Bowl, foliate rim, interior motif of a bird standing on a rock below peach spray panels, similar motif on exterior, Ming dynasty, Wan Li, 5½" diameter, **$450–$700.**

Bowl, interior motif of pagoda and rock with fisherman and boats, riverscape exterior, Ming dynasty, Wan Li, 4½" diameter, **$500–$750.**

Bowl, exterior painted with carp, horse, dragon, and other animals above breaking waves, top and bottom with key-pattern and tooth-pattern bands, six-character Hsüan T'ung mark (and of the period), 8" diameter, **$2,000–$3,000.**

Bowl, everted rim, motif of official and monk with pavilion and fence, the interior with an elder in a roundel below pine branches, K'ang Hsi, 7¾" diameter, **$800–$1,200.**

Chinese porcelain bowl, underglaze blue and white with motifs of dragons and diapers, late 18th century, **$1,500–$1,800.** Courtesy of the Virginia Keresey Collection.

Bowl, everted rim, globular, painted with dragons and flaming pearls, mid-17th century, Transitional, 9½" diameter, **$475–$750.**

Bowl; globular tripod; four roundels of cranes; the base with Yung Cheng mark, but 19th century; 9¼" diameter, **$400–$600.**

Bowl and cover, domed lid, flower-head finial, overall motif of foliage and horses, crack in body, Ming dynasty, early 17th century, 5" high, **$600–$800.**

Bowl and cover, shallow bowl, bud finial, scrolling foliage, Ming dynasty, late 16th/early 17th century, 6" diameter, **$600–$800.**

Box and cover, four lion mask feet, motif of carp and waves, peony sprays and vines at trim, repaired, Ming dynasty, late 16th/early 17th century, 4" square, **$750–$1,000.**

Circular box and cover, soft-paste porcelain, underglaze blue and white with motif of boys in various poses, K'ang Hsi mark (and of the period), 6" diameter, **$1,000–$1,500.** Courtesy of the Virginia Keresey Collection.

Box and cover, ingot-shaped, cover painted with phoenix and lotus within a key-pattern rim, the lower part painted with lappets of cell and dot pattern, the interior divided into two compartments, Ming dynasty, 16th century, 4½" diameter, **$3,000–$4,000.**

Blue and white dish with motifs of gourds, slightly scalloped rim, Ming Dynasty, Wan Li, 6" diameter, **$900–$1,200.**

Chinese blue and white porcelain dish, the center motif of flowers and foliage surrounded by a diaper divided by floral reserves, the border containing flowers and emblems, damaged, Ch'ien Lung, 18th century, 11½" diameter, **$300–$400.**

Chinese underglaze blue and white dish with circular motifs of dragons and flames, K'ang Hsi style, c1800, 5½" diameter, **$250–$375.**

Box and cover, scenic motif on lid within double bands, early 20th century, 3" diameter, **$50–$75.**

Box and cover; lady and attendant with pine branch on lid; four-character Ch'ien Lung mark on base, but early 20th century; 3½" diameter, **$45–$65.**

Brush pot, cylindrical, motif of the Immortals and officials, fritting, K'ang Hsi, 7" diameter, **$1,000–$1,500.**

Brush pot, cylindrical, motif of fisherman and lake with landscape, K'ang Hsi, 5" high, **$1,200–$1,500.**

Brush pot, cylindrical, figures and landscape, 19th century, 5¼" high, **$250– $350.**

Brush pot; cylindrical; two panels of figures on horseback; four-character Ch'eng Hua mark on base, but late 19th century; 5½" high, **$125–$225.**

Candlesticks, tall and square, formed in two parts (as a large bell supporting a slender conical upper section), overall lotus and scroll divided by key-pattern borders, early 19th century, 21" high, **$3,000–$4,000.**

Candlesticks, one with chips, ribbed stems, wide flanges, domed feet with radiating Shou characters, mid-to-late 19th century, 11½" high, **$1,000– $1,500.**

Dish; seated lady watching a boy chasing a butterfly; the border with four panels of tulips dividing larger, fan-shaped panels; Ming dynasty, T'ien Ch'i/Ch'ung Cheng, 14" diameter, **$1,800–$2,500.**

Dish, aster pattern, leaf mark on base, chipping, K'ang Hsi, 13" diameter, **$700–$900.**

Dish, motif of central basket of peony, trellis-pattern border, 18th century, 12" diameter, **$400–$600.**

Dish, scrolling peony on interior, exterior with branches, fritting, K'ang Hsi, 14" diameter, **$400–$600.**

Dish, central spray of finger citrus and peach branches, 18th century, 7½" diameter, **$300–$400.**

Dish, rocky riverscape with bird in flight, chips, Ch'ien Lung, 12½" diameter, **$400–$600.**

Ewer, animal handle with face peering over rim, three leaping horses among Precious Things emblems, minor fritting, early 17th century, 7¼" diameter, **$500–$8,000.**

Ewer, pear-shaped, serpentine spout, scrolling lotus and bands of ruyi heads with plantain leaves on the neck, Ming dynasty, Wan Li, 5¾" high, **$500–$750.**

Ewer, serpentine spout, scrolling lotus on body, ruyi heads on foot, floral sprays on neck, garlic top, damaged (metal mounts, rim, chain, and stretcher), Ming dynasty, first half of the 16th century, 11" high, **$1,500–$2,000.**

Ewer and cover, hexagonal, bulbous spout, arched handle, painted with landscapes and a procession of dignitaries, damages, mid-19th century, 8½" wide, **$300–$350.**

Ewer; serpentine spout; globular body; motif of peony, chrysanthemum, and lotus in molded, petal-shaped panels; trellis pattern on the conical neck; rim chips; K'ang Hsi, 8" high, **$600–$900.**

Garden seat; barrel-shaped; lion mask handles; brocade balls and lotus on top; peacocks and peony at the center between borders of raised studs, waves, and lappets at the base; restored; Ming dynasty, 16th century, 14½" high, **$800–$1,200.**

Garden seat, hexagonal, painted with flowering shrubs between two bands of raised studs, late 19th century, 19" high, **$550–$700.**

Garden seat, blue ground with white sprays of blossoms and two pierced coin symbols, hairlines, c1900, 18" high, **$300–$500.**

Jar, soft paste, oviform, village scene and riverscape, the neck shaved, 18th century, 12½" high, **$600–$800.**

Jar, oviform, motif of scrolling chrysanthemum between bands of lotus, tooth pattern around the shoulder, chipped, c1755, Transitional, 8" high, **$350–$500.**

Jar, square form, two panels of figures and pavilion with riverscape, two panels of calligraphy, second half of the 19th century, 11" high, **$150–$225.**

Jar and cover, Hawthorne pattern, c1900, 8" high, **$125–$175.**

Jar and cover, bird finial, motif of 100 Antiques, cracked, 18th century, 6" high, **$400–$600.**

Jar and wood cover, five boys playing in a garden, 18th century, 6½" high, **$750–$950.**

Jars and wood covers, Hawthorne pattern, early 19th century, 5" high, **pair, $200–$300.**

Jardinière, four large panels of hunters and game birds between ruyi lappets, 19th century, 18" diameter, **$2,500–$3,500.**

Jardinières and underplates, square form tapering to base, continuous scenic motif, mid-to-late 19th century, 9½" wide, **pair, $900–$1,200.**

Jardinières, everted rim, continuous mountainous riverscape with pavilions, three bracket feet with floral sprays, pierced bases, late 19th century, 19½" high, **pair, $1,200–$1,600.**

Jardinières, continuous motif of children, lappets at the foot and ruyi shape lappets at the top, 19th century, 14½" high, **pair, $1,500–$2,500.**

Jardinières, tapering cylindrical form painted with fish and water plants, bases pierced, 20th century, 10" diameter, **pair, $700–$900.**

Jardinières, octagonal with everted rims, stylized lotus and scroll above lappets, the foot reticulated and painted with cloud scrolls, one with restoration on rim, 19th century, 14½" diameter, **pair, $1,200–$1,500.**

Jardinières, rectangular with four bracket feet, a band of lotus and scroll between gadrooned and cloud-scroll borders beneath flange and key-pattern rim, 19th century, 16" long, **pair, $1,500–$2,000.**

Jardinières, circular, painted with four-toed dragons and flaming pearls above wave border, one damaged, early 19th century, 13½" diameter, **pair, $1,500–$2,000.**

Kendi, roundels of flower heads and breaking waves at center, lotus on mammiform spout, lappets around foot, repair to spout, Ming dynasty, early 16th century, 7½" high, **$1,200–$1,800.**

Kendi painted with meandering budding flowers, lozenge symbols at the shoulder, hairlines, Ming dynasty, late 16th century, 7" high, **$750–$1,000.**

Kendi, panels of leaves and peach sprays overall, leaves on neck, mammiform spout, damaged, Wan Li, 7" high, **$300–$500.**

Kendi, meandering hibiscus motif and scrolling foliage, mammiform spout, restored and chipped, Wan Li, 7½" high, **$600–$950.**

Kendi, cranes and clouds on hexagonal scale pattern, emblems at shoulder, crack on spout, Wan Li, 5" high, **$500–$700.**

Kendi, meandering chih lung and flower sprays, foliage at waist, mammiform spout (chipped), 17th century, 7" high, **$600–$800.**

Kendi, panels of riverscapes, lotus sprays on body, onion-shaped spout, ruyi lappets at shoulder, plantain leaves on neck, flared rim, Ch'ien Lung, 9" high, **$950–$1,500.**

Stem cup, two fruiting vines on exterior, roundel of vine at center of interior, key-pattern band on foot, Ming dynasty, 17th century, 5" diameter, **$1,500–$2,000.**

Stem cup, leaping carp and waves in center of interior below a trellis-pattern border, 17th century, 5" diameter, **$600–$900.**

Blue and white porcelain teapot, K'ang Hsi period, some roughness under the lid, **$500–$700.**

Vase, mei ping form, motif of stylized lotus at the center, lappets and key pattern around foot, lappets around shoulder, Ming dynasty, 16th century, 8½" high, **$800–$1,200.**

Vase, double gourd, Buddhistic lions and ribboned balls around center of upper and lower lobes, borders of interlocking foliage and lappet band around foot, damages, Ming dynasty, 16th century, 15½" high, **$2,500–$3,500.**

Vase, pear-shaped, meandering lotus and chrysanthemums with chevron borders, plantain leaves on neck, lappets around foot, badly damaged, 14th century, 9" high, **$250–$350.**

Vase, baluster form, loop handles, meandering lotus overall, plantain leaves on neck, fritting, 15th century, 7" high, **$1,500–$2,500.**

Vase; pear-shaped; dragon handles; two panels of scholars crossing a bridge with riverscape, divided by scholar's utensils and censers; prunus branches and cell pattern around rim; chips on base; K'ang Hsi, 15" high, **$2,700–$3,800.**

Vase, baluster form, pheasant in flight (and other flying birds) with rock-work, hatch pattern around shoulder, camellia and rock-work around neck, minor chips, K'ang Hsi, 18" high, **$3,500–$5,000.**

Left: Underglaze blue and white deep dish, the recessed well decorated with stylized fruit and flower-head medallion within a border containing the eight Taoist Emblems, the exterior with scrolling foliage above ruyi spearhead border, Ch'ien Lung mark (and of the period), 8" diameter. Realized price (including the 10-percent buyer's premium), Christie's East, New York City, **$605.**

Right: Underglaze blue and white baluster vase; the body on a tall, flaring foot and painted with a scene of eccentric Immortals amongst pine, lingzhi fungus, and rock-work between molded bands of geometric devices; the neck further painted with a bird on a gnarled pine amongst bamboo, lingzhi, and pierced rocks; star crack and small gold lacquer rim repair; Yung Cheng (Yongzheng) mark (and of the period); 8⅞" high. Realized price (including the 10-percent buyer's premium), Christie's East, New York City, **$715.**

Chinese underglaze blue and white bowl, lotus and scroll motif in Ming style, mid-19th century, 4½" diameter, **$200–$300.**

Vase, beaker form, panels of archaic vessels and scholar's utensils within floral lozenge borders, damaged, K'ang Hsi, 10¼" high, **$600–$800.**

Vase, baluster form with domed cover, lion mask ears, peony above lappets, ruyi lappets around shoulder, foliage on neck, a body crack painted over— poor restoration, 19th century, 26½" high, **$650–$1,000.**

Vase, blue with white slip relief motif of plum tree and bamboo, mid-19th century, 9" high, **$400–$500.**

Vase, baluster form, dense scrolling peony above band of lotus petals, the shoulder with hatch pattern, tooth pattern around neck, Ch'ien Lung, 15½" high, **$1,500–$2,000.**

Vase, baluster form, scrolling peony between bands of lappets, the shoulder with ruyi lappets, late 18th century, 14¾" high, **$1,200–$1,800.**

Vase; double gourd; five-toed dragons, flaming pearls, and cloud scrolls; lappets on neck; cell pattern around foot; late 19th century, 16" high, **$700–$900.**

Vases, hexagonal, overall lotus meander between ruyi lappets, c1900, 24" high, **pair, $2,000–$3,000.**

Vase, yen-yen shape, painted with zodiac animals, late 19th century, 16½" high, **$650–$825.**

Vase, dappled blue overall, early 20th century, 9½" high, **$100–$150.**

Vase, yen-yen shape, panels of the Immortals in landscapes, flaring neck, drilled and mounted as a lamp, 18th century, 18½" high, **$1,200–$1,500.**

Vases, baluster form, overall chrysanthemum and vines motif, pierced wood covers, pierced and mounted as lamps, c1900, 14" high, **pair, $700–$950.**

Blue and Yellow

Bowl, two yellow dragons above two overlapping petals, plain interiors, each with tiny rim chips, Ch'ien Lung (Qianlong) six-character mark (and of the period), 5" diameter, **$1,000–$1,500.**

Dish, everted rim, centrally painted with five-toed dragon and flaming pearl amongst fire scrolls with a border of two dragons and flaming pearl, repeated on exterior, Tao Kuang (Daoguang) six-character mark (and of the period), 9¾" diameter, **$2,000–$3,000.**

Dish, everted rim, centrally painted with five-toed dragon and flaming pearl amongst fire scrolls with a border of two dragons and flaming pearl, repeated on exterior, rim chips, Tao Kuang (Daoguang) six-character mark (and of the period), **$1,000–$1,500.**

Dish, everted rim, centrally painted with five-toed dragon and flaming pearl amongst fire scrolls with a border of two dragons and flaming pearl, repeated on the exterior, Ch'ien Lung (Qianlong) six-character mark (and of the period), 9½" diameter, **$3,000–$4,000.**

Dish, everted rim, centrally painted with five-toed dragon and flaming pearl amongst fire scrolls with a border of two dragons and flaming pearl, repeated on the exterior, rim chips, Ch'ien Lung (Qianlong) six-character mark (and of the period), **$2,800–$3,500.**

Celadon

Bowl; flat rim; small, molded floral medallion; exterior molded with petals and meander; Ming Dynasty, 15th century, 6½" diameter, **$2,000–$3,000.**

Bowl; shallow, flattened rim; deep, semitranslucent, olive green glaze; gray biscuit foot; kiln adhesions on base; Northern Sung (Song) Dynasty, 6¼" diameter, **$1,000–$1,500.**

Bowl, short foot, inward-curving rim, pale olive green glaze, Northern Sung (Song) Dynasty, 4½" diameter, **$500–$700.**

Bowl, exterior carved with foliage meander, the interior with six ribs rising to the everted rim, the glaze with a large crackle, damage to the rim, Northern Sung (Song) Dynasty, 4¾" diameter, **$500–$750.**

Bowl carved with a single open flower on a peony spray on the interior, translucent olive green glaze, paler on the base, Northern Sung (Song) Dynasty, 8½" diameter, **$3,000–$5,000.**

Dish, the incised interior motif of flowering lotus and four fruiting branches filling the well, Ming Dynasty, 14th/15th century, 13¼" diameter, **$900–$1,200.**

Dish, hexafoil, shallow well, orange-fired foot, pale blue glaze, large crackle, Southern Sung (Song) Dynasty, 6" diameter, **$2,000–$3,000.**

Dish (Lung Ch'uan), flaring rim carved with lotus heads and scroll around a central flower head, blue-green glaze, chips on foot, Yüan Dynasty, 8¾" diameter, **$600–$750.**

Vase, pear-shaped, glaze slightly crackled, damaged, Yüan Dynasty, 6½" high, **$400–$600.**

Vase, ribbed body, short cylindrical neck, everted rim, ivory glaze on interior, olive green glaze on exterior, shallow-cut foot, crack in body, Yüan Dynasty, 8" high, **$600–$800.**

Water dropper (Lung Ch'uan) modeled as a cockerel, olive green glaze, chipped, Yüan/Ming Dynasty, 2¾" high, **$300–$450.**

Chien Yao (Hare's Fur)

Bowl, mottled and streaked glaze thinning at the foot, restored, Sung (Song) Dynasty, 5" diameter, **$700–$900.**

Bowl, conical, streaked and splashed on the interior in a pale olive brown on a chocolate ground, shallow-cut stoneware foot, damaged, Southern Sung (Song) Dynasty, 4¾" diameter, **$400–$550.**

Bowl, cylindrical rim streaked with lavender and cream on a deep brown glaze, shallow-cut buff stoneware foot, Sung (Song) Dynasty, 4¾" diameter, **$700–$900.**

Bowl, conical, everted rim, dark olive brown translucent glaze thinning to brown at the rim, gray stoneware with shallow-cut foot, misfired glaze, Southern Sung (Song) Dynasty, 5½" diameter, **$600–$800.**

Bowl, the interior streaked coffee brown over a crackled darker brown ground, glaze degradation, 4½" diameter, **$600–$900.**

Chün Yao

Bud vases, pear-shaped, cylindrical handles, blue glaze mottled and splashed with lavender, a band of bosses below the neck, 18th century, 3¾" high, **pair, $500–$700.**

Dish; flat, everted rim; pale lavender glaze with large crackled, reddish splash across the interior; minor chips on foot; Yüan Dynasty, 4¼" diameter, **$1,500–$2,500.**

Vase; broad, tapering body; short, trumpet neck; air bubbling in the glaze; deep lavender; reddish brown biscuit foot; Yüan Dynasty, 11¾" high, **$600–$900.**

Copper Red

Bottle, pear-shaped with elongated neck, Buddhistic lion in underglaze copper red around the body, 18th century, 8" high, **$800–$1,200.**

Bowl, three carp on exterior in underglaze copper red, plain interior, scratches on interior, Yung Cheng (Yongzheng) six-character mark (and of the period), 9" diameter, **$5,000–$7,000.**

Bowl; three carp in underglaze copper red on the exterior; plain interior; Yung Cheng (Yongzheng) six-character mark on base, but 19th century; 8¾" diameter, **$300–$500.**

Copper Red and Blue

Bowl painted with four copper red dragons amongst clouds above waves, with a central dragon roundel; Ch'ien Lung (Qianlong) mark on base, but 19th century; 7" diameter, **$300–$500.**

Bowl, the rim mounted in silver, Eight Immortals on the exterior, the interior with Shou Lao in a medallion; Hsüan Te (Xuande) mark on the base, but 18th century; 7¾" diameter, **$600–$800.**

Dish, the center and exterior with red dragon and blue waves, the exterior with a cash-pattern band, Chia Ch'ing (Jiaqing) seal (and of the period), 7" diameter, **$2,200–$3,500.**

Dishes, the well decorated with a red dragon and blue breaking waves, the exterior with dragons and waves, Ch'ien Lung (Qianlong) seal (and of the period), 7" diameter, **pair, $3,500–$5,500.**

Dishes, the well decorated with a red dragon and blue breaking waves, the exterior with dragons and waves, one damaged, Ch'ien Lung (Qianlong) seal (and of the period), 7" diameter, **pair, $1,700–$3,000.**

Jardinière, plain interior, exterior with dragon and breaking waves, hairlines, 18th century, **$1,000–$1,500.**

Vase, beaker form, painted in underglaze blue and copper red with small areas of celadon glaze, the upper part with fishing boats and pines, the center with two chih lung and ruyi sprays, the spreading foot with a pine grove and fisherman, crack on base, rim chips, K'ang Hsi (Kangxi), 17½" high, **$900–$1,300.**

Vase, sloping shoulders with panels of flowers on a cell-pattern ground, the body with pine and prunus, the neck with blue bamboo, cup-shaped lip, 18th century, 16½" high, **$1,200–$1,600.**

Vase, yen-yen beaker form, flying cranes and pines repeated on the neck, 18th century, 18" high, **$1,000–$1,500.**

Crackled (Oatmeal Hue) Glaze

Vase, fluted mouth banded in brown, the body with famille rose floral decoration, brown band at the base, early 20th century, 12" high, **$100–$155.**

Vase, blue and white decoration of scholar's utensils, mid-19th century, 12" high, **$500–$700.**

Vase, famille verte, a continuous motif of warriors on horseback; Ch'eng Hua seal, but late 19th century; 10" high, **$125–$185.**

Vase, Buddhistic lion mask and ring handles, molded key-pattern bands in deep brown around the shoulder and base, late 19th century, 14" high, **$250–$350.**

Vase, pear-shaped, underglaze blue birds above brown bands, neck shaved (reduced), early 20th century, 11" high, **$75–$100.**

Egg and Spinach

Bowls; bodies splashed with leaf green, yellow-ochre, and aubergine over white slip; hairlines; 18th century, 7" diameter, **pair, $600–$800.**

Bowls, flaring rims, damages to each, K'ang Hsi (Kangxi), 7½" diameter, **pair, $800–$1,200.**

Buddhistic lion joss-stick holder, rectangular base, paw on brocade ball, damaged, late 19th century, **$300–$400.**

Buddhistic lion joss-stick holder, rectangular open-work base, paw resting on cub's head, Kang H'si (Kangxi), 14½" high, **$3,500–$5,500.**

Parrot perched on rock-work base, iron red beak, 18th century, **$400–$600.**

Jar, broad baluster form, monster mask handles applied at the shoulders, interior partially glazed green, late 19th/early 20th century, 11" high, **$550–$750.**

Vase, double gourd, 18th century, 7" high, **$1,500–$2,500.**

Fa Hua

Bowl, exterior glazed turquoise with white and green flowering sprays in relief, interior glazed dark turquoise, flaking and chips, Ming Dynasty, 7¾" diameter, **$500–$700.**

Censer, tripod with two turquoise dragons in relief on an aubergine ground, 17th century, 6" high, **$600–$800.**

Censer, tripod, streaked deep aubergine with turquoise splashed, repair on rim, 17th century, 7¾" high, **$700–$900.**

Jar, oviform, three lotus heads and foliage in relief, lappets in relief at the shoulders; turquoise, cream, and aubergine glazes; chip on foot; 15th/16th century, **$2,000–$3,000.**

Jarlet, aubergine with a turquoise interior, 17th century, 3" high, **$375–$475.**

Famille Jaune

Ewer in the form of Buddhistic lion crouching on a brocade ball and clasping one side of a hexagonal baluster, decorated with panels of prunus and trellis, rectangular base, K'ang Hsi (Kangxi) style, c1900, 7" high, **$375–$500.**

Parrots, pierced rock-work bases, mirror image, incised and molded markings indicating feathers, late 19th/early 20th century, 3" high, **pair, $100–$150.**

Left: *Chinese porcelain Buddhistic-lion-form wine pot, famille jaune,* c1900, 7" *high,* **$100–$175.** Right: *Chinese Buddhistic lion with brocade ball, famille jaune, marked* China, c1930, 4" *high,* **$35–$50.**

Teapot, hexagonal, six bracket feet, each panel painted with a standing lady, spout and handle with geometric pattern, Buddhistic lion finial, K'ang Hsi (Kangxi), 7" high, **$6,000–$8,000.**

Vase, pear-shaped, painted with scholars and dignitaries holding fans and sceptres; K'ang Hsi (Kangxi) mark, but late 19th century; 12½" high, **$500–$700.**

Vase, baluster form, continuous motif of pairs of birds perched on tree peony, late 19th century, 15¾" high, **$600–$800.**

Vase, tapering square form, tall flaring neck, each side with a warrior, late 19th/early 20th century, 15" high, **$700–$900.**

Vase; baluster form; panels of lotus, camellia, and other flowers surrounded by birds; K'ang Hsi (Kangxi) mark, but late 19th century; 20½" high, **$700–$900.**

Vase, square form, each side painted with terraces and buildings, late 19th century, 20" high, **$900–$1,200.**

Famille Noire

Fish Bowl, exterior painted with continuous floral sprays, key and chevron border, interior with carp and water weeds, early 20th century, 19¼" diameter, **$1,500–$2,500.**

Immortals, each seated with an attribute, early 20th century, 6½" high, **set of 8, $600–$900.**

74

Jardinière; flattened rim; continuous scene of birds perched on gnarled branches of flowering prunus in shades of green, yellow, white, and aubergine on a black ground; late 19th century, 14¼" high, **$1,200–$1,600.**

Vase, yen-yen form, painted with a pair of pheasants on rock-work, late 19th century, 17" high, **$500–$700.**

Vase, baluster form, warrior on horse-back brandishing his spear, late 19th century, 16" high, **$700–$1,000.**

Vase, baluster form, overall continuous motif of flowers, mounted as a lamp, c1900, 15" high, **$300–$500.**

Vases; square form; each side painted with tall, upright, flowering peony and green, pierced rock-work; late 19th century, 14½" high, **pair, $1,500–$2,200.**

Vases and covers, Buddhistic lion finials, overall motif of flowers and scrolling vines, one restored, one damaged, late 19th century, 20" high, **pair, $1,500–$2,000.**

Vases, square form, mirror image, each side painted with prunus and branches, trumpet necks, late 19th century, 27" high, **pair, $2,000–$3,000.**

Famille Rose

Bowl, shallow, motif in Chinese taste, a rose-colored flowering plum and two colored bamboo on the exterior, plain interior, Ch'ien Lung (Qianlong) six-character mark (and of the period), 4½" diameter, **$3,500–$5,500.**

Bowl, yellow ground, everted rim, densely painted with flowers and foliage, five red bats on the interior, Tao Kuang (Daoguang) six-character mark (and of the period), 7" diameter, **$2,000–$3,000.**

Chinese porcelain figures of two of the Eight Immortals, bisque faces and hands, deep green and blue painted attire, black beards, marked Made In China, *c1930, 6½" high,* ***each, $50–$75.***

Bowl, two roundels of standing ladies, ruby ground with lotus scrolls, plain interior, Kuang Hsü (Guangxu) seal (and of the period), 5½" diameter, **$500–$700.**

Bowls; exteriors painted with a cockerel, hen, and chicks between daisy, peony and rock-work borders; Yung Cheng (Yongzheng) six-character mark on bases, but early 20th century; 4½" diameter, **pair, $600–$800.**

Brush pot, continuous motif of warriors engaged in battle, late 18th/early 19th century, 4" high, **$350–$500.**

Dish, insects and rock-work with flowering peony, tufts of grass and foliage, 18th century, 6" diameter, **$700–$900.**

Dish painted with a lady and Immortal between deer and male attendant, peony sprays forming the border, cracked, 18th century, 15" diameter, **$800–$1,000.**

75

Figure, standing boy (one of the Ho-ho Erxian twins) wearing attire enameled with lotus, holding a blue vase in both hands, early 19th century, 11" high, **$900–$1,200.**

Figure; dragon; red, spiky fins and fangs on a pink, swirling cloud base; late 19th century, 10" diameter, **$1,200–$1,500.**

Figures, Eight Immortals, each on a rectangular base, some with minor chips, early 19th century, 10" high, **$2,500–$3,500.**

Figure, phoenix perched on a rockwork base, mounted as a lamp, silk shade with fringes intact, early 20th century, 9½" high, **$275–$350.**

Figure, Shou Lao, open mouth, holding staff and peach, early 20th century, 24" high, **$400–$600.**

Fish bowl; massive; densely painted with groups of pavilions, groves of willow and pine, scholars relaxing, sages fishing, and geese flying, all below a key-pattern border; the rim with iron red flower heads; early 20th century, 27" diameter, **$3,000–$5,000.**

Fish bowls, relief motif of warriors on horseback in landscapes, 19th century, 21" diameter, **pair, $6,000–$8,000.**

Fruit, gourd, early 20th century, 3" diameter, **$50–$75.**

Fruit, three peaches joined by a molded leafy branch, pinkish glaze, early 20th century, 2½" wide, **$100–$125.**

Fruit, peach, early 20th century, 4½" diameter, **$75–$100.**

Fruit, pomegranate, early 20th century, 4" diameter, **$50–$85.**

Garden seat, miniature, two landscape panels, two pierced cash symbols between raised bosses and foliate ground, Chia Ch'ing (Jiaqing), c1800, 9" high, **$1,250–$1,800.**

Garden seat, barrel-shaped, pierced on two sides with double cash symbols, the central band of birds and peony between bands of stylized lappets and lower band of cell pattern, late 19th/early 20th century, 19" high, **$1,200–$1,600.**

Garden seats, hexagonal, two sides pierced with cash symbols, upper and lower border with pink ground and raised bosses, the body with scrolling pink flowers and celadon vines, lappet border at the base, late 19th/early 20th century, 19" high, **pair, $3,500–$4,500.**

Garden seats, Millefleurs, quatrefoil section, black ground, one with major restoration, c1900, 19" high, **$2,500–$3,500.**

Garden seats, top with pierced cash symbols, upper and lower borders with raised bosses and pink lotus, green scrolling foliage, a center band with scene of wooded mountain landscape, late 19th/early 20th century, 19" high, pair, **$2,500–$3,500.**

Garniture set: pair of vases mounted as lamps and a censer with a wood cover; panels of Precious Things reserved on a floral diaper ground; the censer with four monster mask feet; late 19th century; the censer, 11½" high; the lamps, 12" high, **$1,000–$1,500.**

Garniture set: two beaker-form vases on domed bases, tripod censer and cover with Buddhistic lion finial and two joss-stick holders; each decorated with Precious Things, blue interiors, and key-pattern border; mid-to-late 19th century, 9" high, **$3,000–$4,000.**

Jar, baluster form, a continuous scene of children playing within a fenced terrace, late 19th century, 12½" high, **$700–$900.**

Jar and cover, baluster form, the celadon body painted with a large band of dragons between bands of flower heads and blue key pattern—all on a gold ground, early 20th century, 22" high, **$1,100–$1,700.**

Jardinière, narrow foot, everted rim, overall motif of tables, scholar's utensils, and Shou characters between painted and gilt bands of Buddhistic emblems, early 20th century, 19½" high, **$1,000–$1,500.**

Jardinière, globular, motif of Immortals and attendants by a lakeside between pink and turquoise brocade bands, the lip with Precious Things, early, 16" diameter, 14" high, **$800–$1,200.**

Jardinière, interlocked cash and peach sprays within lappet borders, late 19th century, 14" diameter, **$1,000–$1,500.**

Jardinières, iron red dragons confronting the flaming pearl amidst clouds and above breaking waves, Kuang Hsü (Guangxu) period, 16" diameter, **pair, $1,800–$2,500.**

Jardinières with stands, exteriors with four circular reserves of vases filled with flowers, lappet border under rim, overall motif of floral sprays, Kuang Hsü (Guangxu) period, 15" diameter, **pair, $2,000–$3,000.**

Panel, a central pink dragon on a blue ground with scrolling foliage and key-pattern borders, late 19th century, 26" square, **$1,500–$2,500.**

Plaque, two birds perched on flowering branches, hardwood frame, early 20th century, framed size 22" × 18", **$400–$600.**

Plaque, a dragon and rock-work, wood frame, early 20th century, framed size, 21" × 16", **$350–$500.**

Plaque, scholar seated beside a table on a terrace, hardwood frame, late 18th/early 19th century, framed size 19" × 14", **$2,500–$3,500.**

Plaques, figures and riverscape, hardwood frame, late 18th/early 19th century, framed size 7" × 4", **pair, $1,200–$1,600.**

Plates, ruby ground, painted with green diapered scroll unfurled to reveal a black cockerel perched beside flowering peony, rim chips, Ch'ien Lung (Qianlong) six-character mark (and of the period), 8¾" diameter, **pair, $4,000–$6,000.**

Ruyi sceptre painted to simulate cloisonné, foliage motif overall, three pierced inset plaques with pink Shou characters, Ch'ien Lung (Qianlong) six-character mark (and of the period), 20½" long, **$7,500–$10,000.**

Saucer dish, eggshell, painted with the eight horses of Muwang on a terrace beneath a willow, their bodies pink, white, brown, or gray; Yung Cheng (Yongzheng) mark, but early 20th century; 7½" diameter, **$250–$400.**

Saucer dish, eggshell, two birds seated on pierced rock-work below peony sprays and above daisies, early 20th century, 10" diameter, **$300–$500.**

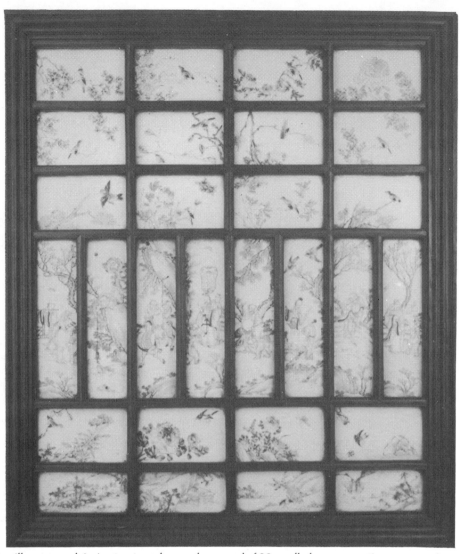

Famille rose porcelain-inset rectangular panel composed of 28 small plaques; a continuous scene of court elders at leisure in a rock-work landscape with pine, prunus, and fruiting boughs; the upper and lower sections with peony and birds; c1900, 26½" × 32". Realized price (including the 10-percent buyer's premium), Christie's East, New York City, **$495.**

Left: Chinese porcelain plate with floral motif in shades of pink, green, and orange; overglaze orange Ch'ien Lung mark on base; c1930, 6" diameter, **$25–$40.** Right: Chinese porcelain plate with motif in orange, green, and pink; overglaze orange mark on base indicating Ch'ien Lung; c1925; 9" diameter, **$65–$95.**

Chinese porcelain teapot in orange and gold with two reserves, c1925, **$65–$95.**

Chinese porcelain vase with a turquoise ground and children in famille rose, elephant head and ring ears, Kuang Hsü four-character mark (and of the period), c1900, 2½" high, **$100–$150.**

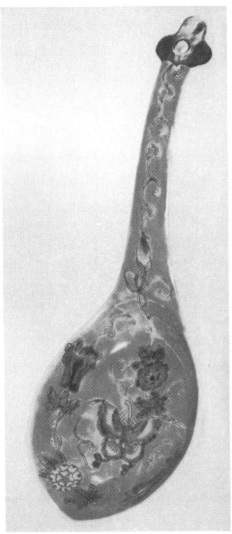

Chinese porcelain spoon, turquoise ground with famille rose motifs of butterflies and flowers, Kuang Hsü period, late 19th century, 7" long, **$150–$250.**

Chinese eggshell-porcelain vase in the style of Ch'ien Lung, famille rose, the base with a four-character commendation mark, early 20th century, 4" high, **$400–$650.**.

One of a pair of Chinese eggshell-porcelain vases in famille rose, mirror image, early 20th century, 9" high, **$700–$900.** Courtesy of Howard and Florence Kastriner.

Chinese porcelain vase with gilt motifs, Ch'ien Lung (Qianlong) six-character mark (and of the period), small wax repair on the foot, 4" high, **$700–$900.**

Saucer dishes, ruby-glazed, bright pink/crimson, white exteriors, late 18th/early 19th century, 7½" diameter, **pair, $1,500–$2,000.**

Sweetmeat dish and cover, mottled pink exterior with green vines and leaves, green interior divided into four key-pattern compartments, late 19th century, 10" wide, **$300–$475.**

Teapot, fluted body painted with panels of flowering trees, early 19th century, 10" wide, **$275–$375.**

Trays, oval, lobed, with an iron red inscription in the center surrounded by lime green bands with pink foliage carried over to the exterior; four short, gilt feet; gilt rims; iron red Chia Ch'ing (Jiaqing) seal on a lime green ground (and of the period), 6½" wide, **pair, $3,000–$5,000.**

Vase, beaker form, gilt and painted with colored peony-laden censers beneath ruyi-shaped lappets, all between puce diapered bands, 18th century, 7¼" high, **$600–$800.**

Vase, bulbous with long neck, continuous motif of pheasants and peony and other blossoms issuing from rockwork, 18th century, 15½" high, **$4,000–$6,000.**

Vase, pear-shaped, Millefleurs on a black ground, loose ring handles; Ch'ien Lung (Qianlong) mark, but early 20th century; 15" high, **$500–$700.**

Vase, pear-shaped, Millefleurs pattern on a gilt ground, loose ring handles; Ch'ien Lung (Qianlong) mark, but late 19th century; 14" high, **$1,000–$1,500.**

Vase, pear-shaped, 100 Deer motif, Ch'ien Lung (Qianlong) seal (and of the period), mounted as a lamp, **$5,000–$7,000.**

Vase, ruby glaze, short-waisted neck, c1800, 7" high, **$1,000–$1,500.**

Vase, hexagonal, pomegranate handles, pairs of birds on rock-work in one band and herons and lotus in another divided by bands of diapers and scholar's utensils, late 19th/early 20th century, 23" high, **$1,500–$2,500.**

Vases, square baluster bodies with blue ground and four rectangular reserves (two calligraphic and two with lotus and cranes), the blue ground with pink dragons, bats and flowers, key pattern around neck and foot, European green interiors and bases, Chia Ch'ing seal (and of the period), 10" high, **pair, $8,000–$12,000.**

Vases, ovoid, painted with 100 Antiques motif on a celadon ground, Buddhistic lion handles, early 20th century, 37" high, **pair, $4,000–$6,000.**

Vases, celadon ground, enameled with birds and flower sprays, mounted as lamps, late 19th century, 16" high, **$700–$950.**

Famille Verte

Bowl, high cylindrical foot, the motif of Precious Things on an ochre-yellow ground, K'ang Hsi (Kangxi), 4½" diameter, **$600–$800.**

Bowl, exterior with four panels of flowers and vases, reserved on a ground of scrolling peony, rim chips, K'ang Hsi (Kangxi), 11" high, **$900–$1,200.**

Brush pot, motif of a Taoist figure on a terrace, restored rim, K'ang Hsi (Kangxi), 5" high, **$500–$700.**

Charger, iron red chrysanthemums within a stripped and diapered border—all enclosed by a wide border of iron red, aubergine, and yellow flower heads; Ch'eng Hua mark, but late 17th century; 14" diameter, **$1,500–$2,000.**

Figures, Buddhistic lions, each figure with loose eyes; rectangular bases decorated with fan-shaped panels of lotus; enameled on biscuit in yellow, green, aubergine, and black; K'ang Hsi (Kangxi), 12" high, **pair, $6,000–$8,000.**

Figure, dignitary with a long beard and impassive expression, the head reserved in biscuit; seated on an aubergine throne; his robe with yellow dragons and aubergine flaming pearls and clouds; K'ang Hsi style, late 19th century, 25" high, **$2,500–$3,500.**

Figure, one of the Erxian twins standing on a square base wearing an apron jacket and holding a vase, chipped, early 18th century, 11" high, **$750–$900.**

Figure, Kuan Yin, hair piled high and coiled beneath a cowl; robes in yellow, green, and aubergine; 18th century, 9" high, **$1,200–$1,500.**

Figures, the Eight Immortals, each seated and each with an attribute, one with a beard and mustache, c1900, 5" high, **$1,000–$1,500.**

Figures, parrots, green feathers, black-and-white beaks, peach-colored rock-work base, late 19th/early 20th century, 7" high, **pair, $600–$800.**

Jar, globular, bands of court ladies and flowered jardinières on a diapered ground, the shoulders with medallions of Precious Things emblems, crack in base, K'ang Hsi (Kangxi), 9" high, **$500–$700.**

Jar, baluster form, continuous scene of noblemen receiving military figures, K'ang Hsi (Kangxi), 13" high, **$1,000–$1,500.**

Jardinière; cylindrical; the body decorated with butterflies above peony and chrysanthemum growing amongst pierced rock-work; the flat, everted rim with a band of scrolling lotus heads; the base pierced; rim chips; K'ang Hsi (Kangxi), 9½" high, **$1,500–$2,500.**

Joss-stick holders, mirror image, Buddhistic lions seated on rectangular bases, front paws raised, one with a cub and one with brocade (pierced) ball, bulging eyes, hexagonal holders issuing from their backs; green, ochre, aubergine/brown; minor damages; K'ang Hsi (Kangxi), 8" high, **pair, $1,200–$1,600.**

Joss-stick holders; Buddhistic lions standing on leaf-shaped stands; deep green, yellow, and aubergine; mounted on ormolu stands; K'ang Hsi (Kangxi), 5¼" high, **$1,200–$1,600.**

Joss-stick holders; Buddhistic lions standing on rectangular bases; green, yellow, and aubergine; late 19th century, 6" high, **$400–$600.**

Kendi, body molded with vertical ribs, motif of continuous landscape, neck with silver mount, restored spout, K'ang Hsi (Kangxi), 9" high, **$1,500–$2,000.**

Planter, three bands of various diapers, four bracket feet, 19th century, 9" long, **$900–$1,200.**

Plate, flowers growing from a pierced rock-work rim with iron red flower heads on a white ground, damaged, K'ang Hsi (Kangxi), 9½" diameter, **$300–$600.**

Saucer dish painted with a seated lady resting against rock-work with two butterflies at her side, damaged, K'ang Hsi (Kangxi), 7½" diameter, **$1,500–$2,000.**

Vase; rouleau shape; boys playing games above a green and orange lappet border; trellis design of birds, fruit, and flowers below the shoulders; the rim with a formal border; late 19th century, 16½" high, **$900–$1,200.**

Vase and cover, continuous riverscape, the cover with leaf-shaped panels of riverscapes and florals, rim and cover restored, K'ang Hsi (Kangxi), 22" high, **$1,200–$1,500.**

Water dropper, long-tailed bird perched on a peach, old damages, spout chipped, K'ang Hsi (Kangxi), 3¾" wide, **$300–$500.**

Funerary Objects

Amphora, straw-glazed, two handles springing from the shoulder and forming dragons' heads biting the cup-shaped rim, damages, small piece of rim missing, Tang Dynasty, 17" high, **$600–$800.**

Brush pot dating from the Tang dynasty, 3½" diameter, **$900–$1,200.**

Figure, an attendant wearing coat and trousers and a cap, the pottery with traces of red pigment, Northern Wei Dynasty, 6½" high, **$1,200–$1,600.**

Figure, an attendant, head bowed, hands clasped and pierced to hold a standard, loose coat and high boots, Sui Dynasty, 10" high, **$1,200–$1,500.**

Figure, a camel standing on four squares on a rectangular base, white-painted red pottery, legs restored, Tang Dynasty, 11½" high, **$1,000–$1,600.**

Figure; a court lady wearing a high-waisted, pleated gown; the gray pottery with traces of pigment; restored; Northern Wei Dynasty, 6½" high, **$300–$400.**

Figure, a dog, ears erect, collar on neck, the glaze a silvery green iridescence, Han Dynasty, 9½" long, **$2,500–$3,500.**

Figure, a dog, recumbent position, drooping ears, arched backbone, ochre glaze, Tang Dynasty, 3½" long, **$2,500–$3,500.**

Figure, an equestrian, the rider's hands raised as if holding reins, the horse's head tucked, yellow glaze, minor restoration, Sui Dynasty, 10½" high, **$3,500–$4,500.**

Figure, an equestrian, glazed green and buff, the horse—head turned to the left—standing on four squares on a rectangular base, rider and horse restored, Tang Dynasty (TLT confirmed dating), 12½" high, **$6,000–$8,000.**

Figure, a lady equestrian, hair tied in a topknot; the horse with an open mouth and looking to the left; the tail, ears, and legs restored; Tang Dynasty (TLT confirmed dating), 14¾" high, **$3,000–$5,000.**

Chinese funerary figurine of a grandmother, traces of red pigment on dress, Tang dynasty, 11¾" high, $1,000–$1,500.

Figure, a horse looking to the left, high ridged saddle and short saddle cloth, some red and black pigment visible, pink buff body, restored, Tang Dynasty, 11" high, **$4,000–$6,000.**

Figure, Lokapalo wearing helmet and armor, left arm raised with clenched fist, standing on a crouching lion, legs cracked, no pigment remaining, Tang Dynasty, **$1,500–$2,500.**

Figure; a soldier wearing breastplate and tunic, the hand socketed as if to hold a spear; gray pottery with traces of red, black, and white pigment; Northern Wei Dynasty, 7" high, **$1,500–$2,000.**

Figure, a soldier wearing a tunic, hands clasped at his chest, restoration to the face, Tang Dynasty, 14" high, **$700–$900.**

Figure, a standing lady, straw glaze, long robe, hair in a high loop, neck and base restored, Tang Dynasty, **$1,000–$1,500.**

Figure, a standing lady, hands clasped, long flowing robe (white and orange with red borders) flaring at the base, pink pigment on face, damaged, Han Dynasty, 12¾" high, **$1,200–$1,800.**

Figure, a standing lady, her robe with traces of white pigment, her hair knotted and having traces of black pigment, restored, Tang Dynasty, 12½" high, **$3,000–$5,000.**

Jar, modified pear shape, the body with bands of wave patterns, glazed green and brown on the red body, damaged, Han Dynasty, 12¼" high, **$900–$1,200.**

Jar, one handle, painted with a band of chocolate brown lozenge which is repeated on the neck, chipped, Neolithic (Second/Third Millenium B.C.), 5¾" diameter, **$650–$960.**

Jar; broad, globular body painted dark brown and reddish brown with lozenges divided by panels of triple lines; chipped; Neolithic (Second/Third Millenium B.C.), 5" diameter, **$800–$1,200.**

Jar; black splashed glaze; two small, looped handles; restored rim and handles; Tang Dynasty, 6½" high, **$1,500–$2,000.**

Jar, red pottery with overlapping square panels of vertical and horizontal lines, chipped, Neolithic (First Millenium B.C.), 14" diameter, **$1,800–$2,500.**

Jar, globular, gray pottery, overlapping trellis pattern on the body, plain band at the shoulder, chipped, Neolithic (First Millenium B.C.), **$2,500–$3,500.**

Jarlet, green- and straw-glazed in a double gourd form, chips on foot, Tang Dynasty, 3½" high, **$1,000–$1,500.**

Pillow, buff pottery with a green glaze, fan-shaped foliate headrest on a grid with interlocking circles, ochre edge with incised wave patterns, waisted body, flanged foot, chip on foot, Ch'in (Qin) Dynasty, 11" wide, **$1,000–$1,500.**

Pillow, red pottery with a green and yellow glaze, the pillow formed as a recumbent lion with fierce expression, unglazed base, minor restoration, Ch'in (Qin) Dynasty, 13" long, **$2,000–$3,000.**

Vase; globular; high, flat foot; spinach green and silver glaze; pierced and mounted as a lamp; Han Dynasty, 16" high, **$800–$1,200.**

Green and Aubergine

Bowls, everted rims, exterior with aubergine five-toed dragons pursuing the flaming pearl above breaking waves, damages to one, K'ang Hsi (Kangxi), 4½" diameter, **pair, $1,000–$1,500.**

Bowls, everted rims, incised with two five-toed dragons and flaming pearls and fire scrolls above waves, plain interiors, hairlines on both, 18th century, 4½" diameter, **pair, $1,000–$1,500.**

Green and Blue

Vase, baluster form, painted in green enamel, outlined in underglaze blue, five four-toed dragons pursuing flaming pearls above waves; Ch'eng Hua mark, but 19th century; 7½" high, **$300–$400.**

Yellow and Green

Bowl, exterior with incised and enameled five-toed dragons and flaming pearls with phoenix above a petal lappet band, the center of the interior with a longevity symbol, K'ang Hsi (Kangxi) six-character mark (and of the period), 4½" diameter, **$5,000–$7,000.**

Dishes, exterior with two five-toed scaly dragons chasing flaming pearls amidst clouds on a yellow ground, white interior, Kuang Hsü (Guangxu) six-character mark (and of the period), 7" diameter, **pair, $1,200–$1,500.**

Saucer dish incised and painted with a green dragon pursuing the flaming pearl on the interior, Kuang Hsü (Guangxu) six-character mark (and of the period), 5¾" diameter, **$750–$1,000.**

Honan

Jar, globular with 27 ribs, unglazed rim, the body with a black glaze stopping short of the cut buff stoneware foot, Sung (Song) Dynasty, 5" high, **$2,500–$3,500.**

Jar, globular with 27 ribs, unglazed rim, the body with a black glaze stopping short of the cut buff stoneware foot, Sung (Song) Dynasty, 8" high, cracked and chipped, **$400–$600.**

Vase, double gourd, the sections joined by rope-twist handles, neck reduced, damaged, Sung (Song) Dynasty, 10½" high, **$400–$600.**

Ming and Ch'ing (Qing) Dynasty Pottery

Figures, Buddhistic lions, one with paw on cub, one with paw on brocade (pierced) ball, green and blue glazes streaked with white, Shekwan ware, early 20th century, 9" high, **pair, $225–$375.**

Figure, Buddhistic lion, glazed black with blue and white streaks and mottling, paw on brocade ball, Shekwan ware, c1900, 7" high, **$100–$150.**

Figure; Buddhistic lion seated on a brown-glazed, waisted, rectangular stand; her paw on a cub; open mouth; collar with descending tassels; extremities chipped; Shekwan ware, c1900, 30" high, **$900–$1,200.**

Figure of Chen Wu seated on a rock-work throne; glazed turquoise, green, and ochre; hands and face unglazed; 17th century, 12" high, **$600–$900.**

Figure of Chen Wu seated on a high-backed throne, his loose-fitting attire glazed purple and ochre, roof tile, mounted as a lamp, Ming Dynasty, 14" high, **$1,000–$1,500.**

Figure of a crab, green glaze with white on pincers, Shekwan ware, early 20th century, 6¾" wide, **$75–$120.**

Figure of a mythological dog; red, green, and blue glazes streaked with white on high points; Shekwan ware, early 20th century, 7½" wide, **$100–$125.**

Figure, Shou Lao seated on a high-backed throne, his robes glazed purple and turquoise, roof tile, mounted as a lamp, 12½" high, Ming Dynasty, **$1,200–$1,500.**

Figures, mirror image, scholars with hands clasped, their faces and extremities unglazed, one restored, mounted as lamps, Ming Dynasty, 15" high, **pair, $2,500–$3,500.**

Tile maker's figure of a Bodhisattva seated beside books on a lotus base above pierced rock-work, glazed green, very old damages, 17th century, 12¼" high, **$700–$900.**

Tile maker's figure of a demon (standing over a cloud) on a cylindrical base; glazed green, ochre, and brown; chipped; 17th/18th century, 14¼" high, **$1,200–$1,600.**

Tile maker's figure of a dragon standing on clouds; glazed yellow, green, and aubergine; 18th century, 23" long, **$1,500–$2,500.**

Tile maker's figure of a standing guardian wearing elaborate armor, glazed green and ochre, mounted on a wood base, chips to the surface, late Ming Dynasty, 22" high, **$1,500–$2,500.**

Tile maker's figure of an equestrian, glazed green and brown, late 19th century, 9½" high, **$200–$300.**

Tile maker's figure of an equestrian, the dignitary wearing his armor, the horse in galloping position; glazed green, amber, and mustard yellow; chips to the surface; 18th century, 13½" high, **$1.000–$1,500.**

Jars and covers; oviform; short, wide necks; the shoulders carved with a lotus band; bud finials on the domed lids; Tank style, late 19th century, 8½" high, **pair, $200–$400.**

Roof tiles, seated Kylin, green glaze, damaged, Ming Dynasty, 11¼" high, **pair, $1,200–$1,800.**

Roof tiles; standing male figures wearing green-, amber-, and cream-glazed attire; Ming Dynasty, 16" high, **pair, $2,500–$4,000.**

Storage jar, glazed black, the neck with a band of bosses and two small loop handles, Ming Dynasty, 24" high, **$1,000–$1,500.**

Vase, mallet shape, two handles, mottled and streaked with a blue-black glaze, Shekwan ware, late 19th century, 7" high, **$200–$285.**

Vase, baluster form, thick blue-black glaze, Shekwan ware, 18th century, 12½" high, **$200–$275.**

Swatow

Box and cover, blue and white with large lotus flowers, rim chips on the inside, 15th century, 4" diameter, **$200–$300.**

Dish, a circular panel of buildings on the well with quatrefoil panels enclosing figures and boats, red and turquoise, 16th century, 15" diameter, **$600–$800.**

Dish; blue and white; painted with a phoenix, peony, and bamboo; panels of peach and foliage on the border; cracked; 17th century, 14" diameter, **$400–$600.**

Dish, blue and white with motif of pheasant and peony within a diaper border, cracked, 17th century, 18½" diameter, **$400–$600.**

Dish; incised peony in green, red, and turquoise between flower heads radiating from a central peony roundel; 17th century, 14" diameter, **$550–$750.**

Jar, blue and white, four loop handles at the shoulders, stylized peony motif, cracked, 17th century, 9½" high, **$200–$300.**

Ting Wares

Bowl, rounded sides, exterior with carved lotus and leaves, Northern Sung (Song) Dynasty, 4" diameter, **$1,200–$1,800.**

Dish molded on the interior with Buddhistic lions with a key-pattern border, ivory glaze, copper rim, crack on base, Sung (Song)/Yüan Dynasty, 5½" diameter, **$2,000–$3,000.**

Dish, circular, carved with a stylized flower under a creamy white glaze, rim in the biscuit, Sung (Song) Dynasty, 4½" diameter, **$1,500–$2,500.**

Dish carved with a central roundel of two fish and waves, plain exterior, glaze stopping neatly around the shallow-cut foot, rim in the biscuit, unglazed base, Sung (Song) Dynasty, 6¾" diameter, **$800–$1,200.**

Tou ts'ai (Doucai)

Bowl painted on the exterior with six lotus blossoms and a foliage meander above ruyi lappets around the foot, plain interior, Tao Kuang (Daoguang) seal (and of the period), 5¾" diameter, **$1,800–$2,600.**

Bowl; a central, full-faced dragon surrounded by six phoenix medallions; the exterior with Shou characters; Hsüan Te mark, but 18th century, **$900–$1,200.**

Bowl, conical, painted with groups of flowers on the exterior and a central lotus on the interior, Tao Kuang (Daoguang) six-character mark (and of the period), 5" diameter, **$1,800–$2,500.**

Dish, the well decorated with lotus heads and scrolling stems around a central flower head, the everted rim decorated with eight flower heads and vines, the exterior painted with bats, 18th century, 9½" diameter, **$800–$1,000.**

Dish; everted rim painted with a flower head and fine, interlinked pearls; the reverse with five iron red bats; 19th century, 6¼" diameter, **$275–$400.**

Dish, a centrally painted duck and flowering lotus plants below a narrow border, the exterior with wading duck and lotus, 19th century, 6½" diameter, **$300–$500.**

Dishes; the interiors painted with a full-faced, five-toed dragon and fire scroll, the borders with a wave pattern; Hsüan Te mark, but 19th century; 7½" diameter, **pair, $300–$500.**

Dishes; the interiors with dragon and clouds bordered by carp and waves; breaking waves on the reverse; hairlines on one; Ch'eng Hua mark, but 18th century; 6½" diameter, **pair, $1,200–$1,600.**

Saucer dish painted with a large flower head on a lotus pod, the exterior with similar motifs, 19th century, **$350–$500.**

Saucer dishes painted with a central Shou roundel within eight Shou characters and bands of scrolls, the exteriors with scrolls and stylized foliage, Ch'ien Lung (Qianlong) six-character mark (and of the period), 8½" diameter, **pair, $3,500–$5,000.**

Vase, everted rim, slender body, painted with birds in flight and flowering branches; Ch'eng Hua mark, but 18th century; 7½" high, **$1,000–$1,500.**

Tz'u Chou (Cizhou)

Bowl, the exterior with calligraphy and foliage, Ming Dynasty, 6½" diameter, **$400–$500.**

Figure of an Immortal seated on a lotus base, ivory with brown cloud scrolls, 20th century, 8" high, **$200–$300.**

Figure of Chen Wu seated on a rockwork base, his hands resting on his knees, 17th century, 8½" high, **$800–$1,200.**

Figure of a recumbent tiger painted deep brown over cream slip, minor cracks, Yüan Dynasty, 3½" wide, **$700–$900.**

Jar, baluster form, continuous scene of noblemen on horseback in a landscape, damaged, Transitional, c1650, 11" high, **$500–$700.**

Jar painted with cranes in flight above an iron red band of wave pattern; the shoulders with a band of prunus, pine, and scrolls; damage to the neck; 18th century, 5¼" high, **$350–$450.**

Jar, globular, painted with alternating panels of five-toed dragons and flaming pearls above crested waves, Wan Li mark (and of the period), cracked and badly scratched, 6" diameter, **$2,200–$3,300.**

Jar, ovoid with painted calligraphy on the upper border, the center with large floral motifs and key pattern, imperfections in the glaze, Yüan Dynasty, 12" high, **$1,500–$2,200.**

Pillow; concave, rectangular, sloping surface with a barbed medallion enclosing a mountainscape; the front painted with a flower, the back with calligraphy; leaf and scroll borders; cracked; Yüan Dynasty, 12¼" high, **$1,200–$1,800.**

Pillow incised through the white slip with a crane in flight above clouds, a flower-head border, old cracks and damages, Yüan Dynasty, 8½" long, **$1,500–$2,200.**

Vase, pear-shaped, trumpet neck, three bands of stylized flowers painted over cream slip, the slip and clear glaze stopping irregularly above the deeply cut foot, glaze fret to rim and foot, small hairlines, Sung (Song) Dynasty, 10" high, **$2,000–$3,000.**

Vase, pear-shaped with a wide band at the mouth, translucent brown splashes on a deep brown opaque ground, damaged, Sung (Song) Dynasty, 5¼" high, **$500–$800.**

Chinese porcelain box and cover, wu ts'ai, dragon-and-cloud and phoenix-and-cloud motifs, Ming dynasty, 1¾" × 1¼", **$600–$900.**

Vase, pear-shaped with a trumpet mouth, cream slip under a translucent glaze, shallow-cut buff stoneware foot, neck chipped, Sung (Song)/Yüan Dynasty, 10" high, **$700–$950.**

Wu ts'ai (Wucai)

Dish; centrally painted with birds in flight, fruiting peach tree, and rockwork; four floral cartouches divided by the cell pattern on the border; late Ming Dynasty, 8" diameter, **$300–$500.**

Saucer dish painted with two boats and islands, hairlines, Ming Dynasty, 6" diameter, **$185–$250.**

Saucer dish painted at the center with a panel of a bird on a berry branch, wide cell ground, borders reserved with fruit panels, restored, Wan Li six-character mark (and of the period), 6¼" diameter, **$350–$550.**

Sweetmeat box; the interior with seven compartments, each decorated with birds and flowering branches; matching exterior; chips on base and rim; Wan Li six-character mark (and of the period), 9" diameter, **$2,000–$3,000.**

90

I Hsing (Yixing) teapot with a blue glaze, square form, faintly impressed mark on base, first half of the 19th century, 6" high, **$800–$1,200.**

I Hsing (Yixing) teapot in double-tree-trunk form; terracotta, blue, and cream with branch-form finish; bamboo-form spout; branch-form handle; early 19th century, 3" high, **$500–$750.**

Tea caddy and cover, octagonal, painted with lappets of flowering branches, rim chip on cover, frittings, 18th century, 4½" high, **$400–$600.**

Vase decorated with horses and a floral ground, Transitional, 12½" high, **$2,000–$3,000.**

Vase; globular, with two panels of dragons on a lotus ground below stiff leaves; the flaring neck with lotus scrolls below a chevron pattern; Wan Li mark, but 19th century; 9" high, **$400–$600.**

Vase, double gourd, the lower half with birds in a wooded landscape below three bands of ruyi heads, the upper part with two phoenixes in flight, Wan Li six-character mark (and of the period), 10" high, **$1,200–$1,600.**

Vases, beaker form, flaring upper section painted with a dignitary beside a bridge, with ladies and attendants within clouds, camellia sprays and rock-work in the central section, peach sprays on the lower sections, the interiors of the necks with scrolling peony, damaged, 17th century, 20½" high, **pair, $2,000–$3,000.**

I Hsing (Yixing)

Box and cover, peach form, yellow with brown splashes, 18th century, **$700–$1,000.**

Brush washer; peach form; yellow with brown splashes; supported on three feet formed by walnut, lychee, and peanut; 18th century, 3¾" wide, **$1,500–$2,200.**

Bulb bowl with enameled flowers and three stub feet, marked China, c1930, 9" diameter, **$100–$145.**

Figure of a seated Lohan wearing flowing robes folding at the base, 18th century, 5½" high, **$2,000–$3,000.**

Flower pot in the form of a tree stump, marked China, c1930, 5" high, 6" diameter, **$150–$220.**

Teapot, rare blue glaze, rectangular with flat cover, early 19th century, 6" high, **$800–$1,000.**

Teapot, compressed globular form, a single molded band at the widest point, loop handle, curved spout, 18th century, 7¼" wide, **$1,000–$1,500.**

Left: I Hsing (Yixing) *water dropper of a boy upon a buffalo, late Ch'ing dynasty,* **$200–$300.** Right: I Hsing *water dropper of a monk reading and seated beside a pig, late Ch'ing dynasty,* **$275–$375.**

Teapot, compressed globular form, loop handle, short spout, olive brown with gritty texture, signed Qu Hua, 20th century, **$900–$1,200.**

Teapot, globular with mushroom-shaped lid, the body with applied fruits and nuts of lighter-colored clay, bamboo-stem-form spout, 19th century, 4½" high, **$600–$800.**

Teapot; green glaze; melon ribbed with leaves and vine around the body; drooping loop handle; short, bent spout; 19th century, 4" high, **$650–$850.**

Teapot, lozenge shape, square handle and spout, bracket feet, c1800, 7½" wide, **$1,000–$1,500.**

Teapot, robin's egg blue, C handle, S-curved spout, domed lid, 18th century, 6" high, **$2,500–$3,500.**

Teapot; robin's egg blue; simulated bamboo handle, spout, and finial; interior of cover chipped; early 19th century, 5¾" high, **$1,200–$1,500.**

Teapot, rounded rectangular form, spout and handle molded as a branch and enameled yellow, applied yellow and green grape leaves, early 20th century, 4½" high, **$100–$150.**

Teapot; tree trunk form; body with applied branches, leaves, and berries; flat cover; 19th century, 5½" high, **$600–$800.**

Tea set: teapot and six cups, all in the form of tree stumps, marked China, c1925, **$100–$150.**

Tea set: teapot, sugar, creamer, and tray; all with applied pewter embellishment; dragon motif; marked Shanghai, China; c1935, **$275–$375.**

Vase, tree stump form, marked China, c1935, 7" high, **$100–$175.**

Vase, beaker form, applied plum blossoms and branches, the flowers in a cream-colored clay, early 20th century, 9" high, **$300–$500.**

Water pot molded as a miniature teapot, short spout, looped handle, bud finial, 19th century, **$400–$600.**

Ch'ing Dynasty

大清順
治年製

Shun Chih
1644–1661

Shun Chih (seal form)
1644–1661

大清康
熙年製

K'ang Hsi
1662–1722

K'ang Hsi (seal form)
1662–1722

大清雍
正年製

Yung Cheng
1723–1735

Yung Cheng (seal form)
1723–1735

大清乾
隆年製

Ch'ien Lung
1736–1795

Ch'ien Lung (seal form)
1736–1795

嘉慶
年製

Chia Ch'ing
1796–1820

Chia Ch'ing (seal form)
1796–1820

大清道
光年製

Tao Kuang
1821–1850

Tao Kuang (seal form)
1821–1850

大清咸
豐年製

Hsien Feng
1851–1861

Hsien Feng (seal form)
1851–1861

大清同
治年製

T'ung Chih
1862–1874

T'ung Chih (seal form)
1862–1874

大清光
緒年製

Kuang Hsü
1875–1908

Kuang Hsü (seal form)
1875–1908

大清宣
統年製

Hsüan T'ung
1909–1912

洪憲
年製

Hsüan T'ung
1909–1912

4

Cloisonné

The name *cloisonné* is derived from the French word *cloison*, meaning *cell*. Basic cloisonné is a metal body with designs made of wire cells which have been filled with enamels.

Creation of a cloisonné object begins with bending and hammering a sheet of metal into the desired shape. The artist then paints the design onto the metal sheet. Once the wires are bent into shapes and placed against the metal to form the partitions, or cells, a layer of enamel (powdered glass) is sifted over them and gently fired to secure the wires in place. (On ceramic bodies, or Japanese Totai, vegetable glue was used.)

Before firing begins, the cells must be packed with enamel in powdered form. The colors of the fused enamel depends on the mixture of natural minerals, and in turn, the temperatures at which the object is fired depend on the colors being used.

Those needing the highest heat are fired first, after which the cells are packed again and refired until they are even with the height of the wires. Finally, the piece is polished—with stones of various coarseness, followed by charcoal, and then with powdered horn mixed with oil—until the proper finish is obtained.

Chinese Cloisonné

Chinese cloisonné, called Ch'ing tai-lan after the period of the Ming Dynasty during which it was developed (1450–56), can have gold, bronze, brass, or copper bodies. Designs usually include a primary motif with a background diaper (repetitive pattern) such as clouds, double T, bats, and so on. These background patterns were used to strengthen the pattern as well as to enhance its aesthetic quality. The motifs, which are somewhat stylized, include popular themes such as the dragon in pursuit of the flaming pearl (the pearl representing truth); the lotus and scroll; Buddhistic symbols; masks; and 1000 Flowers. Objects, both ornamental and occasional as well as functional, include animals, figures, water pipes, snuff bottles, censers, vases, and so forth.

For the most part, Chinese cloisonné marks are reign marks (see the markings listed in the "Prices on Chinese Porcelain and Pottery" section of Chapter 3).

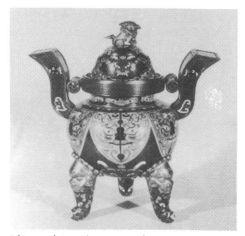

Chinese cloisonné censer with cover, tripod feet, decorated with t'ao-t'ieh (monster masks) in turquoise and green on a dark blue ground, the cover surmounted with a gilt Buddhistic lion, marked Lao T'ien Li, 9½" high, **$1,500–$2,000.** Courtesy of the Edson Collection.

Chinese cloisonné wine set, peach form with red lotus and blue dragons on a turquoise ground, tray 9½" diameter, **$1,000–$1,500.** Courtesy of the Edson Collection.

Japanese Cloisonné

Japanese cloisonné is called Shippo-yaki. Yaki means ware. Shippo has two definitions: beauty or goodness, and Seven Precious Jewels (which can be combinations of pearl, shell, agate, gold, silver, lapis lazuli, coral, and amber).

Japanese Cloisonné Marks

Ando Jubei

Gonda Hirosuke

Gonda Hirosuke

Hayashi Kihyoe

Hayashi Kodenji

Inaba
Cloisonné Company

Hayashi Tanigoro

Kawaguchi

Namikawa Sosuke

Kawade Shibataro

Namikawa Yasuyuki

Ota

Takeuchi Chubei (totai maker)

97

Japanese cloisonné is a bit more complicated than its Chinese counterpart. The body may be silver, copper, papier-mâché, lacquer, pottery, porcelain, or brass. Unlike Chinese cloisonné, which usually has a reign mark if marked, Japanese cloisonné can have factory marks and/or artists' signatures/seals. The enamels can be opaque, translucent, or transparent. Designs featured on Japanese cloisonné are naturalistic and may encompass large or small areas; geometric borders, designs in reserves, or some combination of the two were also used. Scenic and floral motifs were popular. Objects include standard occasional and decorative pieces as well as netsuke, inro, ojime, buttons, pins, tsuba, pipes, and so on.

Japanese cloisonné features a technique known as *counterenameling*, used to prevent large areas from warping. In these objects, the unworked and undecorated reverse is covered with counterenameling, as are interiors and bases.

See the figure on the preceding page for examples of Japanese cloisonné marks.

Types of Japanese Cloisonné

Yusen shippo. Wired enamel.

Totai shippo. Ceramic-bodied cloisonné.

Shōtai shippo (pliqué à jour). Transparent enamel, the body etched away with acid to create a stained-glass effect.

Left: *Japanese totai vase, cloisonné on porcelain, blue ground with floral motifs, modified pear shape,* c1875, 9" high, **$500–$700.** Right: *Japanese totai vase, cloisonné on porcelain, a blue ground and delicate floral motif with insects, the rim and base with diapers and mon, the base marked* Takeuchi Chubei, c1875, 5" high, **$700–$900.**

Musen shippo. Wireless cloisonné.

Yu-musen shippo. A combination of wired and wireless motifs.

Moriage (Cameo). The motif has enamel piled above the surface of the piece, forming a pattern in mild relief. A certain area may have been embossed, and enamels added, layer by layer, before firing.

Akasuke (Pigeon Blood). Transparent red enamel over a copper body. The term is also used to describe yellow, green, blue, and lavender created in the same manner.

Ginbari. Silver foil wrapped around a metal body, applied with translucent or transparent enamel.

Japanese cloisonné box, the ground shaded in pale blue, dove on maple branch, wire and wireless, the base with a Namikawa Sosuke silver-wire mark, restored, c1900, 4" × 5", **$2,000–$3,000.**

Cloisonné Values

Basin, flat rim, black ground with a yellow dragon, the well with four more dragons on the exterior, blue counterenameled base with large Ming mark (but early 20th century), Chinese, 13" diameter, **$250–$400.**

Basin, hexafoil, gilt interior and turquoise ground, the decoration including dragons and Shou characters, some losses in the enamel, Chinese, 17th century, 5½" diameter, **$600–$900.**

Bottle/vase, cylindrical, long neck, turquoise ground with formal lotus meander, Chinese, late 19th century, 15" high, **$400–$600.**

Bulb bowl, Millefleurs, brightly colored, the counterenameling a blue-green, copper rim and base, marked *China*, c1930, 10" diameter, **$200–$275.**

Box and cover, black ground, overall floral motif in colors, the interior lined with wood, base with Inaba mark in silver wire, motif in silver wire, marked *Japan*, c1925, 5" × 4", **$500–$700.**

Chinese cloisonné ashtray, blue ground with T pattern, white flowers, green foliage, blue counterenameling on interior, marked China, c1930, 4" diameter, **$50–$75.**

Enameled, hammered copper box and cover; the flowers and foliage in pastel hues in low relief; sined Ando; Japanese, Meiji period, c1905, 6½" × 4½", **$2,000–$3,000.**

Box and cover, black ground with large pastel flower heads, Japanese, early 20th century, 2½" square, **$275–$375.**

Box and cover, brass wire, phoenix and leaf motif on lid, floral roundels on sides, black ground, Japanese, c1915, 5" wide, **$200–$300.**

Box and cover, circular, black ground, the lid with a yellow dragon, the sides with cloud patterns, marked *China*, c1935, 4" diameter, **$150–$225.**

Box and cover, circular, phoenix and flowers on a green and goldstone ground, Japanese, late 19th century, 4" diameter, **$250–$350.**

Box and domed cover, circular, overall large lotus meandering between gilt rims, turquoise ground, Chinese, 18th century, 2½" diameter, **$1,000–$1,500.**

Box and cover, flattened ovoid form, silver wires, three butterflies on the lid within a brocade border, some damage, a plaque is missing from the base, the work is similar to that attributed to Namikawa Yasuyuki, Japanese, Meiji period, 3½" diameter, **$900–$1,200.**

Box and cover, flattened circular form, silver wire and enamels worked in a motif of three cranes within a brocade border, the base with a silver plaque marked *Namikawa Yasuyuki*, some damages, Japanese, Meiji period, 3¼" diameter, **$2,000–$3,000.** (Note: Correct attribution by means of a maker's seal or mark raises values.)

Box and cover, kiku shape, silver wire, black ground with colorful motif of butterflies, a few minor cracks, Japanese, late Meiji period, 6" diameter, **$1,500–$2,500.**

Box and cover, lobed, motif of a phoenix in colors on an aventurine (goldstone) ground, Japanese, late 19th century, 3" diameter, **$250–$350.**

Box and cover, lozenge-shaped, foliage on the sides, blue T pattern forming squares around the top, Chinese, late 19th/early 20th century, 4½" wide **$200–$300.**

Box and cover, rectangular, the cover with two fans, both decorated with cranes, the yellow ground with scattered floral roundels, the sides with scrolls, crack on the base, Japanese, Taisho period, 4" × 7", **$300–$400.**

Box and cover, silver wire and enamels worked with a bird perched on a cherry branch, pale blue ground, Japanese, c1930, 4" wide **$300–$500.**

Box and cover, silver wire, the cover with a carp on a shaded light blue ground, Namikawa Sosuke seal in silver wire on the base, Japanese, Meiji period, 5½" wide, **$20,000+.**

Box and cover, yellow dragon and flaming pearl motif on a black ground with cloud patterns, Japanese, early Showa period, 3½" × 2½", **$275–$375.**

Box and cover; yellow ground; the lid inset with a pierced, pale celadon jade panel carved with a long life emblem; overall lotus and scrolls and Shou characters; Chinese, late 19th century, 13½" wide **$800–$1,200.**

Boxes and covers, yellow ground with T-pattern wire work, the covers with a central Shou character roundel surrounded by five hard-stone bats, the interiors with blue counterenameling, Chinese, late 19th century, 10" wide **pair, $1,500–$2,000.**

Box and cover enameled in primary colors with a phoenix on a rectangular panel, the ground profusely decorated with fans and flowers, brass mounts, brass interior carved with birds in flight above grasses, Japanese, Meiji period, 5¾" × 4¾" × 3½", **$500–$700.**

Bowl, pliqué à jour, enameled with peony, lilies, and chrysanthemums on a pale green ground, silver rim and foot, cracked, Japanese, Taisho period, 5½" diameter, **$700–$900.**

Bowl, pliqué à jour, maple and prunus on a pale green ground, chrome mounts, Japanese, Showa period, 4" diameter, **$500–$700.**

Bowl, silver wire with butterflies on a deep blue ground, cracked, Japanese, c1900, 3" diameter, **$100–$125.**

Bowl, the center of the interior decorated with a lotus pond on a blue ground beneath a red-ground band of Precious Things, the exterior with scattered flower-head roundels on a turquoise ground, Chinese, 19th century, 15½" diameter, **$2,500–$3,500.**

Candleholders modeled as standing ducks looking to the left and to the right, turquoise bodies with dense dragon scrolls, their heads set with jade sconces, triangular bases, Chinese, late 19th/early 20th century, 11" high, **$900–$1,200.**

Censer, tripod, three bulbous feet, overall lotus and scroll pattern on a medium blue ground, severely damaged, Chinese, 17th century, 9¼" high, **$400–$600.**

Censer, three rounded feet, brass wire worked in numerous mon symbols, the cover with a missing finial, Japanese, c1910, 3½" high, **$100–$125.**

Censer, tripod, decorated with three white phoenix in flight amidst scrolling chrysanthemums on a turquoise ground, the dragon handles replaced, Chinese, 17th century, 4½" wide **$300–$500.**

Censer, tripod, flat bottom, flaring rim, three stub legs and two Buddhistic lion mask handles, turquoise ground with a motif of lotus meander, old damages, Chinese, 17th century, 4¾" diameter, **$900–$1,200.**

Censer and cover; tripod masked legs; chih lung handles; lotus finial; flowering and fruiting peach branches overall in red, blue, and green on a turquoise ground; Chinese, 18th century, 7" high, **$1,500–$2,000.**

Censers, modeled as long-tailed birds looking to the left and to the right, the bodies turquoise, the wings polychrome, gilt beaks and legs, damages to the legs, Chinese, 18th century, 7" wide **pair, $3,000–$4,000.**

Chamber candlesticks; wide, shallow drip pans; apricot ground decorated with clusters of flowering branches; the sides set with twig handles; Chinese, last half of the 19th century, 5½" wide **$500–$800.**

Charger, butterfly and flowers against a medium blue ground, darker blue counterenameling, pitting overall, two cracks, Japanese, late 19th century, 12" diameter, **$300–$500.**

Charger, three standing cranes amongst bamboo, blue ground, the rim with a floral border, copper body, Japanese, c1915, 26" diameter, **$800–$1,200.**

Charger, blue ground with a motif of birds in flight above foliage and flowers, intricate diapered border around the rim, Japanese, c1900, 11" diameter, **$700–$950.**

Charger, foliate form, brass wire and colored enamels worked in a motif of coiled dragons on a goldstone ground, Japanese, late 19th century, 12" diameter, **$350–$550.**

Charger, silver wire and enamels worked in a motif of pheasants and chrysanthemums on a blue ground, narrow diapered border around the rim, some chipping and loss of enamel, Japanese, c1900, **$800–$1,200.**

Charger, the rim with a band of floral lappets, pale blue ground with a hawk in flight above flowering peony branches, surface with minor flaws, Japanese, c1885, 15" diameter, **$1,500–$1,800.**

Cigarette box, hinged cover, black ground with colored kiku, gilt metal interior in katakiribori with birds and bamboo, Japanese, early Showa period, 5" wide **$325–$500.**

Dish, oval, everted rim, phoenix on a diapered floral and foliate ground, blue-green counterenameling, Japanese, c1870, 13½" wide **$700–$900.**

Dish; shallow with flat, everted rim; the center with two confronting five-toed dragons facing the flaming pearl amidst cloud scrolls, the rim with flower-head meanders, the exterior with lotus scrolls; losses to enamel filled in with wax; Chinese, 16th century, 9½" diameter, **$900–$1,200.**

Flask, cylindrical, long neck, two gilt dragon handles, spreading foot, scenic motif above fish and breaking waves, Chinese, late 19th century, 16" high, **$1,200–$1,600.**

Flask; circular, flattened form; the front and back with scenic motifs including deer, pine, and cranes; the neck with overlapping green leaves; Chinese, c1900, 12½" high, **$900–$1,200.**

Figures of cockerels standing on rock-work bases, mirror image, open beaks, green ground with colored feathers and tails, restoration to one, Chinese, 20th century, 9½" high, **pair, $1,500–$2,500.**

Figures of cranes; each standing on flat, circular base; white bodies with polychrome feathers and tail feathers; candle sconces missing; Chinese, 18th century, 18" high, **pair, $5,000–$6,000.**

Figures of ducks, crouching position, dark blue ground, thick and thin wires, colorful feathers, gilt beaks and gilt webbed feet, Chinese, early 20th century, 9" wide **pair, $900–$1,200.**

Figures of standing ducks, heads raised, turquoise ground with polychrome feathers, Chinese, 20th century, 6½" high, **pair, $400–$700.**

Figures of elephants, each with a vase on its back, blue ground, floral scroll motifs overall, one badly bruised, Chinese, early 20th century, 16" high, **pair, $1,800–$2,400.**

Figures of kylin; deep blue-green, scaly bodies; blue faces; gilt horns, manes, tail, and hoofed feet; Chinese, late 19th century, 12" wide **pair, $1,500–$2,500.**

Figures of pheasants perched on grassy rock-work, pierced bases interspersed with flowerheads, the feathers predominately Indian red and turquoise, Chinese, early 20th century, 9½" high, **pair, $1,000–$1,500.**

Figures of quails locking to the left and to the right, detachable backs, gilt legs and beaks, deep blue and white breasts and polychrome feathers, Chinese, early 20th century, 4½" high, **pair, $900–$1,500.**

Jar and cover, Millefleurs on a medium blue ground, bruise on one with loss of enamel, Chinese, c1930, **$70–$125.**

Jar and cover; three legs; globular form; red ground with large phoenix and tail plumage in yellow, blue, and green; the cover with spider mums; silver mounts; minor nicks and dents; marked *Kumeno Teitaro*; Japanese, Meiji period, 6¾" high, **pair, $2,500–$3,500.**

Jar and cover; blue exterior with continuous leafy lotus amidst fan and circular, shaped panels of flowers; turquoise counterenameling; Japanese, first quarter of the 20th century, 12" high, **$200–$300.**

Jar and cover decorated with floral roundels on a black ground, Japanese, Meiji period, 3" high, **$300–$500.**

Jar and cover, floral geometric panels on a muddy turquoise ground, some loss of enamel, Japanese, c1865, 12½" high, **$700–$900.**

Jar and cover, overall design of cherry blossoms on a medium blue ground, the rim of the cover with a black dragon-scale band, marked *China*, c1935, 8" high, **$100–$175.**

Jar and cover, overall florals in an overlapping pattern on a black ground, marked *China*, c1935, 6½" high, **$100–$175.**

Jar and cover, overall T-pattern with large-petaled chrysanthemums scattered on a medium green ground, base marked *China*, c1935, 6" high, **$75–$125.**

Jar and cover, ovoid, silver wire worked with two fish and lilies on a blue-gray ground, Japanese, Meiji period, 5" high, **$600–$900.**

Chinese cloisonné model of a phoenix perched upon a branch of flowering hydrangea mounted as a lamp, the phoenix dated c1900, the mounts dated c1922, the phoenix 14" high, the lamp overall 27" high, **$1,000–$1,500.**

Plaque, concentric green and blue bands of scrolling polychrome flowers, minor surface repair, Chinese, late Ming dynasty, 7" diameter, **$800–$1,200.**

Planter, pink lotus meander and leafy vines overall on a turquoise frond, the foot decorated with florets, Chinese, 18th century, 6" wide **$1,200–$1,500.**

Jardinières, circular, turquoise ground, lotus and scroll pattern overall; the jardinières contain hard-stone trees, spinach jade leaves, agate flowers, and carnelian berries; old damages to both, Chinese, early 20th century, 24" high (to top of trees), **pair, $600–$900.**

Pricket candlesticks; the shafts set into flaring sconces and standing on domed, knopped bases; turquoise ground with lotus scrolls; Chinese, late 19th/early 20th century, 19" high, **$1,500–$2,500.**

Ruyi sceptre, long shaft cast with three panels of peach sprays in relief at the head, center and base of the shaft: turquoise ground with key pattern; Chinese, early 20th century, 22" long, **$700–$1,000.**

Ruyi sceptre, stylized ruyi, oval head set with four enamel-on-copper peaches, additional peaches on the center of the shaft and the terminal, the turquoise ground with lotus meander, Chinese, early 20th century, 20" long, **$1,200–$1,800.**

Smoking set: ashtray, match-box holder, and cigarette jar mounted on a footed tray; all black with a brass-wire T pattern, Chinese, c1925, **$100–$200.**

Smoking set: cigarette jar, ashtray, and match-box holder; floral pattern on a black ground interspersed with T patterns; marked *China*, c1930, **$50–$75.**

Smoking set: tray with two compartments for cigarettes and cigars, a compartment for ashtrays, and a compartment for the match-box holder; deep blue ground with a T pattern in brass wire; marked *China*, c1937, **$200–$300.**

*Chinese cloisonné spittoon, turquoise ground with red and yellow lotus and scrolls, red and blue floral reserves, 5" high, **$900–$1,200.** Courtesy of the Edson Collection.*

Sake bottle (tokkuri); pale blue with a motif of Ju characters in orange, white, and green; Japanese, c1925, 6" high, **$300–$400.**

Specimen set, six round dishes, each decorated with two butterflies within a formal border and exhibiting the various stages of cloisonné manufacture, Japanese, c1890, 5" diameter, **$450–$650.**

Table; a cloisonné plaque of pale blue with a motif of plants, fruit, and scholar's utensils set in a brass table with a lower shelf; the panel Chinese; 19th century, 16½" square, **$700–$1,000.**

Teapot, dark blue lotus leaves on a yellow ground, eight Sacred Emblems and clouds encircling the body, the spout issuing from a makara head, dragon-form handle, domed lid, Chinese, 19th century, 11" high, **$800–$1,200.**

Teapot, pear-shaped, curved spout, domed lid with knopped bud finial, green ground with brightly enameled flower heads, Japanese, early 20th century, 6" high, **$150–$200.**

Tea set, green ground with blue leaf motif, Japanese, early 20th century, **$175–$225.**

Tea set, blue ground with small flower heads overall, covered teapot, covered sugar and open creamer, Japanese, early 20th century, **$250–$350.**

Tray, three-toed dragon in the center with overall geometric designs, a medium green ground, Japanese, late 19th century, 12" wide, **$400–$600.**

Tray, a fruiting vine with two birds flying above, blue ground, formal border, Japanese, late Meiji period, 13" square, **$600–$800.**

Tray; pale blue shaded ground with motif of cock, hens, and chicks; hairlines, cracks, and bruising; signed *Namikawa Sosuke*; Japanese, Meiji period, 12½" square, **$500–$750.**

Tray, rectangular, green ground with Mt. Fuji and scenic motif, Japanese, c1920, 10" long, **$300–$450.**

Vase, archaic form, scrolls forming stiff long leaves between ruyi-head borders at the foot and mouth; red, yellow, green, and blue enamel on a turquoise ground; Ch'ien Lung (Qianlong), Chinese, 18th century, 13" high, **$1,800–$2,500.**

Vase, four-lobed with alternating cranes and butterflies in shaped panels against a red ground, bent lip, dent in base and minor cracks, Chinese, 19th century, 6" high, **$100–$200.**

Vase, black ground with scattered white flowers, Chinese, early 20th century, 4½" high, **$100–$200.**

Vase, akasuke, white chrysanthemums against a red ground (Pigeon Blood), Japanese, early Showa period, 8" high, **$150–$225.**

Chinese cloisonné vase, black ground, cloud pattern, white flowers and shaded green foliage, brass wires, copper body marked China, *c1934, 8" high,* **$75–$125.**

Vase, motif of dense chrysanthemums on a dark green ground, Japanese, late 19th/early 20th century, 5⅞" high, **$250–$350.**

Vase, large yellow flowers scattered on a dark blue ground with overall brass-wire cloud patterns, Chinese, early 20th century, 4" high, **$150–$200.**

Vase, open work with vines and flowers in primary colors, some loss of enamel, Chinese, 6" high, **$150–$225.**

Vase, white flowers and green foliage on a black ground, marked *China*, 4½" high, c1925, **$100–$125.**

Japanese cloisonné vase, silver rim and base, wireless, muted gray ground and pink and white flowers, modified pear shape, late Meiji period, 6" high, $900–$1,200.

Vase, a vertical cylinder between two slender cylinders, parcel gilt base, Chinese, 17th century, 4½" high, **$800–$1,200.**

Vase, baluster form, red ground with brass wire worked in a T pattern with scattered lotus scroll, marked *China*, c1930, 10" high, **$100–$125.**

Vase; baluster form; short, everted neck; silver wire and colored enamels worked in flowering plum branches on a deep blue ground; copper foot and rim; Tadashi seal, Japanese, Meiji period, 3½" high, **$375–$450.**

Vase, baluster form, silver wire and enamels worked with cranes in flight, silver mounts, Ando seal, Japanese, Taisho period, 13" high, **$3,500–$4,500.**

Vase; baluster form; yellow, orange, and purple flowers on a deep blue ground; copper mounts; Japanese, c1900, **$300–$500.**

Vase, baluster form, everted rim, copper wire and pastel enamels worked in a wreath of mums around the shoulder, midnight blue ground, similar pattern on neck, silver foot and rim, Ando mark on base, 14" high, Taisho period, **$3,500–$4,500.**

Vase; baluster form; tall, trumpet neck; copper wire and colored enamels worked in cherry blossoms on branches against a light blue ground; Japanese, c1900, 28" high, **$2,000–$3,000.**

Vase, baluster form, everted rim, dark blue ground, silver wire and colored enamels worked in flowers and butterflies, Tadashi seal, Japanese, Meiji period, 4¾" high, **$250–$375.**

Vase, birds and flowers on a goldstone ground, shaped panels filled with flowers around the shoulder and foot, Japanese, late Meiji period, 10½" high, **$300–$500.**

Vase, black with silver wire worked in a motif of cranes in flight, silver foot and rim, base with Ando mark, c1930, 10½" high, **$1,600–$2,400.**

Vase, bold white and lavender irises and green leaves on a bright turquoise ground, Japanese, early Showa period, 6½" high, **$300–$400.**

Vase, ginbari, lavender ground with two writhing chartreuse dragons in confrontation, Japanese, early 20th century, 6½" high, **$185–$275.**

Vase, ginbari, pale lavender ground with brightly enameled writhing dragon in primary colors, silver wire, Japanese, early 20th century, 7" high, **$200–$300.**

Vase, ginbari, shaded green to gold-orange, the foil with aquatic plants, the body with orange bulgy-eyed goldfish, signed *Hayashi Kodenji*, Japanese, 10" high, **$3,500–$4,500.**

Vase, ginbari, stippled blue ground with pink hibiscus and foliage, Japanese, Taisho period, 14" high, **$900–$1,285.**

Vase, ginbari with incised foil ground, a kingfisher flying amongst large flowering lotus, bruised, Japanese, Taisho period, 12" high, **$700–$900.**

Vase, green-flecked ground (goldstone) with a pink hen and three chicks among flowers and foliage, dented, Japanese, c1900, 8" high, **$100–$200.**

Vase, green-flecked ground (goldstone) with flowering vines in pastel hues, copper rim and foot, Japanese, c1910, 5" high, **$150–$185.**

Vase, green ground with pale green clouds, yu-musen, chrome mounts, Japanese, Showa period, 7" high, **$100–$175.**

Vase, light blue ground with scattered flowers, diaper band around the neck, copper rim and foot, Japanese, 5½" high, c1920, **$100–$175.**

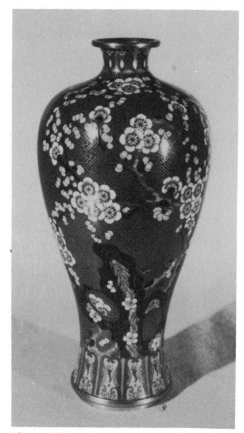

Chinese cloisonné vase, mei ping form, green ground with pink and white plum blossoms, T pattern, lappet border at the foot, signed Lao T'ien Li, *11½" high,* **$900–$1,200.** Courtesy of the Edson Collection.

Vase, long neck, bulbous body, butterflies in colored enamels on a deep blue ground, copper rim and foot, Japanese, late 19th century, 9½" high, **$900–$1,200.**

Vase, long neck, bulbous body, silver wire and enamels worked in a motif of hen and chicks, silver foot and rim, Japanese, 8¾" high, **$1,000–$1,500.**

Vase, mei ping form, the yellow ground with a key pattern, ruyi band at the neck, lappet band at the foot, Chinese, c1925, 14" high, **$200–$300.**

Japanese cloisonné vase in modified mei ping form; the neck with a diapered band in pastel hues; motif of cranes and flowers with silver wire; silver rim and base; minor hairlines in the gray ground; late 19th century, $700–$900.

Vase, mei ping form, overall Millefleurs on a black ground, Chinese, c1935, 12" high, $200–$300.

Vase, moriage, worked in silver wire with branches of pink and white flowers and deep green leaves on a pale blue ground, hairlines, Japanese, early 20th century, 7" high, $800–$1,200.

Vase, moriage, a naturalistic motif of trailing vines on a gray ground, hairlines, base with Ando mark, 9" high, $2,000–$3,000.

Vase, overall swirling patterns divided by a ruyi band at the shoulder, the foot with a dragon-scale pattern, marked *China*, c1930, 10" high, $100–$175.

Vase, ovoid form, the pale blue ground with goldfish and aquatic plants, silver rim and foot, yu-musen, Japanese, c1930, 9" high, $2,200–$3,500.

Vase, ovoid form, two medallions of butterflies above flowers worked in silver wire and colors on a cream ground above and below lappet bands, Japanese, late 19th century, 6" high, $300–$400.

Vase, ovoid form, yellow ground decorated with pink roses and green foliage, chrome mounts, Japanese, Showa period, 6" high, $150–$185.

Vase, ovoid form, akasuke (Pigeon Blood) with white roses and green foliage, chrome foot and rim, Japanese, Showa period, 4" high, $100–$175.

Vase, ovoid form, silver wire worked in hanging blade panels of phoenix and floral panels between gadroon-inlaid borders, silver foot and rim, Ando seal on base, minor chips, 10¾" high, $800–$1,200.

Vase, ovoid form, silver wire worked in a band of peony and foliage on a gray ground, Japanese, c1915, 4½" high, $300–$375.

Vase, ovoid with wide mouth and waisted neck, flaring foot, a mountainscape in pale green and gray on a pale pink ground, chrome mounts, Japanese, early Showa period, 10" high, $300–$500.

Vase, ovoid with a tall neck, worked in silver wires with a motif of butterflies above irises, black ground, formal borders on neck and foot, cracked and chipped, base signed *Kyoto Shibata*, Meiji period, 8" high, $1,500–$2,200.

Japanese cloisonné vase with pale blue-green ground, silver wire, floral motif in pale shades of pink with green foliage, the base with an Ando mark, minor ding on back, early 20th century, **$500–$700.**

Vase, ovoid body worked in silver wire with a bridge spanning a river, the banks with pine trees, pale brown ground, badly cracked on the back (where there is no motif), base marked *Kyoto Namikawa*, Japanese, c1910, 4½" high, **$1,500–$2,000.**

Vase, pear-shaped with short neck, gray ground with hen and chicks worked in silver wire and enamels, minor hairlines, Japanese, late 19th century, 6" high, **$900–$1,200.**

Japanese cloisonné vase, deep blue ground, silver wire, motif of birds and flowers, marked Inaba Nanaho, Meiji period, 5" high, **$3,000–$4,000.** Courtesy of the Edson Collection.

A pair of Japanese cloisonné vases; mirror image; blue ground; silver wire, rims, and bases; diapered band around the base and rim; the motif with numerous flowers, birds, and branches; bases marked Hayashi Kiyoe; 10" high, **$5,000–$7,000.** Courtesy of the Edson Collection.

Japanese cloisonné vase with silver wire, rim, and base; motif of lifelike hydrangeas and sawtooth foliage; marked Hayashi Kodenji on the base; Meiji period, 9¾" high, **$6,000–$8,000.**

Japanese cloisonné vase, green ground, silver wire, motif of standing crane and bamboo, late Meiji period, 4" high, **$125–$185.**

Japanese cloisonné vase with a midnight blue ground, the motif with autumnal leaves and a bird perched upon a branch, diaper border at neck and foot, silver and gold wire, the base with a Hayashi Kodenji mark, 10" high, **$5,500–$7,500.** Courtesy of the Edson Collection.

111

Vase; pear-shaped; a fierce dragon in gray, white, and red on a midnight blue ground; Japanese, late Meiji period, 4½" high, **$200–$300.**

Vase, pliqué à jour, plum blossoms on a blue ground, 5" high, **$900–$1,200.**

Vase, akasuke (Pigeon Blood) with wisteria motif, Japanese, Showa period, 7" high, **$175–$225.**

Vase, red ground with overall brass-wire T pattern, marked China, c1930, 12" high, **$100–$175.**

Vase; red, pink, and purple flowers on a silver blue–gray ground; the base marked Adachi; Japanese, 7½" high, **$500–$700.**

Vase, rust ground with scattered yellow blossoms and green foliage, copper rim and foot, marked China, c1925, 12" high, **$125–$175.**

Vase, silver wire and blue and violet enamels worked in hydrangea on a deep blue ground, silver rim and foot, base with Hayashi Kodenji lozenge mark, Japanese, Meiji period, 3½" high, **$5,000–$6,000.**

Vase, silver wire and enamels worked in a continuous iris pattern on a pale blue ground, lappet band around the shoulders, diaper on rim and foot, repaired, Japanese, late 19th century, 5½" high, **$500–$700.**

Vase, silver wire, rosebuds and one open rose with foliage on green ground, chrome neck and rim, marked Japan, 9" high, **$100–$175.**

Vase, silver wire with birds in flight among wisteria on a deep blue ground, the foot with a diapered band, Japanese, c1910, 9½" high, **$500–$700.**

Vase, silver wire with a bird perched on a flowering branch, pale blue ground, silver rim and foot, chipped, Japanese, c1910, 4" high, **$100–$150.**

Vase, squat body, silver wire worked in a band of peony on a yellow ground, Japanese, c1920, 3½" high, **$250–$350.**

Vase, tapering hexagonal form, silver wire worked in wisteria in shades of lilac on a light green ground, silver rim and foot, base marked Namikawa Yasuyuki, Japanese, Meiji period, 9½" high, **$5,000–$6,500.**

Vases, black ground with silver wire and enamels worked in a bird and bamboo pattern, diapered rims, copper mounts, Japanese, c1910, 8½" high, **$800–$1,200.**

Vases, beaker form decorated with panels of flowers above stiff leaves and bats at the bases, bases poorly restored, Chinese, c1900, 16" high, **pair, $800–$1,200.**

Vases, blue ground worked in silver wire and enamels with numerous flowers, stamped Ota on the base, Japanese, Meiji period, 3½" high, **pair, $700–$950.**

Vases, double gourd, Millefleurs tied with ribbons in relief at the waist, Chinese, mid-Ch'ing (Qing) dynasty, 12½" high, **pair, $5,000–$7,000.**

Vases, midnight blue with wisteria and foliage, one cracked, Japanese, Meiji period, 12" high, **pair, $450–$650.**

Vases, modified mei ping form, turquoise ground with Millefleurs pattern, a lappet band at the base, marked China, early 20th century, 14" high, **pair, $300–$500.**

Vases, globular form, overall floral and leafy scroll motif in colors on a violet blue ground, some enamel loss, Japanese, c1900, 14" high, **pair, $450–$650.**

Vases, rouleau form, the green ground with an overall T pattern, the necks with scrolling lotus, the bodies with large flowers above lappet bands, mounted and pierced as lamps, Chinese, early 20th century, 12½" high, **pair, $400–$600.**

Vases, salmon ground with blue dragons, mirror image, damages on both, Japanese, late 19th century, 8¾" high, **pair, $275–$375.**

Vases, short necks, dark blue ground, irises and foliage in a continuous motif, both dented, Japanese, c1910, 12" high, **pair, $450–$650.**

Vases, silver wire and enamels worked in chrysanthemums and foliage on a pale green ground, Japanese, c1900, 6" high, **pair, $700–$900.**

Vases, slender pear-shaped bodies with black grounds and motifs of egrets above a stream and aquatic plants, copper mounts, Japanese, c1910, 7" high, **pair, $1,200–$1,800.**

Vases; yen-yen shape; each decorated with pine, plum, prunus, and bamboo amidst rock-work; lappet borders; trumpet necks with lotus scrolls; Chinese, c1900, 17" high, **pair, $700–$1,200.**

Vases, yen-yen shape, overall scrolling lotus above stiff leaves at the base, poorly restored bases, Chinese, 19th century, 19" high, **pair, $1,000–$1,500.**

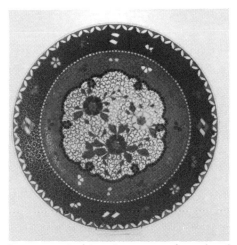

Japanese totai, cloisonné on pottery, bean-shaped cloisons, white ground in the center with floral motif, pale blue and deep blue outer bands, signed Kinkozan, c1875, 7" diameter, **$500–$600.**

Totai

Box and cover, porcelain body, blue ground with motif of a hen and two chicks, diapered border, signed *Takeuchi Chubei*, Japanese, late 19th century, 4¼" X 3¼", **$900–$1,200.**

Bowl, porcelain body, the interior with a floral center medallion, the exterior with a yellow ground and scattered floral mon in colors, marked *Owari*, c1880, 7" diameter, **$900–$1,200.**

Candlestick, panels of butterflies and flowers, autumnal hues, base marked *Noritake*, 8" high, **$300–$400.**

Flowerpot, bucket form, porcelain, blue ground with motif of blossoming peony branches, c1880, 6" high, **$500–$700.**

Flowerpot, porcelain body, blue ground with continuous motif of nesting birds, base marked *Chubei*, c1885, 7½" diameter, **$1,200–$1,800.**

Ginger jar, tree bark, porcelain body, bamboo motif in autumnal hues, c1910, 5" high, **$300–$450.**

Jar and cover, porcelain body, the black ground with a motif of birds perched on branches; markings on base indicating this was one of a pair; 15¼" high, **$2,000–$3,000.**

Mug, porcelain body, orange plum blossoms on a bark ground, base marked Noritake, 7" high, **$300–$450.**

Natsume (tea caddy), the lid with a dragon, the body with a motif of floral mon, the base with a blue and white band, late 19th century, **$900–$1,200.**

Tea set: teapot, sugar, creamer, and six cups and saucers with six cake plates, tree bark with a bamboo pattern, each piece signed Tashiro, c1910, **$700–$1,000.**

Vase; pottery body; moriage motif of wisteria and foliage in bright red, blue, and violet predominating; silver wires; 8" high, **$2,000–$3,000.**

Vase, pottery body, moriage, motif of blossoming peony branches, silver wires, 9½" high, **$2,500–$3,500.**

Vase, serpent handles, motif of irises and butterflies, autumnal hues, base marked Noritake, 8" high, **$350–$575.**

Vase, porcelain body, tree bark with a writhing dragon around the body, autumnal hues, Meiji period, 14" high, **$1,000–$1,500.**

Vase, pottery body, shaded red ground with bird perched on a flowering branch, realistically detailed, c1890, 15" high, **$1,000–$1,600.**

Vase, pottery body, blue ground with bean-shaped cloisonné forming geometric motifs and floral mon, signed Kinkozan, c1885, 5" high, **$300–$475.**

Japanese totai; tree bark; silver wires and autumnal shades with flowers, foliage, and birds; a diaper band at the rim; Meiji period, late 19th century, 15" diameter, **$900–$1,200.**

Vase, porcelain body, bulbous with short neck, red-orange leaves and vines on a tree bark ground, marked Noritake, 4" high, **$300–$400.**

Vase, pottery body, blue ground with scattered floral mon, base marked Kinkozan, c1880, 8½" high, **$600–$800.**

Vases, pair, porcelain bodies, pear-shaped with flaring foot, the neck and foot with underglaze blue and white diapers, the bodies with flowers and foliage on a light blue ground, signed Takeuchi Chubei, c1885, 12" high, **$2,000–$3,000.**

114

5

Ephemera

Confessions of a Paper-holic

For me, the quest for knowledge is an overwhelming desire, akin to an insatiable appetite. Books, magazines, catalogues, or diaries related to or dealing with all aspects of Orientalia—including art, history, travel, industrial arts, and culture—give me a natural high. It's the same kind of high I get from collecting, teaching, writing about, and dealing in Orientalia.

This morning, for instance, two packages arrived. One was from Weatherhill and the other was from an antiquarian book dealer. I didn't know which to open first. The books from Weatherhill were for review in *The Orientalia Journal* (which I publish bimonthly). The other package contained old books and periodicals. I just attacked each, my heart quickening with anticipation as I ripped off the outer wrapping. I got the package from Weatherhill opened first. It contained *Yoshitoshi: Thirty-Six Ghosts* and *Chinese Ceramics: A Short History*. The second package was more difficult to open (this bookseller packs with a vengeance). Even though I knew its contents, my enthusiasm heightened as I reached the materials. The package contained *Japanese Ceramic Art*, by Kikusaburo Fukui (1926); *The Art of Japan*, by Louis Ledoux; *The Catalogue of the Chinese Imperial Maritime Customs Collection at the United States International Exhibition, Philadelphia, 1876*; and several old issues of *Asia Magazine* and *Art Journal*. My pulse began racing as the musty odor of old paper and the pungent aroma of new paper filled my nostrils like fragrant perfume. I couldn't wait to read the materials, and approached each with delight and great appreciation for what it would tell me, for the new knowledge I would gain, and for the enhancement of that which I already knew. How does a collector and dealer of Orientalia become an avid collector of books and related papers? Many years ago, when I began collecting Oriental objects d'art, I realized that owning the Orientalia was not enough. I needed to know as much about what I was collecting as was humanly possible. I needed to know how objects were made, under what circumstances, who the craftsmen were. I needed to know about their culture and history. For a brief time, the public library provided me with books and materials. However, returning borrowed materials always saddened me. I needed and wanted to have access to the materials all the time so that I could have an ongoing learning experience.

With my husband's support, I began to build my own library. At first, I purchased books that were in the index file of the public library—through local bookstores and with the use of a publishers catalogue. Among my first acquisitions was the two-volume set entitled *Potter and Porcelain* by Warren Cox (Crown Publishers). I soon discovered that I was going about the acquisition of books incorrectly. Shortly after acquiring the Cox books I found a first-edition set with the original slipcase in gently used condition for only four dollars (much less than the cost of a new set). At that point, I decided to limit my acquisitions to gently used books which were in and out of print, and to new releases. This was not only less expensive, but the gently used books were far more valuable than new editions of the same titles. The new releases increase in value over the years, but that should not be a criterion for making a purchase.

In addition to book collecting, I added other dimensions to my research/reference library with the acquisition of old periodicals, diaries, photographs, auction catalogues, and catalogues issued by mail-order houses that specialize in products of the Orient. With regard to periodicals, I determined that my needs are limited to editorial content, and that, in contrast to my approach to acquiring books, I would not consider general condition as an important factor. Many old *Asia Magazine* covers are quite valuable, and sometimes the price of the magazine is based upon the collectibility of the cover (for example, Art Deco done by important illustrators is valuable). Acquiring periodicals in less-than-perfect condition (even with the covers missing) lowers the prices and makes them more affordable, especially when you're buying in bulk.

Helpful Hints

Aroma creates problems, especially with old books, periodicals, and new releases, which sometimes have their own pungent odor. The book collector does not want to offend family and friends. I find it best to place small, scented air fresheners in the bookcases and filing cabinets or wherever the paper and books are stored.

When I began collecting books and paper, storage space was a problem. Fortunately, I have an understanding and imaginative husband, who accommodates me by constantly expanding my bookcases and filing cabinets.

I find it best to store periodicals in filing cabinets. Variously sized plastic bags are also helpful in protecting the paper from corrosion, which can be caused by pollutants in the air. Plastic bags also make handling the periodicals much easier.

Some years ago, my husband accompanied me to an antiquarian book fair. To his astonishment, he "loved" the lack of pushing and shoving and the quiet, dignified ambience (quite unlike the antiques events we so often attend). He found Part 2 of Emil Hanover's *Potter and Porcelain*. (Parts 1 and 3 were in my library for some time, but Part 2 was the Far Eastern volume.) This made the experience even more enjoyable and enabled him to share in the collecting experience. Having an extra pair of hands to carry what can sometimes be a very heavy load is helpful, too.

When I teach Oriental Decorative Arts for the Continuing Education Department of New York University, I tell my students—who are collectors, appraisers, interior designers, and dealers—that a good reference/research library is extremely important. A good library helps the collector make the wisest purchases, the appraiser to make the best identification and value judgments, and the decorator and dealer to know positively what they're buying and selling. I cannot stress enough the necessity of being well informed.

Values

Note: All books are in good (or better) condition.

China

Abbate, Francesco. *Chinese Art.* London: Octopus, 1972. **$35–$40.**

Abbate, Francesco. *Chinese Art.* London: Octopus, 1972. **$35–$40.**

Abbot, Jacob. *China and the English.* London: Allman, 1837. **$125–$175.**

Addis, J. J. *Chinese Porcelain from the Addis Collection.* London: British Museum, 1979. **$75–$100.**

Arnold, J. A *Handbook to the West River.* Hong Kong: Canton and Macao Steamboat Co., 1909. **$75–$125.**

Beal, S. *Buddhism in China.* London: S.P.C.K., 1884. **$75–$100.**

Bonnard, Abel. *In China: 1920–1921.* New York: E. P. Dutton, 1927. **$35–$45.**

Brown, Arthur J. *New Forces in Old China.* New York, 1907. **$35–$50.**

The Burrell Collection. Glasgow: Glasgow Art Gallery, 1950. **$40–$60.**

Chen, Shen Tse. *Ancient China's Painters.* Hong Kong, 1978. **$20–$35.**

Cheng, F. T. *Civilization and Art of China.* London: Clowes, 1936. **$30–$50.**

Chinese Porcelain of the Ch'ing Dynasty. London: Victoria and Albert Museum, 1957. **$35–$50.**

Chu, C. C. Peking Rugs and Peking Boys. Peking, 1924. **$75–$100.**

David, Lady. Percival David Foundation of Chinese Art. London: SOAS, 1956. **$35–$50.**

Garner, Harry. Chinese Lacquer. London: Faber, 1979. **$75–$100.**

Gibbs, Howard D. Chinese Imperial Names. New York, 1944. **$45–$55.**

Gompertz, G. M. Chinese Celadon Wares. London: Faber, 1980. **$50–$65.**

Gray, Basil. Early Chinese Pottery and Porcelain. London, 1953. **$75–$100.**

Savage, George. Chinese Jade. London, 1964. **$40–$60.**

Sowerby, Arthur. Nature in Chinese Art. New York, 1940. **$150–$200.**

Some Aspects of Chinese Life and Thought. Shanghai: Kwang Hsueh, 1918. **$40–$60.**

Taylor, I. G. Chinese Jade. London: Grants, 1920. **$40–$60.**

Tredwell, Winifred R. Chinese Art Motives. New York, 1915. **$350–$365.**

Tse, Tsan Tai. Ancient Chinese Art. Hong Kong, 1928. **$50–$75.**

Waley, Arthur. The Analects of Confucius. London, 1949. **$40–$60.**

Wang, Yu-Ch'uan. Early Chinese Coinage. New York, 1951. **$85–$100.**

Warren, George B. Catalogue of Antique Chinese Porcelains. Boston, 1902. **$75–$100.**

Wen, Chen M. An Old Chinese Garden. Shanghai: Chung Hwa, 1921. **$200–$275.**

Werner, E. T. C. Myths and Legends of China. London: Harrap, 1934. **$100–$150.**

Woolf, Bella S. Chips of China. Shanghai: Kelly Walsh, 1930. **$50–$85.**

Yeh, Chien-yu. National Costumes of China. 1957. **$20–$30.**

Yuel, Henry. Cathay and the Way Thither. Tokyo: Kyoyekishosha, 1866. **$150–$200.**

Young, Florence S. H. Pearls from the Pacific. London: Marshall, 1923. **$50–$75.**

Japan

Akiyama, Aisaburo. A Brief History of Pictorial Japan. Tokyo, 1919. **$120–$175.**

Alcock, Sir Rutherford. Art and Art Industries in Japan. London, 1878. **$200–$300.**

Amsden, Dora. Impressions of Ukiyo-E. San Francisco, 1905. **$40–$70.**

Averill, Mary. Japanese Flower Arrangement. New York: Lane, 1933. **$20–$25.**

Brockhouse, Albert. Netsukes. New York, 1924. **$100–$125.**

Caiger, G. Dolls on Display. Tokyo: Hokuseido, 1933. **$125–$225.**

Covell, Jon C. Japanese Landscape Painting. New York, 1962. **$20–$30.**

Dick, Stewart. Arts and Crafts of Old Japan. Chicago, 1905. **$30–$40.**

Dillon, Edward. The Arts of Japan. London, 1922. **$20–$30.**

Dresser, Christopher. Japan: Its Architecture, Art, and Art Manufacturers. London: Longmans, 1882. **$400–$500.**

Evans, Tom. *Shunga: The Art of Love in Japan*. New York, 1975. **$40–$65.**

Franks, Augustus W. *Japanese Pottery* (a reprint of the 1880 edition catalog). London: HMSO, 1906. **$50–$100.**

Gichner, Lawrence E. *Erotic Aspects of Japanese Culture*. Privately Printed. 1953. **$600–$800.**

Gorham, Hazel H. *Japanese Netsuke*. Yokohama, 1957. **$125–$185.**

Gunsaulus, Helen C. *The Japanese Sword and Its Decoration*. Chicago: Field Museum of Natural History, 1924. **$10–$20.**

Hartshorne, Anna C. *Japan and Her People*. Philadelphia: Winston, 1902. **$150–$200.**

Hillier, Jack. *Japanese Drawings*. New York, 1965. **$30–$50.**

Joly, Henry L. *Legend in Japanese Art*. London: Lane, 1908. **$500–$600.**

Kawakatsu, Kenichi. *Kimono*. Tokyo, 1954. **$20–$30.**

Lane, Richard. *Images from the Floating World*. New York: Dorset, 1982. **$40–$60.**

Lawson, Lady. *Highways and Homes of Japan*. London: Unwin, 1920. **$200–$250.**

Photo albums. Late-nineteenth-century albums with hand-colored gravures averaging approximately 8" × 10" can retail at **$300–$500.** Early-twentieth-century albums have values as low as **$150** for a group of 20–30 photos.

Postcard albums with lacquer covers, dating c1900, approximately 30–50 postcards, including hand-colored collotype; photo postcards can retail at **$350–$900,** depending upon condition and type/style of the cards.

Shimonaka, Kunihiko. *Oribe Ware*. Tokyo: Heibonsha, 1958. **$20–$30.**

Shishido, Misako. *The Folk Toys of Japan*. Rutland, VT, 1963. **$40–$65.**

Strange, Edward R. *Catalogue of Japanese Lacquer*. London: HMSO, 1924. **$185–$225.**

Taki, Seiichi. *Japanese Fine Art*. Tokyo: Fuzambo, 1931. **$20–$35.**

Warner, Langdon. *The Craft of the Japanese Sculptor*. New York, 1936. **$50–$100.**

Yashiro, Yukio. *2000 Years of Japanese Art*. New York: Abrams, 1958. **$200–$300.**

The Yearbook of Japanese Art. Tokyo, 1927. **$100–$150.**

Young, A. Morgan. *Imperial Japan 1926–1938*. London: Allen, 1938. **$10–$20.**

6

Furniture

Korean

Korean furniture is simple, making classic use of straight lines. Constructed from woods such as pine, pagoda, paulownia, pear, persimmon, and combinations, this furniture is also marked by distinctive hardware (mostly iron) accents. The pieces which were originally more expensive—those made for the aristocracy—can have white or yellow brass hardware; occasionally, silver was used.

During the Yi Dynasty (1392–1910) furnishings included carved, lacquered, or inlaid storage chests, tables, and folding screens. Among the chests which are of particular interest to collectors of Korean furniture are bin-shaped storage containers or utility boxes used for the storage of household goods and of grain such as rice. Also of interest are the medicine chests, with their many drawers. Sometimes the names of the medicines are painted on or carved into the drawers.

Chinese chest, carved camphor wood, motif of prunus overall, brass mounts and brass label (The Wing On Co Ltd., Shanghai), c1920, 25" long, 10½" deep, 15" wide, **$300–$400.**

Chinese

Chinese furniture has simple, gently curved lines. (Most of the elaborately carved pieces are lacquer furniture or were made specifically for export to the West.) Cutting, joining, and finishing were carefully done.

Like Korean furniture, Chinese furniture employs a variety of woods. Hua-li rosewood (also known as Burmese or East Indian rosewood) has shades ranging from dark to blonde, and is characterized by a translucent, satiny finish. Hung-mu redwood, a cousin of rosewood, is a much darker wood used extensively in the nineteenth and twentieth centuries. It is like American mahogany, but the grain is much finer. Hua-mu burl, displaying the curly patterns of the roots from which it is taken, often appears in inlaid pieces. Chests are often made of camphor wood. Extremely popular among these are the chests with high-relief carving, produced during the 1920s and 1930s.

Note that teak is an Indian wood used exclusively for Indian furniture.

Japanese

The Japanese developed very few forms of furniture. Among the pieces of interest to collectors are clothing stands, cabinets, trays, desks, tables, and tansu (chests of drawers). The Japanese tansu with the finest woods, made for the daimyo and the samurai, had four large drawers, sometimes lacquered in part. The plainer tansu were produced for the poorer classes. Both are of special interest to collectors and both blend with the styles used in interior design today.

In addition to tansu, export furniture of the late Meiji and Taisho periods, as well as that of the early Showa period, is attracting a growing interest, especially those pieces with elaborate carving and/or lacquered motifs.

General Information

When trying to determine whether an ornately carved piece of furniture is Chinese or Japanese, remember the following: Japanese furniture made for Western markets follows the change in styles from Victorian to Art Nouveau to Art Deco. Also, check the carved dragons, if there are any. If they have three toes, 99 percent of the time, the piece is Japanese. Chairs, benches, or settees which have a carved circular motif (a mon) on the seat are always Japanese.

Collectible Oriental furniture does appreciate in value, although the appreciation is low (unless the pieces are proven to be important or of significant provenance). Unfortunately, the same cannot be said for the value of new furniture.

For information on the care and keeping of Oriental furniture, see Appendix D.

Furniture Values

Altar table, hardwood, paneled top and rounded ends, the apron pierced with scrollwork and terminating as fungus, rectangular legs waisted in two places with foliage in low relief, Chinese, 19th century, 87" long, 42" high, 21" deep, **$1,650–$2,700.**

Altar table, hardwood, rectangular, four square legs with scroll feet, the frieze with archaistic scroll brackets and carved on the long side with three bat-shaped scrolling motifs, Chinese, early 19th century, 69" long, 37½" wide, 21" deep, **$3,700–$5,250.**

Altar table, hardwood, rectangular top over a pierced and carved foliate scrolling apron, four square legs and scroll toes, Indonesian, 39" long, **$600–$900.**

Armchair, hardwood, the back pierced and carved with confronting dragons, dragon armrest, ivory eyes, the serpentine seat with a centrally carved Tokugawa mon, cabriole legs, Japanese, Taisho period, **$600–$900.**

One of a pair of Chinese elmwood horseshoe-back armchairs; each with curved, rounded crest rail; rounded stiles; a curved, solid splat shallowly carved with lobed ruyi-head medallion above a sunken, paneled seat; square straight legs with pierced key fret brackets and joined by a footrest and stretchers; 18th century. Realized price (including the 10-percent buyer's premium), Christie's East, New York City, **$1,045.**

123

Armchair, red lacquer, yoke-shaped back, gilt splat, folding leather seat, trestle supports and hinged footrest, gilt metal mounts with foliate scrolls, Japanese, late Edo period, 43½" high, **$1,500–$2,500.**

Armchairs, low with rectangular backs, carved paneled splats and seats, carved arm supports, legs joined by simple stretchers, one leg broken, Chinese, early 20th century, 40" long, **pair, $600–$800.**

Armchairs, hung-mu, the crest rail above an S-scrolled splat, oval marble panel inset on the backs, circular legs, box stretcher on frontal bracket support, Chinese, 19th century, **pair, $2,500–$3,500.**

Armchairs, hung-mu, each with rectangular paneled seat, aprons at front and sides with carved foliage, the front apron extending to the footrail and the stretchers at the bottom with narrow skirts, stepped arms, yoke-shaped backs edged with pierced fretwork, the central splat carved with foliage on the front and back, Chinese, 19th century, 42" high, **pair, $2,500–$3,500.**

Basin stand (folding); six rectangular legs with block finials, joined by upper and lower hexagonal bar stretchers; Chinese, 19th century, 26½" high, **$1,000–$1,500.**

Bed (hardwood opium bed), rectangular, detachable sides and back, the base with scrolled apron carved with two dragons, four carved Buddhistic lion mask feet, the back with three scenic panels flanked by side panels of pine and prunus, in need of restoration, Chinese, 19th century, 77" × 36" × 38", **$900–$1,200.**

One of a pair of hung-mu marble-inset armchairs, stepped backrest carved with cloud scrolls and set with marble plaque below a burl panel, angular scroll arms, the rectangular seat over a simple scroll-carved apron and square straight legs joined by stretchers, Chinese, 19th century. Realized price (including the 10-percent buyer's premium), Christie's, New York City, $935.

Bed; hardwood; rectangular canopy carved with panels of birds, vessels, and dragons above a fretwork ceiling; the upholstered mattress above four drawers; all supported on wide scroll feet; needs some restoration/repair; Chinese, c1900, 93½" × 129" × 33½", **$1,000–$1,500.**

Bed (canopied marriage bed), red- and gilt-lacquered wood, pierced and carved birds and leafy scrolls in high relief on a red ground, Chinese, late 19th century, outside frame 66" wide, overall 90" long, **$2,800–$4,000.**

Bench, back carved with two panels containing bamboo and birds surmounted by two confronting dragons beneath Mt. Fuji, arms with carved dragons, seat with hinged lid, some minor cracking, Japanese, Meiji period, 50" × 59" × 22", $1,800–$2,800.

Bench; the back with two panels of birds and bamboo carved in high relief; below, a view of Mt. Fuji; the arms carved with dragons; the seat carved with three Tokugawa mon within a key-pattern border; in need of some repair; Japanese, late Meiji period, 50" × 60" × 24", **$2,500–$3,500.**

Bench, hardwood, the back carved with open-work trees flanked by two acanthus finials, the arms as sprouting branches, the rectangular seat with scroll-pattern border, floral apron, four back supports, Japanese, late Meiji period, 50" × 26" × 52", **$900–$1,200.**

Cabinet, pine, two parts (three sets of sliding doors and five drawers), Japanese, Meiji period, 60" high, **$900–$1,200.**

Cabinet on stand, rectangular, stepped shelving, two pairs of sliding doors, four hinged doors, brown lacquer ground with gold and black hiramakie and hirame, motifs of birds and insects amongst flowers, old damages and wear, Japanese, late 19th century, 31" × 48", **$5,500–$7,500.**

Cabinet (chandana/tea cabinet), burl keyaki wood, four sliding paneled doors above two glass doors which enclose a cased and sectioned interior, the lower case with a bowed door and a glass door, Japanese, late Meiji period, 30" × 50", **$1,700–$2,500.**

Cabinet; carved red (cinnabar) lacquer; two square hinged doors above two larger doors enclosing a shelf and two drawers—all above a shallow drawer; bracket feet; the front carved with ladies and attendants with children beside pavilions in landscapes—all within borders of key pattern; the top and sides with cell pattern; brass hinges and locks; some old damages; Chinese, 18th century, 14¼" × 26", **$2,500–$3,500.**

Cabinet, hung-mu, two narrow central doors with low-relief carvings of cloud scrolls between upper and lower doors enclosing a shelf and two drawers, metal hinges and lock plates with Shou characters and Shou-character pulls, Chinese, early 19th century, 79" high, **$2,800–$4,000.**

Cabinet; fruitwood; asymmetrical arrangement of drawers, doors, and shelves joined by a bridge; overall motifs of birds, flowers, and foliage inlaid in bone, ivory, and mother-of-pearl; some inlay missing; Japanese, Meiji period, 86" high, **$2,200–$3,500.**

Cabinet; black lacquer; two doors; the front decorated in low relief with mother-of-pearl, hard stone, and gilt in a motif of children playing on a grassy terrace watched by ladies at the sides, all within borders of mother-of-pearl dragons; crackle to the surface; Chinese, c1900, 34" × 52", **$1,000–$1,500.**

Cabinet; two parts; two large doors and four drawers in the lower section; two large and four small doors in the upper section, with one drawer and one cupboard; iron mounts; Japanese, early Meiji period, 68" high, **$1,500–$2,200.**

Cabinet, hardwood, rectangular, a long upper compartment with sliding panels above open shelves and carved with peony blossoms and Shishi, the frame simulating bamboo edged with carved flowers, Japanese, late Meiji period, 16" X 54", **$1,200-$1,800.**

Cabinet; black and gilt lacquer; two doors enclosing an interior of shelves and columns fitted with variously sized drawers above two larger drawers; overall motifs of riverbanks and pavilions on a gilt-lacquered, pierced stand; brass bail handles; some damages, Japanese, Meiji period, 57½" high, **$1,200-$1,800.**

Cabinet, hardwood, glass-encased, extensively carved with irises, four interior shelves, rectangular plinth, four shaped legs, Japanese, late 19th century, 68" high, **$2,500-$3,500.**

Chair, rosewood, reclining, cylindrical headrest above a curved paneled splat back connected to the frame, curved arms with another set of curved arms flanking the paneled seat, a draw front nesting leg support, Chinese, 19th century, 32" high, **$900-$1,200.**

Chest, pine, supported on low legs, the hinged front with plain iron mounts and an iron lock, Korean, Yi Dynasty, 19th century, 37" X 13¼" X 24½", **$600-$800.**

Chest, burl and elmwood, plain top, brass-mounted corners, front with four paneled sliding drawers above two paneled doors mounted with circular brass mounts, shaped apron, short cabriole legs joined by stretchers at the sides, Korean, Yi Dynasty, 19th century, 37" X 37" X 20", **$900-$1,200.**

Chest, black and gilt lacquer, the hinged cover decorated with pairs of confronting dragons and phoenix within a band of red key scrolls on a gilt ground, sides similarly decorated, bronze loop handles, circular lock plate; with matching low table stand; Chinese, c1900, 18" X 37" X 24", **$1,000-$1,500.**

Chest of drawers, hardwood, the front with mock drawers, paneled pull-out drawers and small doors all inlaid in mother-of-pearl with Buddhist emblems, short cabriole feet, Korean, Yi Dynasty, 41" X 39" X 14", **$1,000-$1,500.**

Chest, red lacquer, rectangular with two long drawers above a pair of short drawers, iron hardware and side handles, Japanese, early 20th century, 26½" wide, **$450-$600.**

Chest, camphor wood, high-relief carving of warriors, some on horseback, overall brass mounts and lock plate, Chinese, c1925, 21" X 36" X 24", **$800-$1,200.**

Cupboard, hinged drop front revealing three small drawers, the sides with large carrying handles, brass mounts pierced with swastika, shaped apron, Korean, Yi Dynasty, 19th century, 37½" X 34½" X 18", **$800-$1,200.**

Cupboard, huang hua-li, rectangular, floating paneled top and sides, rounded stiles extending to form feet and joined by curved aprons, doors reveal trays and drawers, Paktong pulls, legs cut down, Chinese, early Ch'ing (Qing) Dynasty, 56" X 28", **$2,000-$3,000.**

A honey-toned camphor and elmwood storage chest, the rectangular top with two removable lids and brass latches revealing slide compartments above a pair of small cupboard doors opening to a plain interior, sunken paneled sides, bracket feet, Chinese, 19th century, 36" high, 34½" wide. Realized price (including the 10-percent buyer's premium), Christie's East, New York City, **$935.**

Desk, hardwood, carved with a dragon coiled around Mt. Fuji above stepped shelving, a cupboard section (beside the shelving) carved with phoenix and foliage, the lower part with two drawers above cabriole legs, Japanese, c1900, 40" × 36", **$1,200–$1,800.**

Desk; hung-mu; the detachable, paneled top rests upon two pedestals with two pairs of drawers; straight legs joined by rectangular box stretchers having interlocking, flattened struts; brass bail handles; Chinese, early 20th century, 30" × 62", **$1,000–$1,500.**

Desk, lacquered wood, hinged top section set on detachable cabinets which are set on a low rectangular support, the two doors reveal shelves and drawers, overall motif of gilt-lacquered birds and flowers on a black ground, brass mounts, warped, nicks around the bottom, Japanese, early Showa period, 62½" high, **$800–$1,200.**

Desk and chair, the upper part surmounted by pierced and carved irises and foliage above two side doors revealing shelves, the apron with pierced and carved foliage, cabriole legs, matching chair, Japanese, late Meiji period, desk 50" high, **$1,000–$1,500.**

Dresser and mirror; keyaki wood; four drawers and beveled, rectangular mirror; Japanese, 20th century, 19" X 37", **$350–$450.**

Game table; floating paneled top; stepped sides, each with a small drawer; four square legs terminating in hoof feet (inward-curving); Chinese, early 20th century, 30" X 33", **$800–$1,000.**

Garden stools, hardwood, barrel form, open sides with four intersecting medallions between rows of bosses, marble circular plaque set in the tops, Chinese, first half of the 20th century, 20½" high, **$1,100–$1,600.**

Ice chest; a two-panel cover fitting over a tapered, square case; brass bail handles; painted red; Chinese, late 19th century, 19⅜" wide, **$650–$750.**

Mirror, rectangular, banded with ivory mosaic work, gilt bronze support, Chinese, 15" X 20", **$500–$700.**

Chinese lantern, hardwood frame with inside-painted glass panels, silk tassles, original hook, one of a pair, electrified, early 20th century, the frame measuring 28" high (not including the length of the tassels), **pair, $2,000–$3,000.**

Mirror, the gilt wood frame with panels carved with the Eight Immortals on a band of floral scrolls, Chinese, c1800, 27½" X 38¾", **$500–$800.**

Mirror, octagonal, the gilt wood frame carved with scrolls, Chinese, early 19th century, 26½" X 37", **$400–$600.**

Money chest, hinged cover, iron pattern of raised bosses around the sides, Japanese, 19th century, 16" X 10", **$300–$500.**

Screen; four panels of embroidered ecru silk, each with varied flowers, foliage, and birds in flight worked in gold thread; black-lacquered frames; Japanese, Taisho period, leaf size 19" X 6", **$2,000–$3,000.**

Screen, Shibayama, two panels, each decorated in gold and silver lacquer and inlaid with mother-of-pearl and coral songbirds and butterflies in a mountainous landscape with a river and waterfalls, the back with songbirds perched on flowering prunus branches, Japanese, late Meiji period, 35" × 73", **$3,500–$5,000.**

Screen; six-leaf; inlaid on one side with hard stones, ivory, and mother-of-pearl within cell-pattern bands above a border of kylin; the motif a continuous battle scene with warriors on horseback; losses to inlay; some surface damage; Chinese, late Ch'ing (Qing) Dynasty, each leaf 15" × 68", **$1,800–$2,800.**

Screen, eight-panel coromandel, a flock of geese amongst reeds and rock-work on a gilt ground, Chinese, late Ch'ing (Qing) Dynasty; each leaf 68½" high, 16½" wide; **$1,500–$2,500.**

Screen, hardwood, four panels, each inset with three porcelain plaques (famille rose with the 100 Antiques motif), the reverse with red lacquer floral motifs, Chinese, late 19th century; each panel 70" high, 20" wide; **$2,000–$3,000.**

Screen, hardwood, four panels, each leaf carved in shallow relief with Immortals and attendants in a mountainous landscape, the reverse with bats and Shou characters, the square feet with archaistic scroll brackets, Chinese, c1900; each panel 74½" high, 17½" wide; **$2,000–$3,000.**

Screen, hardwood, four panels carved with numerous pierced geometric and foliate designs, each panel with two knop finials, Indian, c1900; each panel 78" high, 21" wide; **$650–$900.**

Settee; hung-mu; rectangular backrest with three oval rings above spindle supports, flanked by armrests with single rings and spindles; the paneled seat above a frieze of rectangles on rounded, straight legs joined by side stretchers and footrest; Chinese, c1900, 42" long, **$2,500–$3,500.**

Shodana, an open upper part above two hinged doors—each with an inlaid figure of a dancer in ivory and shell, the interior with three drawers, wood refinished, Japanese, c1900, 41" × 44", **$2,000–$3,000.**

Side chairs; hardwood; finely pierced, circular scroll backs with drop-in, serpentine seats; pierced apron on pad legs with animal heads and feet; Indian, 19th century, 35" high, **pair, $600–$800.**

Side chairs; round top rail supported by a curved, rectangular back-splat; the straight, square legs joined by a low footrest and stretchers; Ming style, Chinese, 19th century, 21" × 16½" × 43", **pair, $1,500–$2,500.**

Side chairs, carved red (cinnabar) lacquer, open rectangular back, center splat carved with flowering trees, straight legs joined by stretchers, overall carving of vines and flower heads, one in need of restoration, Chinese, 19th century, 30" high, **pair, $2,800–$4,000.**

Stand (for kimono), black and gold lacquer decorated with flowering clematis growing upon a trellis, copper mounts, badly chipped and cracked, Japanese, Meiji period, 21½" wide, **$700–$900.**

Stands, hardwood with inset marble tops, five legs joined by a pentagonal stretcher, the legs and rim carved with prunus, Chinese, c1925, 33" high, **pair, $900–$1,200.**

Stand, hardwood, inset marble top, four legs, the apron carved with foliage, Chinese, c1925, 20" high, **$325–$475.**

Stand, wood, carved and pierced with irises and foliage, four cabriole legs, the top with a red lacquer dragon, Japanese, Taisho period, 28" high, **$475–$675.**

Stool, hardwood, rounded frame forming two side legs, Chinese, c1930, 15½" high, **$500–$700.**

Table, hardwood, the rim carved with a lappet border, a pierced apron carved with daisylike flowers, the top set with pink marble, supported on a tripod pedestal base with stylized paw feet, Japanese, late Meiji / early Taisho period, 36" high, **$900–$1,200.**

Table; hardwood console; rectangular, paneled top above a pierced and carved apron frieze of curvilinear foliage; four square, tapered legs; Indonesian, 19th century, **$1,200–$1,800.**

Table, oval form standing on four elephant legs joined by a crossbar, profusely carved overall, 54" diameter × 30" high, **$700–$1,000.**

Table, carved red (cinnabar) lacquer, the top with a flower head and dense checker pattern, the sides with dragons and flaming pearls amongst dense cloud whorls, the latter design repeated on the apron, four rectangular feet, minor repairs, Chinese, late 19th century, 36" long, **$2,000–$3,000.**

Table; polychromed and lacquered; octagonal form; eight open-work, folding legs, each with a flowering plant; profusely decorated and outlined in black and gilt lacquer; Indian, c1900, 28" diameter, **$900–$1,500.**

Table (side table), hung-mu, rectangular top, the narrow sides carved with key fret, four slender cabriole legs terminating in hoof feet (inward-curving), scroll-shaped apron, plain stretcher front, Chinese, early 19th century, 36" high, **$700–$1,000.**

Table; low; black lacquer; rectangular section with open frame; interstices carved to resemble lotus panels; bronze mounts; cracked, Japanese, late 19th century, **$1,200–$1,500.**

Table, hardwood, circular drum form on five inward-curving legs joined by a bottom stretcher, a frieze around the top with fruiting vine, Chinese, c1900, 20½" wide, **$600–$900.**

Table, hardwood, low with inserted burl wood top section, the four inward-curving legs joined by a frieze pierced with dragons, Chinese, c1935, 37" wide, **$600–$900.**

Table; black-lacquered wood; the top inlaid with mother-of-pearl, coral, jade, and painted figures of ladies in a garden; inward-curving legs; glass top; Chinese, c1935, 42" long, 28" high, **$800–$1,200.**

Tables, nest of four, hardwood, rectangular and low, the plain tops with mock bamboo surrounds and legs, joined by friezes pierced with fruiting vines, Chinese, late 19th century, 18" high to 28" high, **$1,200–$1,600.**

Tansu, double-sided kaidan (stepped) with nine steps, keyaki wood, iron mounts, each side with sliding doors, one hinged door, three vertical doors, Japanese, mid-19th century, 85" high, **$3,000–$4,500.**

Tansu/kuruma-wheeled; two sliding, lattice doors; one cabinet and two drawers with locking bar front; iron mounts; late Edo / early Meiji period, 40" high, **$2,500–$3,500.**

Tansu (Issho), kiri wood, four drawers with iron mounts and pulls, Japanese, early 20th century, 36" × 42", **$500–$700.**

Tansu, oak and kiri wood, three drawers and two sliding doors in the upper section, two doors in the center, two drawers in the base, Japanese, late 19th century, 58¼" high, **$1,000–$1,500.**

7

Inro, Netsuke, Ojime, and Related Articles

Because Japanese garments had no pockets, personal accessories had to be suspended from a cord worn around the carrier. In this assembly, known as *sagemono*, the *netsuke* was the toggle used to prevent the cord from slipping through the *obi* (sash). The slide used for making the string tight or loose is called an *ojime*. In putting together the sagemono, the wearer would string the accessory through its runners (one on each side), adding the ojime as a slide, and fastening the netsuke at the end.

134

Top, left to right: Inro, erotic, four-case decorated in orie togidashi on a nashiji ground with a
couple united in sexual congress. Realized price
(including the 10-percent buyer's premium),
Christie's, New York City, **$2,200.** Four-case inro
in iroe takamakie and hiramakie and inlaid aogai
on a bark ground, clothing hung on a rope as if to
air, inlay missing and chips, macabre staghorn
ojime formed as a skull, signed Gyokumin. Realized price (including the 10-percent buyer's premium), Christie's, New York City, **$1,760.**

Bottom, left to right: A sleeve inro; the sleeve
decorated in gold hiramakie, kirigane, and
nasahiji; two scholars on a bridge with rock-work
beside and clouds above; seven-case inro decorated
in iroe hiramakie to represent the grain of wood;
minor chips and old damages; early 19th century.
Realized price (including the 10-percent buyer's
premium), Christie's, New York City, **$1,230.**
Five-case inro in gold hiramakie, nashiji, and
kirigane on a fundame ground; a pensive Dutchman leaning against a tree and watching a group
of four puppies playing in a field; late 19th century.
Realized price (including the 10-percent buyer's
premium), Christie's, New York City, **$2,860.**

Types of Netsuke

Manju netsuke is named for its resemblance to the Japanese rice cakes of
the same shape (round). This form of
netsuke dates from the eighteenth
century, unless it is made of ivory, in
which case it originated around the
mid-nineteenth century. Manju netsuke may be made as one piece or two
halves, and is slightly hollow inside (to
take the cord). There may be a ring at
the back used for the attachment of
the cord; most manju netsuke have
himotoshi (holes), either one or two.

Ryusa is a more deeply carved
variation of the manju. Kagamibuta is
basically like a manju netsuke, but the
lower half is well hollowed and the
opening covered by a convex metal
disc with a loop underneath. The cords
are passed through a hole in the center and are then fastened to the loop
on the lid.

Additional types of netsuke are as
follows:

- **Katabori.** Netsuke made to look like
  animals and figures, carved in wood
  or ivory.
- **Kurawa.** Ashtray netsuke.
- **Ichiraku.** Netsuke that has been
  woven or plaited in the form of baskets, gourds, and so on.
- **Trick or toy netsuke.** Netsuke with
  moving parts.

Inro

The inro was the principle accessory
worn by men. It originated as a box for
holding a seal, and was later divided
into two compartments to carry the
ink as well. In the late 16th / early 17th
century, the inro was further divided
into as many as five—and sometimes
even six—cases or compartments.
Sometimes one or more of these main
compartments was itself divided in
half. At this point in the development
of inro, they became medicine chests
(yakuro) and were used to carry all sorts
of medicines, drugs, and ointments.

Note that the bottom compartment of early inro is generally lined
with silver or gold foil. In addition, inro
(as well as ojime and netsuke) may be
marked with a signature or seal. Like
netsuke and ojime, inro can be found
in a variety of materials and techniques, including ivory, wood, bone,
antler, cloisonné, lacquer, wood, pottery, porcelain, and metal.

FYI (For Your Information): Netsuke

The illustration shows a netsuke of Gama Sennin signed *Chogetsu*. It is supposed to be a nineteenth-century netsuke carved from stag antler. In the last few months, several of this very same netsuke have been bought and sold by various dealers in New York City as well as other parts of the country. It seemed odd that the very same netsuke should suddenly become so available. In fact, upon examining these netsuke I discovered that they were excellent copies executed in some sort of polymer.

It appears that the original netsuke was used to create a mold which has obviously been used a number of times. The reproduction is a quality rendering, finished by hand. Each of the netsuke I examined had a variation in the stain. The darkest was deep brown and the lightest was pale yellow. The weight, feel, size, coloring, and other apparent qualities of these netsuke would fool an expert. Only by using the hot-needle test (penetrating the substance in question with a red-hot needle point and identifying it by the resulting odor emitted) could it have been determined that these netsuke were not authentic.

Netsuke of Gama Sennin with Chogetsu Mark: A Polymer Copy

I wonder just how many of this particular netsuke have been circulating and if other authentic netsuke have been used to create molds. If you see a similar netsuke, or discover other look-alikes which test plastic, please let me know where and when they were offered. Letters should be sent to Sandra Andacht c/o *The Orientalia Journal*, P.O. Box 94, Little Neck, NY 11363.

Other Accessories

- **Tonkotsu.** Tobacco boxes which are larger than inro. Tonkotsu are usually wood, and are carved or decorated with lacquer and/or inlay.

- **Tobako ire.** Pouches that were usually made of tanned leather or pieces of brocade.
- **Kinchaku.** Money pouch.
- **Yatate.** The case which contained the brush and ink; usually bronze.
- **Fudezutzu.** A separate case for ink.
- **Hashi ire.** Chopstick and knife.

Values

Inro

Two-case; bamboo; carved with Chinese scholars, trees, and buildings; some wormage; 19th century, **$250–$350.**

Two-case, hinoki wood (cypress) applied with tsuishu and black tsuikoku with two sides of an ink cake in low relief; chipped, cracked, wormage; attributed to Ritsuo; **$1,900–$2,500.**

Two-case, red lacquer with gold and silver reeds and marsh grasses, coral bead ojime, c1900, **$500–$600.**

Three-case, gold hiramakie, takamakie heidatsu and togidashi on a black ground with a continuous motif of a bird perched on rock-work, chipped, late 18th century, **$1,200–$1,800.**

Three-case, gold and silver hiramakie with five insects on each side, black ground and interiors, relacquered, early Meiji period, **$900–$1,200.**

Three-case; gold and silver hiramakie, hirame, and nashiji with a continuous landscape showing an Emperor standing beside courtiers; top and bottom cases in need of restoration; 18th century, **$1,500–$2,000.**

Two-case silver inro decorated with gold and silver peony and leaves, inlaid coral berries, coral-bead ojime and silver cloisonné manju netsuke, signed Fujimoto Kanekatsu (with kakihan), **$4,000–$6,000.** *Courtesy of the Edson Collection.*

Three-case; hiramakie, mother-of-pearl, and silver on a gold ground; a continuous fence and floral motif; some inlay missing; late Meiji / Taisho period, **$500–$700.**

Three-case; ivory with gold, silver, and red takamakie with floral roundels; age cracks; plain, round, ivory ojime; ivory hako netsuke; the top with gold-lacquer fern; 19th century, **$1,500–$2,200.**

Three-case, mura-nashiji decorated in gold and silver hiramakie and hirame with a continuous motif of flowering chrysanthemums, gyobu interiors, signed *Kajakawa saku*, red tsubo-shaped seal, restored, early 19th century, **$1,885–$2,800.**

Three-case roironuri; gold, silver, red, and brown hiramakie, takamakie, okibirame, and nashiji with the 12 zodiac animals; damaged; coral bead ojime; 19th century, **$600–$950.**

Three-case, wood (natural) with lacquer, mother-of-pearl and enamel depicting lotus leaves in a continuous motif, shibuichi double gourd ojime, early 19th century, Ritsuo style, **$3,000–$4,000.**

Three-case, wood carved in relief with a continuous motif of Shoki pursuing two Oni, ivory ojime carved with the Seven Gods of Good Luck, a wood netsuke of Shoki's hat, 19th century, **$1,500–$2,200.**

Four-case; cherry bark decorated in iroe, hiramakie, and takamakie on a red-brown ground with foliage and flowers; coral glass ojime; late Meiji period, **$1,200–$1,600.**

Four-case; fundame decorated in gold and silver hiramakie, takamakie, and hirame with a hawk on a perch; nashiji interiors; rubbed; chipped; late 18th/early 19th century, **$1,875–$2,650.**

Four-case, hirame and togidashi with a full moon behind pine branches, nashiji interiors, 19th century, **$1,500–$2,500.**

Four-case, ivory, one side carved with Ebisu, the reverse with Daikoku, the panels within floral borders, floral runners, early Showa, **$400–$600.**

Four-case; kinji; decorated in gold, black, and red hiramakie, takamakie, hirame, and nashiji with a cockerel standing on a drum; rubbed and chipped; early 19th century, **$1,800–$2,800.**

Four-case; kinji; decorated in gold, brown, and silver hiramakie, hirame, nashiji, and togidashi with a continuous motif of thatched houses amongst pine trees; slightly damaged and a minor repair to two cases; early 19th century, **$800–$1,200.**

Four-case; kinji with gold, silver, red, and black takamakie, hiramakie, hirame, and togidashi; a dragon emerging from swirling waves; nashiji interiors; early 19th century, **$700–$900.**

Four-case, kinji ground with a motif of berried branches, the berries of inlaid coral, gold takamakie leaves, kinji interiors, signed *Koma Ankyo*, chipped, cracked, 19th century, **$1,200–$1,650.**

Four-case; nashiji decorated in gold hiramakie, takamakie, and hirame with birds perched on branches; nashiji interiors; rubbed; chipped; crack on one cord runner; late 19th century, **$1,000–$1,500.**

Four-case, roiro decorated with a floral spray on one side and a fan-shaped panel of flowers on the reverse in gold and colored takamakie, nashiji interior, chipped and worn, signed *Kagikawa saku* (with red pot seal), 19th century, **$2,000–$3,000.**

Four-case, roironuri decorated in gold and silver togadashi and hirame with a hut beneath leafy branches, nashiji interiors, very badly worn, early 19th century, **$700–$950.**

Four-case, Somada school with a repetitive brocade motif of inlaid aogai on a roironuri ground, 19th century, **$2,000–$2,800.**

Four-case, Somada style, roiro ground with grazing horses in mother-of-pearl and gold foil, much of the inlay missing, 19th century, **$900–$1,200.**

Four-case; Somada school; gold and silver gyobu nashji; inlaid aogai on a roirinuri ground with peacock, mums, and butterflies; the runners with aogai; round ojime and manju netsuke en suite; 19th century, **$5,500–$7,500.**

Four-case, wood, both sides carved with a dragon and clouds, wood bead ojime, wood manju netsuke carved with a dragon, Taisho period, **$500–$800.**

Five-case; one side with a cock perched on a drum; the reverse with a hen and three chicks; Shibayama inlay; gold takamakie, togidashi, and kirigane on akinji ground; some inlay missing; 19th century, **$2,000–$3,000.**

Five-case; gold fundame; gold, red, and black takamakie, hiramakie, and hirame; Shibayama inlaid motif of cranes and peaches; nashiji interiors; signed *Jokasai*; metal ojime; ivory netsuke of a karako; old wear and damages; inlay missing; **$1,050–$1,700.**

Five-case; hiramakie, nashiji, and togidashi with a continuous motif of a village beside a river bank; quite worn; coral bead ojime; 19th century, **$2,000–$2,850.**

Five-case; kinji; decorated in gold, silver, red, and black hiramakie, takamakie, togidashi, and heidatsu with a cockerel standing on a drum; the reverse with a floral spray; chipped; a hairline; orange glass ojime; early 19th century, **$1,500–$2,200.**

Six-case, black with red-lacquer motif of a Koshin mask, another mask on the reverse, 19th century, **$600–$900.**

Six-case, ivory carved in high relief with a continuous Chinese landscape, coral bead ojime, late 19th century, **$2,500–$3,800.**

Netsuke

Ivory, two sumo wrestlers engaged in combat, oval base, signed *Shomin*, 19th century, **$500–$700.**

Ivory, three salmon struggling upstream, late Meiji period, **$175–$300.**

Ivory, a bird emerging from a clam shell, inlaid eyes, 19th century, **$300–$500.**

Ivory, Tokyo school, a Chinese boy dressed in Chinese attire and carrying a basket of fruit, 19th century, **$700–$1,000.**

Ivory, Chokaro Sennin carrying a gourd on his shoulder, age cracks, 18th century, **$325–$500.**

Ivory, a coiled snake, inset horn eyes, signed *Toshitsugu*, Meiji period, **$600–$800.**

Ivory, a Dutchman, his coat engraved and stained with foliate designs, inlaid details, signed *Hidegyoku*, Meiji period, **$425–$600.**

Ivory, Fukurokuju clasping his staff, late Meiji/early Taisho period, **$400–$600.**

Ivory, Gentoku galloping his horse into the Dankai river, lightly stained, signed Mitsuo, 19th century, **$900–$1,250.**

Ivory, a goose preening, boldly carved feathers, age crack, late 18th/early 19th century, **$1,000–$1,500.**

Left: Hirado netsuke of two carp molded in relief (yin and yang), late Edo period, **$900–$1,200**. Right: Hirado netsuke of a sparrow, molded in low relief, late Edo period, **$400–$650**.

Ivory, a grazing horse, head lowered to the left, engraved mane and tail, age cracks, early 19th century, **$1,200–$1,500**.

Ivory, Handaka Sonja seated on a rock with a tiger beside him, signed *Shigechika*, age cracks, 19th century, **$300–$500**.

Ivory, Hotei holding an uchiwa, a karako on his back, signed *Okakoto*, **$300–$400**.

Ivory, a man seated on a cushion, his arms and legs crossed; engraved and stained details; early 20th century, **$600–$800**.

Ivory; a mask of Hannya, the female demon; the tips of her horns cut off, signifying repentance; 19th century, **$200–$300**.

Ivory, a mask of Okina, late Meiji period, **$200–$300**.

Ivory, an Oni in the disguise of Fukusuke, 18th century, **$400–$600**.

Ivory, a peony blossom with finely rendered petals and stamen, the curled stalk forming the himotoshi, signed *Ryuso*, **$600–$900**.

Ivory, a puppy lying on a roof tile, inlaid horn eyes, late Edo period, age cracks, **$425–$575**.

Ivory, a rat seated beside two leaves upon a closed seashell, its tail trailing over the edge, inlaid horn eyes, signed *Rantei*, 19th century, **$800–$1,250**.

Ivory, a recumbent cat, its eyes with inlaid ebony pupils, late Meiji period, **$900–$1,200**.

Ivory, Tomotada style, a recumbent ox, the fur engraved and stained brown, its eyes with inlaid pupils, one missing, 19th century, **$600–$800**.

Ivory, a skull with anatomical detail, Meiji period, **$600–$800**.

Ivory, Masanao style, a sparrow with inlaid eyes, age cracks, 19th century, **$200–$400**.

Ivory, a tortoise with six smaller ones clambering over its carapace, engraved details stained brown, late Edo period, **$500–$650.**

Ivory, Rensai style, a seal netsuke, three frogs on a lotus leaf, age cracks, 19th century, **$475–$600.**

Ivory, a seated Daruma, incised details, 19th century, **$900–$1,200.**

Ivory; a seated, smiling Hotei; boldly carved with incised and stained details; late Edo period, **$450–$650.**

Ivory, a seated Karako, details engraved and stained black, late 19th century, **$300–$400.**

Ivory, Okatomo style, a seated monkey holding its offspring and clutching a stalk of kaki fruit, the legs forming the himotoshi, inlaid eyes, stained details, 19th century, **$750–$1,000.**

Ivory, Kyoto school, a seated tiger with inlaid ebony eyes, engraved and stained details, early 19th century, **$600–$800.**

Ivory, Kyoto school, a snarling tiger seated upon a section of bamboo, incised and stained details, 18th century, **$2,000–$3,000.**

Ivory, a standing Dutchman wearing a wide-brimmed hat, his attire with incised details, 18th century, **$4,000–$6,000.**

Ivory, a standing toy dog, knotted collar, tail looped to form himotoshi, late Meiji period, **$600–$800.**

Ivory, Disappointed Rat Catcher kneeling and holding on to a box while the rat creeps over his shoulder, signed *Tomomasa*, 19th century, **$400–$600.**

Ivory, Urashima (the fisherman) feeding the minogame (turtle) that is his future bride in disguise, contemporary, **$375–$500.**

Ivory, a very plump sparrow, inlaid horn eyes, inscribed *Masanao*, late Edo period, **$500–$700.**

Kagamibuta, in relief, the bronze plate with ''Kinko on the carp'' in various alloys, ivory bowl cracked, 19th century, **$200–$300.**

Kagamibuta; shakudo, silver, and sentoku with a performer wearing a fox mask (scene from a No play); ivory bowl with age cracks; 19th century, **$1,000–$1,500.**

Kagamibuta, in relief, a courtier wearing elaborate garb, the lid with various alloys, ivory bowl, 19th century, **$350–$550.**

Kagamibuta, shakudo plate inlaid with a silver Mt. Fuji and gold clouds, ivory bowl, 19th century, **$400–$600.**

Kagamibuta, the shakudo lid inlaid in gold and silver with a tiger and bamboo, ivory bowl, 19th century, **$900–$1,200.**

Lacquer, in the style of the Nara school, a bearded Mongolian holding a vase, the sword strapped on his back forming the himotoshi, Taisho period, **$1,500–$2,000.**

Lacquer, Somado style, box form with a motif of an uchiwa (single-stick fan), 19th century, **$900–$1,200.**

Lacquer; a boy seated beside his dog; nashiji; red, gold, and black takamakie; 19th century, **$1,000–$1,500.**

Lacquer, a Daruma with arms stretched over his head, black and gold lacquer on a red ground, 19th century, **$500–$700.**

Manju, ivory, a man smoking a tobacco pipe, Shibayama inlay, stained ivory, some inlay missing, late Meiji period, **$375–$500.**

Manju, ivory, carved in shishiaibori, a performer dressed in a loose robe, the details inlaid in mother-of-pearl, signed *Komin*, 19th century, **$450–$650.**

Manju, ivory, carved with Hotei holding an uchiwa and leaning on a sack, the reverse with scroll designs, 19th century, **$425–$650.**

Manju (kamakuri-bori), carved with three apes picking peaches, late Edo period, **$475–$650.**

Manju, Raiden running amongst clouds, *Hoshunsai Masayuki* signature/seal, 19th century, **$1,500–$2,200.**

Manju, Shibayama inlay with kiku and foliage, age cracks, Meiji period, **$500–$700.**

Manju carved with a Samurai's implements and armor, late Meiji period, **$425–$600.**

Manju carved with shaped panels of the 12 zodiac animals, gilt-lacquer ground, 19th century, **$550–$775.**

Manju formed with eight masks, signed *Tomochika*, 19th century, **$500–$750.**

Manju, lacquer, fundame ground with lotus and leaf in silver and gold takamakie, hairlines, 19th century, **$600–$850.**

Manju, porcelain, underglaze blue and white with a mountainscape, early 19th century, **$475–$675.**

Manju, staghorn, pierced and carved with the legend of Ono no tofu, the frog carrying an umbrella, the reverse with pine trees, 19th century, **$1,000–$1,500.**

Manju, walrus, carved with egrets and a variety of flowers, 19th century, **$700–$1,000.**

Manju, walrus, low relief carving of Jurojin, 19th century, **$485–$625.**

Porcelain, a celadon-glazed crane, Seto, late 19th century, **$225–$300.**

Porcelain, a celadon-glazed Jurojin, Seto, Meiji period, **$250–$400.**

Porcelain, a karako seated upon an ox, white glaze, Meiji period, **$250–$375.**

Pottery, a badger in a priest's garb, mid-19th century, **$275–$375.**

Pottery, a bakemono kneeling down with two cha wan, his neck pierced with a pin (a nodding netsuke), **$665–$950.**

Pottery, Kenzan style, a basket of *bakemono* (unreal things) from the story "The Tongue-Cut Sparrow," **$700–$900.**

Pottery, a Daruma, his eyes in gilt, late Meiji period, **$200–$400.**

Pottery, Okame with colored Kiku mon on her kimono, Meiji period, **$500–$700.**

Silver, double gourd with engraved foliage, Meiji period, **$500–$700.**

Silver, gourd shape with leaves and tendrils in relief, Meiji period, **$600–$800.**

Stag antler, a brush pot, three bracket feet, one side carved with a tortoise, signed *Hoshunsai* with kakihan, 19th century, **$2,000–$2,800.**

Left: *Silver netsuke in the form of Daikoku's mallet with applied gold embellishments, Meiji period,* **$1,000–$1,500.** Right: *Carved coral netsuke of the Sneezer, signed* Masakazu, *late 19th century,* **$2,000–$2,800.**

Stag antler, Tokyo school, a Buddhist temple gong (Mokugyo) hollowed out, the handles formed by two confronting dragons, 19th century, **$1,200–$1,600.**

Stag antler, a group of mushrooms on a worn edge basket, 19th century, **$750–$1,050.**

Stag antler, a man carrying a basket of flowers, 19th century, **$150–$225.**

Stag antler, a recumbent boar, eyes with inlaid pupils, 19th century, **$100–$200.**

Stag antler, a sashi netsuke carved as mask of Oni, 19th century, **$800–$1,200.**

Stag antler, a Shishi leaning on a tama, inlaid ebony eyes, early 19th century, **$250–$375.**

Wood, a chestnut naturalistically detailed, (So school), **$1,000–$1,500.**

Wood, a coiled dragon with inlaid ebony and ivory eyes, late Edo period, **$275–$375.**

Wood, Gama Sennin, a toad perched on his back; he holds a staff and wears a mugwort cloak; one crack; late Edo period, **$300–$400.**

Wood, a Kappa astride a cucumber, 19th century, **$600–$800.**

Wood, a karako (child) holding a puppy, 19th century, **$200–$300.**

Wood, a kirin with neck stretched upward, jaws open wide, fincly detailed, 19th century, **$900–$1,300.**

Wood, Tokyo school, a large and small chestnut with an inlaid ivory maggot, signed *Gyokuso*, **$500–$700.**

Wood, a mask of Otobide, inlaid horn eyes, 19th century, **$400–$600.**

Wood, Daikoku's mallet, ivory inlay, Meiji period, **$800–$1,200.**

Wood, a rat clutching a chestnut, nicely patinated, inlaid horn eyes, late Edo period, **$300–$500.**

Wood, a rat clutching a bean, his body curled, the curling tail forming the himotoshi, inlaid horn eyes, one ear damaged, 19th century, **$700–$900.**

143

Wood, a seated monkey (Hear No Evil), his legs crossed to form the himotoshi, signed *Masanao*, late 19th century, **$1,000–$1,500.**

Wood, a seated monkey with inlaid horn eyes, ittobori (single-cut) carving, 19th century, **$200–$300.**

Wood, a Shishimai dancer dressed in full costume, late Meiji period, **$175–$225.**

Wood, Nagoya school, a Shojo sleeping off the effect of sake, finely incised details, signed *Ikkan*, 19th century, **$3,000–$4,000.**

Wood, a tea picker, ittobori carving; the female figure holds a bowl of recently picked tea; 19th century, **$200–$300.**

Wood, a Yamabushi emerging from a large conch shell blowing a horagi, 18th century, **$750–$1,100.**

Wood, an awabi shell, 19th century, **$150–$250.**

Wood, an inebriated man dancing on one foot, late Edo period, **$375–$575.**

Wood, a mask of Oni, signed *Ikko*, 19th century, **$200–$300.**

Wood, Disappointed Rat Catcher, signed *Hisakazu*, 19th century, **$500–$650.**

Wood; the Sneezer; he makes himself sneeze by tickling his nose; late Edo period, **$500–$700.**

Wood, Tokyo school, the Sneezer holding an ivory fan, **$800–$1,100.**

Wood, two frogs on a lotus leaf, c1900, **$150–$250.**

Wood, So school, two Kyogen players, one dancing with a fan, one tapping a drum, inlaid with ivory and ebony, signed *Soya*, **$2,000–$3,000.**

Wood, two sages playing Go, carved details, **$350–$500.**

Ojime

Boxwood in the form of a persimmon, 19th century, **$100–$200.**

Brass and copper with a carp in low relief, 19th century, **$400–$600.**

Cloisonné, round, black ground with flowers in colors, silver wire, c1900, **$375–$525.**

Gold (in the form of a tied purse), c1900, **$750–$1,050.**

Gold, oviform with a floral and butterfly motif, dented, late 19th century, **$900–$1,200.**

Iron (in the form of a finger citron), 19th century, **$300–$475.**

Ivory carved with two Oni faces, Meiji period, **$150–$225.**

Ivory with cranes carved in low relief, late 19th century, **$500–$700.**

Ivory carved overall with five puppies, one spotted, 19th century, **$700–$900.**

Ivory carved in relief with Rakan, 19th century, **$200–$400.**

Ivory carved in the form of an octopus, 20th century, **$300–$400.**

Ivory carved in the form of a peach, early 20th, **$200–$300.**

Ivory carved in the form of a human skull, late 19th, **$150–$250.**

Ivory carved with the Three Wise Monkeys, early Showa period, **$475–$600.**

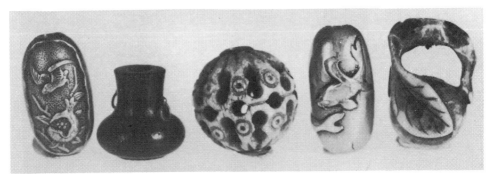

Left to right: *Silver ojime with pomegranate, foliage, and birds in low relief, Meiji period,* **$600–$900.** *Wood ojime in the form of a vase with brass loose ring handles, Meiji period,* **$300–$475.** *Bone ojime with pierced and carved motifs, early 20th century,* **$900–$1,200.** *Silver ojime, carp in relief, 19th century,* **$1,000–$1,500.** *Stag antler ojime carved in the form of a peach and foliage, stained brown, late Meiji period,* **$200–$375.**

Ivory, round, inlaid Shibayama motif of butterfly and flowers, Meiji period, **$750–$1,000.**

Porcelain, underglaze blue and white leaves, the ojime a gourd shape, 19th century, **$300–$500.**

Porcelain, Hirado, underglaze blue and white flower-and-leaf motif, the ojime oval in form, late Edo period, **$900–$1,200.**

Porcelain, iron red and gold with two reserves, signed *Eiraku*, late Edo/early Meiji period, **$900–$1,250.**

Shakudo in the form of Daikoku's mallet with silver and sentoku embellishment, 19th century, **$550–$700.**

Shakudo in the form of a die with gold and silver inlaid stripes, 19th century, **$500–$700.**

Shakudo with a shibuichi dragon, 19th century, **$700–$900.**

Silver with a motif of bird and mums, the center of each mum inlaid in gold, 19th century, **$700–$1,000.**

Silver chased overall with a design of chrysanthemums, late 19th century, **$500–$700.**

Silver, oviform, with a design of dragon and clouds, late Meiji period, **$700–$900.**

Silver, carved and pierced with kiku, late 19th century, **$600–$775.**

Silver in the form of a peach, late Meiji period, **$500–$700.**

Silver in the form of a seashell, late Meiji period, **$400–$600.**

Silver, ovoid, open-work with applied gold kiku, 19th century, **$800–$1,200.**

Silver, round, pierced and carved with peony and foliage, late 19th century, **$450–$550.**

Stag antler carved as a boat, 19th century, **$200–$300.**

Stag antler carved in the form of a mushroom, 19th century, **$225–$325.**

Stag antler carved in the form of a peach, late 19th century, **$200–$300.**

Pipes

Tobacco, long-stem, decorated in gold hiramakie with flowers, silver fittings, Japanese, 19th century, 19½" long, **$500–$700.**

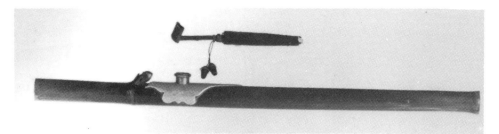

Top: *Japanese pipe in the form of an umbrella, early 20th century,* **$200–$300.** Bottom: *Chinese opium pipe, bamboo with silver hardware,* **$600–$800.**

Tobacco, long-stem, silver with butterflies and kiku, tortoiseshell decorated in hiramakie en suite, Japanese, c1900, **$500–$700.**

Tobacco, short-stem, Banko, two-tone brown with relief calligraphy, Japanese, c1900, **$375–$550.**

Tobacco, short-stem, wood with carvings of birds and flowers, silver fittings, Japanese, c1910, **$150–$225.**

Pipe Cases

Bamboo carved in low relief with four No masks, brass pipe, carnelian glass ojime, late 19th century, **$175–$250.**

Bone carved in high relief with Tobosaku holding a peach, 19th century, **$400–$600.**

Ivory, one side carved with a man leaning on the pole he is holding, the reverse with pine branches, age crack, 19th century, **$300–$500.**

Stag antler carved in relief with scholars playing Go, the upper section with two cranes, signed *Gyokko*, 19th century, **$300–$400.**

Stag antler carved with Ashinga and Tenaga, signed *Shoryu*, 19th century, **$350–$550.**

Stag antler carved with three seals, age cracks, 19th century, **$250–$350.**

Wood decorated in kebori and shishiaibori with a girl and a cat, c1900, **$250–$350.**

Wood lacquered to simulate bamboo, 19th century, **$150–$200.**

Tobacco Pouches

Leather with silver kanamono, ivory bead ojime, and stag antler objihasami; netsuke carved and pierced with gourds; 19th century, **$800–$1,200.**

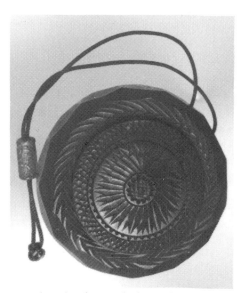

Carved wood tonkotsu with silver and copper ojime, late Edo period, **$250–$350.**

Tonkotsu (box form), wood formed from a section of branch and decorated with stained ivory water lilies, early 19th century, **$375–$575.**

Tonkotsu; wood inlaid with ivory, horn, and shell in a motif of seashells and fish; signed *Tokoku* (school of); late 19th century, **$700–$950.**

Tonkotsu, wood with brown and black hiramakie in a motif of flowering branch and a wasp; chestnut-form ivory ojime; wood netsuke in the form of a lotus pod; 19th century, **$450–$650.**

8

Ivory, Horn, Shell, and Tortoiseshell

Is It Genuine Ivory?

Bernard Rosett

The title of this article is perhaps the question most frequently asked in antiques and art galleries. Since prehistoric days, ivory has been known and loved as an artistic medium. Artificial and substitute materials have been known almost as long.

Ivory comes from the tusks, the upper incisors, of the pachyderm (elephant). Like all teeth, these are mainly composed of calcium phosphate. The structure of a tusk consists of large numbers of minute tubules, each about 1/15,000 inch in diameter, and filled with an oily substance which serves to give nourishment to the tusk.

The fine structure of the tusk explains the great elasticity of the material. The severe depletion of the vast herds of Asian and African elephants (Asian elephant is an endangered species and African elephant is a threatened species) is a direct result of the suitability of ivory for fundamental, ornamental, and occasional objects.

A cross-section of tusk invariably exhibits a reticulated crisscross pattern that is unique to ivory. Also visible is the wood-grain pattern of a longitudinal portion of an ivory sample. The oily tubules mentioned are responsible for the typical gleam and patina of ivory. Another characteristic of ivory is its density: 1.70 to 1.95 times that of water, which often serves to quickly distinguish it from plastics and other light materials. The microstructure of ivory helps to explain its good heat conductivity, whereby it usually feels cold to the touch. Experienced shoppers are often seen touching a suspect piece of ivory to the cheek.

The Bible contains frequent mention of ivory, as in passages describing the glories of King Solomon's temple. The museum at Oxford University in Great Britain boasts ivory works of art from Egypt that predate 3000 B.C. Although the centuries have made them somewhat dry and brittle, they still retain some of the gleam and polish of their youth. Even more ancient is a sample of fossil ivory in the author's possession, preserved by the arctic climate of Alaska, which came from a mammoth some 25,000 years ago. It is stained brown by the minerals in the earth where it has lain so long, but it still bears the characteristic crisscross network of young ivory and is hard and flexible enough to be carved.

There are other natural materials that have some resemblance to elephant ivory, but none have the crosshatched appearance already described.

Hippopotamus teeth (canines and incisors) are the hardest of all the ivory-like materials. The grain lines are wavy and all run in one direction. The surface has a gleaming whiteness. Netsuke are sometimes carved of this material.

Walrus tusks, the upper canines, are also encountered in netsuke and other sculptured work, but are also often seen in Middle Eastern and Scandinavian dagger handles. Walrus "ivory" is often identified by sections of characteristic mottling. Moderately deep carving brings out this handsome effect. The mottled interior has been found to be harder than the outer layer.

Whale teeth are most often encountered in scrimshaw. Whale teeth have a striated grain pattern.

Narwhal tusk comes from the elongated left tusk of a species of arctic whale (now endangered). This often grows to a length of 6–8 feet. It is thought that the mythological unicorn originated in stories of the rarely met narwhal. These tusks are seldom cut into sections, usually being preserved intact as walking sticks. Occasionally, small sections are made into netsuke, which have historically been made of almost any material that might be named. The center of most of the narwhal tusk is hollow, and the transverse and longitudinal sections resemble the pattern of a tree trunk.

Boar's tusks, the upper canines of the wild boar (or of the wart hog), make a particularly fine, white "ivory" beloved by one school of netsuke carvers. The cross-sections of these tusks are approximately triangular. Since these tusks are relatively small (under six inches in length), many carvings contain complete tusks.

Vegetable ivory, which comes from the nut of a tropical South American palm (phytelephas), was often used in the fabrication of buttons. The grain pattern, mostly circular, is dull and indistinct. This material is softer than bone or ivory.

Bone—shinbones or tibia from any reasonably sized animal—is the most commonly used imitation ivory substance. All mammal bones are hollow, the center filled with spongy material. A bone carving will usually show, in transverse section, a pattern of black dots resembling a stubbly beard. A longitudinal section shows the bone channels (foramina) as a series of brown or black streaks. The surface of bone is generally duller than that of polished ivory. A good magnifying glass ($3\times$ to $6\times$) makes it easy to identify many of these materials. Bone is usually less dense than ivory.

Stag antlers, the antlers of reindeer, elk, and the like (sometimes erroneously called staghorn), have long been of common use for knife or dagger handles, as well as for small carvings. Antlers have a spongy center, but the outer zones are denser than bone. The color of an antler varies from yellow to rich brown. The longitudinal section shows many irregular openings, unlike the regular, dark streaks seen in bone.

Plastic ivory substitutes. Many types of plastic have been employed since the invention of celluloid at the turn of the century, in the vain attempt to simulate the properties of ivory. There is even a material called *ivorine* which has alternating streaks of dark- and light-colored plastic to simulate the grain of ivory. This, however, does not approach the density of real ivory, and the grain pattern in no way resembles the crosshatched pattern of ivory.

Even the straight-line pattern is far too regular to deceive a careful observer. It is also much softer than bone or ivory.

The following properties offer more specific guidelines for distinguishing among the materials already discussed here.

- **Hardness or scratchability.** With the point of a sharp penknife scribe a short line on an unobtrusive part of the piece in question. A well-defined incision will be seen in the case of plastic. Bone, ivory, or other animal materials will barely show a scratch.
- **Heat and conductivity.** Plastics are poor conductors of heat. The minute canals of bone or ivory, however, conduct heat quite well. Therefore they feel cool to the touch. A needle or safety pin, heated red hot and quickly applied to an inconspicuous place on the piece in question, is a good method of testing. Animal materials will not be affected, but a small puff of smoke or a brand-like scar are proof of plastic.
- **Solubility test.** A drop of acetone (lacquer thinner) placed on an inconspicuous area of the suspect piece will leave a definite mark if the piece is plastic because it starts to dissolve or soften under the drop of acetone. Animal materials are not affected. For vegetable ivory, a specific test involves the application of a drop of sulfuric acid, which leaves a brown stain on this substance.
- **Grain.** Careful observation through a magnifying glass reveals a great deal of detail, and study of the many grain patterns will aid in identifying the material. It is also important to have good illumination to bring out the fine grain.

- **Color and luster.** True ivory can vary from white to cream to yellow to brown, according to its preparation and history. The color and luster of plastics can be controlled.
- **Density or specific gravity.** As mentioned earlier, bone and ivory are measurably denser than presently used plastics. However, the clever faker can put heavier fillers or ivory dust in his mix to make this a dangerous criterion for the buyer to trust. The author was recently intrigued by a figure of excellent color and high density. The secret was revealed when shaking produced a rattling noise. The plastic piece was filled with buckshot! As in all antique hunting, caution is the key.
- **Smell.** The sense of smell is sometimes helpful in identifying materials. Probably everyone is familiar with the characteristic odor of celluloid that has been subjected to friction. Likewise, some of the acrylics and epoxies have a distinctive sweet odor when rubbed on a wool sleeve. Real bone and ivory are usually odorless unless burned at high temperatures.

Values

Horn (Rhinoceros)

Libation cup carved with a variety of flowers, including peony, chrysanthemum, and sunflower, among rock-work; the handle formed by complex branches of peony by a rock; the plant extending over the rim into the interior beside a large cricket among rocks; the horn a honey tone; Chinese, 18th century, 6" wide, **$7,000–$9,000.**

Libation cup carved with monkeys, deer, birds, and ducks amongst the Three Friends motif (pine, plum, and bamboo), with pine trunks forming the handle and petals forming the interior, Chinese, 18th century, 6½" wide, **$3,000–$4,000.**

Libation cup carved with a sampan moored by a lakeside and two figures on a promontory near retreats in a mountainous landscape, deeply carved pine trees forming the handle and extending over the rim, the horn a deep color, Chinese, 18th century, 6½" wide, **$6,000–$7,000.**

Libation cup carved with a continuous garden scene; main buildings, pavilions, and trees within a household compound; the trunk of a sturdy pine tree forming the handle and extending over the rim into the interior; the horn a dark tone; Chinese, 18th century, 7" wide, **$3,500–$4,500.**

Libation cup carved with overhanging, projecting cliffs rising from breaking waves; a twisting pine forming the handle and extending over the rim; the inside rim carved with formalized clouds; the horn a dark color; Chinese, 17th century, 1¾" wide, **$5,000–$6,000.**

Libation cup carved with a river landscape, a boat with four figures approaching two scholars on a bank, rock-work forming the handle and extending over the rim, the horn a reddish brown color, Chinese, 18th century, 5¾" wide, **$3,000–$4,000.**

Carved ivory box, circular form, with figures and pavilion, all in high relief, Chinese, late 19th century, 2¾" diameter, **$200–$300.**

Japanese ivory card case decorated in a lacquer and Shibayama motif featuring waterfalls and a perched peacock, late 19th century, 4¾" high, **$1,500–$2,000.**

Libation cup carved with pine and other foliage among rocks and a waterfall, the trunk of the pine forming the handle and extending over the rim into the interior, carved rock-work details, the horn a honey tone, minor repair, Chinese, 17th century, 6" wide, **$3,000–$4,000.**

Libation cup carved with mythical animals, including dragons, a tortoise, and a Buddhistic lion, among breaking waves; craggy banks around the rim area; a rocky grotto with a pine tree above forming the handle and extending over the rim; repair to foot and rim chips; Chinese, 17th century, 6" wide, **$5,000–$6,500.**

Ivory

Box and cover carved as an elephant supporting Jurojin and a small boy, Shibayama details, signed *Gyokuzan*, Japanese, c1900, 4¾" high, **$700–$900.**

Box and cover carved and pierced in high relief and low relief with birds, their eyes inlaid in horn, details stained black, age cracks, Japanese, c1900, 5" wide, **$1,000–$1,500.**

Box and cover carved with the Seven Gods of Good Luck, stained details, Japanese, c1920, 3¼" high, **$600–$800.**

Box and cover, double gourd form with relief carvings of flowers, leaves, and gourds over trellis-work, Chinese, 19th century, 4" wide, **$250–$400.**

Box and cover with Shibayama motifs of three cranes standing beneath a prunus, some inlay missing, Japanese, c1900, 3¾" long, **$900–$1,200.**

Brush holder carved and pierced with children, trees, and buildings; Chinese, Kuang Hsü (Guangxu) period, 5¼" high, **$550–$750.**

Brush pot carved overall with numerous figures and pavilions, Chinese, c1885, 4" high, **$800–$1,200.**

Brush pot; cylindrical with incised motifs of birds, insects, bats, and bamboo; Chinese, early 20th century, 4¼" high, **$300–$475.**

Card case densely carved with figures and pavilions, Chinese, first half of the 19th century, 4⅛" long, **$450–$600.**

Letter rack, the arched top carved and pierced with two confronting dragons and flaming pearl, Chinese, c1885, 6" high, **$400–$600.**

Group, two men playing Go, signed *Toshikazu*, Japanese, late Meiji period, 4" diameter, **$1,500–$2,500.**

Group, three dragons, all intertwined, inlaid horn eyes, Japanese, late 19th century, 9½" high, **$850–$1,250.**

Group, four seated Buddhas, dhyana mudra, each on waisted lotus thrones, Burmese, 19th century, 4" high, **$650–$900.**

Group, a father holding his son, the father wearing a kimono jacket and trousers, the boy held at his shoulder, a basket at his feet, cracked, signed *Gyokushin*, Japanese, c1910, 8¼" high, **$1,000–$1,500.**

Model of a bamboo shoot, the interior hollowed and carved and pierced with the old man from the "Tongue-Cut Sparrow" story, signed *Minghoku*, Japanese, Meiji period, 7½" high, **$450–$750.**

Model of a basket seller wearing a kimono jacket and holding a bamboo pole with wares hanging from it, details lightly painted in colors, signed *Masahide*, Japanese, c1900, 6" high, **$700–$1,000.**

Model of Benten wearing elaborate headdress and flowing robe and holding a biwa, signed *Shugetsu*, Japanese, late Meiji period, 12" high, **$1,500–$2,000.**

Model of a Bijin (Japanese beauty), her kimono and obi with chased kiku; she holds a flowering branch; signed *Nobuyuki*; Meiji period, 11¼" high, **$1,200–$1,800.**

Model of a Bijin standing and wearing a patterned kimono and obi, her hands repaired, signed *Shingyoku*, Japanese, Meiji period, 10¾" high, **$600–$900.**

Model of a bird catcher holding a bird in one hand, a basket tied about his waist, the pole missing, age cracks, Japanese, c1920, 12½" high, **$700–$900.**

Model of a Chinese sage holding a writing brush and leaf fan, damaged, Japanese, Taisho period, 8½" high, **$700–$900.**

Model of Daikoku holding a mallet and standing on rice bags, signed *Tamiyuki*, Meiji period, 6⅜" high, **$350–$600.**

Figure of the Disappointed Rat Catcher holding a truncheon, looking over his shoulder as the rat escapes, Japanese, Meiji period, 2½" high, **$900–$1,200.**

Model of a drum seller carrying his wares on a bamboo pole held over his shoulders, Japanese, Taisho period, 5¾" high, **$1,000–$1,500.**

Model of Ebisu carrying a fishing pole (with fish dangling at the end) over his back, signed *Tomokazu*, Japanese, late 19th century, 5" high, **$675–$900.**

Model of an elder smoking a pipe and holding a lantern, his tonkotsu hanging from his waist, signed *Koko*, Japanese, Taisho period, 8" high, **$825–$1,075.**

Model of a farmer carrying a small boy on his back and holding a basket of grain, engraved details stained brown, chipped and cracked, Japanese, c1900, 7½" high, **$300–$500.**

Model of a fisherman seated before a tree repairing his nets, signed *Kyoshu*, Japanese, Meiji period, 10¾" high, **$750–$1,125.**

Model of Fukorokuju holding a staff and uchiwa (single-stick fan), walrus ivory, signed *Tomochika*, cracked, Japanese, late 19th century, 4¾" high, **$325–$500.**

Model of a geisha holding a lantern, her kimono engraved with cranes and stained brown, Japanese, Taisho period, 10" high, **$1,800–$2,200.**

Model of Hotei seated against treasure sack and holding an uchiwa, signed *Gyokumin*, Japanese, Meiji period, 8¼" high, **$400–$575.**

Model of an Immortal holding a fly whisk, the ivory a mellow honey shade, Chinese, Ming dynasty, 8" high, **$2,000–$3,000.**

Model of Kuan Yin standing on a lotus-and-wave base and holding a vase, age cracks, Chinese, late 19th century, 13½" high, **$900–$1,200.**

Model of Liu-hai (an Immortal) with a toad on his shoulder, flowing robe, scroll under left arm, cracked, replaced foot, Chinese, 17th century, 7¼" high, **$1,200–$1,500.**

Model of a phoenix on rock-work, the details picked out in colors and black, cracked, Chinese, c1920, 8½" high, **$500–$700.**

Model of a smiling Immortal wearing flowing robes with wide sleeves, right arm and left leg raised, cracked, extremities damaged, Chinese, 17th century, 7" high, **$700–$1,000.**

Model of an Immortal carrying a ruyi sceptre, age cracks, the patina a soft yellow, Chinese, Ming dynasty, 7" high, **$1,200–$1,600.**

Model of an Immortal with a long beard, chipped foot, Chinese, 18th century, 5½" high, **$750–$1,000.**

Model of a monkey trainer (Sarumawashi) seated on a bench holding a small bowl of rice, a monkey at his side, the details stained brown, signed *Muneharu*, Japanese, late 19th century, 5" high, **$400–$600.**

Model of Ransaikawa and two children, open at each side, signed *Homin*, Japanese, c1900, 4¼" high, **$700–$1,000.**

Model of a rat seated on Daikoku's sack, Japanese, late Meiji period, 5" long, **$525–$675.**

Model of a Samurai holding a fan and leaning on his katana, a wakezashi tucked beneath his obi, engraved and stained details, Japanese, late Meiji/early Taisho period, 7¼" high, **$1,000–$1,500.**

Model of Shou Lao holding a gnarled staff from which a gourd is suspended, age cracks, Chinese, 17th century, 7" high, **$1,400–$1,800.**

Model of a skeleton pulling at a woman's kimono, marine ivory, Japanese, Meiji period, 6" high, **$700–$1,200.**

Model of a standing lady holding the folds of her kimono, a basket of flowers at her feet, the kimono lightly stained and engraved in a floral and geometric pattern, digits broken, signed *Nobuaki*, Japanese, late 19th century, 8" high, **$400–$600.**

Model of a standing lady, Shibayama details on her kimono in a motif of flowers, Japanese, c1885, 9" high, **$2,000–$3,000.**

Model of a standing lady wearing long flowing robes and holding a teapot, finely detailed and painted in colors, Chinese, early 20th century, 10½" high, **$900–$1,200.**

Model of a standing lady wearing a kimono engraved with wisteria, her hair detailed and stained black; she holds a peony blossom; signed *Isshin*; Japanese, late 19th century, 8¼" high, **$775–$985.**

Model of a street vendor holding a pole over his shoulder, drums and baskets suspended from the pole, engraved details stained brown, small pieces missing from the baskets, signed *Eishin*, Japanese, late 19th century, 7½" high, **$500–$700.**

Model of a sumo wrestler with his arms by his side; he wears an elaborate kesho-mawashi; signed *Ryusui*; Japanese, Taisho period, 8½" h, **$975–$1,400.**

Model of a woman holding a floral spray, finely painted in colors, Chinese, early 20th century, 10¾" high, **$900–$1,200.**

Model of a young girl holding her hagoita (battledore), her kimono carved with peony blossoms, Japanese, late Meiji period, 6½" high, **$1,000–$1,500.**

Model of a warrior, marine ivory, the details engraved and stained, Japanese, c1910, 6" high, **$300–$500.**

Models: an Emperor and Empress, each on horseback, Chinese, 20th century, 13" high, **$1,500–$2,200.**

Models of phoenix on rock-work bases, Chinese, early 20th century, 5½" high, **pair, $750–$1,000.**

Models of Shou Lao, mirror images, one leaning left, the other to the right, each with a fan and gnarled staff and long flowing robes, age cracks on each, Chinese, 19th century, 12" high, **pair, $1,000–$1,500.**

Needle case carved with dragons and clouds, Chinese, early 19th century, 6½" long, **$125–$200.**

Plaques carved as a cross-section of a gourd, with 18 Lohan carved in relief (9 on each plaque), details in polychrome, Chinese, 19th century, 7" wide, **pair, $900–$1,200.**

Plaques carved and pierced with crabs, frogs, fish, and seashells; Chinese, c1900, 8½" long, **pair, $1,200–$1,800.**

Plaques deeply carved with figures, mountains, and pavilions; polychrome highlights; Chinese, late 19th century, 12" wide, **pair, $800–$1,200.**

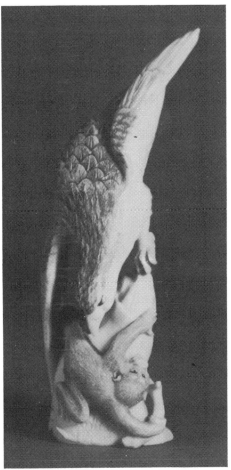

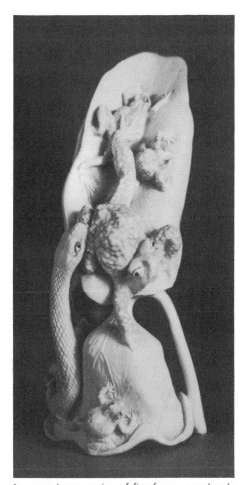

Japanese ivory carving (okimono) of a hawk attacking a monkey, stained details, late 19th century, 5" high, $800–$1,200.

Japanese ivory carving of five frogs—varying in size—and a serpent, all upon an aquatic plant, late 19th century, $800–$1,200.

Plaque painted with Kuan Yin holding a flower; details executed in famille rose; plaque set into a panel for display; Chinese, 18th century, size of wood panel 10" × 6", **$600–$800.**

Puzzle ball and stand, 20 concentric balls carved with various designs, floral exterior, floral base, Chinese, early 20th century, exterior ball 5" diameter, **$1,000–$1,500.**

Seal surmounted by a Buddhistic lion, Chinese, c1900, 3½" high, **$200–$300.**

Table screen carved in relief with a kingfisher perched on a flowering branch, the reverse with figures in a mountainscape, Chinese, 20th century, 7" high, **$350–$500.**

Table screen with Shibayama and lacquered panels featuring birds on flowering branches, some inlay missing, Japanese, c1900, 12½" high, **$1,500–$2,500.**

Takarabune (treasure ship) with the Seven Gods of Good Luck on deck, the wood stand carved as breaking waves, some attributes missing, cracks, Japanese, early 20th century, 19" × 18½", **$2,500–$3,500.**

Takarabune with the Seven Gods of Good Luck on deck, stained and engraved details, Japanese, c1925, 15" long, **$1,500–$2,000.**

Tea caddy; rectangular; densely carved with scenes of scholars, boats, pavilions, and trees; the edges carved as bamboo; sliding top; cracked; Chinese, mid-19th century, 3¾" wide, **$1,000–$1,500.**

Tusk carved in high relief with two dragons and clouds, the eyes inlaid with horn, Maruki seal, Japanese, Meiji period, 32¼" long, **$3,600–$4,200.**

Tusk heavily carved with figures and pavilions, Chinese, 19th century, 35" long, **$2,500–$3,500.**

Tusk vases inlaid in Shibayama with birds, insects, trees, and flowers; silver rims; fitted wood bases; some losses to inlay; Japanese, late 19th century, 11" high, **pair, $2,000–$3,000.**

Tusk vases; Shibayama with lacquer, takamakie, tortoiseshell, and mother-of-pearl; designs of branches, birds, and flowers; cracked, losses to inlay; Japanese, c1900, 14" high, **pair, $5,000–$7,000.**

Vases, tusk on wood stand, carved in low relief with insects and foliage, Japanese, early Meiji period, 15½" high, **pair, $2,200–$3,200.**

Vase carved with four vertical ribs, age cracks, Chinese, 18th century, 4" high, **$400–$600.**

Vases, ovoid, carved with 18 Lohan, each delicately painted in colors, loose ring handles, Chinese, early 19th century, 3¾" high, **pair, $900–$1,200.**

Vase and cover carved and pierced with four panels of landscapes, Buddhistic lion and loose ring handles, Buddhistic lion finial, Chinese, early 20th century, 12½" high, **$1,200–$1,500.**

Vases, trumpet-shaped necks, applied foliage handles, the bodies carved with panels of Lohan, both damaged, Chinese, c1900, 7¾" high, **pair, $450–$600.**

Wrist rests carved in low relief as sections of bamboo, the underside with high-relief landscapes, Chinese, 19th century, 10" long, **$500–$750.**

Shell

Shell, abalone, mounted on three silver ball feet, the shell inlaid with three silver characters reading *health, happiness,* and *long life,* Chinese, c1910, 7" × 8", **$500–$700.**

Shell, abalone, carved with a monkey catching a butterfly, inlaid horn eyes and stained details, Japanese, late 19th century, **$800–$1,000.**

Shells carved in low relief with officials, children, and pavilions; the eyes inlaid; Chinese, late 19th century, **pair, $1,000–$1,500.**

Staghorn

Candlesticks, tree-trunk form with fruiting peach branches, Japanese, late Meiji period, 9" high, **pair, $900–$1,200.**

Model of two monkeys seated beneath a lantern, Japanese, late Meiji period, 5" high, **$300–$450.**

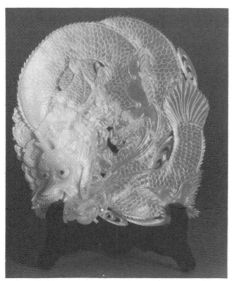

Abalone shell carved in the form of a dragon, inlaid eyes, Japanese, Meiji period, 7" high, **$800–$1,200.**

Parasol handle carved as a kappa holding a sake bottle, inlaid eyes, Japanese, late 19th century, **$300–$400.**

Tortoiseshell

Box and cover; circular; densely carved with figures, pagodas, and trees; sides and base similarly carved; Chinese, early 19th century, 5" diameter, **$1,200–$1,800.**

Shell entirely carved in the style of the Western Chou (Zhou) dynasty, but late 19th/early 20th century, Chinese, **$450–$700.**

9

Japanese Ceramics

Banko Wares

For many years, the name *Banko* has been abused and misunderstood, which in turn has led to great confusion. Collectors and dealers alike have incorrectly used the term *Banko* in conjunction with references to Korean wares, Poo ware, and combinations thereof, in an effort to describe the Sumida Gawa wares attributed to Inoue Ryosai. Because of the misuse of terminology, Banko wares were almost entirely neglected by the collecting community. Today, however, Banko wares are highly collectible.

Rozan (Numanami Gozaemon), also known as Numanami Shigenaga, was the first Banko. Born in Ise Province (now called Mie Prefecture), c1718, he was a wealthy merchant and amateur potter. He used two seals on his wares, *Banko* (meaning 10,000 or *enduring*) and *Fueki* (*eternal* or *unchanging*).

Numanami Gozaemon produced wares in the styles of Ninsei and Kenzan. He also produced wares styled after Korean prototypes, Kochi wares, along with his original formulas. Around 1787, word of this potter's accomplishments reached the capital. Shogun Inyenari was so impressed with these reports that he summoned Numanami Gozaemon to the capital and made him an "official" potter.

During his stay at the capital, Banko was able to study new methods and soon became skilled at using the techniques developed by the Chinese. Among his reproductions or copies were those styled after Ming Dynasty red and green (Wan Li style), famille verte, famille rose, and Delft wares.

The original Banko died at the end of the eighteenth century, and if not for a mere accident, collectors might not even be aware of his work today. Mori Yesetsu (Banko II), born in 1808, was originally a wood carver and bric-a-brac dealer with some degree of skill in the art of the potter. In 1830, he accidentally found the original Banko formulas, which contained descriptions of methods for the manufacture and application of enamels. As it was not uncommon for Japanese marks and seals to be copied, bartered, and/or forged, Mori Yesetsu was able to purchase the recipes and seals (both Banko and Fueki) from the grandson of Banko I.

The wares produced by Mori Yesetsu and his brother Yohei (who adopted the Fueki seal) were somewhat different from those of the original Banko. Mori Yesetsu was inventive and quite creative. Rather than using molds in the manner of his peers, he reversed the process by pressing the clay against the exterior of the mold. With this new method, the wares retained the design on the interior as well as the exterior of the piece. Another result is that the potter's finger marks appear on many forms of the later Banko wares.

For the most part, the paste of these creations was thin and translucent, yet quite strong. From 2 to as many as 12 molds, all having movable and interchangeable parts (basically made of wood), were used to produce many cleverly molded pieces.

In general, each type of Banko ware has distinguishing characteristics. Among the most easily recognizable varieties are marbleized wares, gray wares, tapestry wares, white wares, and brown wares. The marbleized wares are brown and white, with the density of the hues depending upon the ratio of white to brown clay. They are usually quite thin and bear evidence of the potter's finger marks, especially on lids and rims. Gray wares vary in consistency of paste. The early pieces seem quite thick, whereas later pieces are generally thin. Often one finds gray wares with enameled and/or sprigged-on ornamentation, or with stenciled motifs and Chinese-style glazing. Tapestry wares were made of various pale-colored clays, including

Banko marbleized teapot in shades of brown, Japanese, 3½" high, c1900, **$300–$400.**

Banko teapot, white ware with applied flowers in low relief, the flowers in pastel hues, Japanese, late 19th century, 7" high, **$300–$400.**

Banko vase, gray ware, one panel with monkey (in low relief) retrieving fruit, the reverse with cranes in relief among grasses, polychrome and gilt highlights, Japanese, c1880, 8" high, **$650–$950.**

green, white, cream, gray, brown, and blue. The clay was rolled out to a very thin consistency, pressed together, and and then rolled out again and again. Several of these variously colored rolls were slipped together (in and out) and the composite package of clay was then sliced. In turn, the slices were slipped in and out to form the desired patterns and delineations of color. Tapestry wares are thin and translucent and glazed on the interior. They feel gritty to the touch, much like the texture of a blackboard.

Movable handles are peculiar to Banko wares, as are knobs which pivot in their sockets; these were used on teapots, sake pots, and pieces with finials. Motifs found on Banko wares can be incised, impressed, enameled, molded in relief, or applied in relief, and they can be used singularly or in combinations.

Banko II's wares were quite popular in the Japanese domestic market. Before long, numerous potters such as Shibata and Shitomei Sohei were copying his style, including some pieces hand-turned on the potter's wheel. For the most part, these potters produced wares in the district of Yokkahchi. Generally, all the potters who produced wares styled after those of Mori Yesetsu used either a Banko or Fueki mark, either alone or in combination with their own marks and seals.

In the West, the first important recognition of Banko wares came during the 1878 Paris Exhibition, where more than 15 producers of Banko wares participated.

163

Imari

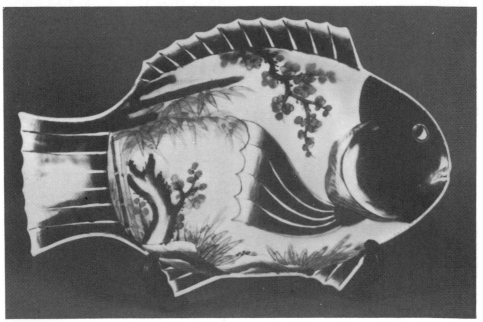

Imari fish-shaped plate; celadon, blue, and white; Japanese, c1875, 11" diameter, **$500–$750.**

Imari refers to a broad group of ceramic wares named for the port town of Imari. These ceramics have been produced since the early part of the seventeenth century in Hizen province (Saga prefecture), northern Kyushu Island, Japan.

The first Imari wares (shoki Imari) show the Korean influence in style and decoration. The basic decorations were executed in underglaze blue and white. Overglaze polychrome decorations were not developed until the middle of the seventeenth century. At that time, Dutch traders brought vast quantities of ko Imari (early Imari) to Europe, where it was greatly admired and sought after. It was so successful that it cut into the Chinese export porcelain market, thus forcing the Chinese to produce Imari.

There are distinguishable variances between Japanese and Chinese Imari. The Japanese porcelain is heavier. Its glaze is thicker and may contain pinholes. It may also show evidence of spur marks (caused by the supports in the kiln). The blue hues found on Japanese Imari are darker than those of its Chinese counterpart, and are often characterized as "runny." Unlike the Chinese Imari, which used a thin, coral red, Japanese Imari was decorated with thick, opaque Indian red. Certain varieties of Japanese Imari can even have lacquered motifs.

Color categories of Japanese Imari include *sometsuke*, decorated in underglaze blue and white; *nishikide*, decorated with patterned polychrome

Imari charger; Indian red ground with cranes in gosu (blue), white, black, and gilt; Japanese, late Edo period, 18" diameter, **$1,200–$1,600.**

Fukagawa kogo (incense box) in the form of a Shishi decorated with mon in blue, red, and gilt; the base and interior with an orchid-spray mark; Japanese, early Meiji period, 2½" high, **$500–$700.**

designs; *gosai*, generally not more than five colors; and *sansai*, decorated in three colors. The descriptions below give further details on popular types of Imari.

Fukagawa

Although the Fukagawa family has been engaged in the production of porcelain since c1650, the wares produced from the Meiji period into the early twentieth century, when Japanese porcelains were first being exported to the West, are of special interest to collectors.

In 1876, the head of the family, Fukagawa Ezaiemon, established a ceramic society called *Koransha* (the company of the fragrant orchid). The markings used on the wares of this company included an orchid spray and leaves. Several members of the society left in 1880 to form new companies, leaving Koransha with the Fukagawa family. In 1894, Chuji Fukagawa, the head of the company at the time, adopted a new trademark, or backstamp: Mt. Fuji. When Fukagawa Porcelain was appointed purveyor to the Imperial Household in 1910, the company became the representative of Japan's chinaware society.

The Fukagawa company has always produced wares of the highest quality, but collectors tend to concentrate on those with the Imari palette and on those judged representative of the arts and crafts movement (*studio ceramics*).

Hirado

Hirado Island is located off the northwest coast of Kyushu, Japan. It was on this island, in the mid-eighteenth century, that the renowned Hirado porcelains were introduced. Although the

Left: *Hirado dragon upon waves, all white, Japanese, late Edo period,* **$750–$950.** Right: *Hirado carp, all white glaze, Japanese, early Meiji period,* **$500–$700.**

daimyo (feudal lord) of Hirado, Matsura Shizunobu, had brought over Korean potters at the the end of the sixteenth century, production of fine-quality porcelains was not initiated there until c1750. At that time, a fine clay (used in combination with other materials) had just been discovered. The resulting porcelain was excellent for its glaze and modeling.

Like other Japanese daimyo, the Lord of Hirado financially supported the production of ceramic wares. Prior to the Meiji restoration (1868), Hirado porcelain wares were produced for the sole use and discretion of the daimyo. Regulations were enacted forbidding the sale of Hirado porcelains. The wares were used as presentation pieces, given to the Court of the Tokugawa and to other daimyo and noblemen. Among these pieces, the ones produced during the late 18th and early 19th centuries are considered the best Hirado porcelains. Still, the collecting community has shown great interest in later Hirado wares,

many of which were uniquely and exquisitely modeled.

The paste of Hirado wares is white (milky) and free of grit, which is sometimes found in the paste of other varieties of Imari. The glaze is lustrous and almost void of the kind of granulation present in the glaze of other Imari porcelains.

Hirado wares produced in the white were so cleverly modeled that any addition of color would have distracted from the overall artistry of the object. Other pieces were done with a single beautiful shade known as *Hirado blue.* Hirado blue is a soft, delicate color which was used to enhance and enrich motifs such as landscapes, floral sketches, and karako (children) at play. The blue was applied to the surface of an article once it had reached the biscuit stage of firing. Hirado blue is not as smudged or runny in appearance as that found in other Imari.

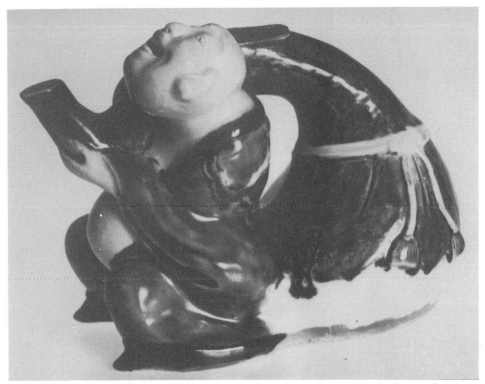

Hirado ewer in the form of Hotei and sack in gosu (blue), brown iron oxide and white, 18th century, **$2,500–$3,500.**

Prices for Hirado porcelain vary from dealer to dealer—as is the case with just about all forms of Orientalia—and are dependent upon profit margins and so on. However, like many other areas of Orientalia, Hirado continues to progress steadily in terms of both prices and appeal to collectors.

Kakiemon

Kakiemon is a name synonymous with the line of potters who worked at the Nangawa kiln, near Arita (a district in Hizen, which was the center for porcelain manufacture). It is also the name given the superb porcelain, motifs, and palette produced by this line of potters during the eighteenth, nineteenth, and twentieth centuries.

Sakaida Kizaemon (Kakiemon I), c1596–1666, was among the first potters to produce porcelain in Japan. He is also acknowledged as the producer of the first overglaze enamels used on Japanese porcelain. During the Kwanei era (1624–1644), he was a student of Takahara Goroshichi, a Korean potter known for his underglaze-blue decorations. Goroshichi and Kizaemon worked together at Shoten-ji temple, a Buddhist monastery where the latter had taken refuge because of the political turmoil of the times. There they produced porcelain wares with blue and white motifs.

At the same time, Kizaemon began experimenting with methods that could enable him to produce colored

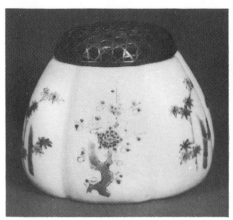

Kakiemon censer with copper lid, the motif in colors, Japanese, c1720, 4" high, **$6,000–$8,000.**

enamel glazes. In the process he used techniques learned from the formulas given to him by a friend named Tokuemon. Tokuemon, an Arita merchant, had been in Hagasaki (approximately 60 miles from Arita) while a Chinese ship was in the harbor, and had bought formulas unknown in Japan from a Chinese potter traveling on the ship. After much experimentation, Kizaemon was successful in producing a red ornamentation (like the color of persimmon), which he presented to the head of the Nabeshima clan in the form of a decoration for an *okimono* for *tokonoma* (an object for display purposes in an alcove). The lord of Nabeshima was so struck by the new glaze that he changed Kizaemon's name to Kakiemon (derived from the Japanese *kaki*, which means *persimmon*).

The earliest Kakiemon polychrome porcelain wares were made from clay obtained from Izumi yama, in Hizen province. This clay was of the highest quality, and the porcelain was thin. The glaze was white, and the clarity of the polychrome enamels added further richness to the wares. Motifs were simple and naturalistic, quite the

opposite of the busy patterns one associates with Imari. They never included diapers or geometric motifs, and generally either two-thirds or one-fourth of a given article was left undecorated.

From the end of the seventeenth century, Kakiemon wares had a more lustrous glaze and richer motifs which did include geometrics in addition to traditional styles.

The Kakiemon palette includes blue (blue-black, blue-gray, and blue-green); iron red (light); yellow; black; and aubergine (eggplant purple). Occasionally gilt has been added. Also note that some early wares have a brown or brownish red edge.

Nabeshima

Officially, the first kiln for Nabeshima was set up at Iwayakawachi, c1628. Toward the end of the seventeenth century, the kiln was moved to Okochiyama. Prior to the Meiji restoration (1868), Nabeshima wares were produced under the patronage of the daimyo of Saga prefecture, Lord Nabeshima. Similar to other wares produced during the Edo period, Nabeshima porcelains were only intended for the use of the daimyo. Nothing less than perfection was acceptable, and only the finest of specimens were used by the daimyo as special presentations and/or gifts. Then, from 1868 on, Nabeshima wares were produced for domestic use and Western export. However, quality and perfection did not decline as quantity increased. Thus, whether late or early, these wares have high market values.

Nabeshima porcelain was produced from the same materials used at other Arita kilns. Yet it is much finer than other Arita wares, which some-

*Nabeshima plate decorated in underglaze blue, Japanese, 18th century, 8" diameter, **$900–$1,200.***

*Nabeshima-style plate with high foot decorated with a comb pattern, the motif a copy of an Utamaro print, Japanese, late Meiji / early Taisho period, 8" diameter, **$400–$700.***

Nabeshima wares, moreover, were enameled with subdued or paler hues, as compared to the more vibrant or brilliant hues found on other Arita porcelains. Among the colors used on polychrome articles are iron red, underglaze blue, yellow, green, and seiji (celadon, which has a green tint). Unlike the slightly raised application of enamels found on other varieties of Arita wares, Nabeshima enamels are flat, becoming one with the glaze.

The motifs found on Nabeshima wares are usually simple, naturalistic, and structurally bold. Designs can cover as little as one-third of the surface of an entire object. Geometric motifs in polychrome enamels were generally used in combination with a monochrome ground to cover the entire surface of an object.

Nabeshima wares are well known for their high foot rim. Generally, bowls and plates have a high foot rim which is enhanced with an underglaze-blue comb pattern. The reverse rims of articles may also be enhanced with repetitive flowers and leaves, or with the cash pattern in underglaze blue.

times have a coarse and roughly textured paste. Another distinction of Nabeshima wares is that their decorators drew outlines in underglaze blue, then filled in the motif using either broad or fine strokes. Other Arita porcelains have somewhat careless drawings, by comparison, for their enamels were applied prior to the outlining process.

Kyoto Ceramics

Left: *Kyoto-ware tea caddy (chaire) with underglaze blue and brown iron oxide motif of the Imperial kiku mon, the base marked* Taizan, *Japanese, early 19th century,* **$800–$1,200.** Right: *Matching furo (brazier), the base also impressed with a Taizan mark, 8" high,* **$1,500–$2,500.**

The early seventeenth century opened a golden age of ceramic production in what was then Japan's capital city as potters filled the orders of Kyoto's prosperous merchants and courtiers, who demanded high-quality ceramic wares for use in the tea ceremony (*Cha no yu*) and for food service. Even in the most ordinary ceramics, Kyoto potters set the standard for style and craftsmanship.

Kyoto-ware chaire (tea caddy), the base with impressed Ninsei mark, an ivory lid, Japanese, 4" high, **$3,000–$5,000.**

Kyoto-ware bowl; the motif of flowers and foliage carried out to the rim, which is cut as buds and blossoming flowers in pale hues and gosu (blue) with gilt highlights; Japanese, 18th century, 10" diameter, **$2,500–$3,500.**

Circular box and cover, the overall motif in green and gosu (blue) kiku mon (16 petals), brown iron oxide bands, the interior decorated with wheels of life in colors and gilt, the base with an impressed Ninsei mark, 6" diameter, **$3,000–$4,000.**

Kyoto-ware bowl with floral motifs and cranes above, the rim cut out to simulate flying cranes, brown iron oxide and gosu (blue), the base signed Kenzan, Japanese, 18th century, **$3,000–$5,000.**

Although the works of certain potters achieved magnificent acclaim, similar characteristics reappear regularly in all ceramics from Kyoto. The works are distinguished by *eclecticism*, a selective use and sophisticated interpretation of many styles and techniques inspired by objects from other periods and cultures. And Kyoto's artists were among the first in Japan to master the overglaze enamel decoration closely associated with Kyoto ceramics.

Among the artists whose works are highly sought by collectors of Kyoto ceramics are Ninsei, Kenzan, Hozan, Eiraku, Ogata Kenzan, and Dohachi. In addition, objects made in the style of these artists are desirable, whether they were produced during the time in which the artist lived, or in later periods.

Satsuma

The collector/dealer who hears the word *Satsuma* thinks of a long-admired form of Japanese ceramics in which faience (pottery) is covered with a glaze that produces a beautiful network of crackles and is itself ornamented with polychrome enamels.

Near the end of the Momoyama period (1574–1603), Shimazu Yoshihiro, the daimyo of Satsuma and Osumi provinces, launched an attack against Korea as a prelude to the conquest of the Chinese Empire. Although the Japanese armies had gained some strong victories, after six years of fighting, they were recalled to their homeland by Hideyoshi Toyotomi. Upon returning to Japan in 1598, Shimazu Yoshihiro brought with him approximately 20 families of Korean potters, who settled in Kagoshima and Kushinko. Shortly before the start of the Edo period (1615–1868), these Korean potters were divided into two groups. One group was relocated in Chosa, Osumi province. The second group was resettled in the area around Naeshiragawa, Satsuma province. Reasonably good clay was found in and around these locations, and the potters soon began to practice their craft.

Early productions included articles for use in Cha no yu. Monochromes, flambé glazes, same gusuri (sharkskin glaze), bekko gusuri (tortoiseshell glaze), and shiro gusuri (white glaze) were all popular. Objects were generally small in size and mod-

Satsuma-style tea set decorated in colors and gilt with Rakan, Kannon, and dragon; Japanese, c1925, **service for 6, $200–$250.**

Satsuma jar and cover decorated in green, gosu (blue), red, white, and gilt; bird finial; the lid with a Shishi motif; Japanese, late 18th century, restored, 8" high, **$1,200–$1,500.**

Left: *Satsuma covered box decorated in gosu (blue), red, and gilt; Japanese, late Edo period, 4" diameter,* **$1,500–$2,000.** Right: *Satsuma covered box with 1000 Butterflies motif in gosu, red, and gilt; late Edo period, 4" diameter,* **$1,500–$2,000.** Courtesy of the Edson Collection.

eled after Korean prototypes. Grandiose objects such as palace vases and urns were, for the most part, products of the Meiji period (1868–1912), and were made for Western export.

It was not until the Kwansei era (1787–1800) that Satsuma wares were decorated in the manner recognized today. The employment of poly-chrome enamels, including silver and gold, was initiated, with artists using gold under the direction and instruction of Shimazu Narinobu, the daimyo at that time.

Early motifs were simple, elegant, graceful interpretations of nature. They included florals, birds, insects, and animals (both real and mythological), used singularly or in combinations. Shortly before the end of the Edo period (1850–68), figures in the forms of processionals, Rakan (Buddhist disciples), warriors, and so on were incorporated into motifs.

At the London International Exposition in 1862, Satsuma was displayed for the first time in a Western country. This was followed by displays in Paris (1867) and in Vienna (1873), and at the Philadelphia Centennial in 1876. From its first appearance in the West, Satsuma was extremely well received and in overwhelming demand. As a result, the so-called imitation Satsuma wares were created (near the beginning of the Meiji period) to meet the new demand. Actually, the "imitations" should be classified as Satsuma:

For the most part, there is little variation in the quality of the paste, or in the technique and methods of decorating, used to produce these wares. For the layman, in fact, they are hardly distinguishable from the productions of Kagoshima prefecture.

Satsuma was created by individuals whose great technical skills were combined with gracefulness of form and a careful mixture of compounded hues. The endless variety of wares produced attest to their excellence.

Sumida Gawa Wares

As stated at the beginning of the Banko section, a great deal of confusion has resulted from the abuse and misinterpretation of the *Banko* name, especially in relation to Sumida Gawa wares. Therefore, it is important to eliminate the rumors at fault, all of which have run rampant here in the USA:

- Sumida Gawa wares were made in Formosa.
- They were made by Korean prisoners of war.
- They were made on Poo Island, (a nonexistent place) which was washed away by a typhoon.
- The wares were produced from 1840 to 1910 for the French and English markets.
- They were produced by a colony of midgets.

Unfortunately, many who buy, sell, and collect Sumida Gawa ceramics have helped perpetuate similar myths. These rumors should be completely disregarded, and neither *Korean ware, Poo ware, Banko ware*, nor any combination thereof should be used to describe Sumida Gawa wares.

The Asakusa district of Tokyo actually saw the birth of Sumida Gawa wares. Tokyo is located on East Central Honshu, on the Kanto plain. This region is intersected by the Sumida Gawa (*gawa* means *river*), for which the ceramics produced nearby were named. Until the arrival of Inoue Ryosai, a Seto potter, there had been little in the way of porcelain manufacture in Tokyo. Then, in 1875, Inoue Ryosai formed a partnership with Shimada Sobei, a pottery dealer, and established a porcelain kiln in the Asakusa district. Materials for the production of his wares were likely secured from Aichi prefecture, where Seto is located, so there was little difference in the quality of his paste as compared to that of Seto (Owari) producers. His style of decoration, for the most part, was more in line with that of the Tokyo school. The Asakusa kiln

Sumida Gawa vase, red ground with morning glories and foliage in high relief, pinched form, white flambé curtain glaze, Japanese, c1900, 10" high, **$550–$750.**

produced pottery wares, including articles for use in Cha no yu, as well as porcelain wares contemporary to the late nineteenth and early twentieth centuries, which were fashioned there until the end of the Taisho period.

It appears that during the late 1890s, porcelain-bodied wares with heavy transmutation (flambé) curtain glazes and applied figures in relief

were developed; the earliest Sumida Gawa wares date from this time. (In 1899, a Sumida Gawa vase standing 48 inches high and having a porcelain body, red ground, and applied motifs of the 500 Buddhist Disciples won First Prize in a Tokyo exhibition.) Hayata Takemoto, with whom Inoue Ryosai had worked earlier in establishing a kiln for the daimyo of Settsu Province (Osaka prefecture), was a specialist in the use of transmutation glazes, especially in the Chinese style. It seems reasonable to assume that his working relationship with Hayata Takemoto allowed Inoue Ryosai to develop the glazes so closely associated with the later Sumida Gawa wares.

The earliest wares usually had a red, green, or black ground, distinguished sometimes by a leathery look. The smaller, ornamental pieces, especially figures, were often entirely covered with glaze.

In 1924, the kiln was moved from the Asakusa district to Yokohama. Despite the change in location, the name of the wares remained the same. Several new hues, however, were added to the palette: orange, brown, blue, and lavender.

Among the other characteristics of later pieces is an unglazed ground which may be flicked off with a fingernail or removed with a strong hand and a dampened cloth. Some of these pieces were made with the use of a mold (including the figures done in relief), which can be detected by examining the interior of an object and/or its motif. In general, motifs—which feature monkeys, dragons, scenics, florals, Rakan, elders, and karako—are applied in high relief.

Japanese Pottery and Porcelain Marks

Kiyen factory

Akahada/Kishiro maker

Akahada

Sampei Gashu maker

Kashiu Mimpei maker

Kashiu Sampei maker

Cho maker

Eizan maker

Kichi maker

Maker's mark

Yoskiage

Good Fortune / Long Life

Good Fortune

Good Fortune

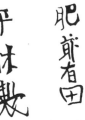

Hibarabayashi maker

176

Japanese Pottery and Porcelain Marks

Zoshuntei maker

Mori Chikara, Mikawachi
(maker and place)

Fukagawa maker

Yamaka maker

Fukagawa maker

Hichozan Shimpo maker

Shimodo maker

Hirado

Found on Hirado wares

Mikawaji

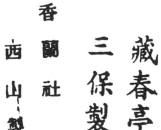

Zoshuntei maker

Happiness

Banko (impressed mark)

Japanese Pottery and Porcelain Marks

Banko (impressed mark)

Yusetsu maker (Banko)

Fuyeki maker (Banko)

Banko (impressed marks)

Banko—Tekizan maker

Ganto—Sanzin maker

Fuyeki maker

The Yofu factory

Banko ware

Kutani (place name)

Kutani (place name)

Kutani (place name)

Kutani (place name)

Kiokuzan maker

Yuzan maker

Kutani/Kayo (place name)

Kochoken maker

Japanese Pottery and Porcelain Marks

Tozan maker

Iwazo maker

Kawamoto Masukichi
maker / Seto, Japan

Kawamoto Hansuke maker

Rokubeye maker

Iwata, Aichi, Japan

Toyosuke maker

Eizan maker

Owari (place mark)

七寶會社

Nagoya (place mark)

Kawamoto Masukichi maker

Hokuhan maker

Gyokuzan maker

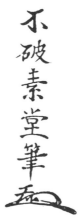

Fuwa Sodo maker

Ide maker

Kai maker

Nakajima maker

薩
摩

Satsuma (place mark)

Satsuma (place mark)

Hoju maker

Hohei maker

Hoyei maker

Japanese Pottery and Porcelain Marks

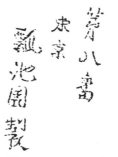

Koko maker

Siekozan maker

Kinko factory maker

Hiocheyen Tokyo maker

Gosaburo maker

Gozan maker

Tsuji/Tokyo, Japan
(maker and place mark)

Kozan (Makuzu) maker

Denka maker

Myakawa Kozan maker

Makuzu Kozan maker

Meizan maker

Kenya maker

Ryozan maker

Inoue Ryosai

Inoue Ryosai

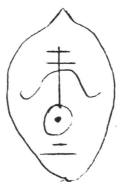
Inoue Ryosai

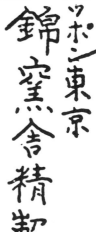
Kinsho Company, Tokyo
(maker and place mark)

Japanese Pottery and Porcelain Marks

Kitei maker   Zoroku maker   Hichibeye maker   Sahei maker   Seifu maker

Raku   Eiraku maker   Eiraku maker   Kanzan Denshichi maker   Makuzu Kozan maker

Shuzan maker   Kinunken maker   Taizan maker   Taizan maker   Tanzan maker

Bizan maker

   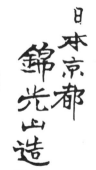

Seikozan maker   Shuhei maker   Kanzan maker   Kinkozan

Hozan maker   Awata (place mark)   Ryozan   Kinkozan   Dohachi   Kenzan

Japanese Pottery and Porcelain Marks

Dai Nippon (Great Japan)

Ninsei

Japanese Pottery and Porcelain Values

Arita

Dish; Kakiemon style and palette; central roundel of phoenix on rock-work with flowers; the rim with rocks, pine, plum, and bamboo; late 17th century, 8" diameter, **$1,500–$2,000.**

Dish, underglaze blue with scrolling floral motif, 19th century, 5" diameter, **$50–$75.**

Dishes, blue and white, each painted with three fish, floral scroll on the reverse, 18th century, 8½" diameter, **pair, $1,500–$2,000.**

Ewer, underglaze blue and white, three square panels, two with foliage and figure, the other with herons on plum branches, the neck with a band of stylized flower heads, loop handle, minor chips, late 17th century, 9" high, **$1,200–$1,600.**

Arita censer in the form of a treasure ship (tarakabune) with a deck which can be lifted off, the back of the sail with perforated openings in the form of cash, polychrome and gilt, Japanese, late 18th century, 8" long, **$1,200–$1,600.** Private collection.

Arita ash pot; square form; blue, Indian red, green, gilt, and colors; supported on four legs; two panels; Shishi and cash symbols; Japanese, c1800, **$700–$900.** *Courtesy of Richard A. Bowser.*

Jar and cover, underglaze blue and white, ovoid form with a motif of phoenix and flowering trees with formal borders, the cover restored, late 17th century, 20" high, **$1,500–$2,500.**

Jar and cover, octagonal ovoid form, underglaze blue and white, the motif consisting of flowers and rock-work beneath formal bands, restoration to cover and rim, late 17th century, 25¼" high, **$3,500–$5,000.**

Kendi, ribbed globular body with underglaze foliate branches, the neck and everted rim similarly decorated, early 18th century, 8" high, **$700–$1,000.**

Model of a leaping carp, iron red, underglaze blue and gilt, fin restored, 18th century, 4¾" high, **$600–$800.**

Model of a seated tiger, white biscuit, naturalistic detail, late Edo period, 5" high, **$900–$1,200.**

Arita joss-stick holder in colors and gilt, Japanese, late 18th / early 19th century, 3" long, **$500–$700.**

Arita model of a puppy, white biscuit, black pupils, Japanese, late Edo period, 3" high, **$1,000–$1,500.**

Model of a sleeping cat; red, black, and gilt; the tail curled to one side; late 19th century, 7" long, **$300–$500.**

Vase and cover, ovoid, underglaze blue and white, panels of kiku bordered by cloud bands, the cover similarly decorated and surmounted by a tear-shaped finial, early 18th century, 19" high, **$1,500–$2,200.**

Arita model of a monkey, white biscuit, Japanese, early 19th century, 4" high, **$700–$950.**

Vases, beaker form, gosai with motif of dragons and flowers, raised ribs and animal-head ears, archaic style, one with minor repair, late 18th century, 10" high, **pair, $600–$800.**

184

Banko bowl with monkeys around the rim, the interior with a crackle glaze, the monkeys' garb in colors, Japanese, c1910, 7¾" diameter, $700–$950.

Left: *Banko candlestick in the form of an iris with applied iris and leaves, shades of green and lavender, Japanese, c1890,* $200–$300; *right: Banko vase, one of a pair, gray ware with basketweave motif and applied branches, colors and gilt, Japanese, c1880, 3½" high,* $400–$600. Courtesy of Richard A. Bowser.

Wine pot and cover, underglaze blue and white, a continuous band of chrysanthemum flower heads, loop handle, rim and spout with karakusa (scroll), knop finial, late 18th century, 7½" high, **$700–$900.**

Banko

Bowl; marbleized; round; decorated with flowers, butterflies, and insects; late 19th century, 6½" diameter, **$700–$900.**

Censer in the form of a house, the roof perforated, c1910, 4¾" high, **$275–$350.**

Group of monkeys: Hear, See, and Speak No Evil; c1920, 3" high, **$150–$185.**

Banko censer in the form of Hotei's *sack with Hotei and child in low relief, primary colors, Japanese, c1900, 3" diameter,* **$300–$400.**

Group of monkeys: Hear, See, and Speak No Evil; c1920, 5½" high, **$300–$400.**

Group of monkeys: Hear, See, and Speak No Evil; 6½" high, **$400–$500.**

Group of monkeys, one holding a broom, c1915, 7" wide, **$350–$475.**

Group of monkeys grasping for a fish, c1915, 6½" wide, **$400–$500.**

Humidor, marble and white glaze with no masks in low relief, 6½" high, c1920, **$450–$600.**

Humidor, a contorted face, gray ware, 6" high, c1920, **$450–$600.**

Nodder, a child carrying a fan, c1920, 4½" high, **$400–$600.**

Two Banko monkeys, each holding a vase, Japanese, c1910, 3" high, **each, $200–$300.**

Nodder, Fukusukesan, gray ware, c1900, 3" high, **$350–$450.**

Nodder of Fukusukesan seated on a monkey, c1910, 5" high, **$500–$700.**

Nodder of Fukusukesan, c1910, 7" high, **$600–$700.**

Nodder, a monkey reading a book, c1910, 5" high, **$300–$500.**

186

Banko teapot in the form of a quail, gray ware with colors and gilt highlights, insect finial, Japanese, c1900, **$375–$450.**

Banko teapot, gray ware with the Three Wise Monkeys in low relief, the teapot in the form of a pumpkin, deep green the primary color, Japanese, c1910, **$350–$475.**

Banko vase in brown tapestry with applied flowers in low relief, polychrome and gilt, impressed Banko mark in base, c1900, 6" high, **$350–$500.**

Banko vase with a scenic motif in relief, ring handles, beige and brown, Japanese, c1930, 7" high, **$100–$150.**

Bizen ewer with applied gourds and foliage in relief, twisted handle, modified double-gourd form, Japanese, early 19th century, 16" high, **$750–$950.**

Plate, gray ware, the clay in basket-weave form, late 19th century, 7" diameter, **$375–$500.**

Teapot, four military generals in relief, Taisho period, **$300–$400.**

Teapot, gray with enameled motifs of 100 Treasures in relief, reed handle and tea strainer, c1900, **$375–$500.**

Teapot (with strainer) in the form of Ebisu holding a fish, gray ware with colored enamels, Taisho period, 6" × 7", **$275–$375.**

Teapot in the form of a cat, the head as the lid, the raised paw as the spout, gray ware with dainty enameled flowers, c1915, **$400–$500.**

Teapot in the form of a duck, woven reed handle, c1915, **$300–$400.**

Teapot, glazed white in imitation of Chinese blanc de chine, applied lotus, late 19th century, **$400–$500.**

Teapot; gray ware in the form of a house; the roof as the lid; applied flowers, branches, and birds; reed handle; c1910, **$350–$450.**

Teapot in the form of a goat, gray ware with enameled flowers, c1920, **$375–$475.**

Vase, gray ware, motif of enameled crustaceans, impressed Banko seal, c1875, 8" high, **$650–$800.**

Vase, gray ware, in the form of a Japanese lantern, painted green at the top and bottom, red body, naturalistically enameled motif of running rabbits, 8½" high, c1900, **$350–$500.**

Vase, gray ware, painted green in a basket-weave pattern with a cat and mouse motif, late Meiji period, 6½" high, **$275–$375.**

Vase, brown ware, with an enameled motif of flowers, late 19th century, 6" high, **$450–$650.**

Wall pocket, gray ware enameled in colors and gilt, in the form of Daikoku with sack and mallet, Taisho period, 7" X 5" X 2", **$200–$275.**

Wall pocket in the form of Hotei; gray ware painted green, yellow, and red; Taisho period, 7½" X 4½" X 2", **$200–$275.**

Wall pocket, gray ware in the form of a hawk perched on a branch, Taisho period, 4¼" X 8¼", **$300–$375.**

Wall pocket in the form of a woman with a green basket on her back, early Showa period, 9½" high, **$125–$175.**

Bizen

Censer modeled as two birds, finely detailed, late Edo period, 4½" high, **$2,800–$3,500.**

Chaire (tea caddy), cylindrical, string cut foot, dark brown glaze, ivory lid, late 18th century, 2½" high, **$400–$600.**

Dish; octagonal; raised sides; impressed motif of leaves, insects, birds, and dragons; deep brown glaze; early 18th century, 7" diameter, **$500–$800.**

Figure of Hotei leaning on treasure bag, a fan in one hand, late 19th century, 6" high, **$400–$600.**

Hanaire, cylindrical and irregular in form, with pinched neck, brown with splashed ash glazes, 18th century, 11" high, **$700–$900.**

Bizen sake bottle, pinched form, with Daikoku in low relief, Japanese, late Edo period, 6" high, $300–$500.

Storage jar, the shoulders with an incised band and three applied loop handles, 19th century, 27½" high, **$100–$185.**

Tokkuri (sake bottle), pear-shaped with a dark ash glaze, 17th century, 7⅝" high, **$400–$600.**

Wall pocket in the form of a section of bamboo, Meiji period, 11½" high, **$100–$150.**

Vase, bulbous with tapered neck, brown body splashed with lighter brown glaze, 18th century, 10" high, **$1,000–$1,500.**

189

Censer surmounted by a Shishi and tama, the body with flying phoenixes, the entire piece in red-orange and gilt, the base with impressed Eiraku (Hozen) mark, early 19th century, 6" high, $2,000–$2,500.

Eiraku

Cha wan (tea bowl), green-brown glaze, pottery, impressed mark, c1870, **$900–$1,200.**

Bowl, Chochin style, flowers and Shishi with key fret border, late Edo period, impressed mark, 8" diameter, **$1,500–$2,200.**

Vase, globular, decorated in red-orange with phoenix and butterflies above clouds, porcelain, Eiraku seal, early Meiji period, 7" high, **$1,200–$1,800.**

Fukagawa punch bowl with the dragon and cloud motif, the base with an orchid-spray mark, gilt highlights, Japanese, late 19th century, c1885, 16½" diameter, **$1,000–$1,500.**

Fukagawa vase with café au lait (coffee hue) ground and mon, various chrysanthemum forms in colors and gilt, orchid-spray mark on base, Japanese, early Meiji period, 4" high, **$750–$975.**

Fukagawa

Plate; Imari palette; ribbed, fluted, and scalloped; paneled motif of flowers, trees, and maple leaves; center with a kiku spray; Koransha orchid spray mark; early Meiji period, 10" diameter, **$900–$1,200.**

Jardinière; globular; ribbed with motif of peony and sparrow in shaped reserves; blue, red, and gilt; base marked Fukagawa sei, late 19th century, 14" diameter, **$800–$1,200.**

Jardinière; globular; painted in blue, red, yellow, and gilt with continuous tree peony; the base marked Fukagawa sei, late 19th century, 15½" diameter, **$600–$900.**

Spittoon, cherry blossom mouth and plum blossom interior, the upper band with dragon and pearl, the vertical bands with plum and diapers, Mt. Fuji mark, c1905, 10½" high, **$2,000–$2,750.**

191

Hirado bottle with underglaze blue motif of birds perched on branches, Japanese, late Meiji period, c1900, 13½" high, **$900–$1,200.**

Fukagawa vase with motif of irises in red, blue, and gilt; the base with an orchid-spray mark; Japanese, early Meiji period, 8" high, **$500–$750.**

Vase, bulbous with short neck, birds on branches, Mt. Fuji mark, c1915, 6" high, **$200–$300.**

Vase, colors and gilt with courtiers holding fans, the shoulder and foot with stylized phoenix, Fukagawa in red characters, 16" high, **$1,200–$1,500.**

Vase; iron red, blue, and gilt with a band of cranes and waves below a lappet border; the neck with ruyi bands; late 19th century, 23" high, **$1,500–$2,000.**

Vase, motif of fish and blossoming plum trees, Mt. Fuji mark, c1910, 6⅞" high, **$300–$500.**

Vases, pair, each with misty forest scenes in underglaze blue and gilt above and below floral bands, Meiji period, 10" high, **$900–$1,200.**

Vases; ribbed; ovoid with flared necks; panels of cranes, pheonix, and prunus; c1890, 12" high, **pair, $1,500–$2,200.**

Vases; ovoid with inward-curving rims; painted with panels of cranes amongst pine and bamboo reserved on a ground of kiku mon and scrolling foliage; red, blue, and gilt; Koransha mark, 19th century, 25" high, **pair, $7,000–$10,000.**

192

Hirado covered box in the form of a seashell; the shell finial with a pearl inside; blue, brown iron oxide, and white; motifs of crustaceans and shells; late Edo period, 5" diameter, $1,000–$1,500.

Hagi

Cha wan, light celadon glaze with lacquer restorations, brocade bag, 17th century, 3¼" high, **$900–$1,200.**

Hibachi, rectangular, finely crackled with underglaze blue leaves, late 18th century, 3" high, **$400–$600.**

Hirado

Bottle, globular with an elongated neck, underglaze blue and white with karako, the neck with ruyi sceptre below stiff leaves, late Edo period, 8" high, **$1,000–$1,500.**

Bottle/vase, globular body with phoenix and a leafy branch, the long neck with inverted stiff-leaf border, late Meiji/early Taisho period, 12" high, **$1,500–$2,000.**

Bowl and cover modeled as a seashell and decorated with small shells in low relief, iron oxide and underglaze blue, late 18th century, 5" wide, **$1,000–$1,500.**

Box and cover, underglaze blue and white in the form of a rat on a melon, chipped, late Edo period, 4½" high, **$600–$800.**

Candlesticks, underglaze blue and white, each modeled as a karako holding a branch, petal rim, damages to both, late Meiji period, 5" high, **pair, $400–$600.**

Censer, globular, underglaze blue and white, pierced lid, the body with plants and karako, early Meiji period, 3" high, **$600–$800.**

193

*Hirado, Hotei and sack, underglaze blue and white, Japanese, late Edo period, 2" × 1½", **$900–$1,200.***

Cup, the center with a basket-weave band, the top band with a continuous landscape, late Meiji period, 4½" high, **$700–$900.**

Ewer, underglaze blue and white, a seated karako with a dog in his arms, the dog's head forming the spout, the cover modeled as a hat, c1910, 7¾" high, **$350–$500.**

Ewer, brown and cobalt blue in the form of a Hotei and treasure sack, a late 19th-century copy of an 18th-century specimen, 8" long, **$500–$700.**

Group, Shishi (five in all) clambering over one another, underglaze blue and white, chips to tails and ears, late 19th century, 7⅜", **$600–$900.**

Jar and cover, conch shell with applied barnacles and seashells, brown and underglaze blue, 6" diameter, 19th century, **$900–$1,200.**

Joss-stick holder in the form of a rabbit, cash-shaped opening at the top, repair to one toe, early 19th century, 6" high, **$1,000–$1,500.**

*Hirado bucket with underglaze blue motifs of birds above breaking waves, 7" high, Japanese, early Meiji period, **$500–$700.***

Model of a cockerel, the tail feathers arched upwards, white ware, 19th century, 6½" high, **$600–$800.**

Model of a puppy, white glaze, bow tied around his neck, late 19th century, 4½" long, **$700–$900.**

Model of a Shishi in underglaze blue and white, late 19th century, 5" high, **$350–$550.**

Model of a recumbent tiger, white glaze, 19th century, 7½" long, **$650–$800.**

Teapot, brown and underglaze blue with stippled ground, white flower heads and foliage, late 19th century, 5½" high, **$300–$500.**

Vase, ovoid, high shoulder, flared mouth, incised plum-branch motif, all white, Meiji period, 12½" high, **$800–$1,200.**

Vase, applied tripod dragon feet, the globular body decorated with a blue cloud pattern, damaged, c1910, **$300–$500.**

Vase, globular, underglaze blue dragon motif and a dragon in relief around the neck, the dragon's spikes broken, c1900, 7½" high, **$300–$400.**

Kakiemon

Bottle; hexagonal with a tall neck; underglaze blue, iron red, green, and yellow with pine, prunus, and bamboo amidst rocks; chip and hairline; late 17th century, 10¾" high, **$7,000–$9,000.**

Bottle/vase with a motif of cherry and peony blossoms, 18th century, 9" high, **$1,800–$2,500.**

Bowl, exterior divided into 10 panels alternating with ladies and blossoms, brown rim, star crack in base, c1700, 8½" diameter, **$2,500–$3,500.**

Kakiemon bottle, the motif of a phoenix in colors, the reverse with sparse cloud forms in colors, Japanese, early 18th century, 13½" high, **$4,000–$6,000.**

Bowl, lobed form, Three Friends (pine, plum, and bamboo) motif on the interior, exterior with peony sprays in colors, brown-edged rim, chipped, 18th century, 7" diameter, **$3,000–$4,000.**

Bowl, oval, typical palette with a band of dragons bordered by waves, exterior with flower heads, late 18th century, 8¾" long, **$1,200–$1,800.**

Bowl, pierced-ring rim, Kakiemon palette, motif of morning glory against a trellis, hairline and rim chip, late 17th century, 6½" diameter, **$2,000–$3,000.**

Bowl, Kakiemon style, painted colors and gilt with phoenix and clouds, the exterior with butterflies and flowering branches, late 19th century, 9½" diameter, **$400–$600.**

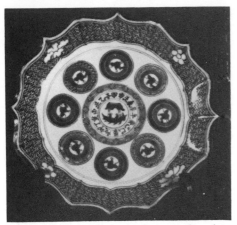

Underglaze blue and white Kakiemon zodiac plate, Year of the Horse, brown edge, Japanese, c1726, 8" diameter, **$2,000–$3,000.**

Imari bowl; Indian red, blue, and gilt; scalloped rim; four reserves on the interior and exterior, divided by panels of diapers; the center with a vase filled with flowers; Japanese, early 19th century, 9" diameter, **$700–$950.** Courtesy of Leon and Toni Andors.

Bowl; everted, brown-edged rim; the interior with two birds above pine and prunus and banded hedges within a floral band in colors and gilt; late 17th century, 5½" diameter, **$1,500–$2,200.**

Bowls, kiku form, typical palette, courtesans amongst flowering plum, the well of each with a stylized floral motif, 19th century, 6½" diameter, **pair, $800–$1,200.**

Censer; hexagonal; three ball feet; iron red, green, yellow, aubergine, and blue; two birds above prunus and rocks; no cover; late 17th/early 18th century, 5¼" high, **$7,000–$9,000.**

Dish; lobed; foliate with two floral sprays, a bird perched on a branch, a Shishi, and a moth; rim chips; late 17th century, 9¾" diameter, **$2,000–$3,000.**

Kendi; globular with short spout, tall neck, everted rim; blue, red, and green motif of flowers and foliage; spout damaged; no stopper; late 17th century, 8" high, **$3,500–$5,000.**

Mizusashi (water jar), underglaze blue and white with flowering peony and rock-work on the body and lid, 18th century, 8" high, **$2,000–$3,000.**

Saucer dish, foliate rim, underglaze blue, iron red and colors with gilt, two birds amongst rocks, the reverse with a band of plum blossom, brown-edged rim, c1700, 11" diameter, **$2,500–$3,500.**

Saucer dish; green, blue, red, black, and gilt with Three Friends motif; rim chips and hairlines; late 18th century, 4½" diameter, **$700–$900.**

Teapot and cover, typical palette, continuous band of plum blossoms and grasses, karakusa on spout and handle, kiku knop finial, finial restored, end of the 17th century, 5¾" long, **$700–$900.**

Vase, ovoid, painted with prunus trees and chrysanthemum amongst rock-work, c1800, 10" high, **$2,500–$3,500.**

Karatsu

Bottle/vase, globular body, long neck, black-brown with cream-colored neck, late Meiji period, 10" high, **$300–$400.**

Cha wan, high foot, motif of plum blossoms in iron oxide, Edo period, **$300–$400.**

Imari

Barber's bowl; iron red, underglaze blue, and gilt with flowering shrubs; the everted rim with kiri and phoenix; late 17th century, 10¾" diameter, **$750–$1,050.**

Bottle, Three Friends motif, Kakiemon style, 18th century, 12⅞" high, **$1,650–$2,175.**

Bottle/vase; long neck with butterfly mon and floral patterns in iron red, underglaze blue, and gilt; c1870, 10" high, **$300–$400.**

Bowl; sansai; scholar's table, chest, and mon with floral, scroll, and bat motifs; c1830, 6" diameter, **$700–$900.**

Bowl, sansai, the motif with a center medallion of phoenix and paulownia, 16 petals forming the contour; the interior with radiating bands of mon diapers, crane, and florals, which are repeated on the exterior; the foot decorated with X's and O's; c1775, 7¾" diameter, **$3,500–$4,500.**

Bowl, gosai, scalloped with a central medallion of pomegranates and foliage in underglaze blue and gilt, a band of blossoms and leaves form the contour, wide band of six panels with reserves, pseudo Ming mark, c1800, 8" diameter, **$750–$900.**

Bowl; sansai; fluted, ribbed, and scalloped; a motif of florals and phoenix; c1800, 6" diameter, **$700–$900.**

Bowl; gosai; a center medallion with a Torri gate in a waterscape; the border divided into three reserves, each featuring waves and carp; c1860, 6" diameter, **$375–$500.**

Censer, square with canted corners, four panels with shrubs and flowers on a diaper ground, a pierced wood cover added later, pseudo Cheng Hua mark, late Edo period, 7" square, **$1,200–$1,600.**

Charger, gosai, mum and leaf motif with six alternating bands of tree and veranda with beehive and bird, raised enamels, the reverse with leaf and scroll in an underglaze blue, c1870, 12" diameter, **$1,700–$2,200.**

Charger; sansai; shell-shaped; fluted, ribbed, and scalloped; the motif featuring kame and garden; the reverse with blue scrolls; c1885, 13" diameter, **$900–$1,200.**

Charger, gosai, phoenix and six varied floral cartouches, impressed Katkana mark, c1925–34, 12½" diameter, **$200–$300.**

Charger, gosai, center medallion of kanne kike with three fan reserves of florals and alternating mon, the reverse with underglaze blue bats, c1870, 13¼" diameter, **$1,000–$1,500.**

Charger; gosai; fluted, ribbed, and scalloped; three sprays of peony and foliage in the center; three phoenix cartouches divided by three bands of kiku and mon; the reverse with red and underglaze-blue rhinocerous horn and coin patterns; c1870, 12¼" diameter, **$1,800–$2,500.**

Charger; sansai; fluted, scalloped, and moderately ribbed; flower/phoenix and two alternating mon overall; c1850, 14" diameter, **$1,000–$1,500.**

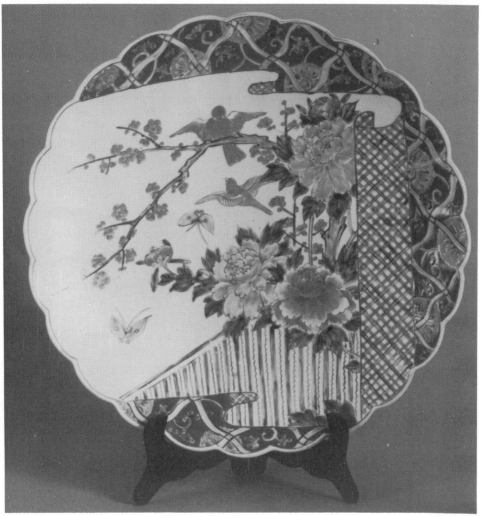

Imari charger with scalloped rim; red, blue, yellow, green, aubergine, and gilt; Japanese, late 19th century, 18" diameter, **$550–$800.**

Charger; sansai and gilt; the central roundel containing peonies and bamboo branches; the rim with shaped panels filled with phoenix on a cherry branch, Shishi, and Buddhistic emblems; chipped; crack in base; Genroku period, 22" diameter, **$2,500–$3,500.**

Charger, blue and white, a village scene, Meiji period, 22" diameter, **$2,000–$2,500.**

Dish; sansai; persimmon center medallion; motif of fruit, foliage, and scrolls; c1850, 7½" diameter, **$175–$225.**

Dish, sansai, the pattern featuring pine and a four-petaled leaf with six alternating mon and floral bands, underglaze blue scrolls on the reverse, c1880, 6¼" diameter, **$150–$225.**

Dish, sansai, fish form with mon and floral motif, Meiji period, 4¾" diameter, **$300–$500.**

Imari pitcher, vertical diapers in colors and gilt, Japanese, late 19th century, 8" high, **$400–$500.**

Dish, sansai, fish form with floral motif and gilt highlights, Meiji period, 15" diameter, **$700–$1,100.**

Dish, sansai, in the form of a boat, the stern with a notch, the exterior ornamented with waves, the interior with floral motifs and diapers, Meiji period, 12" × 7¼", **$800–$1,200.**

Model of Chonin holding a fan, his undergarments iron red and gilt, his kimono black, 7" high, **$900–$1,200.**

Model of a bijin holding a scroll; her kimono decorated with florals in red, blue, and gilt; c1890, 16" high, **$900–$1,200.**

Left: Imari figure with musical instrument in blue, red, green, and gilt; c1920, 6" high, **$100–$150.** Right: Imari figure with fan; her kimono in gilt, blue, and red; Japanese, c1890, 3½" high, **$350–$550.**

Model of a bijin playing a biwa, gosai, her kimono decorated in floral patterns, c1910, 6" high, **$300–$500.**

Model of a bijin seated and playing with a cat, mounted as a lamp, c1920, 5" high, **$125–$185.**

Plate, sansai, slightly scalloped, the center with a flower vase and low table, floral border with landscape cartouche, five spur marks on the base, late 18th century, 11" diameter, **$3,000–$4,000.**

Plate, sansai, scenic landscape center medallion with six panels of mon and garden views, the reverse with underglaze blue scrolls, c1880, 8¾" diameter, **$300–$400.**

Plate, gosai, scalloped rim, the center with a dragon medallion, three large leaf cartouches and overall motifs of cherry trees, the reverse with underglaze-blue and red cash and ginger, c1800, 8½" diameter, **$700–$900.**

200

Plate, sansai, fluted and scalloped, three-leaf pattern with reserve of Kotobuki (*congratulations*) and diaper mon, the reverse with underglaze-blue treasure bags, c1800, 8½" diameter, **$900–$1,200.**

Plate; sansai; fluted, ribbed, and scalloped with floral medallion in the center and 12 radiating bands of varied floral motifs; c1830, 8½" diameter, **$900–$1,200.**

Plate; gosai; fluted, ribbed, and scalloped; the center medallion surrounded by radiating bands of florals and paulownia; the reverse with underglaze-blue pearl and ginger; c1860, 9½" diameter, **$300–$425.**

Plate, gosai, motif of fungus and scrolls on the reverse, the center with a flower vase, the border with sages in landscapes, c1850, 8½" diameter, **$300–$400.**

Plate, gosai, hexagonal, the center with a floral cartouche, the border with alternating bands of flowers and birds, scrolls and cash on the reverse in underglaze blue, c1880, 11" diameter, **$850–$1,200.**

Plate; octagonal; the motif featuring clouds, insects, and flower baskets; c1800, 7½" X 9¼", **$1,000–$1,500.**

Plates in the form of abalone shells, blue and celadon with gilt highlights, the motif of pine and plum with diapers, the plates molded in low relief, c1875, 8½" X 9½", **pair, $500–$600.**

Plates; sansai; shell-shaped; fluted, ribbed, and scalloped; phoenix and tree pattern in Chinese style; c1875, 9" diameter, **pair, $350–$475.**

Platter; oval; fluted, ribbed, and scalloped; the motif including waves, cranes, pine, and kame diapers with kiku; the reverse with cash and scroll motifs and moon year characters in underglaze blue; c1850, 9½" × 12½", **$700–$900.**

Platter, oval, a band of shells and medallions of scholar's utensils on the rim, the center with wisteria and toys which have wheels in the form of the wheel of life, late Edo period, 13" wide, **$600–$900.**

Saucers, sansai, petal-shaped, slightly ribbed, dragon medallion surrounded by six formal cartouches, c1850, 5" diameter, **set of 6, $1,000–$1,500.**

Tokkuri, sansai, rectangular with canted shoulders, short neck, dragon and vines, body crack, late 17th century, 7" high, **$700–$900.**

Tokkuri; rectangular; angled shoulders; short neck; panels of cranes; red, blue, and gilt; late 18th century, 7¼" high, **$1,200–$1,600.**

Umbrella/cane stand, sansai, the upper and lower bands with underglaze-blue flowers, the center with flowering branches and fence-work, stenciled patterns, c1910, 24" high, **$800–$1,200.**

Umbrella/cane stand, underglaze blue and white with overall floral motifs, stenciled patterns, c1910, 24" high, **$400–$600.**

Vases; sansai; fluted, ribbed, and scalloped with overall floral reserves; c1860, 8" high, **pair, $1,200–$1,500.**

Kutani

Bottle/vase painted with shaped, scattered reserve filled with figures and landscapes; c1910, 11" high, **$350–$500.**

Bowl, the interior painted with a bird beside a flowering plant, clouds on exterior, Yoshidaya, early 19th century, 4½" high, **$1,000–$1,500.**

Bowl, underglaze blue in a floral motif, 17th century, 8½" diameter, **$300–$500.**

Bowl and cover, the domed cover with a section of bamboo forming the finial, painted red-orange and gold with shaped panels of courtiers seated on horseback with attendants, the bowl with panels of birds and branches, white interior, marked *Dai Nihon Kutani*, c1890, 10½" diameter, **$300–$450.**

Censer; AO; the domed, pierced cover with a Shishi finial; the body with a dragon chasing the pearl above waves; colors and gilt; marked *Fuku* on base; late 19th century, 6" high, **$250–$350.**

Censer, three short legs, the body with orange and gilt foliage, the lid missing, marked *Fuku*, 11" high, c1900, **$300–$400.**

Censer modeled as a Shishi, the head forming a pierced cover, orange and gilt, marked *Kutani*, c1900, 4½" high, **$175–$250.**

Charger, the central motif of six cranes flying over a beach above minogame (turtles) on rocks, the red sun rising in the horizon within a floral border, Taisho period, 18" diameter, **$900–$1,200.**

Chopstick rest, double gourd with an orange cord, Meiji period, 3" long, **$100–$150.**

Dish decorated in red and gilt with shaped panels of flowers, cockerel, and hen; the base marked *Kutani*; late 19th century, 14" diameter, **$600–$900.**

Dish, the well with the Seven Gods of Good Luck in a woodland setting, the border with flowers and scrolls, red and gilt, c1880, 14" diameter, **$900–$1,200.**

Figure of a bijin, polychrome and gilt, c1920, 12" high, **$200–$300.**

Figure of a standing Hotei with treasure sack and fan, brown-toned skin, colored attire, impressed Kutani mark on the base, the base with a cheese-cloth finish, c1935, 8" high, **$100–$125.**

Figures; Seven Gods of Good Luck; orange, green, brown, and gilt attire; each with an attribute; c1925, 3" high, **set, $200–$300.**

Figure of a hawk perched on a tree stump, naturalistic decoration, late 19th century, 12" high, **$300–$400.**

Figure of a sleeping cat, gold splashes on the body, a red ribbon collar with gilt bell, Showa period, 10" long, **$150–$200.**

Plate, iron red and sepia with gilt floral sprays within gilt foliage border, the exterior with a leaf-blade band in iron red, c1910, 9" diameter, **$200–$300.**

Plate, red and gilt with sepia flowers, the exterior with a red diapered band, late Meiji period, 8" diameter, **$100–$150.**

Plate, red-orange and gilt with fan-shaped panels of women doing various domestic chores, rim restored, marked *Kutani*, late 19th century, 10½" diameter, **$500–$700.**

Sake bottle (tokkuri); AO; rectangular; tall neck; everted rim; green, blue, aubergine, and black with panels of riverscapes and landscapes; Yoshidaya revival; marked *Fuku* on base; early 19th century, 10½" high, **$2,000–$3,000.**

Sake bottle (tokkuri), double gourd, AO with motif of vines, marked *Kutani* on the base, c1875, 8½" high, **$300–$400.**

Sake bottle (tokkuri); double gourd with designs of dragon and kirin with clouds, waves, and geometric patterns; Yoshidaya revival; marked *Fuku* on base; early 19th century, 8" high, **$1,200–$1,800.**

Sake bottle; pear-shaped; 1000 Faces in red, black, and gilt; c1915, 6" high, **$200–$300.**

Teapot, orange and gold with flowering branches, c1915, 5" diameter, **$125–$175.**

Tea set: teapot, covered sugar and creamer, six cups and saucers, and six cake plates; scenic motif featuring Mt. Fuji; marked *Kutani*; c1910, **$275–$350.**

Tea set: teapot, open sugar and creamer, six cups and saucers; eggshell porcelain; red-orange and gilt with landscape motif; c1910, **$250–$300.**

Tea set: teapot, covered sugar and creamer, eight cups and saucers, two serving plates, and eight cake plates; orange and gold with samurai and attendants and a riverscape; marked *Dai Nihon Kutani*; c1910, **$300–$500.**

Kutani vase with applied foliage and toad; the body decorated with insects; white, red-orange, and gilt; Japanese, late 19th century, c1885, 4" high, **$300–$400.**

Kutani tray, two open-leaf-form handles, scalloped rim, motif of hawk perched on branch above breaking waves, red-orange and gilt, Japanese, late 19th century, 16" diameter, **$750–$950.**

Vase; AO; ribbed; oviform; tall, slender neck; panels of various diapers; early 19th century, 7" high, **$800–$1,200.**

Vase, AO, birds flying above peony, marked *Fuku* on the base, c1900, 8" high, **$200–$300.**

Vase, gourd-shaped, red-orange and gilt motifs of birds perched on flowering branches, c1885, 8½" high, **$225–$300.**

Vase; 1000 Faces pattern; orange, black, and gilt; c1900, 6" high, **$150–$200.**

Vase, oviform, red-orange foliage and blossoms overall with gilt highlights, marked *Kutani* on the base, c1890, 14" high, **$600–$800.**

203

Box in the form of a cloud with a floral motif, the interior decorated with blue and gilt, the base marked Kenzan, Japanese, 18th century, 5" wide, **$2,500–$3,500.**

Tea bowl (cha wan) with white glaze, gosu (blue), and brown iron oxide floral motifs on exterior and interior; signed Kenzan; Japanese, 18th century, **$3,000–$5,000.**

Kutani vase with a panel featuring Kinko on a carp, red-orange and gilt, Japanese, late 19th century, c1885, 6" high, **$500–$700.** Courtesy of Richard Bowser.

One of a set of *mukozuke* (set of 5), *Kyoto ware*, with motifs of maple leaves in colors on a beige-cream ground, each piece signed Kenzan, **$3,000–$5,000.**

Kyoto-ware ash pot; gosu (blue), green, and cream with carved motif of flowers and scrolling foliage; Japanese, late 18th century, 4½" high, **$1,500–$2,200.**

Kenzan

Basket, cherry and hawthorne motif, Kenzan style, late 19th century, 6" high, **$250–$350.**

Bowl; irregular, shallow form; painted with a bamboo pattern in white slip and underglaze iron brown; the base signed and dated 1705, 10" diameter, **$3,000–$5,000.**

Kyoto-ware bottle (tokkuri), the body carved with flowers and foliage in gosu (blue), green and cream, Japanese, 18th century, 10" high, **$3,500–$5,500.**

Bowl, motif of bamboo in iron brown and white; signed *Kenzan*, but actually only done in his style; late 18th century, 11" diameter, **$1,000–$1,500.**

Bowl; irregular form with a pierced rim; bamboo and snow motif in white slip and underglaze iron brown; the base with a white reserve signed *Kenzan*; early 18th century, 9" diameter, **$1,500–$2,000.**

Dohachi

Box and cover modeled as a bird and decorated in blue glazes, seal on the base, early 19th century, **$800–$1,200.**

*Kyoto-ware censer, open-work lid, the motif including mon and foliage in colors and gilt, the base with a Ninsei impressed mark, Japanese, 5" high, **$2,500–$3,500**.*

Bowl, a motif of maple leaves in colors, Dohachi seal, early 19th century, 6" diameter, **$700–$1,000**.

Figure of Okame, kimono in colors and gilt, marked on the base, early 19th century, 6" high, **$1,200–$1,650**.

Kyoto Ceramics

Box and cover in the form of a brocade ball; green, blue, red, and gilt; Ninsei style; early 19th century, 1½" high, **$800–$1,200**.

Box and cover in the form of a mandarin duck painted in colors and gilt; Ninsei style; early 19th century, 3⅞" long, **$1,000–$1,500**.

Box and cover; circular with chrysanthemums overall in gilt, gosu blue, and red on a cream ground; Ninsei seal; 18th century, 2⅞" diameter, **$2,200–$3,200**.

Box and cover; circular with red, green, blue, and gilt Buddhistic symbols on a cream ground; inscribed *Ninsei* on the base; 18th century, 3½" diameter, **$3,500–$5,000**.

Censer modeled as a Shishi, its head forming the cover; ochre, blue, and iron oxide details with gilt lacquer repairs; late 18th/early 19th century, 7¾" high, **$1,200–$1,500**.

Kyoto-ware tea bowl (cha wan), the black ground decorated with butterflies in colors and gilt, Ninsei style, Japanese, late 19th century, **$300–$400.**

Kyoto-ware bottle, underglaze motif of Three Friends (pine, plum, and bamboo), Japanese, late 17th/early 18th century, 8" high, **$2,000–$3,000.**

Kyoto-ware cha wan decorated with a mandarin duck, Japanese, late Edo/early Meiji period, **$300–$500.**

Kyoto-ware chaire (tea caddy) with wood lid; the black body decorated with diapers in gilt, red, and blue; base with impressed Ninsei mark; 3" high, **$4,000–$5,000.**

Censer, pierced and molded with lotus and foliage in pastel hues, the base with a diapered band, Meiji period, chips on rim, 10½" high, **$700–$900.**

Censer and cover painted with leaf-shaped panels of flowers; signed Kenzan, but actually only done in his style; late 19th century, 2" high, **$800–$1,200.**

Chaire, globular form, everted rim, mottled brown glaze, ivory lid, the base marked Ninsei, but actually only done in his style; early 19th century, **$600–$900.**

Cha wan decorated with brown slip, Indian red, and gilt, flowering plum branches; the base marked Kenzan, but actually only done in his style; early 19th century, 3" diameter, **$600–$900.**

Kyoto-ware ewer decorated in colors and gilt, the base with a Taizan mark, Japanese, early 19th century, **$750–$1,000.**

Cha wan, raised ring foot, the gray glaze with plum blossoms in iron red and iron oxide, Kenzan style, early 19th century, **$500–$700.**

Jar and cover; green, blue, and gold motif of willow trees; Ninsei style; early 19th century, 8¾" high, **$1,200–$1,800.**

Mizusashi, cylindrical, a variety of open and closed fans in colors and gilt, inverted lid with loop handle signed *Gyozan* and sealed *Cho*, late Edo period, 6" high, **$1,200–$1,600.**

Mizusashi; cylindrical; inverted lid with loop handle; a motif of standing cranes in blue, black, and iron red with gilt highlights; signed *Gyozan*; late Edo period, 8" high, **$1,000–$1,500.**

Figure of Hotei carrying treasure sack and holding a fan, colors and gilt, realistically modeled, late Edo/early Meiji period, 12" high, **$1,200–$1,800.**

Sake bottle; bulbous; short neck; flowering chrysanthemum and lotus in red, white, green, and gilt on a creamy glaze; early 19th century, 8½" high, **$1,000–$1,500.**

Kyoto-ware mizusashi (water jar) for the tea ceremony, bands of motifs upon a crackled ground decorated in overglaze colors, by Eiraku Hozen, Japanese, early 19th century, 7" high, **$3,000–$5,000.**

Sake bottle; cylindrical; short spout; crackled glaze; blue, white, and green motif of camellia sprays; late 18th century, 8⅜" high, **$2,000–$3,000.**

Sake bottle; cylindrical with short neck; two lobed-handle bosses; blue, green, and gilt motif of pine trees below a band of scrolling foliage in iron red; late 17th/early 18th century, 6½" high, **$2,500–$3,500.**

Sake bottle, double gourd, green and blue motif of plum and bamboo, early 19th century, 12" high, **$900–$1,200.**

Sake bottle, rectangular, short neck, blue overall, each side with a panel filled with a blue mountainscape on a cream ground, chipped on corners, hairline on foot, last half of the 18th century, 6" high, **$800–$1,200.**

209

Kyoto-ware vase; four handles; bright shades of red-orange, blue, colors, and gilt; base marked Kiyomidzu; Japanese, late 19th century, 12" high, **$650–$950.**

Sake bottle; ribbed; ovoid form; sparsely decorated with pine, plum, and bamboo; late 18th century, 7¾" high, **$1,500–$2,200.**

Sake bottle; squat form; elongated neck; blue mountainscapes on a large, crackled glaze; early 19th century, 8½" high, **$600–$800.**

Vase; globular; a motif of 100 Treasures in red, blue, and gilt; green and aubergine; 18th century, 11" high, **$3,500–$5,000.**

Kyoto-ware vase; modified, elongated pear shape; decorated with flowers and foliage; a diaper band above in colors and gilt; the base marked Taizan; Japanese, c1870, 8" high, **$500–$700.**

Demitasse set with rose red flowers and green foliage, gilt trim, marked Shofu Nagoya, Japanese, c1935, **service for 6**, **$125–$150**. Courtesy of Mrs. Florence Simon.

Made in Japan

Bank in the form of a cat, one paw raised, porcelain, decorated with polychrome flowers, 14½" high, **$150–$200.**

Dinner set, Seiji ware (celadon) in a pale green with Mt. Fuji in white slip (low relief):

Bread and butter plate, 6" diameter, **$10–$20.**

Breakfast plate, 8¼" diameter, **$15–$25.**

Butter tub, perforated bottom, **$50–$75.**

Creamer and sugar, **$75–$100.**

Cream pitcher, **$50–$75.**

Cup and saucer (tea), **$15–$25.**

Cup and saucer (demitasse), **$25–$35.**

Dinner plate, 9¾" diameter, **$35–$45.**

Egg cup, **$20–$30.**

Mayonnaise server and spoon, 6½" diameter, **$35–$50.**

Oval platter, scalloped, 9½" wide, **$50–$75.**

Oval platter, scalloped, 10½" wide, **$60–$80.**

Oval platter, scalloped, 15" wide, **$75–$100.**

Salad bowl, 8½" diameter, **$50–$75.**

Soup bowl, 7¼" diameter, **$35–$45.**

Tea plate, 7¼" diameter, **$15–$25.**

Teapot (four-cup capacity), **$45–$65.**

Teapot with removable strainer (six-cup capacity), **$50–$75.**

Tile, 6½" diameter, **$25–$50.**

Tile, 6" square, **$25–$45.**

Tray in bamboo basket with open handles, 8½" × 14½", **$100–$150.**

Vegetable dish/cover, round, 10" diameter, **$25–$45.**

Vegetable dish/cover, oval, 10½", **$27.50–$40**

Vegetable dish with three feet, round, **$50–$75.**

Vegetable dish, oval with three feet, 7¼" wide, **$35–$45.**

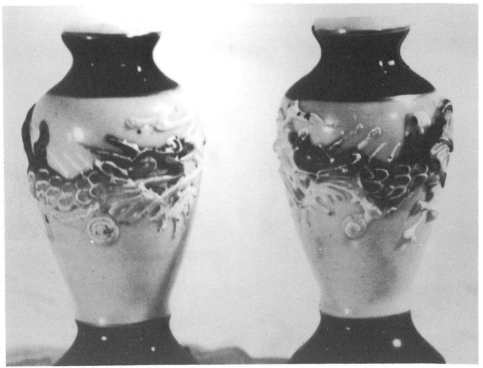

A pair of salt and pepper shakers; yellow ground with moriage dragons in gray, blue, and pink; black band at top and base; Japanese, c1920, $10–$15.

Figures, the Seven Gods of Good Luck, porcelain with luster colors and gilt, mounted on a long stand, c1930, each figure 7" high, **$300–$500.**

Flower bowl, nine white swans surrounding the blue, blue luster, 8" diameter, **$175–$200.**

Phoenix Pattern—Blue and White
    Cereal bowl, 6" diameter, **$18–$22.**
    Cup and saucer, (tea), **$10–$15.**
    Creamer and sugar (loop handle), **$40–$50.**
    Egg cup, **$15–$20.**
    Platter, 12" wide, **$40–$55.**
    Platter, pierced handles, 11", **$35–$45.**
    Salad bowl, 7½" diameter, **$20–$22.50.**

Scalloped dish; muted black-gray ground with moriage dragon in gray, blue, and pink; the wicker handle missing; Japanese, c1930, 8" diameter, $50–$75.

    Scalloped bowl, 5½" diameter, **$15–$18.**

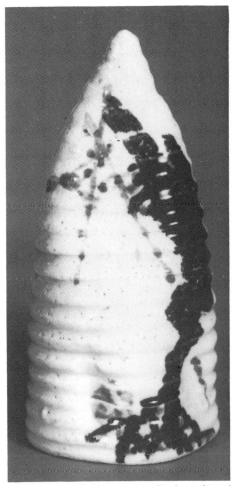

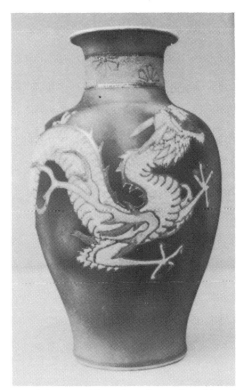

Porcelain vase with coralene dragon in gold and yellow, Japanese, c1925, 6" high, $125–$175.

Pottery wall pocket decorated in black, pink, and bright blue with foliage and plum blossoms; Japanese, 8" long, c1935, $75–$100. Courtesy of Mark Fogel.

Serving bowl, oval, 10" wide, **$45–$55.**

Teapot (cozy), **$65–$95.**

Teapot, 7½" wide, **$40–$55.**

Teapot, 9" wide, **$50–$60.**

Sweetmeat set: seven fan-shaped dishes around a central round dish (each piece with a floral motif), and black lacquer box with matching motif on the cover; 12" diameter, **$125–$175.**

Tea set: teapot, sugar and creamer, and six cups and saucers; moriage; a floral pattern on a deep green ground; marked *Made in Japan* (with a plum-blossom trademark); c1930, **$150–$175.**

Tea set: teapot, covered sugar and creamer, and six cups and saucers; moriage; a landscape motif in autumnal shades; c1925, **$100–$200.**

Tea set: teapot, sugar and creamer, six cups and saucers, and six cake plates; tan and blue luster; **$100–$125.**

Mokubei

Vase with underglaze-blue motifs of Chinese Lohan on a crackled white glaze, signed, 19th century, 10" high, **$700–$900.**

Nabeshima

Dish, underglaze blue and white, two mandarin ducks amongst water weeds and grasses, comb pattern on the foot, tasseled cash on the reverse, late 19th century, 8" diameter, **$500–$700.**

Dish, underglaze blue and white, camellias on a pale blue ground, comb pattern on the foot, tasseled cash on the reverse, late Edo period, 7½" diameter, **$500–$600.**

Dish, underglaze blue and white, chrysanthemums and foliage, comb pattern on the foot, 18th century, 8¼" diameter, **$800–$1,200.**

Dish, underglaze blue and white, everted rim, motif of flowering camellia branch, the reverse with tasseled cash, tapered comb pattern on the foot, 18th century, 8¼" diameter, **$4,000–$6,000.**

Dish, polychrome motif of peonies, comb pattern on the foot, the reverse with tasseled cash, two hairlines, 18th century, 7¾" diameter, **$1,000–$2,000.**

Saucer dish, polychrome motif of wisteria and foliage curling upward, comb pattern on the foot, gold lacquer repairs on the rim, 18th century, 4¼" diameter, **$2,500–$3,500.**

Saucer dish; a motif of plum blossoms, foliage, and peaches in iron red, blue, and green; comb pattern on the foot; three groups of cash on the reverse; late Meiji period, 8" diameter, **$600–$750.**

Nabeshima dish decorated with a takarabune (treasure ship) in colors and gilt, comb pattern on foot, early Meiji period, 8" diameter, **$600–$800.**

Nabeshima plate with an underglaze blue motif of a flower basket, Japanese, 18th century, 8" diameter, **$1,800–$2,200.** Private Collection.

Noritake (Art Deco)

Ashtray, circular, orange luster, 3½" diameter, **$15–$25.**

Ashtray, orange luster border, hexagonal, the well with a standing lady, 4¼" wide, **$75–$100.**

Ashtray, flower form, orange luster with a seated nude on the rim, 7" wide, **$275–$375.**

Dish with lemon and flowers in relief, bright orange luster ground, the motif in bright yellows and greens and black, Noritake, Japanese, c1925, **$100–$150.** Courtesy of Mark Fogel.

Dish with center handle hand-painted in shades of green and blue, green and gilt rim and handle, base marked Noritake, Japanese, c1930, 9" diameter, **$100–$125.** Courtesy of Mark Fogel.

Box (powder), blue and orange luster with blue bird finial, 4½" wide, **$150–$185.**

Cake plate, round with two open handles, cobalt and gilt border, the center with a lake scene at dusk, 10½" diameter, **$125–$150.**

Candlesticks, a lake scene in autumnal hues, 5½" high, **pair, $150–$225.**

Celery dish, oval with open handles, lake scene in autumnal hues, 12½" long, **$50–$100.**

Chamber sticks, orange luster, black-rimmed loop handles, 2½" high, **$100–$150.**

Condiment set: salt and pepper, mustard pot and spoon, toothpick holder, and tray; orange and blue luster with small floral motifs; 5" diameter, **$150–$175.**

Decanter, primary hues with a Mexican motif, 8½" high, **$300–$400.**

Dresser doll, bobbed hairdo, cylindrical form, gold luster with red-orange plum blossoms, 5½" high, **$275–$325.**

Humidor, continuous desert scene in shades of red, 5½" high, **$320–$375.**

Humidor, lake scene in autumnal hues, 4" high, **$175–$225.**

Inkwell, clown form, primary colors, 4" high, **$285–$350.**

Luncheon set: four kidney-shaped plates and four cups; gold luster border with a floral motif in primary colors on the plate; a floral motif on the interior of the cups; 7" long, **each, $50–$75.**

Plaque, autumnal lake scene with water fowl, 10" wide, **$175–$225.**

Smoking set: two-handled oval tray, match holder, and cylindrical cigarette container; blue luster with floral sprays; 7" long, **$220–$260.**

Sweetmeat set: blue and gold luster with six fan-shaped dishes surrounding a circular dish, each with a motif of fruit in primary colors; **$150–$225.**

Tea set, orange luster and white with a motif of roses and foliage, **service for 6, $275–$350.**

Tea set: teapot, sugar and creamer, four cups and saucers, and four cake plates; two shades of orange-luster borders with gold-luster bodies and black bands; knop finials; **$200–$275.**

Tea set: teapot, sugar and creamer, six cups and saucers, and six cake plates; deep orange with a pattern of two perched cockatoos; **$300–$400.**

Tea set: teapot, sugar and creamer, and six cups and saucers; a desert scene in shades of red; **$225–$325.**

Vase, orange luster with geometric bands and stiff-leaf (archaic) motif, 8¾" high, **$175–$225.**

Vase, jack in the pulpit, autumnal lake scene, 7¾" high, **$225–$325.**

Vase; tree-trunk form with a peacock in red, blue, yellow, and green; 5" high, **$250–$275.**

Wall pocket, blue luster with a motif of a lake scene in autumnal hues, 8" high, **$100–$135.**

Wall pocket, orange luster below and above a lake scene with swans at sunset, 8" high, **$100–$150.**

Pottery bowl with purple flambé glaze on the interior and exterior, the base marked Nippon, *Japanese, c1900, 6" diameter,* **$175–$200.** Courtesy of the Virginia Keresey Collection.

Black pottery box and cover decorated with calligraphy, the base marked Nippon, *Japanese, c1900, 4" diameter,* **$100–$150.** Courtesy of Kyle Husfloen.

Nippon Era Ceramics

Bowl, open handles, lakeside scene with swans in autumnal hues, **$100–$150.**

Bowl, two open handles, windmill scene, 6½" diameter, **$100–$125.**

Bowl, two open handles, orange and gold border, interior and exterior with ladies standing in a garden, **$125–$175.**

Bowl, two reticulated handles, autumnal hues with a lakeside scene and a moose, **$100–$125.**

Bowl, cobalt with gilt trim, interior with fan-shaped reserves of seated Rakan, 7" diameter, **$100–$150.**

Bowl, cobalt and gold with red and pink roses, 8" wide, **$175–$225.**

Bowl in a woven silver basket with twisted silver handles, pale blue exterior, white interior with small blue flowers, 4½" diameter, **$150–$185.**

Bowl, red ground, dark blue border, Bird of Paradise motif, 9¼" diameter, **$150–$185.**

Candlesticks, Gouda style, 7½" high, **$225–$325.**

Chocolate set: pot (10½" high) and six cups and saucers; slip-trailed dragon (moriage); the ground shaded black-gray and pink with blue and pink flames; gray dragon; **$350–$450.**

Chocolate set, orange and gilt handles and trim, bijin amongst cherry trees in a village scene, **$375–$500.**

Dish, the central motif of flower vases in pastel hues, the border with alternating yellow and blue reserves, 9½" diameter, **$150–$200.**

Baking dish and cover, pottery, bamboo design in brown and green, 6" diameter, **$75–$100.**

Fruit basket, wicker handle, bamboo motif in green on a white porcelain, 7" diameter, **$100–$125.**

Fruit dish; black ground with flowers and bird perched on a branch in yellow, blue, and pink; a blue border; Chinese-style motif; 7⅛" diameter, **$100–$125.**

Fruit dish; black ground with flowers and birds in yellow, blue, and pink with a blue and yellow border; Chinese-style motif; 8½" diameter, **$125–$175.**

Fruit dish; black ground with flowers and a bird perched on a branch; shades of blue, yellow, and pink; 10" diameter, **$175–$220.**

Humidor, Rakan molded in relief, 7½" high, **$1,000–$1,500.**

Humidor, windmill scene in shades of brown and yellow, **$300–$400.**

Jar and cover, moriage dragon motif in shades of gray, 7" high, **$250–$350.**

Juice set: elephant-form pot and six tumblers; moriage dragon in shades of gray with pink and blue flames; **$300–$400.**

Juice set: covered pitcher (9½" high) with six tumblers; Satsuma style; diapers in gold and red; the panels with figures of children; **$300–$450.**

Nut set: one large bowl (6" diameter); small bowls (each 3" diameter); scalloped with iris motif; **$100–$150.**

Pitcher, cobalt and gold with brilliant red roses, 8" high, **$350–$475.**

Pitcher, Satsuma style, scalloped foot and rim, diapers in gold and red, two scenic panels with children at play, 7" high, **$200–$275.**

Plaque, three herons huddled amongst marsh grasses, 8½" diameter, **$200–$300.**

Plaque, Egyptian scene, two camels and two riders, 10" diameter, **$200–$300.**

Plaque, oval, two dried salmon in relief, 18" wide, **$1,000–$1,500.**

Plate, cobalt and gold with red spider mums, 9" diameter, **$225–$300.**

Plate, moriage, slip-trailed dragon motif in shades of gray, 8" diameter, **$100–$150.**

Smoking set: humidor, cylindrical cigarette container, match holder, and tray; Egyptian scene with camel and rider; **$500–$600.**

Snack set, pale blue with huddled white herons, tray 8½" long, **service for 4, $200–$300.**

Tea set, lotus finial, a motif of pink cherry blossoms and branches, **6 pieces, $275–$325.**

Tea set: teapot, sugar and creamer, and six cups and saucers; moriage dragon motif in shades of gray; **$200–$300.**

Tea set: teapot, sugar and creamer, and six cups and saucers; orange ground with silver dragons; Chinese style; **$250–$325.**

Tea set, Satsuma style, motif of Rakan and Kannon, gilt trim, knop finials, **service for 6, $225–$350.**

Vase, beaker form, black with irises and a band with a continuous lake scene, 10½" high, **$200–$275.**

Vase, cylindrical, motif in Longwy style, 10½" high, **$200–$250.**

Vase, green pottery in a woven silver basket, marked *Awaji Nippon*, 12" high, **$125–$175.**

Vase, yellow pottery in a woven wicker basket, marked *Awaji Nippon* (with an impressed trademark of a bird), 14½" high, **$200–$250.**

Vase, moriage, square form, a motif of plum blossoms and branches with perched birds, dragon and ring handles, biscuit ground, 9" high, **$225–$300.**

Vase, moriage dragon motif in shades of gray, **$200–$250.**

Vase, moriage, motif of cranes and lotus, 10" high, **$200–$300.**

Vase, moriage, motif of flowering prunus branches, 10" high, **$200–$300.**

Vase, moriage, bird perched on a flowering branch, two open handles, 12" high, **$200–$300.**

Wall pocket, pottery, black with bird (in relief) painted in colors and gold, 12" long, **$200–$300.**

Occupied Japan

Ashtray, interlocking square form, decorated with a bird perched on a flowering branch, orange and gold, base marked *Kutani Occupied Japan*, 4" long, **$55–$85.**

Candy dish and cover; circular; Imari palette with motif in red, blue, and gold; 6½" diameter, **$100–$125.**

Candy dish, magenta lacquer with gold flowers on the lid, 7" diameter, **$100–$175.**

Kutani porcelain dish in Kakiemon style, the base marked Occupied Japan, *7" diameter,* **$100–$150.**

Raku ash pot with knife-cut motifs, Japanese, 18th century, 7" diameter, **$900–$1,200.**

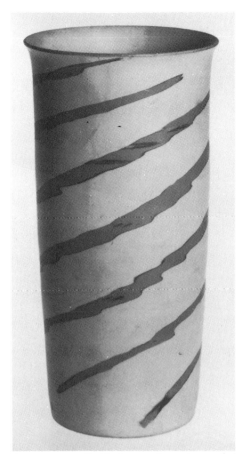

Pottery vase, cylindrical, one of a pair, marked Occupied Japan, 14" high, **$100–$175.**

Figures, Dutch boy and girl, each carrying buckets suspended from strings, blue and white, 4" high, **$15–$20.**

Figures, mandolin players, attire with lace trim, marked *Moriyama*, 6½" high, **$200–$250.**

Figures, Dutch boy and girl, polychrome, 3½" high, **$20–$25.**

Figures, Thai dancers, polychrome, 5¼" high, **$45–$65.**

Figures, Imari style, male and female dressed in Japanese costumes, polychrome, 6½" high, **$200–$300.**

Group; a Japanese gentleman with a lady by his side (she appears to be cleaning his ear); Imari palette; 9" long, **$250–$300.**

Group, a seated bijin playing with cat, Imari palette, 4" high, **$200–$300.**

Sake set: a whistling bottle and six cups; white with red dragons; **$75–$100.**

Sake set: a whistling bottle and five cups; moriage with gray dragons; **$75–$100.**

Tea set: teapot and five cups; traditional; Imari palette; **$100–$125.**

Tea set: teapot, sugar and creamer, six cups and saucers, and six cake plates; hand-painted with bright orange flowers and green foliage; gilt trim; **$100–$175.**

Oribe

Bowl, short foot ring, turned rim, brown slip and green glaze with autumnal flowers and trellis pattern, gold lacquer repair, late 17th/early 18th century, 9" diameter, **$2,000–$3,000.**

Dish, round and scalloped, green glaze with incised cranes and foliage, rim chips, 17th century, 7" diameter, **$1,200–$1,800.**

Censer, cream body with a green glaze and brown flower and trellis pattern, late 19th century, 8¾" high, **$300–$500.**

Cha wan, fences and plum-blossom design, late Edo period, **$250–$325.**

Mukozuke, boat-shaped dishes, loop feet, green and white glaze on a brown ground with interlocking diamond shapes, the exterior with wave patterns, two restored, early Edo period, 7½" long, **set of 5, $700–$900.**

Raku *cha wan* (tea bowl) with black glaze and splash of white and green, Japanese, Edo period, **$1,500–$2,000.**

Raku

Cha wan, black glaze stopping short of the foot, chips on the rim and foot, impressed Raku seal, 18th century, **$300–$400.**

Cha wan, black and brown glaze stopping short of the foot, 18th century, 4½" diameter, **$1,800–$2,500.**

Cha wan, flaring mouth, short ring foot, black glaze, Raku seal, 19th century, 5⅞" diameter, **$600–$900.**

Cha wan, short ring foot, temmoku glaze, impressed Raku seal, 19th century, 2⅞" high, **$800–$1,200.**

Cha wan, short ring foot, mottled red glaze, impressed seal (Cho Raku), 19th century, 3" high, **$700–$1,000.**

Patterned Dinnerware

Tree in the Meadow

This pattern, otherwise known as the Sunset Pattern, is highly collectible (like the Azalea pattern below). Its scenic motif features a house set with a tree in the background. The motif is generally found in autumnal hues, but has been identified in shades of blue and green, as well. Values for Tree in the Meadow Dinnerware are comparable, for the most part, to the values listed for Azalea.

Azalea

The Azalea pattern contains pink and white azalea blossoms. The blossoms have yellow stamens and red shafts. The foliage is yellow-green with dark green accents between the blossoms. Prices are as follows.

Bouillon (two handles), **$15–$20.**
Bouillon, **$20–$25.**
Basket, **$100–$185.**
Bonbon dish, **$25–$40.**
Bowl (two handles), **$15–$20.**

Two sets of creamers and sugars in the Azalea pattern. See listing for current values.

Satsuma bottle decorated in colors and gilt with a floral motif, Japanese, c1900, 8" high, **$300–$500.**

Bowl (soup), **$15–$25.**
Bread and butter plate, **$10–$15.**
Butter tub with liner, **$35–$45.**
Cake plate, **$45–$55.**
Celery dish, **$100–$125.** (Tree in the Meadow, **$30–$45.**)
Cheese dish, **$100–$125.**
Chocolate cup and saucer, **$20–$25.**
Coffee pot, **$400–$500.**

Creamer, **$20–$35.**
Cup and saucer (demitasse), **$30–$45.**
Cup and saucer (tea), **$20–$30.**
Dinner plate, 9¾" diameter, **$20–$30.**
Egg cup, **$20–$30.**
Four-o'clock-tea cup and saucer, **$25–$35.**
Gravy dish, **$40–$55.**
Ice cream set (seven pieces), **$220–$250.**
Jam jar (with under-plate), **$75–$100.**
Lemon plate, **$20–$30.**
Luncheon plate, **$20–$30.**
Mayonnaise set (three pieces), **$30–$45.**
Mustard set (three pieces), **$40–$50.**
Nut dish, **$17–$22.**
Oatmeal bowl, **$12–$15.**
Pickle dish, **$20–$25.**
Platter, 12", **$40–$50.**
Platter, 14", **$40–$60.**
Platter, 16", **$300–$350.**
Relish dish (two-handled), **$125–$175.**
Salad plate, **$15–$25.**
Salt and pepper, **$20–$30 (and up).**
Sauce dish or berry bowl, **$10–$15.**
Spoon holder, **$45–$55.**
Sugar (covered), **$20–$30.**
Sugar (open), **$17–$22.50.**
Sugar shaker, **$75–$100.**
Tea and toast set (one cup and tray), **$20–$25.**

Satsuma punch or fruit bowl decorated in the United States, colors and gilt, signed Mabel Dibble, 1909, *18" diameter,* **$900–$1,200.**

Teacup and saucer (breakfast), **$20–$30.**

Tobacco jar, **$250–$325.**

Vase, **$200–$250.**

Vegetable dish (oval or round), covered, **$100–$125.**

Vegetable dish, open and divided, **$100–$125.**

Satsuma

Basket, flattened circular form with a motif on each side featuring seated children in colors and gilt, signed *Hattori*, late Meiji period, 3" high, **$175–$225.**

Bowl, black matte ground on the interior and exterior with gilt flowers and birds, early Showa period, 8½" diameter, **$200–$300.**

Bowl decorated with clouds and two dragons on the interior below a lappet border; the exterior with mums; iron red, blue, and gilt; signed Masanobu; c1810, 8" diameter, **$3,500–$5,000.**

Bowl; deep, rounded form with shaped panels filled with women engaged in a variety of domestic pursuits; the panels divided by bands of diapers; colors and gilt; late 19th century, 6" diameter, **$400–$600.**

Bowl, hexagonal, the motif with mums and butterflies on the interior, the exterior with a band of flower heads at the rim, c1930, 6" diameter, **$100–$175.**

Bowl; the interior with shaped panels filled with bamboo, dragons, plum blossoms, and phoenix on a formal ground; the exterior with phoenix, key pattern, and lappets on the rim; signed Masanobu (with blue Shimazu mon); first quarter of the 19th century, 12" diameter, **$4,000–$5,000.**

Bowl, the interior with a seated Kannon, colors and gilt, the exterior with gilt diapers, late Meiji period, 8" diameter, **$400–$500.**

Bowl, lobed rim, roundels of kiku and kiri mon in blue and gilt on the interior and exterior, signed Shokuzan, early Meiji period, 8½" diameter, **$1,000–$1,500.**

Bowl, the interior with a peacock on rock-work amongst blue and salmon-hued peony and flowering prunus, the exterior with roundels, a diaper border, signed Chikusai, Meiji period, 12¼" diameter, **$700–$950.**

Bowl, black matte ground on the interior and exterior with a motif of gilt butterflies overall and a diaper border, chipped, early Showa period, c1930, 4" diameter, **$100–$150.**

Bowl, flower form, decorated with figures in a village scene with a lake, colors and gilt, Taisho period, 5¼" diameter, **$150–$185.**

Bowl in the shape of Mt. Fuji, the interior with samurai on horseback, the exterior with floral roundels and diapers, signed Kinkozan, late Meiji period, 6⅛" wide, **$500–$850.**

Bowl, square form with canted corners, the interior and exterior in the 1000 Flowers pattern in colors and gilt, signed Yozan, Meiji period, 4¾" diameter, **$300–$500.**

Bowl; the interior with objects for the scholar's table; the rim with lappets; the exterior with chrysanthemum and foliage; iron red, blue, white, and gilt; late Edo period, 5" diameter, **$2,000–$3,000.**

Box and cover, fan-shaped, the lid decorated with figures picnicking beneath flowering cherry trees, the sides with diapers, c1910, 4½" wide, **$500–$600.**

Box and cover, hexagonal, the lid with ladies in a garden, colors and gilt, signed Kinkozan, c1920, 3" wide, **$300–$400.**

Box and cover; the lid with sprays of flowers and rock-work in gilt, blue, and colors; the sides with brocade patterns; late Edo period, 6" diameter, **$1,200–$1,600.**

Box and cover, the lid with a writhing gold dragon, signed Kozan, Meiji period, 3¼" diameter, **$300–$475.**

Box and cover, flower form, the exterior with gold phoenix, the interior with bamboo and prunus, early Meiji period, 3" diameter, **$650–$800.**

Left: *Satsuma box with floral motif in colors and gilt, late Edo / early Meiji period,* **$700–$900.** Right: *Satsuma box and cover with floral motif in gosu (blue), red, and gilt; the interior painted with flowers; late Edo period, 3¾" diameter,* **$1,800–$2,400.**

Box and cover in the form of a drum, overall motif of fruit and flowers, colors and gilt, 3" diameter, c1900, **$350–$550.**

Bucket, the body with a continuous landscape and birds in flight, gilt handle and bar, c1885, 7" high, **$200–$300.**

Bucket, the body with blue and lavender morning glories and green foliage, gilt trim, c1890, 6½" high, **$225–$325.**

Censer and cover decorated with panels of warriors and court ladies, the cobalt blue ground with gilt foliate scrolls, signed *Kinkozan*, late Meiji period, 5" high, **$2,000–$2,700.**

Censer and cover decorated with figures in a garden, trailing purple and white wisteria and gilt highlights, Meiji period, 6" high, **$400–$600.**

Censer and cover; the sides with panels of figures including bijin, courtiers, and entertainers (as well as birds) in a landscape; the pierced cover with overall gilt diapers; hairlines, Meiji period, signed *Seikozan*, 6" high, **$2,000–$3,000.**

Censer and cover decorated with children playing various games, the pierced cover and ground with 1000 Flowers, restored chips and finial, hairline, signed *Yabu Meizan*, c1910, 3½" high, **$2,000–$2,500.**

Censer and cover, samurai and attendants within diapered patterns in colors and gilt, late 19th century, 8" high, **$200–$300.**

Censer and cover; the body with panels of foliage and mums; the ground with scattered mon and scrolls; angular handles; mask and tongue legs; Shishi finial; gilt, iron red, and blue; rim cracks; signed *Masanobu*; early 19th century, 9" high, **$2,800–$3,700.**

Censer and cover; the silver lid pierced with peony; the cylindrical body decorated with foliate roundels on a diaper ground; iron red, gilt, white, black, and turquoise; early 19th century, 4" high, **$1,500–$2,000.**

Censer and cover, reticulated overall, gilt borders, c1910, 4" high, **$1,000–$1,500.**

Chaire with a continuous scene of children in colors and gilt, 2½" high, Meiji period, **$600–$800.**

Satsuma censer (sans lid) decorated with floral motifs in colors and gilt, signed Kinkozan, *c*1910, 4" diameter, **$900–$1,250.** Courtesy of Howard and Florence Kastriner.

Cha wan decorated with fan-shaped panels filled with flowers and foliage, Meiji period, **$300–$500.**

Cha wan decorated with phoenix and flowers, late Edo/early Meiji period, **$500–$600.**

Censer and cover; hexagonal; each side with floral lappets in colors and gilt; pierced shakudo, shibuichi, and silver lid; blue mon on the base; late Edo period, 6" high, **$3,500–$4,500.**

Censer and cover, lozenge form with fan-shaped panels of kiku surrounded by dragons and clouds, a mixed alloy lid, the base with a blue mon, late Edo period, 7" high, **$2,000–$3,000.**

Censer and cover, the body with 1000 Flowers pattern, replacement lid (pierced wood), signed *Yabu Meizan*, c1900, 3" high, **$1,000–$1,500.**

Censer and cover; the silver lid pierced with peony; the cylindrical body decorated with foliage roundels on a diaper ground; iron red, gilt, white, black, and turquoise; early 19th century, 4" high, **$1,500–$2,000.**

Censer and cover, reticulated overall in a basket-weave pattern, c1910, 4" high, **$1,000–$1,500.**

Chaire, a continuous scene of children in colors and gilt, 2½" high, Meiji period, **$600–$800.**

Charger, foliate, colors and gilt, Rakan and Kannon and their attributes, diapered rim, the halos in raised gilt, c1915, 12" diameter, **$700–$1,000.**

Cha wan decorated with fan-shaped panels filled with flowers and foliage in colors and gilt, Meiji period, **$300–$450.**

Cha wan decorated with phoenix and flowers, late Edo/early Meiji period, **$500–$600.**

Cha wan decorated with the Seven Gods of Good Luck and their attributes; iron red, blue, and gilt, with a diapered rim and a lappet band; the base with a blue mon; c1860, 4" diameter, **$1,000– $1,500.**

227

Seto Satsuma charger with Kanzan and karako in colors and gilt, late Edo period, Japanese, 15½" *diameter,* **$1,000–$1,500.**

Cricket cage, the pierced body held by a cloth formation (which is also the handle), painted with fans and flowers, finial missing, late Meiji period, 8" high, **$500–$700.**

Dish, colors and gilt with a large gathering of Rakan and attendants in a landscape, diaper band around the rim, signed H*ododa*, Taisho period, 12" diameter, **$450–$650.**

Dish, kiku form, the diapered petals radiating from a central panel of figures, colors and gilt, c1910, 6⅜" diameter, **$800–$1,200.**

Dish supported by a monkey at one end and a dog at the other, landscape motif, the dog's neck cracked and restored, signed K*inkozan*, late Meiji period, 6½" long, **$400–$600.**

Satsuma ewer; motif of Rakan, Kannon, and dragon; gilt and colors; Japanese, 1915–25, 6½" high, **$500–$700.**

Satsuma ewer with cover, decorated in colors and gilt, the base signed Toyosai, late Edo period, **$1,800–$2,700.**

Dish, the interior with karako playing within a formal band which is bordered by chrysanthemum sprays, signed Meizan, 5¾" diameter, **$800–$1,200.**

Dish, leaf shape with motif of a suzuribako (writing box) in colors and gilt, Meiji period, 9¾" diameter, **$425–$575.**

Dish, colors and gilt with three birds amongst flowers and grasses, floral border, signed Kinkozan, late Meiji period, 8" diameter, **$600–$800.**

Figure of a bijin holding a handscroll, her robes decorated in clouds motif, colors and gilt, one hand restored, hairlines coming up from the base, late 19th century, 14½" high, **$500–$750.**

Figure of a seated Daruma; his robe and cowl in iron red, blue, and gilt, and decorated overall in repetitive kiku mon; mid-19th century, 7½" high, **$1,500–$2,500.**

Figure of Daikoku holding mallet and standing on a rice bail; his attire in red, blue, white, gilt, black, and turquoise; mid-19th century, 8" high, **$2,000–$2,700.**

Figure of an elder seated on a tatami mat, colors and gilt, early 20th century, 5" wide, **$400–$600.**

Figure of a standing elephant; the saddle decorated in blue, iron red, gilt, and colors; c1800, 7" high, **$3,500–$4,500.**

Figure of a standing elephant; brown body with orange, green, and gold saddle; early Showa period, 6" high, **$200–$275.**

Figure of Hotei; his robes in black, green, and gold with phoenix medallions; late Meiji period, 10½" high, **$700–$1,000.**

229

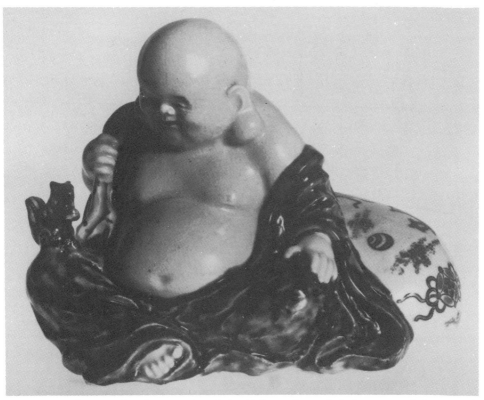

Satsuma, seated Hotei with sack, a squirrel perched at his knee, colors and gilt, Japanese, early Meiji period, 6" high, **$500–$750.**

Figure of Hotei seated on sack and holding a fan, hands and feet repaired, late Meiji period, 10¼" high, **$200–$375.**

Figure of an Immortal; his patterned robe in colors and gilt, his beard and mustache black; he holds a fan which has been restored; hairlines and chips; Meiji period, 27½" high, **$1,200–$1,800.**

Figure of Kannon, her robes and cowl heavily gilded with repetitive geometric designs, c1900, 12" high, **$375–$500.**

Figure of Kannon; her robe and cowl decorated in brown, red, orange, blue, and green with gilt accents; overall floral diapers; c1925, 12" high, **$200–$300.**

Figure of Kannon, her loose robes and cowl in colors and gilt, repaired hands, early Showa period, 16" high, **$200–$300.**

Figure of Kanzan; attire decorated in floral patterns, colors, and gilt; signed *Gahokoku*; Meiji period, 10" high, **$1,000–$1,500.**

Figure of Okame holding a fan, her robes in colors and gilt with floral motifs, late 19th century, 12" high, **$400–$600.**

230

Satsuma mizutsugi with motif of fans, moriage motifs within the fans, color and gilt, late 18th / early 19th century, **$2,000–$3,000.**

Satsuma model of a dog, Bekko (tortoiseshell) glaze, Japanese, late Edo period, 8" high, **$3,000–$5,000.** Courtesy of Howard and Florence Kastriner.

Figure of Rakan seated on rock-work, his loose-fitting robe decorated in colors and gilt, damaged, early Meiji period, 10¼" high, **$750–$1,000.**

Figure of a Shishi with gilt, circular designs; early 19th century, 7" high, **$1,200–$1,500.**

Figure of a Shishi and tama, brown with colors and gilt, Showa period, 7½" high, **$100–$125.**

Figure of a standing woman, her kimono in colors and gilt with a motif of maple leaves and streams; she holds a fan; early Meiji period, 12½" high, **$1,000–$1,500.**

Figure of a woman; her robes in brown with red, orange, green, and gilt mon; Showa period, 14" high, **$150–$185.**

Jar and cover, ovoid body with three panels of peony between formal borders, matching lid with knop finial, c1850, 9" high, **$1,800–$2,500.**

Jar and cover, two panels with village and lakeside scenes, the ground with 1000 Flowers, cover painted to match, signed *Yabu Meizan*, late Meiji period, 10" high, **$2,500–$3,500.**

Jar and cover, the body with oval reticulated panels between panels showing figures in a garden with maple and wisteria, the shoulder and foot with flowers, reticulated cover, signed *Kinkozan*, late Meiji period, 8" high, **$2,500–$3,500.**

Jar, the ovoid body decorated with peony and Shishi, colors and gilt, cover missing, marked *Satsuma yaki* (in gold on a black reserve), c1915, 9" high, **$200–$275.**

Jardinière decorated with the Seven Gods of Good Luck, colors and gilt, signed *Dai Nihon Satsuma yaki*, Meiji period, 11¼" diameter, **$700–$900.**

Jardinière; panels of samurai and attendants; brown ground decorated with trailed yellow, red, and blue enamels; c1915, 9" diameter, **$225–$375.**

Napkin holder; cylindrical; Three Friends motif in iron red, blue, gilt, and colors; late Edo period, 4" high, **$800–$1,000.**

Napkin holder, cylindrical, decorated with Tomoe mon in colors and gilt, late Meiji period, 3¾" high, **$400–$600.**

Plate, cobalt and gilt ground surrounding a central motif of three women in a garden, late Taisho period, signed *Kinkozan*, 8" diameter, **$1,000–$1,500.**

Plate, colors and gilt with a seascape, several boats, the narrow border worked in a gilt diaper, signed *Kinkozan*, late Meiji period, 9½" diameter, **$400–$500.**

Plate, fan shape supported on three stub legs, motif of maple leaves in autumnal colors and gilt, c1930, 10" wide, **$175–$275.**

Plate; iron red, blue, and gold; a mountainscape; the border with a lappet band which is carried over to the reverse; marked *Satsuma yaki* with a blue mon on the base; late Edo period, 10" diameter, **$3,000–$4,000.**

Plate, rectangular, dragon and Rakan in gilt and colors, late Taisho period, 8½" × 12", **$300–$500.**

Plate, the central motif (warrior's headgear and flowers) in colors and gilt, a gilt diaper border, c1900, 8½" diameter, **$600–$775.**

Plate, two girls in low relief in a garden scene, a gilt diaper border, the motif in colors with heavy gilt, Taisho period, 7" diameter, **$200–$300.**

Teapot decorated with a mass of flowers on the lid, spout, handle, and two-thirds of the body; signed *Kinkozan*; late Meiji period, 7" high, **$300–$500.**

Teapot, discus form with alternating bands of flowers and foliage, supported on three legs, bail bamboo handle, early Showa period, 5" diameter, **$200–$275.**

Teapot modeled as a cockerel and decorated in colors, blue, and gilt; realistic in appearance; legs restored; handle damaged; early 19th century, 7½" long, **$1,200–$1,600.**

*Kyoto Satsuma oval platter, a wizard and his monkey, colors and gilt, Japanese, early Meiji period, 16"
wide, **$500–$750.***

Teapot decorated with figures of seated
Rakan and dragons, with Kannon; in
colors and gilt; marked *Hododa*; early
20th century, **$250–$375.**

Tea set: teapot, sugar and creamer, six
cups and saucers, and six cake plates;
a motif of bamboo in green with gilt
highlights; c1935, **$200–$300.**

Tea set; brown ground with Rakan,
Kannon, and dragon; dragon spouts;
c1935, **service for 6, $250–$350.**

Tea set: teapot, covered sugar and
creamer, six cups and saucers, and six
cake plates; each piece decorated with
wisteria pattern; c1935, **$300–$475.**

Tea set, each piece decorated with a
woman seated next to a child in a garden setting, c1920, **service for 4,
$300–$500.**

Tea set: teapot, covered sugar, open
creamer, and six cups and saucers;
overall motif of 1000 Flowers; signed
Yabu Meizan; c1905, **$2,000–$3,000.**

Tokkuri; double-gourd form with two
diapered panels and two panels of
scattered kiku and foliage; blue, iron
red, and gilt; first half of the 19th century, 6½" high, **$1,500–$2,500.**

Tokkuri, double-gourd form with birds
and flowers in colors and gilt, the neck
with gilt diaper, Meiji period, 8½" high,
$350–$550.

Tokkuri, the body with brown and blue
glazes and flowers and foliage in gilt,
Edo period, 7½" high, **$2,000–$3,000.**

Umbrella stand, brown ground with
panels of warriors and attendants,
overall designs in trailed colored
enamels, c1915, **$300–$550.**

233

Satsuma vase in beaker form; applied motifs of young girl, her dog, basket of fruit, trees, foliage, and grasses; Mt. Fuji in low relief; colors and gilt; Japanese, c1900, 16" high, **$3,500–$5,500.** *Courtesy of Howard and Florence Kastriner.*

Vase, two reserves of figures on a floral ground, c1930, 6" high, **$200–$300.**

Vase, baluster form with a continuous rural scene (including huts and a procession), the neck and foot with cobalt and gilt scrolls, signed *Kinkozan*, Taisho period, 6" high, **$1,000–$1,500.**

Vase, barrel form with birds perched on flowering prunus branches above and below gold diaper bands, Taisho period, 9" high, **$200–$300.**

Vase, beaker form, decorated with figures in a garden, signed *Ryozan*, late Meiji period, 6" high, **$450–$600.**

Satsuma cylindrical vase on tripod feet, colors and gilt with a floral motif, base marked Kinkozan, *Japanese, c1915, 5" high,* **$500–$700.**

Vase, colors and gilt with Rakan molded in relief on a scenic ground, the neck with a band of dragons, chipped rim and foot, late Meiji period, 14" high, **$300–$500.**

Vase, two panels of figures in garden landscapes divided by a cobalt ground filled with gilt flowers, signed *Shuzan*, late 19th century, 5¾" high, **$300–$475.**

Vase, a processional, the shoulders with a floral band, colors and gilt, cracked, signed *Kinkozan*, c1900, 4" high, **$150–$200.**

Satsuma vase with motif in colors and gilt, Japanese, c1955, 8" high, **$75–$100.**

Satsuma vase with handles in the form of Daikoku's mallet; the motif in gosu (blue), gilt, and red; base with blue mon; late Edo period, 5" high, **$1,500–$1,800.**

Vase decorated with 100 Antiques between ruyi bands and chrysanthemum lappets; iron red, blue, and gilt with colors; blue mon on the base; 9" high, **$2,500–$3,500.**

Vase, double gourd, cobalt blue with gilt dragons, signed Kinkozan, late Meiji period, 4" high, **$400–$600.**

Vase, double gourd with panels of courtiers kneeling before a daimyo, the ground with brocade patterns, colors and gilt, late 19th century, 5" high, **$375–$485.**

Vase, globular with a short neck, the body with two Shishi and tama on each side, lappet band on the foot and neck, late Edo period, 7½" high, **$1,200–$1,800.**

Vase, globular, colors and gilt with chrysanthemums and butterflies above and below lappets, marked Satsuma yaki (and with blue mon), Edo period, 11" high, **$3,000–$4,000.**

Vase, hexagonal with Rakan molded in relief, a writhing dragon in relief, colors and gilt, late Taisho/early Meiji period, 11" high, **$500–$700.**

Vase, motif of flowers and grasses beside a stream, the shoulder with butterflies and a fan, colors and gilt, 6" high, c1915, **$300–$400.**

Vase, a peacock in colors and gilt perched on a flowering branch, colorful plumage, late 19th century, 8½" high, **$450–$600.**

Vase, a continuous scene of figures in a village beside a lake, the shoulder with birds and flowers, colors and gilt, c1915, 4" high, **$200–$300.**

Vase, baluster form, molded in low relief with warriors and women in gardens, cobalt blue ground with gilt scrolls, signed *Kinkozan*, c1910, 8" high, **$500–$750.**

Vase, continuous pattern of Immortals and attendants beneath trees, colors and gilt, late 19th century, 4" high, **$300–$400.**

Vase; the motif includes three egrets, bamboo, and flowering grasses in colors and gilt; signed *Kinkozan*; 6½" high, **$450–$675.**

Vase; ovoid body; decorated with orchids and a stream; the shoulder with phoenix and kiri leaves; iron red, blue, green, and gilt; the base marked *Satsuma yaki*; late Edo period, 17" high, **$4,000–$6,000.**

Vase, the body decorated with frogs in various poses in colors and gilt highlights, early Meiji period, 7" high, **$500–$700.**

Vase, double gourd, decorated with figures overlooking a lake, a village scene in the background, brocade borders, colors and gilt, rim and foot damaged, signed *Yabu Meizan*, c1910, 4¾" high, **$700–$950.**

Vases, ovoid form, colors and gilt with chrysanthemum and bamboo fences above and below a blue border with gilt floral roundels, marked *Satsuma yaki*, Meiji period, 11" high, **pair, $1,200–$1,800.**

Satsuma vase; modified pear shape; gosu (blue), gilt, and red; late Edo period, 8" high, **$3,000–$4,500.**

Satsuma mizusashi (water jar) with delicate motifs of peacocks and foliage highlighted in gilt, late Edo period, 6" high, **$1,500–$1,800.**

Satsuma water coupe, undecorated, early 20th century, 4" high, **$200–$300.**

Vases; slender baluster form with motifs of vases and koro in iron red, blue, gilt, and colors; marked *Satsuma yaki*; late Edo period, 7½" high, **pair, $1,500–$2,000.**

Vases, brown ground with Rakan in colors and gilt highlights, early Showa period, 12½" high, **pair, $200–$300.**

Vases decorated with pheasants and bamboo in colors and gilt highlights; the neck, foot, and side panels in cobalt blue with gilt foliage; c1920, 8" high, **pair, $300–$500.**

Vase, 1000 Flowers motif in colors and gilt, signed *Kinkozan*, Taisho period, 7" high, **$1,000–$1,500.**

Vase, modified mallet shape, the four squared sides with two panels of gardens and diaper neck, the panels within the diaper contain village scenes with townspeople, rim and foot in colors and gilt, Tokyo school, late 19th century, 9" high, **$900–$1,200.**

Vase; modified pear shape with slender neck; alternating bands of flowers, diaper, and figures in a processional; signed *Meizan;* c1900, 4½" high, **$1,500–$2,500.**

Vase; oviform; iron red, blue, gilt, and colors with birds flying below wisteria and above capped waves; blue mon on the base; late Edo period, 8" high, **$2,000–$3,000.**

Satsuma blank decorated in the United States with a motif of pink cockatoos and flowers in shades of pink and fuchsia, c1926, 8" high, $300–$500.

Vase, ovoid, scholars beneath trees in colors with gilt highlights, applied chrysanthemum-form handles, Taisho period, 5¾" high, **$200–$300.**

Vase supported on the back of a Shishi, the vase with panels of figures, chipped, hairlines, c1920, 9" high, **$600–$800.**

Vases decorated in orange and gold maple leaves and branches, signed *Kinkozan*, c1920, 4½" high, **pair, $300–$450.**

Vases, mirror image, the shoulders with a procession of figures attending a festival, the neck and foot with gilt diapers, c1910, 18" high, **pair, $1,500–$2,100.**

Satsuma Decorated Blanks

Bowl, Bouquet Pattern, Pickard Studios, Chicago, 8" diameter, **$600–$800.**

Box and cover, stub feet, decorated with irises and spring flowers in pastel hues, dated September 1919, 6½" diameter, **$500–$700.**

Box and cover supported on four legs, a geometric pattern in gilt and black, c1920, 6" diameter, **$350–$450.**

Bowl, a geometric pattern in varied shades of orange and deep red with black and gilt trim, signed L.G., 1919, **$300–$500.**

Humidor decorated with a geometric pattern on the lid and body, gold and black, **$650–$800.**

Vase; motif of orange, blue, green, and yellow flowers; dated 1923; 7" high, **$450–$500.**

Vase, a band of pink and blue flowers around the center, signed H.D., 1923, 7" high, **$300–$500.**

Vase, black rim, the body with green and orange geometric designs, signed M.D., 1913, 5½" high, **$400–$600.**

Seto

Bottle/vase, pear-shaped, crackled olive brown glaze, late 17th/early 18th century, 12½" high, **$600–$800.**

Cha wan, cream glaze with blue-green curtain glaze, early Meiji period, **$100–$200.**

Dish ("horse's eye"); large, brown-glazed spiral patterns around a plain, deep well; brown rim; late Edo period, 10" diameter, **$500–$700.**

Plate, pale celadon crackled glaze with enameled motif of a tortoise and frog, late 19th century, 7" diameter, **$300–$375.**

Seto-ware triple gourd bottle with applied tie, brown glazes, lacquer repair at the lip, Japanese, 8" high, 18th century, **$900–$1,200.**

Seto-ware vase with scaleless dragon in high relief, the vase with a flambé glaze, Japanese, c1900, 7" high, **$300–$500.** Courtesy of Richard A. Bowser.

Seto-ware stemmed bowl, the body with reticulated floral motifs, the interior of the bowl decorated with carp, all in greens and blues, Japanese, 18th century, 6" high, **$4,000–$5,000.**

Tokkuri, brown glaze to cream, late Edo period, 6" high, **$300–$400.**

Tokkuri, modified pear shape, short ring foot, decorated in underglaze blue on a light brown ground with birds and tree, late 17th/early 18th century, **$500–$700.**

Tazza decorated in underglaze blue with herons and willow below a key fret band, the foot with pierced floral mon and enameled foliage, 18th century, 12¾" high, **$5,000–$6,000.**

Stemmed bowl, the interior in aubergine and mustard with symbol of long life, the exterior a blue-green with blue motifs of insects, the base marked Makuzu Kozan, late 19th century, 5" high, **$2,000–$3,000.**

Kozan censer in celadon with a white slip motif of clouds and cranes, the base with a Kozan mark, the lid copper with perforations in the form of Tokugawa mon, Japanese, c1900, 5" high, **$1,500–$1,800.**

Shino

Dish, round with underglaze blue flowers on a white ground, 17th century, 6" diameter, **$2,000–$3,000.**

Shiragaki

Storage jar, baluster form, tapered to foot, rolled lip, four applied handles, olive green glaze, 18th century, 12½" high, **$700–$900.**

Storage jar, ovoid body with short neck, textured surface, brown glaze, 17th century, 20" high, **$500–$700.**

Soma

Bottle, globular body, tall neck with raised rim, gray crackled glaze, horse motif in brown slip, 19th century, 10" high, **$1,000–$1,500.**

Cha wan with Soma mon and horse motif, early 20th century, **$200–$250.**

Studio Ceramics

Bottle, squat and square, temmoku glazes, fitted wood box signed Kawai Kanjiro, 7" high, **$2,000–$3,000.**

Censer with silver lid; the floral motif featured on two panels of the body is cut out in the lid; the base is signed Tomimoto Kenkichi; Japanese, 5" high, **$2,500–$3,500.**

Box and cover, the cover of flower form, 3⅛" diameter, Kanjiro, **$600–$900.**

Box and cover, circular, pottery decorated with cranes nesting in a pine tree beneath a full moon, colors and gilt, signed Taizan, c1900, 5⅛" diameter, **$800–$1,200.**

Ewer in the form of an animal with archaistic motifs and mon with rabbits; gun metal, blue-green, and white; Japanese, Tanzan, c1910, **$1,800–$2,500.**

Inkwell with silver mounts, glass inserts, motif of crustaceans and waves in green, silver pen with writhing dragon in low relief, Japanese, c1910; the inkwell, **$500–$750,** *the pen* **$300–$500.** Courtesy of Richard A. Bowser.

Boat with removable roof, all white, the base with an impressed Kozan mark, c1905, Japanese, 18" diameter, **$1,000–$1,600.**

Oil dish in deep mustard-brown and brown-black, scenic motif, Seto style, the base with impressed Makuzu Kozan mark, late 19th century, Japanese, 6" diameter, **$1,800–$2,400.**

242

Two sake ewers in blue-green, white, and beige with motifs within motifs and diapers; each marked Tanzan; c1900, the largest 6" high. Left: Restored, **$500–$800.** Right: **$1,500–$1,800.**

Bowl, leaf form, porcelain, the blue ground with stem and ribs in low relief, impressed mark (Makuzu Kozan), late Meiji period, 12¼" long, **$1,500–$2,200.**

Bowl, porcelain, flower heads on a white ground, the base with a seal (Seifu), late 19th century, missing lid, **$500–$700.**

Brush pot, hexagonal, cream glaze over splashed iron abstract patterns, wood box, Shoji Hamada, 7¾" high, **$900–$1,200.**

Censer, tripod, globular body, celadon glaze, signed Seifu, porcelain, late 19th century, 3" high, **$1,000–$1,500.**

Cha wan, blue and yellow peony sprays, the base marked Seifu, early 20th century, **$300–$500.**

Dish, circular, colored glazes depicting leaves in a river bed, signed Ro (Rosanjin), 7½" diameter, **$1,500–$2,500.**

Dish, square, gray with orange-brown streaks, a motif of grass in white, Shino style, Rosanjin, 10½" square, **$2,500–$3,500.**

Dish, squared with upturned corners, Iga style, Rosanjin, 7½" diameter, **$900–$1,200.**

Model of two egrets in pottery, the details painted gray, beaks broken, marked Kozan (Miyagawa Kozan), c1885, 4¾" high, **$600–$900.**

Mizusashi, cylindrical, the ground shaded pink to white with clouds and Mt. Fuji, the cover glazed black to simulate lacquer, Seifu, c1900, 7¼" high, **$2,000–$3,000.**

Pitcher in blue-green, white, beige, and black with motifs within motifs, together with caricatures; Japanese, Tanzan, c1900, 8" high, **$1,500–$2,200.**

Vase; conical form; turquoise, beige, brown, and blue-green glazes with white accents; a play of motif within motifs; the base marked Tanzan; *Japanese, c1900, 7" high,* **$1,500–$1,800.** Courtesy of Howard and Florence Kastriner.

Plate, underglaze blue and white with a moon through bamboo, the motif carried over to the reverse, late 19th century, signed *Seifu,* 8¼" diameter, **$1,000–$1,500.**

Plate enameled in gilt and colors with ferns and daisies, signed *Taizan,* c1910, 8½" diameter, **$600–$800.**

Vase, flattened rectangular form, red and blue iris spray on a cream ground within blue bands, Kawai Kanjiro, 9" high, **$700–$1,000.**

Vase, café au lait ground with blue and white roundels filled with birds and foliage, porcelain, signed *Kawamoto Masakichi,* c1880, 18" high, **$5,000–$7,000.**

Vase, globular body, round ring foot, everted rim, motif of kiri and phoenix set against a scrolling vine, underglaze blue and white and café au lait with celadon ground, porcelain, signed *Kawamoto Masakichi,* 10¼" high, **$3,000–$4,000.**

Vase, copper red ground with a motif of morning glories in lavenders, signed *Kozan,* c1900, 6½" high, **$1,400–$1,800.**

Vase, baluster form, a dragon and waves in colors and underglaze blue, the base marked *Makuzu Kozan sei,* c1905, 10" high, **$1,400–$1,800.**

Vase, baluster form, decorated in shaded-green-to-mauve ground with a motif of wisteria coming down from the neck, the base marked *Makuzu Kozan,* 12½" high, c1900, **$2,500–$4,000.**

Vase, underglaze blue and red with band of foliate scrolls, Ju characters and stylized longevity symbols, cracked, signed *Katie zo,* 11½" high, Meiji period, **$400–$600.**

Vase, baluster form, underglaze blue and white with bamboo and leaf motif, signed *Makuzu Kozan,* c1900, 24½" high, **$3,500–$4,500.**

Porcelain vases with pink and green motifs, mei ping form, the bases signed Makuzu Kozan, *Japanese, c1910, 3½" high,* **each,** **$900–$1,200.**

Vase, ovoid form, porcelain, pale green graduated glaze with motif of huddled herons, signed *Seifu,* Meiji period, 4" high, **$700–$900.**

Vase, porcelain, copper red glaze, impressed mark (Seifu), 5" high, **$900–$1,200.**

Vase, beaker form, pale pink with white herons and plum blossoms, signed *Makuzu Kozan,* c1900, 7" high, **$1,500–$2,200.**

Vase, bulbous with a short neck, yellow ground with underglaze blue and white dragons and clouds, marked *Kozan sei* (Miyagawa Kozan), late 19th century, 7" high, **$1,200–$1,600.**

Vase decorated with three fish, pottery, colors and gilt, base marked *Makuzu Kozan,* late 19th century, 4" high, **$2,000–$3,000.**

Vase; double gourd; decorated with flowers, stems, and foliage on a brown ground; restored; base marked *Tanzan;* late 19th century, 4¾" high, **$800–$1,200.**

Vase decorated with cranes in flight above breaking waves, colors and gilt, marked *Tanzan,* c1900, 4" high, **$750–$950.**

Vase, hexagonal with birds flying amongst flowering peony branches, marked *Taizan,* 9" high, **$600–$850.**

Left: *Double gourd vase, deep blue ground with silver overlay motifs of maple leaves and scrolls.* Right: *Vase, deep-chocolate-colored ground with silver overlay irises and foliage. Both marked* Tanzan, *5" high,* **each, $900–$1,200.** Courtesy of Howard and Florence Kastriner.

Vase, globular form, trumpet neck, pottery, motif of maple leaves in gilt and autumnal hues against a cream-colored glaze, base signed *Makuzu Kozan* (seal), late 19th century, 9⅜" high, **$3,500–$5,000.**

Vase, globular, the motif of peaches and foliage in underglaze blue and copper red, base marked *Kozan*, c1900, 6" high, **$2,000–$2,500.**

Vase, double gourd, underglaze blue and white with groups of birds in flight above flowering branches, signed *Kawamoto Masakichi*, c1885, 15" high, **$1,500–$2,200.**

Vase, baluster form, pastel-hued magnolia and foliage, chip on base, underglaze blue seal, Ryosai, c1900, 7½" high, **$800–$1,200.**

Vase, baluster form, blue and violet morning glories in low relief, base signed *Ryosai*, c1890, 10" high, **$1,200–$1,800.**

Sumida Gawa bowl with three figures peering over the rim, red ground, Japanese, early 20th century, 6½" diameter, $225–$300.

Porcelain vase with carved motif of flowers and grasses, the full moon above, five curled legs, shades of pale blue and white, eggshell porcelain, Japanese, c1905, 6" high, $900–$1,200.

Vase, beaker form, underglaze blue and white with a motif of bamboo stalks, signed *Ryosai*, late 19th century, 8⅜" high, **$1,000–$1,500.**

Vase, globular form with a tall neck, graduated celadon ground with a pink and white floral motif, marked *Ryosai*, c1885, 8" high, **$1,000–$1,500.**

Vase, baluster form, light green graduating to pink and yellow with blossoming peony branches, marked *Shofu*, c1885, 7½" high, **$700–$900.**

Vase, oviform, shaded green to white, two herons in a pond with marsh plants, marked *Shofu*, c1885, 9" high, **$600–$900.**

Vase, ovoid, carved with kiku on a pale blue glaze, signed *Seifu*, c1900, 5¼" high, **$3,200–$4,000.**

Vase, ovoid with a graduated green ground and a motif of cranes in flight, impressed Seifu mark, late 19th century, 3½" high, **$900–$1,200.**

Vase; cylindrical with three bands containing pomegranates and foliage, scrolls, and chrysanthemums; signed Taizan; c1890, 6" high, **$800–$1,200.**

Vase, double gourd with birds perched on flowering prunus in colors and gilt, pottery, the base signed Taizan, c1900, 7½" high, **$1,200–$1,500.**

Vase, flared neck, bulbous body, decorated with panels of flowering branches, base marked Taizan, c1905, 7½" high, **$1,000–$1,500.**

Vase, creamy pink crackled glaze with a motif of a goose and marsh grasses under a full moon, lacquer repair on rim, signed Tanzan, 8" high, c1900, **$1,200–$1,500.**

Vase; double gourd; muted shades of green, brown, and blue in a leaf motif; marked Tanzan; late 19th century, 7½" high, **$600–$800.**

Vase decorated with three Tai fish in shades of brown and ochre on creamy glaze, rolled lip, pottery, marked Tanzan, c1900, 7" high, **$1,200–$1,800.**

Vase; bulbous body with long, tapered neck; a motif of flowers in colors and gilt on the neck and down one-third of the body; pottery; the base marked Ito Tozan; c1900, 9" high, **$600–$900.**

Sumida Gawa

Ashtray, black ground with the Seven Gods of Good Luck peering over the rim, late Meiji period, 5½" diameter, **$400–$500.**

Ashtray in the form of a badger, cartouche, c1910, **$250–$350.**

Ashtray, red body with a boy seated on the rim, cartouche, c1925, 2½" diameter, **$200–$300.**

Ashtray, circular with a house near the rim, impressed mark, 4" diameter, **$175–$225.**

Bottle/vase, a skeleton carrying a sake bottle, plus a badger on rock-work, 7⅜" high, **$900–$1,200.**

Censer (and cover) on three legs, elephant handles, the finial in the form of an elder, lid perforated, 5" high, **$400–$500.**

Coffeepot, Toby form, blue glaze, 9" high, **$400–$600.**

Cookie jar, temple form with a figure seated on the lid, the roof forms the lid, 9" high, **$500–$700.**

Flower bowl, three children peering over the rim, red ground, 3½" × 7", Taisho period, **$250–$325.**

Flower dish for cut flowers, ten men peering over the rim, green body, Taisho period, 9" diameter, **$300–$400.**

Figure of Hotei and sack (which is glazed blue), incised mark, 8" high, **$700–$1,000.**

Figure of Daruma; large, loose-ring earrings; black and white cowl and flowing robe; impressed mark on base; 9" high, **$700–$1,000.**

Figure of Rakan seated on a temple bell, his robe and cowl glazed, the bell with a red ground, 9" high, **$900–$1,200.**

Group, Three Wise Monkeys, 3" × 4", c1925, **$300–$400.**

Hanging basket, canoe form, five monkeys climbing into the canoe, cartouche, 12" × 4" × 3", **$1,000–$1,500.**

Sumida Gawa pitcher in the form of a man, his queue forming the handle, purple glazes, Japanese, early 20th century, 4¾" high, $250–$325.

Sumida Gawa vase with floral motif in high relief, early 20th century, $500–$750. Courtesy of Gardner Pond.

Humidor in the form of a man, his face contorted, his arms wrapped around his knees, the lid with a finial in the form of a boy, incised mark, 5½" high, **$600–$900.**

Jardinière; pale curtain glazes; worn red ground; large, bold morning glories and foliage in relief, cartouche, 5" × 6", **$450–$650.**

Jardinière and stand, red ground, writhing dragons in gray, the bowl 12" diameter, total height 26", **$2,500–$3,500.**

Mug, a goat in relief, black ground, cartouche, **$200–$275.**

Pitcher, red ground, black glaze, figures in various poses (drinking sake and burning incense, for example), cartouche, 12" high, **$700–$950.**

Shoe, red ground and curtain glazes, applied design of a child near the toe, incised mark, 6" long, **$500–$600.**

Teacup and saucer; red ground; glazed around the rim, handle, and border of the saucer; both pieces with a child engaged in play near a vase; incised mark; 3¾" high, **$200–$300.**

Teapot in the form of a sampan with a boy, a woven reed handle and waves at the base, incised mark, 7" long, **$700–$900.**

Teapot; red ground; curtain glaze on the handle, spout, lid, and upper body; the decoration includes a child at play; incised mark, 7" high, **$400–$600.**

Teapot, reed bail handle, black ground, blue curtain glaze, applied figures shooting a cannon, incised mark, **$700–$900.**

Toothpick in the form of a man's head, incised mark, 2" high, **$250–$350.**

Vase, green ground, two children on one side, a seated elder on the reverse, incised mark, 7" high, **$275–$325.**

Vase, irises in low relief on a red ground, cartouche, 24" high, **$2,500–$3,500.**

Vase, oviform with red ground, covered with monkeys wearing haori, damage to some of the monkeys, c1915, 14" high, **$1,000–$1,500.**

Vase, pinched form, black ground with a tiger on rock-work, incised mark, 8½" high, **$800–$1,200.**

Vase, red ground with Benten seated on rock-work and playing a biwa, low relief, 11" high, **$400–$500.**

Vase, the Seven Gods of Good Luck in low relief, marked *Made in Japan*, 8" high, **$200–$300.**

Vase with figures of two elders on rock-work, cartouche, 7" high, **$500–$700.**

Vase, one side of the base modeled as a grotto with a family of monkeys in various poses (being seated at a table and drinking tea, for example), cartouche, 18" high, **$2,000–$2,700.**

Vase, red ground with an octopus in relief, cartouche, 2¼" high, **$500–$600.**

Vase, red ground with three children in low relief, incised mark, 8" high, **$200–$300.**

Takatori

Cha wan, short ring foot, temmoku glaze stopping short of the body at the foot, Edo period, **$500–$700.**

Mizusashi, square form, mottled brown glaze, several cracks repaired with gold lacquer, wood cover, 18th century, 6½" high, **$2,000–$3,000.**

Mizusashi, white and blue curtain glaze over brown-black glaze, Meiji period, 6½" high, **$300–$400.**

Sake bottle, pear-shaped, brown crackled glaze, 18th century, 9" high, **$700–$900.**

Tamba

Chaire, ivory lid, late Edo period, 2½" high, **$600–$750.**

Chaire, the body with vertical knife marks and partly covered with brown glaze, ivory lid, 2¾" high, Edo period, **$450–$650.**

Jar, pear-shaped, black glaze splashed on a brown ground, a spout at the foot, late Meiji period, 21½" high, **$400–$600.**

Sake bottle, brown with black running glaze, Meiji period, 8⅞" high, **$100–$200.**

Sake bottle, buff pottery with white slip design, Meiji period, 10½" high, **$200–$300.**

Tokoname

Humidor, dragon and cloud motif in low relief, early Showa period, **$100–$250.**

Jardinière, dragon and cloud motif in low relief, marked *Made in Japan*, c1930, 15" diameter, **$250–$325.**

Teapot, dragon handle and spout, c1900, **$350–$450.**

Tea set, traditional and miniature, each piece 1¾" high, teapot with handle at a right angle, **$200–$300.**

Tokoname planter with dragon and cloud motif in low relief, Japanese, late Meiji / early Taisho period, 7″ × 9″, **$300–$400.**

Vase, dragon and cloud pattern in low relief, c1925, 6″ high, **$75–$100.**

Vase, dragon and cloud pattern, c1920, 9½″ high, **$100–$150.**

Vase, dragon and cloud pattern, c1915, 14″ high, **$150–$200.**

Yatsushiro

Bowl, mishima inlay, gray with white flowers, late Edo period, 7″ diameter, **$300–$400.**

Cha wan, gray with white inlay motif including a "cross" (Namban), Edo period, **$800–$1,200.**

Mizusashi, mishima inlay, floral band, late Meiji period, 6″ high, **$700–$900.**

251

10

Lacquer

Chinese Lacquer

Lacquer was commonly applied to wooden objects, sealing off their surface with a protective coating. Originally, however, the Chinese had an altogether different use for this preservative. Because it turns black when exposed to air, lacquer was first used—with a stylus—for writing on bamboo slips wrapped together or tied to form books. During the Han Dynasty lacquer was colored by the addition of metallic salts: Vermilion, or cinnabar, was produced with sulfide of mercury. With the discovery of ways to generate other hues, including black, brown, yellow, silver, gold, turquoise, olive green, and purple, lacquer became as popular for its ornamental value as it had been for its practicality.

Producing lacquer ware was a lengthy process. A base such as wood had to be planed very thin, then polished, after which a piece of paper, silk, or linen was applied to its surface. Next, layer after layer (20 to 30 coats) of lacquer was smoothed on, with each coat drying thoroughly. When enough coats had been applied, the lacquer could be painted. If the lacquer was to be carved, 200–300 coats were applied to create the necessary thickness.

Japanese Lacquer

The Japanese, besides using standard forms of lacquer production, created many aesthetically appealing innovations: raised work in colors; marbled lacquer; inlaid shell, gold, and silver leaf; pear-skin finishes; relief work using shell, foil, and so on *prior* to the application of the final coat; and using metal filings instead of gold or silver foil on the surface. Their lacquer wares may have metal, wood, paper, or ceramic bodies (bases).

Among the functional and decorative objects produced in Japanese lacquer are netsuke, inro, ojime, and hair ornaments.

Dating Chinese Lacquer

During the T'ang Dynasty, the dry hollow method of producing lacquer ware was developed. Layers of cloth saturated in lacquer were pressed onto a clay or wooden mold. When the lacquer had dried, the mold was removed, and the resulting cloth-based piece could be painted.

Sung Dynasty objects included red lacquer with carved landscapes, as well as small boxes with gold or silver bodies. In addition, mother-of-pearl inlay (lac burgauté) was used for Imperial wares. (As lac burgauté evolved, it also included gold and silver foil inlays.)

The Yüan Dynasty brought new techniques such as red lacquer carved in deep relief, painted lacquer with gold relief, and pierced lacquer.

During the Ming Dynasty, some pewter bodies were used for Chinese lacquer ware, and reign marks were added. Ming designs were bold; with the onset of the Ch'ing dynasty, designs became intricate and delicate by comparison.

Red lacquer was especially prominent in the Ch'ien Lung period of the Ch'ing Dynasty.

Korean Lacquer

Korean lacquer is highly polished with a mirror finish. It is usually found on metal bases. Most prominent are black or red objects sparsely decorated with mother-of-pearl motifs. Patterns include flowers, dragons, and flying cranes.

Lacquer Values

Lacquer book cover decorated in silver and gold takamakie and applied in aogai and ivory, Hotei sitting on bag of treasures before a frog dressed as a fisherman and two seated mice dressed in priest's garb, minor damages, chips and scratches, Japanese, c1883, 15½" × 12½". Realized price, Christie's East, New York City, $825.

Album for postcards, motif of flowers and birds with Shibayama inlay (mother-of-pearl, coral, and horn) on a black ground, Japanese, c1910, 14" × 11", **$200–$300.**

Box and cover; black ground; the cover, a group of gourds in takamakie, aogai, and gold hiramakie; signed *Zeshin*; Japanese, late 19th century, 3" diameter, **$3,000–$4,500.**

Box and cover, black, the lid carved with elephants and soldiers, a green floral border, Thai, 19th century, 11" long, 8" wide, 4½" deep, **$200–$300.**

Box and cover, black with gold and silver togidashi in a motif of huts and Mt. Fuji, Japanese, c1910, 2" square, **$150–$200.**

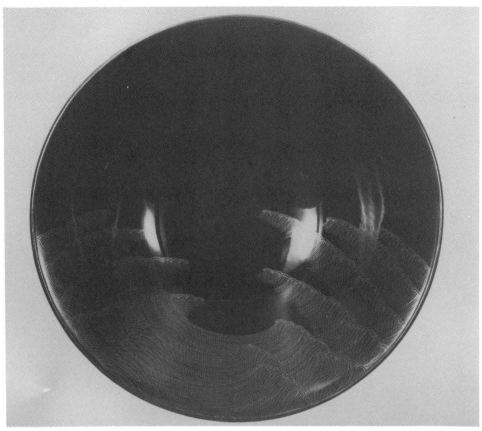

Lacquer bowl with gilt motif of waves in Korin style, silver rim, Japanese, late Meiji period, 14" diameter, **$1,000–$1,750.**

Box and cover, circular, gold hiramakie on a red ground with kiku and trellis pattern, nashiji interiors, Japanese, late 19th century, 3" diameter, **$1,500–$2,200.**

Box and cover, circular, the domed lid inlaid with a mother-of-pearl floral spray in brown lacquer, overall mother-of-pearl coin pattern, old minor damages, Korean, Yi dynasty, 18th century, 4" diameter, **$800–$1,200.**

Box and cover, fan-shaped, nashiji interiors, kinji ground, the lid covered with mums, Shibayama inlay, Japanese, late 19th century, 6" wide, **$1,500–$2,000.**

Box and cover (kogo); red lacquer ground with black motifs of insects, flowers, and foliage in a continuous motif (continued on the reverse); Japanese, 4" diameter, Taisho period, **$1,000–$1,500.**

256

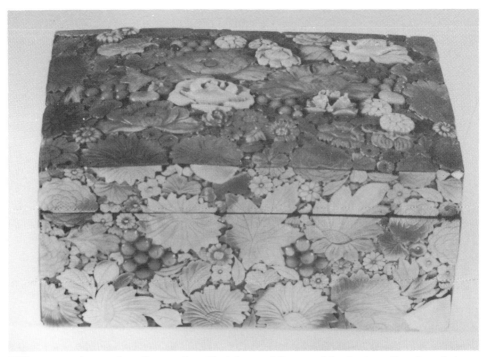

Shibayama-on-lacquer box; the overall motif of flowers, foliage, and berries in mother-of-pearl, ivory, coral, and jade; Japanese, late 19th century, 4½" × 3¾", **$3,500–$5,500.**

Box and cover, fish form, red and black, Japanese, c1935, 12" long, **$100–$150.**

Box and cover, guri, carved with scroll design, age cracks, Japanese, 18th century, 4¼" diameter, **$600–$900.**

Box and cover, lac burgauté, circular, inlaid with gilt foil in hexagonal cells around a mother-of-pearl flower head, Chinese, 18th century, 2" diameter, **$350–$500.**

Box and cover, lacquer and leather, hand-painted with landscape scenes on a brown ground, brass fittings, Chinese, c1920, 15" long, 9" wide, 8" deep, **$125–$185.**

Box and cover, lacquer and leather, hand-painted with landscape scenes on a red ground, brass fittings, Chinese, c1920, 15" long, 9" wide, 8" deep, **$200–$275.**

Box and cover, rectangular, cinnabar (red) lacquer carved overall with peony sprays, black interiors, the lid with a carved white serpentine oval plaque set in the red lacquer, Chinese, c1925, 9" × 12", **$400–$600.**

Box and cover, rectangular, brown ground decorated with tsuba and kozuka in gold and colored takamakie simulating various alloys, restored, Japanese, c1900, 4½" × 7¾" × 5", **$1,800–$2,500.**

Box and cover, round, cinnabar lacquer, black interiors, the lid carved with Shou Lao, overall scrolling vines, Chinese, late 19th century, 4" diameter, **$350–$500.**

Left: *Gofun brush with top in brown lacquer with gilt motifs, Japanese, c1900, 3" high,* **$250–$375.**
Right: *Box and cover (kogo), nashiji with gold motifs of bamboo and long-tailed tortoise (kame), Japanese, late 19th century, 3" high,* **$900–$1,250.**

Box and cover, round, cinnabar lacquer, the cover with a relief garden landscape and figures of three Immortals, overall squared spiral ground, Chinese, mid-to-late 19th century, 5½" diameter, **$500–$750.**

Box and cover; tsuishu; round; carved in relief: one side with a Rakan, the other with cell patterns; Japanese, 19th century, 3" diameter, **$700–$1,000.**

Box and hinged cover, rectangular, the cover with relief motif of birds and flowers, pewter interiors, Chinese, early 20th century, 9" diameter, **$200–$300.**

Box, tiered, cinnabar carved lacquer, old damages, Chinese, Ch'ien Lung (Qianlong), 18th century, 11½" high, **$1,500–$2,500.**

Candy dish and cover, orange and gold with silver mums on the lid, orange interiors, Japanese, c1935, 10" diameter, **$50–$75.**

Carved red lacquer (cinnabar) cylindrical tiered box, the top with a scenic motif, black lacquer interiors, Chinese, 18th century, 6" high, minor damage, **$1,200–$1,800.**

Censer, gold hiramakie, roiro ground, sparse motif of bamboo sprays, nashiji interior, Japanese, c1915, 3" diameter, **$100–$185.**

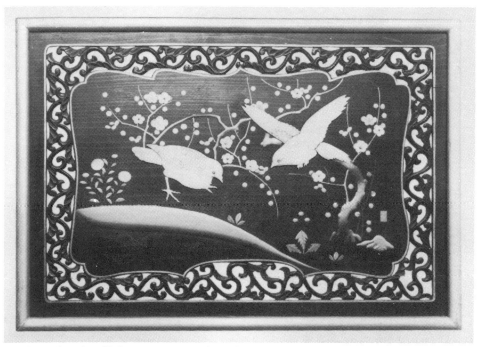

Wood panel with gold lacquer, ivory and mother-of-pearl inlay, Japanese, c1900, 20" × 14",
$800–$1,200.

Chest and cover decorated in gold hiramakie with mon, nashiji ground, copper mounts, cracked and faded, Japanese, Edo period, 25" × 60", **$6,000–$8,000.**

Coasters (6) with matching container box, black with gold peony blossoms, Japanese, c1935, **set, $20–$30.**

Document box (bunko) and cover; gold hiramakie, nashiji, takamakie, and hirame on roironuri ground with pine, grasses, and flowers in a continuous pattern; silver rims; chipped and cracked; cover warped; Japanese, late 18th/early 19th century, 10" wide, 13½" long, 3¾" deep, **$2,000–$3,000.**

Inro storage box (inrobako) with five drawers, detachable front lid, gold and silver togidashi with water plants and grasses on a mura nashiji ground, silver pulls and mounts, chipped and cracked, warped, three drawer pulls missing, Japanese, late Meiji period, 10½" × 11¼" × 8¾", **$1,200–$1,800.**

Jewelry box, black lacquer with painted scenic motif, musical, Japanese, c1955, 12" × 10" × 12", **$50–$75.**

Kodansu; one hinged door enclosing three drawers; the kinji ground decorated in shades of gold and orange takamakie, hiramakie, kirigane, muranashiji, and togidashi; buildings and landscapes; the drawers with grasses; silver mounts; mura nashiji interiors; Japanese, 19th century, 4¾" × 4" × 3½", **$5,700–$7,000.**

Lacquer mirror stand, nashiji with gold motifs and scrolls, Japanese, late Edo period, **$1,800–$2,500.**

Lazy Susan, orange and gold with gold and silver mums in low relief, Japanese, c1935, 12" diameter, **$50–$75.**

Mirror case, gold hiramakie and togidashi with dragonflies, nashiji interior, badly chipped, Japanese, early 20th century, **$200–$400.**

Model of Buddha seated with legs crossed, dry lacquer, jeweled necklaces showing through open robes, red and gold, old damages, Chinese, 17th century, 16½" high, **$900–$1,200.**

Model of Buddha seated on hexagonal lotus base with hands clasped around the right knee; traces of red, black, and gilt; some old damages; Chinese, 17th century, 14½" high, **$800–$1,200.**

Model of Daikoku's mallet, gold with wood-grain body, restored, Meiji period, 5½" long, **$900–$1,200.**

Model of a dignitary seated on a throne; red, gold, and black lacquer; beard made of human hair; some flaking; Chinese, c1900, 10½" high, **$200–$300.**

Model of Kuan Yin, carved cinnabar lacquer, the robes with repetitive square patterns and flower heads, both hands raised, Chinese, late 19th century, 12½" high, **$900–$1,200.**

Model of Shou Lao holding a staff and peach, cinnabar, his robe with Shou characters and cell patterns, some chipping at the bottom of the robe, Chinese, late 19th century, 14" high, **$900–$1,200.**

Panel (taken from a cabinet door and framed), black and gold takamakie with two birds perched on a branch beneath the full moon, Japanese, Taisho period, framed size 15" X 20", **$200–$325.**

Sake barrel, red and black, the sides carved in relief to simulate twisted ropes, Japanese, late Meiji period, 23" wide, **$400–$600.**

Sake kazu (wine pot), globular with gold kiku and scrolls on a silver ground, black lacquer handle, Japanese, late Meiji period, 5½" diameter, **$400–$650.**

Screen, three-panel, each panel with a continuous scene of children playing, the upper portion of each panel having floral clusters and old damages, Chinese, early 20th century, each panel 18" X 72", **$1,000–$1,500.**

Sewing box, oblong, black and gilt, hinged cover, interior with ivory accessories, Chinese, early 19th century, 14" wide, **$1,200–$1,600.**

Lacquer tea caddy (natsume) with silk brocade pouch, motif of maple leaves flowing upstream, late Edo period, **$1,500–$2,500.**

Shrine (portable zushi), black case containing Amida Nyorai standing on a lotus pedestal, gilt wood figure of Bodhisattva on each door, copper hinges, mandala missing, Japanese, early Meiji period, 28½" high, **$3,000–$4,000.**

Tabako-bon in gold and silver hiramakie, hirame, and heidatsu with flowering cherry trees; one wide drawer below two smaller drawers, the top with silver liners and silver covers; silver carrying handle; cracked and chipped; Japanese, late 19th century, **$2,500–$3,500.**

Tabako-bon, rectangular, rounded corners, gold hiramakie and heidatsu with mother-of-pearl inlaid motif of maple and cherry branches floating in a river, silver rims, nashiji interiors, scratched and minor chipping, Japanese, late Meiji period, 11½" × 9" × 6", **$4,500–$6,500.**

Tabako-bon; roironuri decorated in gold, silver, and red takamakie, hiramakie, hirame, nashiji, and heidatsu with red-capped Manchurian cranes in the sunset above peony blossoms and branches; the base fitted with a drawer below two smaller drawers; the top with two copper liners and silver covers; sentoku carrying handle; damaged; Japanese, late 19th century, 9" wide, **$1,200–$1,500.**

Tea caddy (natsume) in gold hiramakie and heidatsu on a red-brown ground with a motif of seashells, nashiji interior, chipped and cracked, Japanese, early 19th century, 3½" high, **$650–$850.**

Table screen, cinnabar, rectangular, carved with figures before a pavilion, the reverse with ladies in a landscape, the base and sides carved with lotus heads and foliage on a spiral pattern ground, restored, Chinese, c1900, 16" high, **$800–$1,200.**

261

Tray, black with sparse gold plum branches, Japanese, c1930, 15¼" X 20", **$150–$250.**

Tray, lac burgauté inlaid with iridescent shell in a scenic motif with pairs of figures, Chinese, 18th century, 4½" square, **$375–$485.**

Tray, cinnabar, canted rectangular form, the central pattern with children in a garden, the border with peony scrolls that continue on the underside, Chinese, early 19th century, 9" X 11", **$900–$1,200.**

Tray for kimono, gold hiramakie with a mon, nashiji underside, Japanese, c1920, 25" long, **$1,000–$1,500.**

Tray, oval, gold takamakie on a nashiji ground with a scene featuring Samurai with banners, Japanese, late Meiji / early Taisho period, 14¼" long, **$300–$400.**

Tray, oval, motif of a warrior on horseback, gilt on black, Burmese, c1900, 18¼" diameter, **$150–$300.**

Tray, lacquer/papier-mâché, red ground with gold designs of birds in flight, marked Made in Japan, c1930, 7½" X 13", **$200–$275.**

Tray, lacquer/papier-mâché, black ground with gold motif of blossoming branches, marked Made in Japan, c1930, 10½" X 13½", **$150–$225.**

Tray, rectangular, gold takamakie on a nashiji ground with a motif of clam shells, Japanese, late Taisho / early Showa period, 15½" long, **$300–$500.**

Tray, red with an incised pattern of a peacock and tree peony, overall cell pattern, cracked, Chinese, early 19th century, 18" wide, **$600–$800.**

Tray, round, lacquer/papier-mâché, black ground with sparse decoration of flowers in colors and gilt, marked Japan, c1935, 12½" diameter, **$200–$250.**

Tray and box, silver with gold and black hiramakie dragonflies, Japanese, Taisho period, 9" wide, **$500–$700.**

Vase, archaic beaker form, black surface on pewter inlaid with mother-of-pearl and gold foil, a continuous mountainscape, some losses, Chinese, early 18th century, 10½" high, **$600–$800.**

Vase with detachable stand, cinnabar carved with Shou roundels and floral bands, old damages, Chinese, early 19th century, 14" high, **$575–$750.**

Vase, ovoid form, trumpet neck, kinji ground with writhing dragon and nashiji interior, Japanese, late Meiji period, 8" high, **$1,000–$1,500.**

Vase and cover, cinnabar, carved with sages and attendants set in rocky landscapes, Chinese, 20th century, 10" high, **$225–$325.**

Vases; carved cinnabar lacquer; globular form; two panels, each inlaid with jade, mother-of-pearl, and coral in a motif of cranes and pine with trellis; carved ground; key pattern at the shoulders and necks; Chinese, c1900, 19½" high, **pair, $1,500–$1,900.**

Writing box (suzuribako); brown ground with mura nashiji decorated with a cherry tree, pine, and prunus in gold, silver, and colored togidashi; the interior with a fitted tray, ink stone, and water dropper (suiteki); cover chipped and cracked; Japanese, 19th century, 8¼" X 9½", **$2,500–$3,500.**

Suzuribako (writing box), black lacquer with gold and silver flowers and foliage, the interior with ink stone and water dropper, Japanese, late Meiji / early Taisho period, **$1,000–$1,500.** Private collection.

Writing box, hiramakie and togidashi on a roiro ground with motif of a large pine, gold hiramakie interior on a nashiji ground with wide-leaf bamboo, silver water dropper, the cases of the writing implements in gold nachiji with silver fittings, corner chipped and repaired, Japanese, Meiji period, 9¼" wide, 10⅝" long, 2⅜" deep, **$4,000–$5,000.**

Writing box; gold, silver, and red hiramakie inlaid in aogai on a gold-speckled black ground; motif of a gateway, trees, and foliage; the interior with nashiji ground and a willow motif; fitted with ink stone and silver water dropper; chips and crack; Japanese, late 18th / early 19th century, **$3,500–$5,000.**

11

Metalwares
Chinese Bronze

Emperor Huang Ti, the Yellow Emperor (2852–2597 B.C.), is recorded as having conceived of the idea for casting metal, thereby opening the door to the development of decorative and functional metalworks. The first bronze vessels, however, were not cast until approximately 2205 B.C., during the reign of Emperor Yu, the fifth emperor to follow Huang Ti. His reign saw the production of the tripod, in the form of three-legged bronze cauldrons. Eventually, the tripod became a symbol of Imperial power.

Collectors consider Shang/Yin era vessels as the focal point among early bronze pieces. Produced for religious and court ceremonies as well as domestic purposes, these vessels helped determine the rank or standing of a household; the more bronze a person or family owned, the more highly they were esteemed.

Early bronze pieces were finished with tools. Some of them were inlaid with black pigment or with gold and/or silver. They could also be partially gilded, and inlaid with semiprecious stones (mainly turquoise). Shang bronzes might even be ornamented with geometric motifs, animal designs, or bands of designs. A frequently used motif was (and still is) the *t'ao t'ieh*, or monster mask, a grotesque face having two eyes, eyebrows, nostrils, and only an upper lip.

Shang bronzes should be covered with a patina (corrosion produced by oxidation of the metal) which is a bluish green, yellowish, or reddish efflorescence. This patina is highly prized.

The defeat of the Shang brought about a new reign, the Chou Dynasty. Chou bronzes fall into periods: early, 1027–900 B.C.; middle, 900–600 B.C.; and late, 600–256 B.C., followed by the Warring States period, 255–222 B.C. At first, Chou bronzes were copies of Shang pieces, distinguished only by their more elaborate designs. Then came the heavier objects of the middle period, with handles and legs decorated with lower relief (not as sharp or high as Shang specimens). Vessels such as the ting had straight legs, and the yü, ku, tsun, and chüeh were no longer produced. Furthermore, the production of bronze animal forms dissipated.

Late Chou bronzes were given more delicate and intricate motifs. There was more use of silver, gold, and/or copper inlays. Pieces included dagger hilts, swords with turquoise stones inlaid, realistic human figures, animals, and personal accessories such as belt hooks, combs, hairpins, mirrors, and so on. Longer inscriptions were another characteristic of later Chou bronzes.

The short-lived Ch'in Dynasty, 221–206 B.C., was an oppressed time—a time during which bronzes with historical inscriptions were melted down. Following it was the Han Dynasty, 206 B.C.–220 A.D., when bronze was fashioned in a variety of functional forms (and sizes) such as dishes, bells, ewers, and basins. During this time, casting was done with the lost wax method. An exact model of the desired vessel was produced in wax, around which a clay mold was formed. A few holes were left in the clay mold so that the wax could be melted, drained, and replaced with molten metal. When the bronze hardened, the mold was usually broken off. If a mold composed of several pieces was used, the pieces could be separated to allow removal of the cast bronze, in which case the mold could be reused.

Han vessels, for the most part, contained 83 percent copper and 17 percent tin. Inlays included gold, silver, turquoise, and the addition of malachite; many pieces were silvered or gilded overall. Bowls, for instance, were usually void of motifs and covered with silver.

In general, bronzes of the Han Dynasty were simpler and more realistic than those from previous eras. Real animals were depicted instead of mythological ones, and the animals were elongated to produce the effect of motion: Horses, for example, are shown with outstretched feet.

During the Ming Dynasty, new processes for variegating the surface of the metal were developed. Reign marks came into use, and vessels based on ceramic shapes, in addition to those with fish-form, rope, phoenix, and elephant handles, were developed.

Included among bronze surfaces were chestnut brown, yellow gold, and crab apple, some of which featured gold raindrop forms or forms similar to gold snowflakes (splashed gold).

In the succeeding dynasty and into the twentieth century, fine Chinese bronzes continued to be produced. Collectors, therefore, have a tremendous range of objects to study. Accordingly, they must consider many factors—among them, stylistics, patina, and markings—in order to make proper age and value identifications. Early specimens often need TLT testing in order for their ages to be accurately determined.

Japanese Alloys

About 200 B.C., during the Han Dynasty, the influence of Chinese and Korean art and industry in producing metalwares reached Japan. The Japanese, quick to learn new methods from travelers, were not satisfied with copying bronze and iron objects, and began to produce their own: mirrors, swords, and bells, for instance. With the introduction of Buddhism in the sixth century A.D. and the resulting demand for images and other religious articles, Japanese metalwork progressed still further. By the eighth century, coinage had been introduced. Finally, the civil wars of the twelfth century brought weapons and armor into great demand, and with that, families of quality metalworkers and swordsmiths rose in prominence.

Later developments continued to strengthen the need for metalwork. With the advent of the tea ceremony, the manufacture of kettles and other utensils became significant. The opening of trade with the West in the sixteenth century led to the introduction of firearms.

During the Tokugawa period, 1615–1868, peace reigned and the art of the metalworker flourished. The bronze makers' art included architectural accoutrements, shrines cast entirely in bronze, and gates for temples. Large bronze lanterns were produced to line the courtyards of shrines.

As both the science of preparing metals and the art of designing them advanced, the Japanese developed a number of interesting alloys. Plentiful copper, known to some collectors for its successful application in hammered and enameled objects, was used chiefly in alloys such as bronze, shakudo, shibuichi, and sawari.

Shakudo is 3 to 6 percent gold. Suitable treatment by pickling and polishing produces a beautiful glossy patina of dark brown or bluish black on objects formed from this alloy. Shakudo makes a perfect ground for inlaid designs of gold, silver, and/or copper.

Komai compact, inlaid gold and silver scenic view with Mt. Fuji in the background capped in silver, Japanese, c1920, **$100–$150.**

Similarly, *shibuichi* has physical properties which make it excellent for inlays. It may consist of one part silver to three parts copper, one part silver to two parts copper, or a fifty-fifty mix of the two. The value of this alloy is dependent, in part, on its patina. When shibuichi is first cast, its color is that of pale gun metal. Its beauty comes with the gray tones that the mix produces.

Sawari, a mix of copper, tin, and lead, was used quite often for creating Buddhistic ceremonial articles.

Gold

Few gold objects were produced because the use of this metal was restricted in Japan. However, it was very popular in the gilding of copper, bronze, and so on, as well as for inlays and as part of the alloy shakudo. Gold was also suitable for lacquering, or was used alone in small articles such as ojime, menuki (sword pegs), and pouch clasps.

Komai match safe with inlaid gilt designs and a grape-and-leaf border around the reserves, Japanese, c1900, **$1,500–$1,850.**

Komai

In 1855, the Komai family originated a form of damascene (or Japanese *zogan*) used to ornament swords, guns, and various types of sword furniture. With the major changes brought about by the Meiji restoration, beginning in 1868, the Samurai were no longer allowed to wear swords, so the Komai family, like many others, had to find another form of livelihood. They applied their damascene craft to creating objects in Western and traditional Japanese styles. Their wares were very well received in the West and are highly prized today.

There were two makers of Komai wares working in Kyoto: S. Komai and O. Komai. Each used a different mark, but the quality of their work is the same. Komai-*style* works, on the other hand, look like genuine Komai, but were produced with a different metal body.

The following outline describes the process used to create damascene ware.

1. On a ground of steel, double hatch lines were cut with a chisel.
2. The outline of the design was drawn on paper and transferred onto the ground by means of the tracing method, in which a design could be copied through paper onto the ground with a small needle point.
3. Some combination of gold, silver, and/or copper was then pounded into the ground, following the pattern of the copied dots.
4. At this point, approximately 20 coats of lacquer were applied, each being baked onto the object before the next application.
5. The object was then rubbed and polished to a bright finish.

Chinese Silver

Silver has always been abundant in China. Among the many articles produced from this abundance, perhaps the finest are those of the T'ang Dynasty. During this period, silver was alloyed with tin and lead, cast into the desired shape, and finished with hammering. Handles and ring feet were soldered on, and sometimes a lining was added, especially when the motif came through to the other side. Many of the objects produced feature a ground closely packed with circles that were punched with a die on which the lines and surfaces of the design had been traced.

Yuan Dynasty silver, for the most part, had plain, beaten surfaces, with a floral medallion or flower-and-phoenix motif. During the Ming Dynasty, the limited amount of silver produced was either cast, engraved, traced, or finished with repoussé.

Chinese silver of the Ch'ing Dynasty enjoyed immense export popularity. This silver matched the shapes of Chinese export porcelains and was, for the most part, designed to meet the requirements of Western tastes, with patterns based on English and American patterns.

The following remarks from Charles L. Tiffany tell a great deal about why Chinese silver was in such demand. They were made following a visit to a silversmith on Old China Street, 1844.

> He can manufacture any article—from a salt spoon to a service plate—in the most elegant manner. He will line a pitcher with its coating of gold or produce a favorite pattern of forks in a very short time. The silver is remarkably fine and the cost of working it a mere song. Its intrinsic

value is, of course, the same as in Europe, but the poor creatures who perspire over it are paid only enough to keep the breath in their bodies. Filigree baskets or card cases seem to be favorites with these silversmiths. It is much cheaper to have a splendid service of plate in China than in any other country, and many Europeans send out orders through supercargoes.

The earliest Chinese maker of export silver was Pao Yun (c1810–1840). He was joined by a number of other makers who worked during the early to mid-nineteenth century (or shortly thereafter), many of whom copied English hallmarks. Some used initials and/or Chinese marks: W was used by Wo Shing or Wohing; an H, by Lee Ching of Hong Kong and Hoachings; WH, by Wang Hing from Queens Road, Hong Kong; CW, by Cum Wo. SS is associated with Synshing, and YS is associated with Yutshing.

Japanese Silver

Although pure silver ore is rare in Japan, lead ore containing considerable proportions of silver is common, and from ancient times has been the major source of silver for the Japanese. Extraction of the silver begins with the smelting of the lead ore, followed by cupellation, a process which involves melting the metal in a porous cavity in the ground so that the lead sinks into the pores, and leaves only the silver. The extraction process is very wasteful of lead, and as a result, silver has

Silver opium clock, the lid with T-pattern openwork, hallmarked, Chinese, late 19th century, 4½" square, **$400–$650.**

found only a small place in Japanese metalwares. However, during the last 200–250 years, a method has been used to extract silver from copper ore.

Japanese silver has been used in conjunction with cloisonné and the art of enameling, as well as for inlays and in the alloy shibuichi, which is valued for its patina. Since the eighteenth century, kettles, vases, ornaments, and such—some of which are masterpieces of chasing—have been produced. Other works of Japanese silver include personal accessories and occasional objects. Unlike the Chinese counterparts, these objects were made with an emphasis on Japanese style rather than on Western styles.

Japanese silver objects generally have a higher silver content than Chinese silver objects.

Left: *Silver basket with tall bail handle, four legs, woven silver, Japanese, c1900, 4" high (to top of handle),* **$600–$800.** Right: *Silver censer with applied gilt mon, Japanese, late Edo / early Meiji period, 3" high,* **$500–$700.**

Other Chinese Alloys

Often, Chinese silversmiths worked in other metals, including gold. One such metal was *paktong*, an alloy made of copper, nickel, and zinc, and used exclusively for export objects such as candlesticks.

Pewter was another metal popularly used for exports, with the largest amount of pewter exported from China during the nineteenth century, around the time of the U.S. Centennial. Chiefly used for tea caddies, incense-stick holders, pricket sticks, jars, teapots, and so on, pewter was sometimes inlaid with brass, copper, or semiprecious stones (especially in the late Ch'ing Dynasty and early twentieth century).

Archaic Chinese Bronzes

Michael B. Krassner

Archaic bronzes are considered by many collectors to be the finest examples of Chinese art, and it is only within the present century that Shan/Yin, Chou, and Han bronzes have come onto the Western market.

The following are types of bronze vessels from the Shang/Yin to the Han Dynasties (1525 B.C.–220 A.D.). They served as models for countless copies through the centuries.

Li. A tripod vessel with hollow legs (one of the most ancient pottery forms) and having two upright loop handles through which a stick could be passed for lifting. Used for cooking meat.

Ting. Similar to a Li, but with solid legs; also used for cooking meat. This is referred to in early Chinese dictionaries as *a sacred vessel for blending the* Five Tastes (acrid, sour, salt, bitter, and sweet), *a vessel for cooking food, or a vessel for boiling well-cooked food.*

Hsien. This is really two vessels: a steamer, formed like a li, with an upper part consisting of a colander with handles. Used for cooking vegetables and cereals. One of these vessels bears the inscription *For use while campaigning, while traveling, wherewith to make soup from rice and millet.*

Kuei (or Chiu). A bowl, with or without a cover, sometimes with handles, resting on three or four feet, or on a hollow base. Used as a container for grain.

Tou. A shallow dish—with handles and a cover—on a round base; used for offering fruit. The circular projection on the cover served as a foot when the cover was inverted.

Fu. A rectangular covered dish with straight, sloping sides, sometimes with four feet. (The cover is almost a duplicate of the vessel.) Used for cooked cereals.

Hsu. A shallow oval dish with handles and cover. As with the tou, the projection on the cover served as a foot when inverted. This is not a ritual vessel. Many are inscribed *Traveling Hsu* and were used during expeditions.

I (also written Yi and Ih). A ewer from which water was poured, often shaped like a sauce boat. The name *i* is also used as a general term for sacrificial vessels.

Kuang. A squat vessel, elongated from front to back, with a handle at the back and a cover extending over an open spout. Also shaped like a sauce boat, but larger than an i (as described above).

Hu. A large wine vessel with a bulbous body, narrow neck, and usually, ring handles. Used for storing food.

Lei. A large vase, or jar, for wine. It is like a hu, but with the widest part of the body just below the neck.

Tsun. A ceremonial wine vessel which is rectangular and has a flaring lip.

Chia. A round tripod, or square and four-legged, vessel with a handle on one side and two uprights on the lip. The legs are hollow so that when the vessel is filled with wine or water and pushed down onto a glowing bed of coals, the maximum surface will be exposed to the heat.

Ku. A tall, slender wine beaker with a wide foot and trumpet mouth.

Chüeh (formerly written Chio). A tripod cup with a handle and a pointed lip.

Yu. A large, deep, covered vessel with a flaring lip, with or without handles, for storing wine or water.

P'an. A shallow basin (usually round) for washing. Used in ceremonial rites and in domestic life.

Chien (or Hsi). A large, deep basin with two handles, also used for washing.

Note: In addition to the vessels listed here, there were many which were made in the form of animals—notably tigers, elephants, goats, deer, and birds.

Bronze Shapes

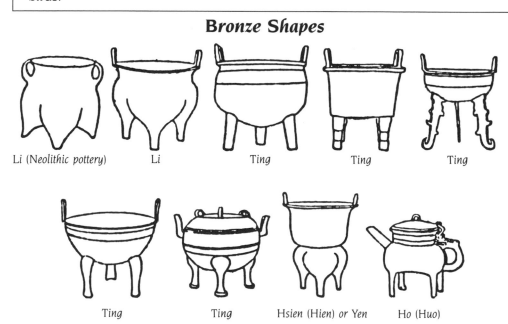

Li (Neolithic pottery) Li Ting Ting Ting

Ting Ting Hsien (Hien) or Yen Ho (Huo)

Bronze Shapes

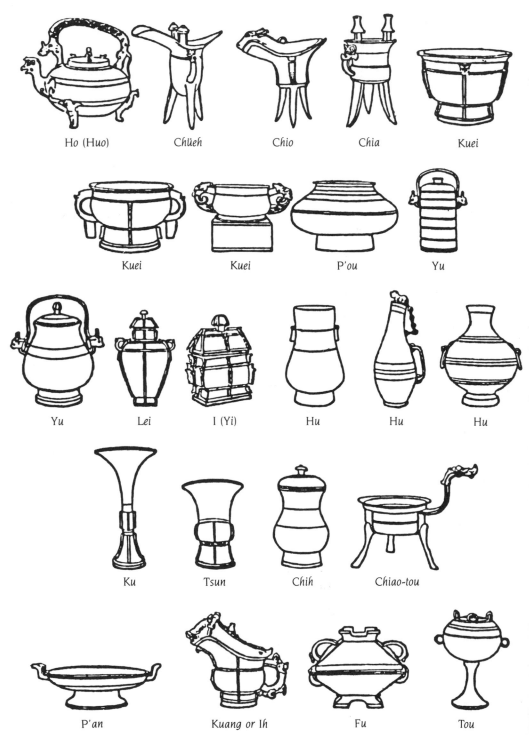

Ho (Huo) Chüeh Chio Chia Kuei

Kuei Kuei P'ou Yu

Yu Lei I (Yi) Hu Hu Hu

Ku Tsun Chih Chiao-tou

P'an Kuang or Ih Fu Tou

Bronze Shapes

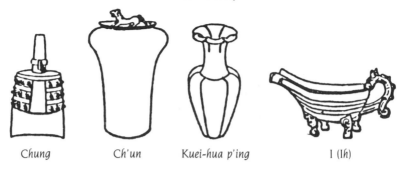

Chung   Ch'un   Kuei-hua p'ing   I (Ih)

Values

Antimony

Box and cover, wood lining, embossed floral motif, Japanese, c1930, 6" × 3¼" × 1¾", **$50–$75.**

Crumb tray and scraper, embossed phoenix and dragon design, Japanese, c1935, 7½" × 7¼", **$45–$65.**

Flower holder, frog form, Japanese, c1925, 4½" × 3" × 1⅝", **$50–$70.**

Flower holder, turtle form, marked *Made in Japan,* c1930, 4¼" × 3¼" × 1¼", **$40–$60.**

Photograph frame with embossed bamboo design, Japanese, c1915, 3" × 3¾", **$40–$65.**

Picture frame with embossed chrysanthemum design, Japanese, c1910, 4" × 5⅜", **$50–$60.**

Brass

Ashtrays, oblong with fluted edge, marked *China,* c1935, **nest of 4, $25–$45.**

Bonbon dish, fluted edge and base, engraved with a floral motif, marked *China,* c1925, 3" × 5½", **$45–$65.**

Finger bowl, two handles, embossed floral motif, marked *China,* c1930, **$30–$50.**

Bowl engraved with two confronting dragons, hardwood stand, both pieces marked *China,* c1915, 14" diameter, **$125–$175.**

Candelabra, two-light, marked *China,* c1930, 4¾" × 9⅜", **$35–$65.**

Candelabra, three-light, the center holder upon an S shape, marked *China,* c1937, 8¾" high, **$75–$100.**

Candlesticks, dragons entwined on stems, marked *China,* c1935, 4" high, **$45–$65.**

Censer, four stub feet, two bamboo-form handles, the body with radiating bamboo leaves, Japanese, c1925, 5½" high, **$150–$220.**

Censer, tripod, the body with a carp and wave design, the lid with lotus blossoms and leaves, Japanese, c1925, 4" × 5", **$125–$175.**

Cigar box, wood roller top painted with a landscape, Japanese, c1930, 8½" high, **$50–$75.**

Brass mini-teapot with glass bead finial and glass flowers, foliage in low relief, Chinese, c1925, 2½" high, **$50–$75.**

Dinner bell and hardwood stand, the bell embossed with a dragon, the stand similarly carved, marked China, c1925, overall height 15", **$150–$250.**

Dinner gong, set of three bells, graduated in size, strung on silk cords, decorated with red flowers, striker missing, Japanese, c1925, **$50–$75.**

Figure of a bull standing on a rectangular base with flat, lobed rim; arched tail; beaded trappings and bells around his neck; Indian, 19th century, 5½" high, **$300–$450.**

Kettle (for hot water) with stand and alcohol lamp, hammered, Fuku character surrounded by etched floral patterns, silver lining, Japanese, c1915, **$200–$325.**

Smoker's set: tray, cigarette holder, cigar holder, ashtray, and match-box holder; etched floral motif; Japanese, c1930, tray size 12" X 9", **$125–$175.**

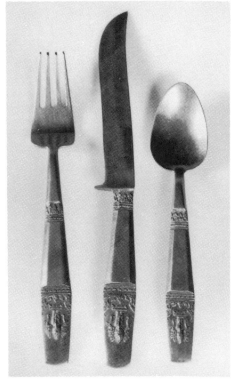

Brass flatware service with carving knife and fork and salad servers, each piece decorated with Ganesh, marked Siam, c1928, **service for 8, $200–$350.**

Brass vase with gold and silver fish, foliage and waves on a gun metal ground, the work incised overall, Japanese, c1955, 12" high, $100–$125.

Smoker's set: round cigarette jar, ashtray, and match holder on a brass smoking stand with removable round tray; Chinese, c1925, 21¾" high, **$300–$500.**

Spittoon (Bidri) with overall design of leaves within bulbous medallions, shoulder and neck in a herringbone pattern, Indian, 19th century, 8½" high, **$325–$500.**

Tray incised with panels of calligraphy within a trellis border, Indian, early 20th century, 22½" diameter, **$200–$300.**

Vase (Bidri), straight flaring sides decorated with silver-inlaid flowers and scrolling stems, Indian, 19th century, 8⅜" high, **$375–$550.**

Vases (Bidri), squared foot with turned stem and ribbed ovoid body, tall neck with floral mouth, overall silver-inlaid flowering plants, Indian, 19th century, 14" high, **pair, $900–$1,200.**

Bronze

Bottle/vase; long, tapered neck; enameled butterflies scattered over the body; Japanese, c1900, 8" high, **$1,200–$1,600.**

Bowl; lotus-petal band around the base; lion mask loose-ring handles and scrolling lotus band below the rim; Hsüan Te (Xuande) mark, but early Ch'ing (Qing) dynasty; 5½" diameter, **$700–$1,000.**

Box and cover, circular, decorated with birds and grasses, the patina overcleaned and scratched, Japanese, c1915, 4¾" diameter, **$75–$100.**

Cauldron; tripod; annular handles; vertical rope pattern on the sides between cicada lappets; C-, L-, and S-shaped scrolls, encrustation and damage, Chinese, Han dynasty, 9" wide, **$800–$1,100.**

Censer in the form of a standing duck, the feathers incised, traces of gilt, Chinese, 17th century, 6" wide, **$950–$1,350.**

Censer in the form of Kinko seated on a carp (the figure of Kinko is removable), Japanese, late Edo period, 12" long, **$1,600–$2,200.**

Censer in the form of a Takarabune (treasure ship), Japanese, c1900, 5¾" high, 4½" wide, **$175–$225.**

Bronze tripod censer with two open-loop handles; Chinese; the base with Wan Li mark, but early 20th century; 5" diameter, **$75–$100.**

Censer, globular, two bamboo node-shaped handles, three legs, Hsüan Te (Xuande) mark but early 20th century, Chinese, 7½" wide, **$325–$450.**

Censer; rectangular form; four feet with rope handles; the sides with Buddhistic symbols; Ch'eng Hua (Chenghua) mark, but 19th century; Chinese, 4½" wide, **$250–$375.**

Censer cast on three short feet, late Ming dynasty, Chinese, 11¾" diameter, **$1,000–$1,500.**

Censer; three conical feet with wide, arched loop handles at the rim; Chinese, 18th century, 6½" diameter, **$900–$1,200.**

Censer; tripod; gilt-splashed; wide, flaring sides; pierced upright handles; flat base; elephant-head feet; Hsüan Te (Xuande) mark, but early Ch'ing (Qing) dynasty; 5½" wide, **$1,000–$1,500.**

Censer, tripod, mask feet, continuous motif of dragon and flaming pearl, S-shaped handles, Tao Kuang (Daoguang) six-character mark (and of the period), cover missing, Chinese, 20" high, **$1,000–$1,500.**

Censer, tripod with bamboo-form handles, the body with phoenix in flight, repatinated, Japanese, c1875, 13" wide, **$500–$700.**

Dish, tripod, bucket form, flared lip, bracket feet, encrustation, Korean, Koryo dynasty, 4" diameter, **$500–$700.**

Drum, ribbed, waisted circular form, the top cast with a star medallion and concentric bands, four open-work frogs on the rim, the sides with double pierced strap-work handles, Shan States, Chinese, 24¼" diameter, 18¼" high, **$2,000–$3,000.**

Figure of Avalokitesvara, gilt, on stepped rectangular plinth, the feet on a lotus base, jeweled tiara, arms draped with flowing robes, Sino-Tibetan, 19th century, 7½" high, **$600–$900.**

Figure of a beetle, naturalistic, articulated joints, Japanese, c1930, 1½" long, **$300–$500.**

Figure of a carp, naturalistic, gilt eyes, signed *Seizan*, Japanese, late Meiji period, 12¾" long, **$1,600–$2,200.**

Figure of a cock; his feathers in shibuichi, shakudo, and sentoku; comb painted red; gilt eyes; Japanese, Taisho period, 14¼" high, **$700–$1,000.**

Figure of a crane on a shaped base standing before a plum branch, in need of re-soldering, Japanese, c1900, 14" high, **$150–$250.**

Figure of a crayfish, naturalistic, articulated body, Japanese, c1930, 4½" long, **$550–$750.**

Figure of a seated Benkei wearing a kimono and leggings, holding an oni clutching a basket, gilt details, signed *Miyao*, Japanese, Meiji period, 14" high, **$7,000–$9,000.**

Figure of Buddha standing on a tiered octagonal throne wearing shoes with pointed toes and a long robe with elaborate flammiform decoration in relief, both hands held forward in abhaya mudra, the face with a downcast expression, the tiered crown with double conical finial flanked by flammiform ear lappets, Thai, 19th century, 22" high, **$300–$400.**

Figure of Buddha (Mon-D'varavati style) encrusted green patina, Thai, 20th century, 18½" high, **$300–$500.**

Figure of Buddha, gilt, hands joined and upturned over crossed legs, necklace at the chest, Chinese, 17th century, 7" high, **$950–$1,600.**

Figure of Buddha, gilt, robes over one shoulder, seated (with legs crossed) upon a double lotus base, one hand upturned, the base with impressed vajara, Chinese, 18th century, 10" high, **$1,500–$2,000.**

Figure of Buddha, gilt, seated in dhyanasana on a stepped lotus base, the base reduced, Tang dynasty, Chinese, 3¾" high, **$500–$700.**

Figure of Buddha seated in dhyanasana on double lotus base, Sino-Tibetan, 19th century, 6" high, **$400–$600.**

Figure of Bodhisattva, gilt, wearing a cowl trailed across the shoulder, flowing robes, Sino-Tibetan, 18th century, 3½" high, **$300–$500.**

Figure of Bodhisattva Amitayus seated in dhyanasana on a draped throne with foliate support corners, Chinese, late 18th century, 7" high, **$650–$950.**

Figure of Amitayus Buddha seated in dhyanasana on a rectangular throne, jewelry includes rosette earrings, bracelets, domed chignon, Sino-Tibetan, 18th century, 7¼" high, **$700–$900.**

Left to right: *Gilt bronze figure of a multi-armed deity seated in dhyanasana, the primary left hand in dhyana mudra and the right slightly raised, the secondary hands raised, the right holding a vajra; wearing a flowing dhoti with coral-studded pectoral jewelry and diadem; a double lotus base; gilt-rubbed; Tibet, late 18th / early 19th century, 7¾" high. Realized price (including the 10-percent buyer's premium), Christie's East, New York City,* **$825.** *Gilt bronze figure of a Lama seated on a double-cushion throne engraved with foliage, the right hand raised in vitarka mudra, the left in dhyana mudra and wearing a cap and loose robes with floral incised borders, sealed, Tibetan, 18th century, 6½" high. Realized price (including the 10-percent buyer's premium), Christie's East, New York City,* **$660.** *Gilt bronze figure of seated Vajrasaftra seated in dhyanasana with the left hand raised in dharmackra mudra (turning an invisible wheel of the law), the right hand raised holding a vajra and wearing a dhoti with pectoral jewelry and diadem, a double lotus base, Tibetan, late 18th / early 19th century, 6¾" high. Realized price (including the 10-percent buyer's premium), Christie's East, New York City,* **$1,210.**

Figure of Buddha seated in dhyanasana on a tiered, waisted throne and wearing a sanghati decorated with linear incisions, his right hand in bhumisparsa mudra, his left hand in dhyana mudra, his face downcast, the tightly curled hair with a pointed finial, Burmese, 18th century, 9¾" high, **$450–$650.**

Figure of Buddha seated in dhyanasana, hands raised in mudra, the interior of the oval base with a cylindrical tube, encrustations, minor damage, Tang dynasty, 5¼" high, **$1,250–$1,875.**

Figure of Buddha seated on a double lotus base, robes open, gilt traces overall, minor damage to three fingers, Ming dynasty, Chinese, 13" high, **$1,500–$2,500.**

Figure of Buddha seated in dhyanasana on double lotus base, hands in dhyana mudra, holding a pearl, Chinese, 17th century, 11½" high, **$1,200–$1,800.**

Figure of Buddha seated in a lotus position on a lotus plinth, Korean, Yi dynasty, 7" high, **$500–$700.**

Figure of a standing Buddha, right hand in varada mudra, mandorla missing, Korean, Koryo dynasty, **$1,000–$1,500.**

Figure of Dakini Vajravarahi standing in ardhapanyankasana, dancing on a prostrated figure on a lotus throne wearing a long billowing scarf, a garland of severed human heads and a five-leaf crown, a flammiform aureole with skulls and vajras in relief behind, Nepalese, 19th century, 19" high, **$800–$1,200.**

Bronze model of a dragon with tama, Japanese, early Meiji period, 12" long, **$1,800–$2,200.**

Figure of Dharmapala Mahakala in yab-yum with his Sakti, seated in dhyanasana on a double lotus throne, three ferocious heads, each with a third eye, wearing skull crowns, flaming red pigmented hair behind, the primary right hand holding the triratna, his remaining five hands in karana mudra, his upper left hand holding a mirror, his sakti with her arms around his neck, Sino-Tibetan, 18th century, 4½" high, **$2,500–$3,500.**

Figure of Dharmapala Yama standing in pratyalidhsana on the back of a bull lying on a prostrated nude figure on a lotus throne, the figure with both hands raised, the bull wearing a jeweled harness with knop finial on his back, the base plate incised with visvavajra, Sino-Tibetan, 18th century, 11" high, **$1,500–$2,000.**

Figure of Dharmapala Mahakala standing in pratyalidhasana, six arms, his primary right arm missing from the elbow joint, his primary left arm holding a kapala, his remaining hands in karana mudra to hold attributes, three heads with three bulging eyes, open mouth with tongue and fangs, skull crowns, necklaces including severed human heads, scroll-incised borders around his waist, Sino-Tibetan 19th century, 12" high, **$600–$800.**

Figure of a dignitary, hands clasped at the chest, Korean, Yi dynasty, 10½" high, **$600–$900.**

Figure of a female holding a tray, she stands on a circular base, Indian, 19th century, 9" high, **$125–$200.**

Figure of Ganesha cast recumbent on an oval dais, Thai, 19th century, 8" long, **$300–$450.**

Figure of Ganesha in dancing position, six arms held out on either side, each holding an attribute, the figure adorned with jewelry and a domed crown, Thai, 20th century, 30" high, **$1,000–$1,500.**

Figure of a grasshopper with articulated joints, signed *Yoshi*, Japanese, c1930, 3½" long, **$350–$550.**

281

Bronze elephant, realistically modeled, Japanese, c1910, 5" high, **$250–$375.**

Bronze tiger, realistically modeled, upon a carved wood stand, Japanese, c1900, 24" long, **$2,000–$3,000.**

Figure of Guandi seated and wearing flowing robes over his armor, a dragon in relief on his stomach, the base with four bracket feet, traces of gilt, Ming dynasty, Chinese, 16" high, **$1,800–$2,500.**

Figure of a guardian, fierce expression, arms raised, hair in top knot, some damages, Tang dynasty, 4½" high, **$1,200–$1,800.**

Figure of a guardian, long robes, holding a scroll and standing on a lotus base, gilt decoration, 17th century, Chinese, 14" high, **$850–$1,250.**

Figure of a Kerala (a deity) standing with her right hand raised and holding the stem of a padma; the left hand in kati mudra on her hip; wearing a long dhoti flanked by sashes knotted at the hip; her jewelry includes armlets, anklets, necklaces, large earrings, and a conical headdress with three large flower heads and a knop finial; South Indian, 18th century, 11" high, **$700–$1,050.**

Figure of Mahakala, gilt, on a rectangular lotus base, holding skull cap and chipper, his other four hands with drums and naga heads, Tibetan, 6" high, **$700–$900.**

Figure of Parvati standing in tribhanga on a square pedestal, South Indian, 20th century, 18¾" high, **$200–$300.**

Figure of a rabbit, the hair realistically executed, signed *Shosai chu*, Meiji period, Japanese, 6½" long, **$900–$1,200.**

Figure of a rat, realistically executed, movable tail, Japanese, c1910, 7" long, **$300–$400.**

Figure of a seated monkey holding a peach, Japanese, early 20th century, 4½" high, **$700–$900.**

Bronze figure of Laksmi, the consort of Vishnu, standing in tribhanga on an oval double lotus base set on a rectangular plinth, her right hand raised in katamukha mudra and her left hanging in lola at her side, her knopped hair with a lotus medallion backed by small open-work floral disc mandorla, dark brown patina, South Indian, 17th / 18th century, 25" high. Realized price (including the 10-percent buyer's premium), Christie's East, New York City, $1,540.

Left: *Bronze inkwell in the form of a fishing basket; basket-weave body; the lid with sentoku, shakudo, and gilt fish; glass insert; Japanese, c1910, 3" high,* **$250–$350.** Right: *Bronze inkwell in the form of a teapot, applied silver motifs of birds on one side and flowers on the reverse, silver finial and chain, glass insert, Japanese, c1915, 4" high,* **$250–$350.**

Left: *Bronze place-card holder in fan shape with gilt flowers, basket, and trim; Japanese, c1900, 3" wide,* **$300–$400.** Right: *Sentoku drum-form box and cover with silver wires and trim, the hinged lid with No masks, Japanese, c1900, 4" diameter,* **$300–$400.**

Figure of Shoki, the demon killer, brandishing his sword, Japanese, late 19th century, 10" high, **$400–$650.**

Figure of Siva, the multi-armed deity, holding attributes and sitting astride an ox on a rectangular plinth, Thai, 19th century, 11" high, **$400–$625.**

Figure of Virabhadra standing on a square, tapering base with both hands held out in front of him; his right hand holding a khadga, his left holding a khetaka; he wears a long dhoti and jewelry; Indian, 19th century, 15" high, **$450–$660.**

Figure of Vajrapani (on a lotus base) leaning to the right with a snake under each foot, two snakes over his shoulders, another snake behind his tiara, Sino-Tibetan, 18th century, 7" high, **$1,200–$1,850.**

Figure of a warrior standing on rockwork, wearing a tunic and holding a weapon, parcel gilt, Chinese, 17th century, 14" high, **$750–$1,000.**

Flower bowl with floral motif inlaid in silver, Japanese, c1910, 7¼" × 2¼", **$250–$375.**

Group, yab-yum, Vajradhara seated in dhyanasana on an associated repoussé single lotus throne, his primary hands in Karana mudra, the secondary hands holding a vajra and clutching his Sakti (who also holds attributes), Nepalese, 17th century, 4" high, **$1,700–$2,500.**

Jardinière, rounded with three stub feet, the body cast with two dragons in low relief, signed *Toshitsugu*, Meiji period, Japanese, 11½" diameter, **$550–$725.**

Mirror cast in low relief with pine and birds, Muromachi period, Japanese, 4" diameter, **$350–$575.**

Mirror (miniature), gilt, circular, cast on one side with lotus and petals surrounding a plain boss, encrusted, Tang dynasty, **$1,750–$2,500.**

Mirror, raised octofoil border, a central boss, encrustations, Han dynasty, 4¼" diameter, **$1,200–$1,750.**

Mirror, silvered with six mythical animals around a central boss, encrusted, Six Dynasties, 5½" diameter, **$800–$1,275.**

Mirror; TLV with foliate lappets around a central domed boss divided by smaller bosses, dragon scrolls, and TLV motifs; encrustation; Han dynasty, Chinese, 7" diameter, **$600–$850.**

Pricket candlesticks, bands of archaistic motifs, large central pans and bell-shaped bases, Chinese, 17th century, 23½" high, **$800–$1,200.**

Seal, Buddhistic lion finial with collar and bell around its neck, Chinese, 19th century, 2½" high, **$100–$150.**

Stem bowl cast in Chou style with archaistic U-shaped and E-shaped geometric motifs, a wave pattern on the foot, Chinese, 18th century, 7" high, **$900–$1,400.**

Tazza, their baluster bodies cast with birds on leafy branches, branch-form handles, Japanese, c1900, 11½" high, **pair, $800–$1,275.**

Temple bell, panels of raised studs and suspension hook, Japanese, 18th century, 21" high, **$1,000–$1,600.**

Vase with applied shibuichi, shakudo, and sentoku wisteria around the shoulders; Japanese, c1890, 8" high, **$600–$850.**

Vase, beaker form, the body with a dragon in high relief, Japanese, c1920, 12" high, **$375–$500.**

Vase, beaker form, the center with four gilt archaistic zoomorphic heads divided by vertical flanges with key pattern and two gilt bands, early Ch'ing (Qing) dynasty, Chinese, 7½" high, **$625–$975.**

Vase, gilt-splashed, high foot and trumpet neck, early Ch'ing (Qing) dynasty, 6½" high, **$750–$1,200.**

Bronze *kame* (tortoise) with vase upon the top of its shell, the vase realistically designed with cranes and pine, plum, and bamboo (Three Friends motif) in relief, Japanese, early Meiji period, 7" high, **$800–$1,200.**

Vase; gilt-splashed; flattened ovoid form; four bosses in a band at the shoulder; tapered foot; Hsüan Te (Xuande) mark, but 19th century; Chinese, 14" high, **$1,800–$2,500.**

Vase inlaid in silver with a bamboo grove, Japanese, c1900, 13½" high, **$2,000–$3,000.**

Vase, modified pear shape, the body with two carp, their eyes gilt, Japanese, c1900, 7" high, **$900–$1,200.**

Vase, pear-shaped, cast with three t'ao t'ieh and loose ring handles, key-pattern bands and cicada lappets, Chinese, 19th century, 21" high, **$3,000–$4,000.**

Bronze vase, modified pear shape with elongated neck and applied dragon, Japanese, c1900, 8" high, **$500–$700.**

Vases, pear-shaped, elongated necks, inlaid with flowers, the details in silver and gilt, Japanese, c1910, 12½" high, **pair, $2,000–$3,000.**

Vase, yen-yen shape, dragon loop handles on the flaring neck, globular body with three dragon-and-cloud scrolls above and below lappet bands, overall gilt splashes, Chinese, early 18th century, 20" high, **$3,500–$4,500.**

Water dropper, Shishi form, Japanese, c1900, **$175–$225.**

Yatate, dragon form, Japanese, Showa period, 6¾" long, **$100–$200.**

Yatate, open-work handle, dragon on bowl, Japanese, Showa period, 9" long, **$125–$225.**

Copper

Figure of Bodhisattva Avalokitesvara Padmapani seated in rajalilasana on a double lotus throne, his right hand resting over his knee, his left on the edge of the throne and holding the stem of a padma flowering at his shoulder; wearing a dhoti, long scarf, and jewelry; his knotted chignon with traces of blue pigment; the limbs with traces of gold; Tibetan, 18th century, 4⅝" high, **$600– $900.**

Figure of a dragonfly, articulated joints, Japanese, c1935, 2¼" long, **$275–$475.**

Figure of Guatama Buddha wearing monastic robe, right shoulder and arm bare, face and limbs gilded, curled hair with blue pigment, Tibetan, 19th century, 6½" high, **$350–$550.**

Figure of the Suryu (Sung god) seated in sattvasana on a double lotus base; hands raised in front and holding flowering stems; wearing armlets, anklets, and a five-pointed crown set with garnets and other stones; gilt traces overall; Nepalese, 18th century, 6" high, **$900–$1,200.**

Plate, oval with a basket-weave motif, the center with two sentoku women holding fans, Japanese, c1900, 9" long, **$175–$250.**

Teapot, squat globular form, domed cover, zoomorphic handle, curved spout, the sides with repoussé medallions, Tibetan, late 19th century, 11½" high, **$400–$625.**

Tray, basket-work border, the center with a seated Rakan, Japanese, c1910, 11½" wide, **$500–$700.**

Vase, basket form, waisted neck, globular body, the shoulders with applied crustaceans, Japanese, Taisho period, 4" high, **$300–$500.**

Vase hammered and enameled with sea shells and crustaceans, signed *Ando*, Japanese, c1910, 7" high, **$3,000–$4,000.**

Vase hammered and enameled with flowering plum branches, signed *Ando*, Japanese, c1910, 7" high, **$3,000– $4,000.**

Figure of a Lama seated in dhyanasana on a double lotus throne, right hand raised in nitaraka mudra, left hand in dhyana mudra, elaborate robes, hair with traces of black paint, the base with an incised medallion, Tibetan, 16th/17th century, 6¾" high, **$2,000–$3,000.**

Figure of Yi-dam Samvara in yab-yum with his Sakti standing in alidhasana on two prostrated four-armed deities holding attributes, Nepalese, 18th century, 6" high, **$1200–$1500.**

Copper and Silver

Amulet box; pointed arch form; repoussé decoration depicting triratna above, akirtimukha below, eight emblems between; contents include bone rosary, brass Syamatara, and brass Buddha; Tibetan, 19th century, 4" high, **$300–$400.**

Water jar (mizusashi), silver body with applied copper fan shapes filled with various flowers in low relief, the lid with loop handle, Japanese, c1890, 6½" high, **$900–$1,200.**

Teapot, silver with applied copper fan-shaped panels filled with foliage, silver lining, bail handle, silver and copper open-work finial, Japanese, c1895, 5" high, **$550–$750.**

Iron

Model of a crayfish, fully articulated, Japanese, early 19th century, 10" long, **$1,200–$1,800.**

Model of a dragon, Japanese, c1910, 10" long, **$100–$150.**

Model of a dragon standing on all four legs, Japanese, c1925, 9" long, **$125–$200.**

Model of an elephant, trunk raised, Japanese, c1930, 6" high, **$100–$150.**

Teapot, cranes in relief on each side, bronze lid and bail handle, Japanese, late 19th century, 7" high, **$150–$250.**

Teapot, ishi (stone) finish, bail handle, Japanese, late Edo period, 8" high, **$400–$600.**

Vajra, slender, either end with four arched ribs and four-sided pointed projections, brass finials, Tibetan, 17th century, 7" high, **$200–$300.**

Komai cabinet with three drawers, each side and each drawer with inlaid gold and silver motifs, Japanese, Meiji period, 2½" × 2½", **$3,500–$5,000.**

Komai box with inlaid gold and silver scenic motif, grape-and-leaf border, Japanese, Meiji period, 2⅜" diameter, **$2,000–$3,000.** Courtesy of the Edson Collection.

Plaque, rectangular, repoussé and carved with Benten holding a biwa, signed Miochin, late Edo period, Japanese, 13" × 11½", **$1,400–$2,200.**

Komai

Box and cover, fan shape with motifs of bamboo, signed Komai, Japanese, c1900, 6¾" wide, **$2,500–$3,500.**

Left: Komai box and cover with inlaid silver and gold scenic motifs, the interior with an incised gilt liner, Japanese, c1925, 5" × 3¾", **$1,200–$1,800.** Right: Komai box and cover, the motifs inlaid in gold and silver, the interior of the lid with a silver wire inscription that dates this piece 1951, Japanese, 5" × 3½", **$900–$1,200.**

Komai flask-form vase with circular panels featuring scenic motifs, silver and gold inlay with grape-and-leaf borders, Japanese, Meiji period, 6" high, **$3,000–$5,000.** Courtesy of the Edson Collection.

Cabinet, two doors open to reveal six drawers, scenic motifs overall, Japanese, c1900, 5½" high, **$2,850–$3,800.**

Cabinet in the form of a shrine; two doors open to reveal three small drawers; decorated overall with birds, flowers, and landscapes; signed Komai; Japanese, c1910, 4" high, **$3,200–$4,500.**

Chest; hinged lid and two drawers; the motifs including various landscapes, buildings, and Mt. Fuji capped in silver; Japanese, c1900, 2½" × 3" × 2⅜", **$3,000–$4,000.**

Dish, circular, decorated with alternating phoenix and dragon pattern around a central circular panel of quail and grasses, Japanese, c1910, 6½" diameter, **$1,500–$1,800.**

Vase, beaker form, two shaped panels of huts and pine, grape-and-leaf ground and borders, marked Komai, Meiji period, Japanese, 4¾" high, **$2,500–$3,500.**

Vase; Komai style; pear-shaped with trumpet neck; decorated with shaped panels of pavilions, rocks, trees, sailing boats, and so on; Japanese, c1915, 5" high, **$200–$300.**

Pewter

Boxes and covers; circular; the covers decorated with vines, leaves, and fruit inlaid with oval agates; Chinese, early 20th century, 7" diameter, **pair, $300–$500.**

Cosmetic box with a central Shou character, Chinese, c1900, 4" long, **$100–$175.**

Candlesticks, square, the drip pans with scrolls, the stems with Shou characters, Chinese, c1920, 28" high, **pair, $350–$500.**

Tea caddy; high, rounded shoulders; low, cylindrical neck; knop finial; undecorated; Chinese, late 19th century, 9" high, **$100–$150.**

Vase, hexagonal with a motif of standing figures, Chinese, c1900, 11" high, **$125–$175.**

Sentoku

Bottle/vase inlaid with gold, silver, and bronze motifs of birds and marsh grasses; Japanese, c1920, 7" high, **$600–$800.**

Vase, nanako ground with floral motifs in low relief, Japanese, c1910, 8¾" high, **$350–$475.**

Shakudo

Model of a standing crane, the feathers with some silver inlay, Japanese, c1905, 11⅝" high, **$350–$550.**

Model of a dragon, hinged legs and jaw, some whiskers missing, Japanese, first half of the 19th century, 14½" long, **$1,800–$2,500.**

Vase, baluster form, decorated in iro-e hirazogan with five red-capped Manchurian cranes and bamboo, Japanese, early 20th century, 6⅜" high, **$700–$900.**

Vase inlaid with two quails; their bodies decorated with gilt, shibuichi, silver, and sentoku; Japanese, c1880, 3" high, **$500–$750.**

Silver

Bottle; globular with writhing dragon applied around the rim and forming two handles; the body with repoussé motifs of dragons and flaming pearl; handles resoldered; marked *Luen-wo, Shanghai*; Chinese, 19th century, 6" high, **$375–$500.**

Bowl, hexagonal, each panel chased and embossed with fruiting and flowering trees, gilt traces on interior, marked HC, Chinese, c1900, 8" diameter, **$600–$900.**

Bowl, rounded, decorated with painted foliate arches and swirls of foliage below a scroll border, Thai, 20th century, 10" diameter, **$250–$400.**

Bowl, circular, two dragons in relief, Chinese, late 19th century, 5" diameter, **$600–$800.**

Bowl, scrolled feet cut as dragons, hexagonal panels embossed and chased with fruit and foliage, Chinese, late 19th century, 6" diameter, **$475–$675.**

Bowl and cover with underplate decorated with the 12 zodiac signs and petal motifs, bird finial, Burmese, 19th century, 6" diameter, **$300–$500.**

Box and cover, round with repoussé irises, the ground hammered by hand, minor dent, Japanese, c1918, 3¾" diameter, **$650–$900.**

Box and cover in the form of a helmet, gold-inlaid mon and clouds, Japanese, early Meiji period, 2½" high, **$800–$1,200.**

Left: *Silver box and cover with kiku mon on lid, incised motif of flowers and birds, four legs, Japanese, early Meiji period, 3½" diameter,* **$500–$700.** Right: *Silver box and cover, six legs, the lid decorated with mon and foliage, Japanese, early Meiji period, 3" wide,* **$450–$650.**

Box and cover, circular, the lid with enameled floral roundels, some losses, Japanese, late Meiji period, 4" diameter, **$800–$1,200.**

Censer and cover enameled with flowers and foliage in relief on a stippled ground, squat form with three bracket feet, Japanese, late Meiji period, 4" high, **$5,000–$7,000.**

Censer, parcel gilt, domed foot with rope-work border, either side with a figure of Samvara in yab-yum with his Sakti, foliage ground, three arched dragon handles, a plaited silver chain for suspension, Tibetan, 19th century, 9" high, **$400–$600.**

Censer with applied panels worked in silver wire and enamels in motifs of phoenix and flowers, Japanese, late 19th century, 4½" high, **$2,500–$3,500.**

Silver filigree card case with dragon and flaming pearl motif, Chinese, last half of the 19th century, **$700–$900.**

Centerpiece with seven removable fluted flower holders, Chinese, c1910, 25" long, 10" high, **$750–$1,000.**

Cigarette box with inlaid shibuichi, the lid with Daikoku sitting and leaning on a sack, Japanese, c1940, 3" wide, 8½" long, **$300–$400.**

Cigarette case with an embossed dragon, gold wash on interior, holds ten regular-sized cigarettes, Chinese, c1925, **$200–$300.**

Cocktail shaker and six tumblers with tray, the tray with glass center, tumblers with silver sleeves, overall dragon motif in very low relief, marked .950, Japanese, c1930, **$950–$1,500.**

Cosmetic box and hinged cover, undecorated, encrustations, Chinese, Sung (Song) dynasty, 2" diameter, **$1,200–$1,850.**

Silver wine ewer with lacquer stand and wood box, Japanese, early Meiji period, 7" high, **$1,800–$2,500.**

Silver mallet (Daikoku's mallet) with gold incised motifs, Japanese, Meiji period, 19th century, 7" long, **$1,500–$2,200.**

Fruit basket, six overlapping shell shapes forming the basket, the handles in the form of a twisted leaf, Japanese, c1900, **$500–$700.**

Goblets, plain bowl, entwined dragons on the stems, Chinese, c1925, 5" high, **pair, $200–$300.**

Kettle, the body embossed with studs, plain cover and spout, bail handle, stamped *jun gin* (silver), Japanese, c1885, 12" high, **$3,500–$4,500.**

Loving cup, plain bowl, bamboo-form stem, mounted on a black wood base, Chinese, c1900, 6¾" high, **$1,000–$1,500.**

Model of an elephant standing on an oval base and wearing a foliate blanket, the mahoot in front, the bowdah with two figures, Indian, 19th century, 10" high, **$600–$850.**

Model of a junk, three lateen sails, four flags at the stern, seven cannons on the deck, three Chinese sailors, Chinese, 10th century, 9" long, **$400–$550.**

Model of a ricksha, Chinese, c1920, 3" high, **$100–$125.**

Mug, flared cylindrical form, molded rim and foot, applied loop handle, Chinese, late 19th century, 4" high, **$500–$750.**

Photograph frame, the border pierced and enameled in colors with a motif of heron and wisteria, some enamel missing, some dents, Japanese, c1890, 9½" high, **$1,200–$1,500.**

Photograph frame, bamboo design in low relief, Japanese, c1912, 3½" × 4", **$400–$600.**

Plaque, repoussé, depicting Kali, her principal hands holding a kapala, secondary hands holding shield and sword, Tibetan, 19th century, 11" high, **$400–$600.**

Plate; parcel gilt; circular with a raised center medallion and petal-shaped flutes, each with a pointed terminal; Indian, 19th century, 12" diameter, **$700–$900.**

Left to right: *Silver salt and pepper shakers in the form of stone lanterns, Japanese, early Showa period, 4"* high, **$200–$300.** *Silver salt and pepper set in the form of a kettle and brazier, loose ring handles and spoon, Japanese, early Showa period, 4½" high,* **$250–$350.**

Silver salts in the form of planters with gilt interiors, Chinese, c1890, 3" diameter, **pair, $250–$350.**

Punch bowl with two dragons in high relief, silver liner, marked *Yokohamma Sterling*, .950, Japanese, c1915, 14" diameter, **$5,000–$7,000.**

Rose-water sprinklers, bulbous body, raised foot, elongated neck, a layer of scrolling filigree, Indian, 19th century, 12½" high, **$500–$750.**

Salts, boat-shaped with concave rims, oval feet, Chinese, late 19th century, 4" wide, **$350–$500.**

Salt and pepper set in the form of ricksa, marked .950, Japanese, early Showa period, 3" high, **$250–$350.**

Salt and pepper in the form of lanterns, marked *jun gin*, .950, Japanese, c1930, 2¾" high, **$275–$400.**

Silver tongs with dragon-and-cloud pattern in high relief, Japanese, c1885, $500–$750.

Sherbet cups (eight to the set), each with dragons in high relief, plain stems, Chinese, c1925, 4⅜" high, **each, $150–$175.**

Stem cup, U-shaped bowl engraved with songbirds perched on bamboo branches, bamboo-form stem, signed WH (Wang Hing), Chinese, c1900, 10" high, **$1,000–$1,500.**

Teapot on bamboo-form stand, covered sugar and open creamer, the covers formed as lotus leaves with twig finials, each piece with relief lotus buds and leaves around the body, marked *Hung Chong, Shanghai,* Chinese, late 19th century, **$2,000–$3,000.**

Silver and enameled vase, motif of enameled irises and foliage in high relief accompanied by motif of water fowl, stippled ground, Japanese, Meiji period, 19th century, 6" high, $1,800–$2,400. Courtesy of the Edson Collection.

Teapot, the body in the form of a section of bamboo, the sides with bamboo leaves in green and ochre enamels, loop handle forming the finial, Japanese, c1905, **$1,000–$1,500.**

Tea service: teapot, covered sugar, and open creamer; decorated with repousse birds and bamboo; bamboo finials; marked WH 90 (Wang Hing); Chinese, c1900, **$1,800–$2,400.**

Thermos bottle decorated with the Three Friends motif (pine, plum, and bamboo), marked .950, Japanese, c1910, **$400–$625.**

Water jar (mizusashi) hammered and overlaid with designs rendered in copper, Japanese, late 19th century, 6½" high, **$2,000–$3,000.**

Whiskey bottle, cornered and punched form, overall design of dragons, corked stopper inserted into silver knop finial, Chinese, c1930, **$375–$500.**

Wine cup, the bowl with dragons in low relief, the stem entwined with dragons, Chinese, c1925, 3½" high, **$125–$175.**

12

Paintings

Chinese Artists

The following list of artists and dates should prove helpful as you attempt to identify paintings, scrolls, and so on, as exactly as possible. It includes a number of artists not mentioned in the price guide (further below).

Bian Sho	c1730–1750
Cai Jia	c1730–1782
Chen Banding	1878–1970
Chen Fang	1896–?
Chen Fushan	b. 1905
Chen Hongshou	1598–1652
Cheng Po	20th century
Chen Shun	1483–1544
Chen Zi	c1650–1697
Cheng Shifa	b. 1921
Cheng Suson	18th century
Dai Jin	1388–1462
Dai Xi	1801–1860
Dao Chao	active in the early-to-mid-17th century

Deng Fen	1892–1964	Li Yihong	b. 1941
Deng Shiru	1743–1805	Lin Fengzi	1886–1959
Ding Jing	1695–1775	Ni Tian	1855–1919
Ding Yanyong	1902–1978	Pan Tianshou	1898–1971
Du Qizhang	20th century	Peng Yulin	1816–1890
Fang Zeng	b. 1938	Pu Ru	1896–1963
Fei Danxu	1801–1850	Qi Baishi	1863–1957
Fu Baoshi	1904–1965	Ren Yi	1840–1895
Fu Shan	1605–1690	Ren Yu	1853–1901
Gao Dai	17th century	Shi Lu	1918–1982
Gao Jianfu	1879–1951	Sun Xingyan	1752–1824
Gu Yun	1855–1896	Wang Chong	1494–1533
Guan Liang	b. 1900	Wang Su	1794–1802
Guan Shangue	b. 1912	Wang Zhen	1866–1938
Hong Yi	1880–1942	Wang Zuetao	1903–1984
Hu Xigui	1839–1883	Weng Tonghe	1830–1904
Hua Yan	1682–1756	Wu Changshuo	1844–1927
Huang Junbi	b. 1898	Wu Shixian	b. c1916
Huang Shaoqiang	1901–1942	Xie Zhiguang	1900–1976
Huang Yi	1744–1841	Xu Beihong	1895–1953
Huang Zhou	b. 1925	Xu Gu	1824–1896
Jin Nong	1687–1764	Yang Shanshen	b. 1913
Ju Cao	1811–1865	Yang Yisun	1812–1881
Ju Lian	1828–1904	Yu Yue	1821–1906
Kang Yuwei	1850–1927	Zhang Daqian	1899–1933
Lain Jian	1747–1799	Zhang Shuqi	20th century
Li Keran	b. 1907	Zhang Yehu	Southern Sung
Li Xiongcai	b. 1910	Zhu Qizhan	b. 1891

Values

Chinese Paintings

Ancestral portrait, shoulder length, an elderly woman, ink and color on silk, matted and framed, late 19th century, framed size, 12" × 19", **$400–$600.**

Ancestral portrait, a family, colors on paper, three noblemen in blue robes, three women in red robes and hair ornaments, the robes with mandarin badge of a phoenix, each seated on draped thrones, 19th century, 55" × 90", **$2,500–$3,500.**

Ancestral portraits, a mandarin couple, ink and color on silk, early 19th century, unframed, each measuring 38½" × 73½", **pair, $2,000–$3,000.**

Oil on canvas, American merchantman at Whampoa, wood frame, late half of the 19th century, framed size 16½" × 22", **$2,800–$3,800.**

Oil on canvas, a British merchant ship in Hong Kong Harbor, c1850, 17½" × 23", **$3,500–$5,500.**

One of a pair of ancestral portraits, the patriarch dressed in a dark blue robe with embroidered green cuffs, bright colors on pith paper, trimmed and framed, Chinese, late Ch'ing dynasty, framed size 23" × 45½", **pair**, **$1,500–$2,200.**

Oil on canvas, portrait of a beautiful Chinese lady, seated, wearing a red robe, her hand resting on a table, her hair adorned with ornaments, gilt frame, 19th century, framed size 18" X 24", **$5,500–$7,500.**

Oil on canvas, a Chinese beauty smoking a pipe, seated on a bed, surrounded by female attendants, wood frame, 19th century, framed size 18" X 22", **$1,500–$2,500.**

Oil on canvas, elegantly attired figures in a pavilion and water garden, hardwood frame, Chinese school, early 19th century, framed size 17" X 24", **$2,000–$3,000.**

Oil on canvas, a river landscape, Chinese school, mid-19th century, framed size 13" X 19", **$650–$900.**

Portrait of an official seated on a throne chair, his robe red with a phoenix mandarin badge, framed, 19th century, framed size, 38" X 60", **$800–$1,200.**

Painted leaves, album, ink and color, each leaf painted with a Lohan and attribute, 19th century, 5" X 7", **set of 10, $1,000–$1,500.**

Watercolor on pith paper, an album of insect specimens, 20 paintings in all, 19th century, 16" X 12¾", **$1,200–$1,600.**

Watercolor on pith paper, from *Methods of Torture and Punishment*, framed, some foxing and stain, 19th century, framed size 11" X 14", **$100–$150.**

Traditional

Fan painting, ink on paper, *Plum Blossoms*, accompanied by a poem, dated 1760, 20¾" X 6¾", **$3,500–$4,500.**

One of a set of four paintings, colors on pith paper, black lacquer frames, Chinese, late 19th century, frame size 10" X 15½", *each*, **$100–$150.**

Fan painting, ink and color on gold-dusted silk, *River Landscape*, Zou Zhe, dated 1652, 20" X 7½", **$1,800–$2,500.**

Fan painting, ink and color on paper, landscape, signed *Zheng Wuchang*, one artist's seal, 21¾" X 7¾", **$400–$700.**

Fan painting (mounted as an album leaf), ink and color on paper, *Lotus*, accompanied by a two-line poem, Gongshou, one artist's seal, one collector's seal, **$1,200–$1,500.**

Fan painting, ink and color on gold-dusted paper, *Peach Blossoms*, inscribed with a poem, Ju Cao, dated 1857, two artist's seals, **$625–$900.**

Hanging scroll, ink on paper, *Lotus*, Pu Ru, signed, four seals, one collector's seal, 12¾" X 42", **$1,500–$2,500.**

Hanging scroll, ink on paper, *Old Tree, Rock, and Bamboo*, Lo Mu, two artist's seals, one collector's seal, 17" × 59", **$1,000–$1,500.**

Hanging scroll, ink and color on paper, *Parrot on Branch*, Ding Yanyong, signed and sealed twice, dated summer of 1978, 26½" × 53½", **$2,500–$3,500.**

Hanging scroll, ink and color on paper, *Peonies and Rock*, Ju Lian, two artist's seals, dated 1882, 19¾" × 38⅞", **$1,200–$1,600.**

Hanging scroll, ink and color on light paper, *White Robed Kuan Yin*, Zang Daqian, two artist's seals, dated 1946, 16¾" × 33", **$3,500–$4,500.**

Hanging scroll, ink and color on paper, *Sparrows* (perched on leafy branches) signed *Yang Shashen*, one artist's seal, dated 1983, 18" × 25⅛", **$1,000–$1,500.**

Hanging scroll, ink and color on silk, *Wild Ducks*, in the style of Bian Jingzhao (with his seal), 19th century, 21½" × 155", **$1,000–$1,500.**

Hanging scroll, ink and color on paper, *Flowering Prunus*, Shi Lu, signed twice, two painted seals, 26¼" × 54½", **$5,000–$7,000.**

Hanging scroll, ink and color on paper, *Shepherdess*, Cheng Shifa, two artist's seals, 1961, 17⅛" × 23¾", **$650–$900.**

Hanging scroll, ink and color on paper, *Landscape*, Li Huasheng, two artist's seals, 18" × 27¾", **$600–$800.**

Hanging scroll, ink on paper, *Calligraphy in Zing Shu* (running script), Wu Changshuo, one artist's seal, dated 1926, 19¼" × 46", **$1,000–$1,500.**

Hanging scroll, ink and color on paper, *Camellias and Birds*, Yu Fei'an, three artist's seals, 20¼" × 35¾", **$800–$1,200.**

Hanging scroll, ink and color on paper, *Camellia and Two Birds*, Huang Binhong, two artist's seals, 13¼" × 23¾", **$1,500–$1,875.**

Japanese Paintings

Fan painting, sumi on paper, mounted as a hanging scroll (kakemono), Sugawara no Michizane riding an ox, Kano school, early Edo period, 19½" × 9½", **$1,500–$2,200.**

Fan painting, colors and gofun on gold paper, red camellias with a thick trunk, painted in the Rimpa manner, early 20th century, 7½" × 12½", **$600–$800.**

Fan painting, sumi and colors on a mica ground, a branch of maple leaves, old repairs, framed, 19th century, framed size 18" × 10", **$500–$650.**

Hand scroll; ink, colors, and gofun on gold pigment paper; a landscape and townscape with temples and shops; Sumiyoshi school; 19th century, 15½" × 24½", **$5,000–$7,000.**

Hanging scroll, ink and colors on silk, *Warrior in Full Armor*, Eigaku Kano (1785–1863), 16" × 45", **$900–$1,200.**

Hanging scroll, ink and colors on silk, *Stalking Tiger*, Suido Yamada (1892–1969), 16½" × 50", **$700–$950.**

Hanging scroll, ink and colors on paper, *Cat and Kitten*, Takeuchi Seiho (1864–1932), 11¾" × 18½", **$700–$950.**

Set of four fusuma depicting Tales of the Genji, *colors on gold paper, Japanese, Tosa-Sumitoshi School, 17th century, each panel 28½" × 68½", some damages. Realized price (including the 10-percent buyer's premium), Christie's East, New York City,* **$6,600.**

Hanging scroll, ink and colors on silk, a flock of geese amongst water grasses and reeds under a full moon, signed *Seiko Shai*, dated Meiji 16 (1883), 32¾" × 74", **$1,000–$1,500.**

Hanging scroll, sumi and colors on silk, a puppy amongst dandelions and grasses, late Edo period, 8¾" × 14½", **$700–$850.**

Hanging scroll, a tiger appearing through bamboo, creased and damaged, 19th century, 12" × 15½", **$400–$600.**

Hanging scroll, colored lacquer on paper, gourd on a vine, signed *Zeshin*, 7½" × 11½", **$6,000–$8,000.**

Hanging scroll, ink and colors on silk, *Hanna tsuki* (Messenger of Flowers), a lady and two servants, one of whom is carrying a floral bouquet, in the style of Zeshin (with his signature), 14" × 23¼", **$575–$700.**

Hanging scroll, sumi on paper, Jurojin and a gnarled staff by a large pine tree, signed *Minamoto Gyokutan*, Taisho period, 15½" × 40", **$375–$600.**

Hanging scroll; ink, colors, and gofun on silk; mandarin duck and aquatic plants; signed *Seiko sho*; dated Meiji 16 (1883), 32¾" × 74", **$900–$1,200.**

Hanging scroll, sumi and colors on paper, a pair of monkeys and their young, Sosen school, dated 1896, 20¼" × 39", **$900–$1,200.**

Hanging scroll, sumi and colors on silk, rabbits amongst autumn grasses, signed *Chokusui*, late 19th century, 16½" × 34½", **$550–$775.**

Hanging scroll; ink, colors, and gofun on silk; *Sparrows and Peonies*; signed *Anko Shoshi*; 20th century, 16½" × 50¼", **$400–$600.**

Two from a series of four paintings—watercolor and gouache on pith paper—depicting various river barges, junks, and sampans plying the shallow waters; Canton School, Chinese, 19th century, 16" × 12" image size, framed and glazed. Realized price (including the 10-percent buyer's premium), Christie's East, New York City, $1,980.

Hanging scroll, sumi and colors on silk, two sparrows on a spray of millet, creased, old damages, 19th century, 11¾" × 15¾", **$300–$450.**

Hanging scroll, sumi on silk, wooded mountainous landscape with buildings, Kano school, 19th century, 14½" × 23½", **$650–$900.**

Painting, sumi and colors on paper, a boy with a falcon on his arm, framed, 19th century, framed size, 9" × 23", **$300–$500.**

Painting, sumi and colors on silk, a monkey eating a peach, Hokusai style, framed, 19th century, framed size 10¼" × 17", **$900–$1,200.**

Screen; two-leaf; sumi, colors, and gofun on paper; Hotei playing with four karako in a lakeside scene; old damages; early Meiji period, leaf size 33½" × 63", **$1,200–$1,600.**

Screen, two-leaf, sumi and colors on gold paper, flowering peony, Kano school, 19th century, leaf size 31" × 80", **$1,000–$1,500.**

Screen, two-leaf, sumi and colors on gold-sprinkled paper, an eagle perched on a branch, stained, old repairs, 19th century, leaf size 29" × 59", **$1,000–$1,500.**

Screen, two-leaf, sumi and colors on paper, a group of three cranes standing beneath a large pine, signed *Ichigyoun hitsu*, some old damages, 19th century, leaf size, 36¾" × 66½", **$3,000–$5,000.**

Screen; two-leaf; sumi, colors, and gofun on paper; flowers in a stream; late 19th century, leaf size 23" × 41", **$500–$700.**

Screen; four-leaf; sumi, colors, and gofun on silver-ground paper; autumn leaves scattered amongst rock-work below a full moon; 19th century, leaf size 25" × 51½", **$2,000–$3,000.**

Screen; six-leaf; sumi, colors, and gofun on silver-ground paper; a stag and deer with autumnal flowers; signed *Koasai*; stained and damaged; Meiji period, leaf size 18½" × 43", **$750–$1,200.**

Screen; six-leaf; sumi, colors, and gofun on gold paper; flowers above boldly breaking waves; 19th century, leaf size 24" X 62½", **$4,000–$6,000.**

Screen; six-leaf; sumi, colors, and gofun on silk; Mt. Fuji, pine, and flowering cherry trees; old repairs; late 18th century, leaf size 24" X 60", **$1,800–$2,500.**

Watercolor on paper, three carp and water reeds, late 19th century, framed size 12½" X 18", **$400–$600.**

Watercolor on paper, women gathering kelp at the seashore, Hiroshi Yoshida, dated 1902, 8½" X 18½", **$1,000–$1,500.**

Southeast Asian Paintings

Pata, depicting Krishna, divided into five horizontal scenes with red borders; in the central panel, a cross-legged figure playing the flute and wearing princely garments, flanked by two gopis offering vessels and two courtiers wearing hive-shaped hats, two bulls seated below, trees and the sky beyond; the four surrounding panels depicting episodes from the life of Krishna, including Balakrishna approaching his mother, who sits churning butter; the two upper panels depicting Jalasaya Vishnu, a couple peering from the balcony of a house, a couple receiving ablutions, Krishna about to behead a princely couple, a similar couple worshipping Vishnu in a temple; cloth surround and lining; Nepalese, 19th century, 42" X 30", **$600–$900.**

Pata, depicting Siva and Parvati, divided into five horizontal scenes; the middle panel subdivided into four square panels flanking the central figures of the six-armed Siva and his wife seated on Nandi Bull and a ferocious lion, the god with three eyes; Siva wears a tiger skin, a garland of severed human heads, and jewelry—his green consort, yellow shawl and orange trousers; flanked by Ganesha and Brahma to the left, Vishnu and a red four-armed deity to the right; a mountainous ground, clouds above; the four panels depicting Siva legends; cotton surround and lining; Nepalese, 19th century, 42" X 30¼", **$800–$1,200.**

Thangka depicting four Arhats—Ajita, Kalika, Panthanka, and Cudapanthaka—each wearing elaborate robes decorated with gilt ornamentation, their faces and lips gilded, their robes in green, red, and blue; each seated on a red lacquered throne surrounded by attendant figures; a landscaped ground; three seated figures of Buddha at the top; a Dharmapala and Sakti at the center; dark red border with silk surround; Tibetan, 18th century, 28½" X 18¼", **$2,000–$3,000.**

Thangka depicting four Arhats: the seated figures of Panthanka holding a pustaka and Abheda holding a stupa above, Pindolabharadvaja holding a patra and pustaka below (to the left), and the fourth holding a patra; a cakra below, a tupa on a pedestal at his left; each figure in elaborate red, green, and orange brocade robes; two with halos; two seated on foliate thrones; the sky above; the ground landscaped with flower sprays, offerings, and other symbols; Tibetan, 18th century, frame size 28" X 16", **$2,000–$3,000.**

Thangka depicting Bodhisattva Maitreya seated in European manner upon an elaborate throne supported by lions, a pavilion with tiered orange roofs behind; in his right hand, the stem of a padma flowering at the shoulder, supporting a cakra; in his left hand, a water ewer; he wears a five-leaf crown, earrings, and other jewelry; gilded body; his robes red, green, and blue; a rayed aureole and green halo behind; numerous Chinese devotees, monks, and bodhisattvas surrounding him; Sino-Tibetan, 18th century, frame size 32¼" X 26", **$750–$1,000.**

Thangka depicting Buddha seated in dhyanasana on a lotus throne with a red frontal apron adorned by a pair of gilt phoenixes, his hands in bhumispara and dhyana mudra; he wears a red robe with gilt flower heads; a rayed aureole with foliate border behind; numerous figures surrounding him; landscape background; creased and worn; Tibetan, 18th century, frame size 24½" X 20¼", **$450–$600.**

Thangka depicting the Dharmapala Vajrabhairava standing in pratyalidhasana on animals, birds, and Hindu deities on a green and blue lotus throne; in yab-yum with his pale blue–bodied Sakti, who holds a blood-filled kapala; the dark blue–bodied deity with 16 legs and 34 arms, each holding a gilt attribute; his central head that of a ferocious bull, flanked by six other heads, surmounted by a red dharmapala head with that of Manjusri on top; wearing skull- and severed-human-head garlands as well as beaded jewels; Mahakala in the center foreground, flanked by Kubera and Yama with his sister Yami; birds and deer in the landscaped ground; Tibetan, 18th century, frame size 16" X 14½", **$550–$900.**

Thangka depicting Guatama Buddha seated in dhyanasana on a white lotus throne, his right hand in bhumisparsa mudra, his left in dhyana mudra holding a patra, wearing a saffron and red sanghati decorated with gilt medallions, the disciples Moggalanna and Sariputra standing in the lower corners, the upper half with a monk, red brocade surround, Tibetan, 19th century, 17½" X 13¼", **$300–$500.**

Thangka depicting a lion-headed Dharmapala riding a mule treading on a human corpse on a lotus throne in a sea of red, swirling blood; his ferocious head that of a lion; three white lions in his blue hair; a dvaja in his right hand, a kapala in his left; he wears boots, an elaborate robe, and a skull crown; a sword at his side; the foreground flanked by animals; the whole surrounded by flames with birds holding entrails in their beaks; Tibetan, early 20th century, 24½" X 16", **$900–$1,200.**

Thangka depicting Vajrasattva seated in dhyanasana on a lotus throne; a vajra in his raised right hand, a ghanta in his left; wearing blue and red gilt-decorated robes, gilt jewelry, and a five-leaf crown; a rayed blue halo with red border and an orange halo behind; Gautama and Aksobhya Buddha above; blue silk brocade surround; the reverse with floral cotton lining; 19th century, 20½" X 13¾", **$450–$600.**

13

Points for the Rug Buyer

In order for the buyer to be knowledgeable enough to distinguish the quality or grade of a rug, he or she must study all types of Persian rugs, focusing on a number of features. For instance, a good rug, whether finely or coarsely knotted, will have a firm, compact body. The thinner the lengthwise *warp* threads—and the *woof* threads which cross them at right angles—the more compact the weave will be. These threads can be observed on the back of a rug or in the selvage and fringe.

Single-knot rugs are the most closely woven rugs. The Ghiordes, or double knot, is found in rugs such as those from the Bijar district.

The best Persian rugs have cotton, linen, or silk, rather than wool, for the warp and woof. Moreover, a good rug will have carefully finished edges and will not be unduly crooked. It should have a distinct design and clear colors, as well.

Marks of Distinction

As a rule, Kashan and Kerman rugs show the finest knotting and closest weave. Kashan rugs are knotted with silk, but either silk or wool is acceptable. Similarly, Fereghan and Sarouk rugs are distinguished by their fine weaving, but it is not as fine as that of the Kermans or Kashans.

Bijars, though coarsely knotted, are firmly woven, usually with a double woof, which makes the rugs very heavy. Tabriz rugs are, as a rule, more finely woven than Bijars, but are not as fine as Sehnas, which are single-knot rugs.

The rugs of the nomad weavers, including Kurdish, Shiraz, and Bakhtiari, are generally coarsely knotted; Tekke Turkoman rugs, which are more finely woven than other nomad rugs and are equal in quality to Tabriz rugs, are the exception. The others have wool for warp and woof. Of this group the common characteristics include a wide, striped selvage ending in a long fringe.

Values for Rugs and Carpets

Note: Carpets are generally larger, and rugs, generally smaller, than ten feet.

Bakhtiari rug, dark green Millefleur ground with oversized stepped pendant medallion (ivory), smaller dark blue floral scalloped medallion, dark blue floral spandrels, red primary border of floral sprays, two pair of narrow guard borders, 6'7" X 4'11", **$2,000–$3,000.**

Bijar rug, red ground, gold petal-form center medallion with blue pendant palmettes and gold floral spandrels, navy blue primary border, a pair of ivory floral guard borders, selvage break, very worn, late 19th century, 12'5" X 5'5", **$5,000–$6,000.**

Chinese carpet, blue ground with overall pattern of stylized clouds, scattered cranes, central crane medallion, pale orange key-fret border, narrow guard stripes, worn, early 20th century, 17'6" X 10'4", **$1,500–$2,000.**

Chinese carpet (Peking); ivory ground covered with trees, mountains, and the Eight Horses of Mu Wang; blue primary border with floral medallions; three pair of guard borders; worn; losses; animal stains; late 19th century, 1'4" X 6'3", **$6,500–$8,500.**

Chinese carpet (Nichols), deep blue with scattered floral sprays and butterflies, gray primary border with prunus blossoms, three guard borders, 17'7" X 11'5", **$6,000–$8,000.**

Chinese carpet, cream field with central blue floral-spray medallion, smaller floral medallions at corners, narrow blue guard borders, 11'9" X 9', **$2,000–$3,000.**

Chinese carpet, cream field with blue and magenta floral sprays at the corners, narrow blue guard border, c1925, 11'6" X 8'10", **$2,000–$3,000.**

Chinese rug, ivory field with colored floral sprays in geometric style, outer guard border with Shou characters in deep blue, c1925, 11'8" × 9', **$1,500–$2,550.**

Chinese carpet, deep blue field with flowering vases and meandering scroll on deeper blue guard border, c1910, 7'6" × 4'2", **$2,000–$3,000.**

Chinese rug, indigo field with flaming pearls and clouds surrounding five dragons, wave-pattern guard border in colors, late 19th century, 7' × 4', **$3,500–$5,000.**

Chinese rug, blue field with royal blue clouds, cream guard border with magenta flowers, outer guard border with dragons, damage, moth deterioration, animal stains, c1925, 9'5" × 7'2", **$1,000–$1,500.**

Chinese rug, pale orange ground with blue and white dragons, deep blue guard border, 4' × 7', **$1,200–$1,600.**

Chinese rug, black ground with Shou Lao surrounded by Immortals in colors, damaged, 6' × 6'2", **$900–$1,200.**

Kashan carpet; ivory ground with all-over pattern of scrolling vines, rosettes, and palmettes; five guard borders; 8'11" × 6'1", **$5,000–$7,000.**

Kashan carpet, red ground with three concentric petal-form medallions in blue, blue and green floral sprays, navy blue floral spandrels, navy blue border of palmettes, three pair of guard borders, worn, refringed, 12'2" × 8'10", **$5,000–$6,000.**

Kerman carpet; navy blue with floral medallion in cream, burgundy, and green; elaborate floral border; worn; 14'3" × 10'4", **$2,200–$3,600.**

Kurdish rug, deep blue ground covered by three vertical rows of flower heads, zig-zag inner designs and spandrels, deep blue meandering vine primary border, one pair of narrow claret floral guard borders, worn, losses to guard borders, 6'11" × 4'2", **$700–$900.**

Kurdish runner, red with five blue medallions, brown floral spandrels, three guard borders, worn and losses, 12'11" × 3'5", **$1,100–$1,800.**

Kurdish runner, navy blue ground, diagonal rows of pentagonal devices, inner trefoil guard border surrounded by an ivory plant leaf and T-device border, repaired and worn, 3'10" × 10'7", **$900–$1,200.**

Sarouk Fereghan mat, cream with pattern of meandering vines and botehs, deep blue primary border, one pair of guard borders, worn and unraveling, 1'8" × 1'6", **$500–$650.**

Sarouk Fereghan rug, red with blue floral pendant medallion and floral sprays with beige floral spandrels, deep blue primary border with floral arrangements, one pair of red guard borders, badly worn and reduced, late 19th century, 4'8" × 3'5", **$800–$1,200.**

Sarouk runner, claret ground with all-over pattern of floral bouquets and sprays, deep blue primary border of flowering vines, two pair of guard borders, repaired and worn, 15'5" × 2'9", **$2,000–$3,000.**

Shiraz rug, midnight blue ground, rust stepped medallion enclosing a smaller blue platform medallion, elaborate vines and rosettes with cream platform medallions in each corner, deep blue border of stylized vines and rosettes, three pair of guard borders, some wear and repair, 6'10" X 4'5", **$1,500–$2,200.**

Tabriz rug, melon ground with oval center medallion, overall Millefleur with burgundy spandrels, ivory primary border with vines and palmettes, three pair of guard borders, 7'7" X 4'8", **$4,000–$6,000.**

Tekke Turkoman carpet, red-brown ground, four rows of gulls, 12 per row, red-brown border with sunburst design, one pair of guard borders with serrated leaf skirts, refringed, 11' X 7', **$3,500–$4,500.**

Tekke Turkoman rug, red ground covered with two rows of octagonal cloverleaf gulls (6 per row) and star devices, a deep blue primary border with interconnecting leaves, two guard borders with striped kilims, 5'3" X 3'10", **$900–$1,150.**

Tekke Turkoman runner, red ground, two rows of gulls, 22 per row, alternating diamond-shaped devices, ivory primary border with palmettes, six narrow guard borders, kilim stripes at each end, 16' X 2'11", **$2,000–$2,700.**

14

Snuff Bottles

During the seventeenth century, the taking of snuff became a popular Chinese practice. Although it was not acceptable for the Chinese to smoke tobacco, snuff was considered medicinal. Accordingly, the snuff bottle, developed in the latter part of the century, was based on the concepts for the Chinese medicine bottles (yao ping).

In the late nineteenth century, the snuff bottle became a cabinet bottle, purchased for collecting purposes. Many of these cabinet bottles were not well-hollowed. At the same time, motifs were more flamboyant.

Today, snuff bottles (antique and contemporary) are highly prized and collected worldwide, and their values continue to rise steadily.

Note: Bottles are not always available with the original cap and spoon. These are interchangeable and, for the most part, do not affect values.

Values

Agate, flattened form, a broad white band around the center, early 19th century, **$400–$600.**

Agate, striated, ovoid, smoky gray with brown stippling, 19th century, **$200–$300.**

Agate/moss, honey-colored with spinach green masslike tendrils, well hollowed, 19th century, **$400–$600.**

Agate/moss; ovoid with mask and ring handles on the shoulders; red, gray, and gold; 19th century, **$800–$1,200.**

Agate/moss, rectangular, honey with blue-green inclusions, 19th century, **$300–$400.**

Agate/shadow, ovoid flattened form with a carved bird and flowers, late 19th century, **$700–$900.**

Agate/shadow carved to depict a bird and fruit beneath a tree (the design incorporating the natural inclusions in the stone), 19th century, **$800–$1,200.**

Agate/shadow, carved, two men seated under a pine, late Ch'ing (Qing) dynasty, **$1,500–$2,000.**

Agate/shadow; carved; an elder, rockwork, and pines; an inscription on the reverse; **$2,500–$3,500.**

Amber carved in low relief with bats on one side, the reverse with a pavilion and pine, late 19th century, **$600–$900.**

Amber, small size, relief carving of fruiting vines overall, late Ch'ing (Qing) dynasty, **$200–$300.**

Amethyst, eggplant form with carved leaves, **$1,000–$1,500.**

Amethyst, mask and ring handles on the shoulders, the stone a pale purple, late Ch'ing (Qing) dynasty, **$1,000–$1,500.**

Amethyst; baluster form; carved with pine, peony, and deer; late Ch'ing (Qing) dynasty, **$1,000–$1,500.**

Bamboo carved as a fruit, the shoulders with small leaves, **$00–$600.**

Bamboo carved in the form of three seed pods, leaves in relief, 19th century, **$225–$325.**

Canton enamel, ovoid, yellow ground painted with phoenix and waterfowl in a landscape, early 18th century, **$5,000–$7,000.**

Canton enamel painted with a continuous scene of children at play and a young woman holding flowers, ruyi band on the foot and shoulders, restored, four-character Ch'ien Lung (Qianlong) mark (and of the period), 18th century, **$6,000–$8,000.**

Canton enamel, ovoid form, mandarin ducks and aquatic plants beneath tree peony, the reverse with a bird perched on a branch, famille rose, restoration on shoulder and neck, early 18th century, **$6,000–$8,000.**

Canton enamel; a continuous landscape with figures, pavilions, and mountains; blue and white; minor fusion flake on shoulder; 18th century, **$3,000–$4,000.**

Canton enamel, yellow ground with a dragon-and-cloud pattern, 19th century, **$600–$800.**

Canton enamel, turquoise ground with yellow and blue dragon and clouds, early 19th century, **$1,000–$1,500.**

Left to right: *Enamel-on-copper snuff bottle, dragon and flaming pearl, late 19th century,* **$500–$600.** *Opal snuff bottle with carp and waves, 20th century,* **$900–$1,200.** *Lac burgauté bottle inlaid with gold and silver foil and mother-of-pearl, late 18th / early 19th century,* **$1,000–$1,500.**

Chalcedony, Tzu chou–style carving with figures and rock-work, **$400–$600.**

Chalcedony carving of a sage, the reverse with pine and riverscape, blue, late 19th century, **$700–$900.**

Chalcedony, ovoid with reddish brown areas on a gray field, 19th century, **$300–$500.**

Cloisonné, baluster form, lotus and scrolls on each side, Ming style, late 19th century, **$300–$500.**

Cloisonné, double-gourd form, blue ground with lotus and scrolls, late 19th century, **$300–$400.**

Cloisonné; flattened ovoid form; butterflies and flowers in white, yellow, and pink on a turquoise ground; late Ch'ing (Qing) dynasty, **$250–$350.**

Cloisonné, open-work with a pattern of phoenix and flowering scrolls in colors and gilt, early 20th century, **$600–$900.**

Cloisonné; turquoise ground with a pattern of butterflies and foliate sprigs overall in red, white, blue, and black; late 19th century, **$300–$400.**

Coral in the form of a carp leaping through waves and spitting a pearl (which forms the stopper), **$750–$950.**

Coral carved overall with tree peonies, **$1,500–$2,000.**

Coral, rectangular form, carved in relief with phoenix and foliage on one side, a dragon and clouds on the reverse, **$800–$1,200.**

Glass, double-gourd form, black with gold speckling, early 19th century, **$350–$500.**

Glass, egg yolk yellow, carved with a band of stiff leaves around the shoulders, 19th century, **$900–$1,200.**

Glass; flattened form; an oval panel on each side; deep blue; Ch'ien Lung (Qianlong) mark, but 19th century; **$300–$500.**

Glass, octagonal and faceted, deep ruby red, early 20th century, **$200–$300.**

Glass, pale green with red circlets of varying sizes, **$150–$275.**

Inside-painted glass decorated with a boy riding a water buffalo, signed Ma Shao Xuan, dated 1905, **$1,000–$1,500.**

Inside-painted glass decorated with butterflies and kittens on both sides, 20th century, **$150–$225.**

Inside-painted glass decorated with a continuous scene of carp, pike, catfish, and aquatic plants; signed Zhou Leyuan; **$1,000–$1,600.**

Inside-painted glass with a continuous scene of standing ladies and rock-work executed in vivid colors, signed Ye Zhong San, dated 1908, **$800–$1,100.**

Inside-painted glass with a continuous scene of figures within a landscape, **$160–$200.**

Inside-painted glass decorated with two ladies amongst flowering branches on one side, the reverse with a scholar and his attendant in a landscape, pear-shaped, **$300–$400.**

Inside-painted glass, large size, decorated with equestrians against a mountainscape, the reverse with ladies and attendants, early 20th century, **$300–$400.**

Inside-painted glass, double bottle, rectangular form, decorated with four landscapes, late 19th century, **$500–$700.**

Inside-painted glass, rectangular, decorated with birds and squirrels, early 20th century, **$300–$400.**

Inside-painted glass, rectangular, decorated with flowers and vases, c1925, **$100–$150.**

Overlay glass, five-color, the white ground decorated with a floral spray on each side, early 19th century, **$1,000–$1,500.**

Overlay glass, five-color on a milk white ground, carved with bats and Buddhist emblems, 19th century, **$1,000–$1,500.**

Overlay glass, five-color on milk glass, double-gourd form with a motif of Buddhist emblems, **$600–$800.**

Overlay glass, blue glass carved through to the white glass with a low-relief motif of a horse and pine, **$600–$800.**

Overlay glass, blue on milk glass, bats and cranes, late Ch'ing (Qing) dynasty, **$400–$550.**

Overlay glass carved in red with chih lung and scrolls, last half of the 18th century, **$900–$1,200.**

Overlay glass, red overlay on bubble-suffused glass, carved with carp and aquatic plants, waves around the base, 18th century, **$2,000–$2,500.**

Overlay glass, bubble glass with red overlay, carved with flowering sprays on each side, 19th century, **$600–$900.**

Overlay glass, red overlay on clear glass, birds and pavilions above crested waves, **$1,500–$2,000.**

Overlay glass, pear-shaped, carved with a red overlay in a continuous scene of pavilions and pines, late 18th century, **$1,200–$1,800.**

Overlay glass, red overlay carved through to a yellow ground with five bats encircling a Shou character, 19th century, **$500–$700.**

Overlay, snowflake glass with red bats overall, 19th century, **$350–$550.**

Hair crystal, **$250–$350.**

Hair crystal, ovoid form, thick clouds of black tourmaline needles, early 19th century, **$600–$800.**

Hair crystal, flattened ovoid form, tourmaline needles enclosed by iridescence, 19th century, **$1,000–$1,500.**

Hair crystal, flattened form, clear stone with fine black tourmaline needles, well hollowed, early 19th century, **$800–$1,200.**

Hornbill carved with two figures under a pine, **$700–$900.**

Hornbill carved with figures in landscapes, **$600–$750.**

Ivory carved as a dragon on waves, **$400–$600.**

Ivory carved as a writhing dragon, **$300–$400.**

Ivory, cylindrical, carved in deep relief, a court scene, late 19th century, **$700–$1,000.**

Ivory, oviform, carved with a hen and chicks, late Ch'ing (Qing) dynasty, **$700–$900.**

Ivory, polychrome double bottle of Emperor and Empress, heads as stoppers, **$400–$600.**

Jade, black, carved in relief, a monkey seated on a rock passing a peach to another monkey, the reverse with Lui Hai holding a string of cash before a toad, 19th century, **$2,500–$3,500.**

Jade, celadon pebble bottle with russet areas, **$225–$375.**

Jade, white, carved in low relief on each side with a large peony, **$700–$900.**

Jade, white, carved as a finger citron, last half of the 19th century, **$500–$750.**

Jade, white, low-relief carving of a pavilion and pine with an elder, mid-19th century, **$600–$900.**

Jade, white with overall carved wickerwork pattern, early 19th century, **$900–$1,200.**

Jadeite, apple green, mottled, rectangular form, first half of the 19th century, **$2,000–$3,000.**

Jadeite, lavender with concave foot rim, **$1,500–$1,800.**

Jadeite, lavender, ovoid form, an overall lattice design, 19th century, **$900–$1,200.**

Jadeite, pale green with emerald flecks and black splashes, 19th century, **$600–$900.**

Jasper carved with branches on a blue-gray ground, **$250–$350.**

Ku Yüeh Hsüan; milk glass painted with birds perched on branches; Ch'ien Lung (Qianlong) mark, but early 19th century; **$1,200–$1,600.**

Ku Yüeh Hsüan; milk glass painted with lotus, peony, and leaf scrolls; leaf band on collar and foot; famille rose; Ch'ien Lung (Qianlong) four-character mark (and of the period), **$4,000–$6,000.**

Ku Yüeh Hsüan, milk glass painted with a continuous motif of flowering branches, famille rose, 19th century, **$900–$1,200.**

Lac burgauté, two brown panels, one inlaid in mother-of-pearl with a long-tailed bird perched on a flowering branch, the reverse with peony clusters, **$1,600–$2,200.**

Lac burgauté, butterfly form with red-orange panels on each side, Shibayama inlay in a floral motif, 20th century, **$700–$950.**

Lac burgauté, octagonal with diapers around a central flower head, 19th century, **$800–$1,000.**

Lac burgauté, rectangular and squat, a shaped panel on each side with a landscape motif, **$400–$600.**

Lacquer; red (cinnabar); carved in deep relief with ladies on a balcony; Ch'ien Lung (Qianlong) mark, but early 20th century; **$150–$225.**

Lacquer, cinnabar, carved in high relief with figures and a pavilion, late Ch'ing (Qing) dynasty, **$400–$600.**

Lapis carved with warriors, **$275–$400.**

Malachite, flattened ovoid form with a circular panel on each side, late 19th century, **$900–$1,200.**

Mongolian silver, cylindrical, inset with turquoise and coral forming small flower heads, late Ch'ing (Qing) dynasty, **$200–$300.**

Mongolian silver inlaid with coral and turquoise on each side, forming large flower heads; late Ch'ing (Qing) dynasty, **$500–$700.**

Mongolian silver, reticulated filigree centered with turquoise on each side, 19th century, **$700–$900.**

Mother-of-pearl carved in relief with five bats around a Shou character, the reverse with a dragon, **$500–$700.**

Opal carved with a dragon on one side and a phoenix on the reverse, **$500–$600.**

Opal in the form of a carp on waves spitting out a pearl (which forms the stopper), **$700–$900.**

Opal, rectangular, two children carved in relief, **$400–$600.**

Porcelain, a motif of two puppies on each side, early 20th century, **$200–$300.**

Porcelain, a green grasshopper on each side, last half of the 19th century, **$400–$600.**

Porcelain, a green grasshopper on each side, early 20th century, **$175–$225.**

Porcelain, a green and orange four-toed dragon and flaming pearl on each side, early 20th century, **$100–$125.**

Porcelain, a red dragon writhing around the bottle, late 19th century, **$400–$600.**

Porcelain in the form of a recumbent elephant supporting a vase on its saddle, famille rose, late 19th century, **$350–$475.**

Porcelain, 1000 Flowers pattern, famille rose on a black ground, c1925, **$100–$175.**

Porcelain molded in relief; a writhing dragon; reticulated ground; famille rose; Ch'ien Lung (Qianlong) mark, but from the Tao Kuang (Daoguang) period; **$800–$1,200.**

Porcelain molded in relief, children playing, famille rose, Tao Kuang (Daoguang) period, **$800–$1,200.**

Porcelain molded in the form of a recumbent Buddhistic lion, famille rose, early 19th century, **$600–$900.**

Left to right: *Porcelain snuff bottle with fish and aquatic plants in relief, famille rose, Tao Kuang period,* **$700–$900.** *Porcelain snuff bottle; underglaze blue, copper red, and white decorated with the Eight Immortals; early 19th century,* **$350–$550.** *Ku Yüeh Hsüan snuff bottle, famille rose, motif of flowers and foliage with insects, 19th century,* **$1,200–$1,500.**

Porcelain, moon-flask form with a Rose Mandarin pattern, early 19th century, **$500–$700.**

Porcelain reticulated and molded in relief with dragons and clouds, glazed blue, c1900, **$400–$600.**

Porcelain, Rose Medallion, baluster form, c1880, **$300–$400.**

Porcelain, white glaze, molded in high relief with 18 Lohan, c1800, **$1,000–$1,500.**

Porcelain, yellow glaze, writhing dragon molded in relief, mid-19th century, **$700–$900.**

Porcelain, blue and white, motif of a standing lady and her attendant, early 19th century, **$300–$500.**

Porcelain, underglaze blue and copper red with a lotus motif, early 19th century, **$200–$300.**

Porcelain, a seated Lohan and pine tree on each side, famille rose, early 19th century, **$500–$700.**

Porcelain, each side with red-orange Buddhistic lions and clouds, early 20th century, **$125–$175.**

Porcelain; blue and white; a continuous landscape; Ch'ien Lung (Qianlong) mark, but late 19th century; **$150–$225.**

Porcelain; blue and white; riverscape with boats in relief; Ch'eng Hua (Chenghua) mark, but late 19th century; **$400–$600.**

Porcelain, underglaze blue and copper red, cylindrical with continuous motif of warriors and horses, 19th century, **$175–$225.**

Porcelain, underglaze blue and copper red, cylindrical with the 12 animals of the zodiac, late 18th century, **$700–$900.**

Left to right: *Porcelain snuff bottle, famille rose, 18 Lohan in relief, each with attribute, early 19th century,* **$900–$1,200.** *Malachite gourd-form snuff bottle, 20th century,* **$700–$900.** *Glass snuff bottle, milk glass with red overlay motif, late 18th century,* **$700–$950.** *Ivory snuff bottle with archaic motifs, late 18th century,* **$1,000–$1,500.**

Porcelain, underglaze blue and copper red with scholars and attendants in a landscape, early 19th century, **$300–$400.**

Porcelain/soft paste, blue and white with a motif of 100 Children, **$900–$1,200.**

Porcelain/soft paste; blue and white with camels and attendants; Yung Cheng (Yongzheng) mark, but late 18th century; **$500–$700.**

Porcelain/soft paste, cylindrical form with the Eight Horses of Mu Wang, late 18th/early 19th century, **$500–$700.**

Porcelain, cylindrical, Rooster Pattern, famille rose, Kuang Hsü (Guangxu) mark (and of the period), **$700–$900.**

Porcelain, cylindrical, figures in a landscape, famille rose, early 19th century, **$400–$600.**

Porcelain, each side decorated with ducks and spring flowers, blue mask and ring handles on shoulders, Tao Kuang (Daoguang) mark (and of the period), **$800–$1,200.**

Porcelain, flattened ovoid form covered with a blue glaze, Kuang Hsü (Guangxu) mark (and of the period), **$300–$425.**

Rock crystal carving of an Immortal, **$150–$250.**

Rock crystal, faceted hexagonal form, first half of the 19th century, **$400–$600.**

Rock crystal painted on the inside with fan-tailed fish and aquatic plants, signed *Ye Zhong San* and dated 1911, **$1,000–$1,500.**

Rock crystal painted on the inside with 18 Lohan and their attributes, signed *Ye Zhong San* and dated 1919, **$2,000–$3,000.**

Rock crystal painted on the inside with a continuous landscape and mountain-scape with a sage and attendant, signed *Zhou Leyuan*, **$1,000–$1,500.**

Rock crystal, rectangular, carved with pine trees, last half of the 19th century, **$200–$300.**

Rose quartz carved in relief on one side with two cranes and pine and a deer and pine on the reverse, **$350–$450.**

Soapstone, gray, low-relief carving of prunus and rock-work, the shoulders with mask and ring handles, **$300–$400.**

Tiger's eye carved with a bird perched on a flowering branch, **$225–$350.**

Tourmaline, green, flattened ovoid form carved with a standing lady on one side and a pine on the reverse, c1900, **$600–$800.**

Tourmaline, pink, modified peach form with carvings of fruit, **$500–$700.**

Turquoise carved with birds in high relief, late Ch'ing (Qing) dynasty, **$500–$700.**

Turquoise carved with flowers and vines in high relief, **$275–$400.**

Turquoise, flattened rounded form, the dark stone with light patches, early 19th century, **$1,500–$2,000.**

I Hsing (Yixing), blue glaze with an oval scenic panel on each side, 19th century, **$700–$1,000.**

I Hsing, two oval panels with landscapes executed in the famille rose palette, first half of the 19th century, **$900–$1,200.**

I Hsing, ovoid, melon, ribbed, **$1,200–$1,600.**

Snuff Saucers

Canton enamel, landscape on a yellow ground, late 18th/early 19th century, **$500–$700.**

Glass, deep red, **$100–$150.**

Chinese Date Marks Found on Inside-Painted Snuff Bottles

甲子	1744-1804-1864-1924	
乙丑	1745-1805-1865-1925	
丙寅	1746-1806-1866-1926	
丁卯	1747-1807-1867-1927	
戊辰	1748-1808-1868-1928	
己巳	1749-1809-1869-1929	
庚午	1750-1810-1870-1930	
辛未	1751-1811-1871-1931	
壬申	1752-1812-1872-1932	
癸酉	1753-1813-1873-1933	
甲戌	1754-1814-1874-1934	
乙亥	1755-1815-1875-1935	
丙子	1756-1816-1876-1936	
丁丑	1757-1817-1877-1937	
戊寅	1758-1818-1878-1938	
己卯	1759-1819-1879-1939	
庚辰	1760-1820-1880-1940	
辛巳	1761-1821-1881-1941	
壬午	1762-1822-1882-1942	
癸未	1763-1823-1883-1943	
甲申	1764-1824-1884-1944	
乙酉	1765-1825-1885-1945	
丙戌	1766-1826-1886-1946	
丁亥	1767-1827-1887-1947	
戊子	1768-1828-1888-1948	
己丑	1769-1829-1889-1949	
庚寅	1770-1830-1890-1950	
辛卯	1771-1831-1891-1951	
壬辰	1772-1832-1892-1952	
癸巳	1773-1833-1893-1953	

甲午	1774-1834-1894-1954	
乙未	1775-1835-1895-1955	
丙申	1776-1836-1896-1956	
丁酉	1777-1837-1897-1957	
戊戌	1778-1838-1898-1958	
己亥	1779-1839-1899-1959	
庚子	1780-1840-1900-1960	
辛丑	1781-1841-1901-1961	
壬寅	1782-1842-1902-1962	
癸卯	1783-1843-1903-1963	
甲辰	1784-1844 1904-1964	
乙巳	1785-1845-1905-1965	
丙午	1786-1846-1906-1966	
丁未	1787-1847-1907-1967	
戊申	1788-1848-1908-1968	
己酉	1789-1849-1909-1969	
庚戌	1790-1850-1910-1970	
辛亥	1791-1851-1911-1971	
壬子	1792-1852-1912-1972	
癸丑	1793-1853-1913-1973	
甲寅	1794-1854-1914-1974	
乙卯	1795-1855-1915-1975	
丙辰	1796-1856-1916-1976	
丁巳	1797-1857-1917-1977	
戊午	1798-1858-1918-1978	
己未	1799-1859-1919-1979	
庚申	1800-1860-1920-1980	
辛酉	1801-1861-1921-1981	
壬戌	1802-1862-1922-1982	
癸亥	1803-1863-1923-1983	

15

Wood-Block Prints

Wood-block prints, *ukiyo-e*, are also referred to as "prints of the floating world." This art form was developed in the last half of the seventeenth century, with artists and skilled engravers initially creating prints to satisfy the Japanese domestic market.

Design of the wood-block print began with the artist painting a picture or design on thin paper. The engraver then pasted this paper, face down, on a cherry wood block, and transferred the outline onto the wood with the use of gauges and other tools. Both sides of the block were used and a block was needed for each color.

Utamaro, oban tate-e, an okubi-e portrait of a beauty holding a sake cup, signed Utamaro hitsu, publisher's seal unidentified, good impression, color slightly faded, spurious mica ground, slightly soiled. Realized price (including the 10-percent buyer's premium), Christie's, New York City, **$4,950.**

The result of the engraver's work was a negative in high relief. The painter, following the artist's instructions, painted the colors on each block with brushes. Finally, dampened papers were aligned and laid, in turn, on each block, then hand-rubbed with a pad, producing the color prints. The blocks were recharged after each impression.

Among the various subjects which are of interest to dealers and collectors in today's market are *sumo-e* (wrestler prints), *bonsai* (botanical prints), *bijinga* (prints of beautiful women), *shunga* (erotic prints), *shibai-e* (prints depicting actors), *nagasaki* and *yoko-hama* (prints depicting foreigners), *uchiwa-e* (fan prints), and landscapes.

Size-related terms used to describe wood-block prints include *chuban* (usually 7½" × 10"), *hashira-e* (usually 4¾" × 28¾"), *hosoban* (usually 5⅝" × 13"), and *oban* (usually 10" × 15"). *Oban tate-e* is a print which is large in width, while *aiban yoko-e* is a print which is large in length.

The Artists

Following are brief descriptions of the artists whose works are listed below.

Eisen (1790–1848): Painter, print maker, and illustrator.

Goyo Hashiguichi (1880–1921): Print maker.

Harunobu (1724–1770): An important, influential painter and print maker.

Kawasee Hasui (1883–1957): Painter and print maker.

Hiroshige (1797–1858): Painter and print maker. His first published work was in the field of illustrated books. He is among the most important Edo period artists.

Hiroshige II (1826–1869): Print maker and adopted son of Hiroshige. He also used the name *Shigenobu* (was known as Hiroshige II from 1858 until 1865).

Hiroshige III (1843–1894): Print maker. Pupil of Hiroshige who adopted the name *Hiroshige* III after Hiroshige II retired—c1865.

Hokkei (1780–1850): Print maker and painter; a student of Hokusai.

Hokusai (1760–1849): Major painter and print maker who worked in many styles.

Paul Jacoulet (1902–1960): French artist who lived and worked in Japan.

Kobayakawa Kiyoshi (1897–1948): Painter and print maker; pupil of Kiyokata.

Kotondo (1900–?): Theatrical designer and print maker.

Kunichika (1835–1900): Print maker and pupil of Kunisada.

Kunisada (1786–1864): Painter and print maker. For the most part, his prints are signed *Kunisada* until 1844, when he took the name *Toyokuni* III.

Kunisada II (1823–1880): Son-in-law of Kunisada I.

Kuniyoshi (1797—1861): Painter and print maker; pupil of Toyokuni. His works are often sealed with the marks on the right.

Shinsui (1896–1972): Painter and print artist; pupil of Kiyokata. Ito Shinsui was a specialist in highly stylized paintings of women. His prints do not date earlier than 1916.

Shunsho (1726–1792): Painter and print maker. Among his pupils were Shucho and Hokusai.

Toyokuni I (1769–1825): Painter and print maker; student of Toyoharu.

Toyokuni II (1777–1835): Student and son-in-law of Toyokuni I. Signed his works *Toyokuni* II after his father-in-law died; then went back to his earlier name, *Toyoshige*.

Utamaro I (1754–1806): Major painter and print maker.

Yoshida, Hiroshi (1876–1950): Western-style painter and print maker who signed his name in English.

Yoshitoshi Taiso (1839–1892): Illustrator and print maker; student of Kuniyoshi.

The Artists' Signatures

Keisai (Eisen)	Kikumaru	Kiyochika	Kiyohiro	Kiyomasu	Kiyomine	Kiyomitsu	Kiyonaga
Kuniaki	Kunichika	Kuniharu	Kunihiro	Kunihisa	Kunikage	Kunikazu	Kunimaru
Kuniyasu	Kuniyoshi	Kyosai	Mangetsudo	Kitao Masanobu	Okumura Masanobu	Masayoshi	Munehiro
Sharaku	Shibakuni	Shigeharu	Shigemasa	Shigenaga	Nishimura Shigenobu	Shigenobu (Hiroshige II)	Yanagawa Shigenobu
Shundo	Shunei	Shunjo	Shunko	Kashosai Shunsen	Katsukawa Shunsen	Natori Shunsen	Shunsho
(Early) Toyokuni	Toyokuni	Toyokuni II	Toyokuni III	Toyonari	Toyonobu	Toyoshige	Tsukimaro
Yoshimaru	Yoshimitsu	Yoshimori	Yoshinobu	Yoshitaki	Yoshitora	Yoshitoshi	Zeshin

Kiyonobu Kiyoshige Kiyotada Kogyo Koitsu Koryusai Koson Kotondo

Kunimasa Kunimasu Kuninaga Kuninao Kunisada Kunishige Kuniteru Kunitora

Nagahide Sadatusa Sadahide Sadahiro Sadakage Sadamasu Sadanobu Sadatora

Shiko Shinsai Shinsui Shoson Shoun Shucho Shumman Shuncho

Shuntei Shunzan Sugakudo Toshihide Toshikata Toshinobu Toyoharu Toyohiro

Urushibara   Early Utamaro (Ga)   Utamaro (Fude)   Yoshichika   Yoshida   Yoshiiku   Yoshikazu   Yoshikuni

325

Values

Individual Prints

Eisen, oban tate-e, *The Somen Falls* (Somen no taki), from the series *Famous Places of Mt. Nikko* (Nikkozan meisho no uchi), signed *Keisai Eisen ga*, Eisen seal, trimmed, soiled, wormage, binding holes, good color and impression, **$1,500–$2,000.**

Eisen, oban yoko-e, *Station 5*, from *The Sixty-Nine Stations of the Kisokaido*, signed *Keisai ga*, publisher seals Takanouchi and Hoeido, soiled, creased, wormage, good impression and color, **$1,500–$2,000.**

Goyo, oban tate-e, *The Teahouse Waitress Onao*, signed *Goyo ga*, dated Taisho 9 (1920); excellent condition, impression, and color; **$2,000–$3,000.**

Goyo, oban yoko-e, *Moon over Kobe*, signed *Goyo ga*, one artist's seal, fair condition, **$700–$900.**

Goyo, oban yoko-e, *Moon over Kobe*, signed *Goyo*, one artist's seal, dated Taisho 9 (1920); good impression, color, and condition; **$2,000–$3,000.**

Goyo, oban yoko-e, *Mandarin Ducks*, signed *Goyo ga*, one artist's seal, dated Taisho 9 (1920); good impression, color, and condition; **$1,200–$1,600.**

Harunobu, chuban tate-e, Hotei wading across a stream with a beauty and young boy, signed *Harunobu ga*, good color and impression, creased, soiled, small tear, **$1,700–$2,200.**

Harunobu, chuban tate-e, waitress Osen and man with cat on his lap in a teahouse, signed *Harunobu ga*, faded, soiled, wormage, **$3,500–$4,500.**

Harunobu, chuban tate-e, a young couple collecting fireflies, signed *Suzuki Harunobu ga*, good impression, faded, crease to upper right-hand corner, **$5,000–$7,000.**

Harunobu, chuban tate-e, a beauty and a falconer with view of Mt. Fuji through an open window, signed *Harunobu ga*, good impression, faded and toned, **$2,100–$2,600.**

Hasui, aiban tate-e, *A Bride at Dagokuden Heian Shrine* (Kyoto Daigokuden), from the series *Views of Japanese Scenery* (Nihon fukei zenshu), signed *Hasui*, Kawase seal, published by Watanabe, dated Taisho 2 (1922); good impression, color, and condition; **$800–$1,200.**

Hasui, aiban tate-e, *The Okayama Castle* (Okayama-jo), dated Taisho 11 (1922); very good impression, color, and condition; **$1,200–$1,500.**

Hasui, dai oban tate-e, *Mt. Fuji from Yoshida*, signed *Hasui*, published by Watanabe, dated Showa 19 (1944), good condition, **$1,000–$1,500.**

Hasui, oban tate-e, *Senon Temple at Chii Mountain in Korea* (Chosen Chiizan Senonji), signed *Hasui*, dated Showa 15 (1940), published by Watanabe, good color and condition, **$500–$700.**

Hasui, aiban tate-e, *Nono Shrine, Kyoto* (Kyoto Nonomiya), dated Taisho 12 (1923), signed *Hasui*, red seal, published by Watanabe; good impression, color, and condition; **$1,500–$2,000.**

Hasui, oban tate-e, *Pines at Miho Seashore* (Miho no matsubara), signed *Hasui*, Tama seal, published by Watanabe, dated Showa 6 (1931), fair condition, **$400–$500.**

Hiroshige, oban tate-e, Sudden Shower at Atake *from the series* One Hundred Views of Famous Places in Edo, *signed* Hiroshige ga, *good impression, color faded,* **$2,000–$3,000.**

Hiroshige; *oban tate-e*; Komagata Temple, Azuma Bridge (*Komagata-do, Azumabasahi*), *from the series* One Hundred Famous Views of Edo; *signed* Hiroshige ga *and published by Uoya Eikichi; very good impression, color, and condition. Realized price (including the 10-percent buyer's premium), Christie's, New York City,* **$638.**

Hasui, aiban tate-e, *The Sugukuji Temple* (Nagasaaki Sufukuji), from the series *Views of Japanese Scenery*, signed Hasui, Kawase seal, published by Watanabe; good impression, color, and condition; **$900–$1,200.**

Hasui, oban tate-e, *The Great Buddha at Kamakura* (Kamakura Daibutsu), published by Watanabe, dated Showa 5 (1930), good impression and color, minor stains, **$350–$450.**

Hiroshige, oban tate-e, *The Sea at Satta* (Suruga Satta no kaijo), from the series *Thirty-Six Views of* Mt. Fuji, signed Hiroshige ga, published by Tsutaya Kichizo, good impression and color, stained on top right side, **$3,000–$3,500.**

Hiroshige, oban tate-e, an album of the complete series *Thirty-Six Views of* Mt. Fuji, soiled, wormage, trimmed, **$1,200–$1,500.**

Hiroshige, oban yoko-e, *View of Mt. Fudesute* (sakanoshita), from Hoeido's *Tokaido* series, good impression and color, repair to top left margin, **$1,500–$2,050.**

Hiroshige, oban yoko-e, Seki, early-morning departure from the main fortress (the inn), good impression and color, repairs to top edge, **$1,700–$2,200.**

Hiroshige, oban yoko-e, *Asukayama, Edo,* from the series, *Thirty-Six Views of Mt. Fuji,* good impression and condition, **$1,500–$2,100.**

Hiroshige, uchiwa-e, the lovers Umegawa and Chubei beneath the willow tree, signed *Hiroshige ga,* published by Enshuya Matabei, good color and impression, trimmed, **$1,600–$2,200.**

Hiroshige, oban tate-e, triptych, a panoramic view of the Kameido Temangu Shrine (from the Toto meisho series *Famous Views of the Eastern Capital*), signed *Oju Ichiryusai Hiroshige ga,* Ichigyusai seal, fair impression, worm holes, soiled, **$600–$800.**

Hiroshige, oban tate-e, *Hilltop View, Yishima Tenjin Shrine* (Yushima Tenjin Sakaue-Chobo), dragon 4 (1856), good impression and color, retouched, creased left margin, slight staining, **$800–$1,200.**

Hiroshige, oban yoko-e, *Mishima Huts and Tress in Blue and Black* (Hoeido Tokaido), good impression and color, center fold, some staining, **$3,000–$4,000.**

Hiroshige, oban yoko-e, (Hoeido Tokaido) Futakawa, good impression and color, **$2,000–$3,000.**

Hiroshige, oban yoko-e, (Hoeido Tokaido) Futakawa, tea shop at Sarugababa Plain, good impression and color, center fold, stains near figures, lain down, **$800–$1,200.**

Hiroshige II, oban tate-e, *The Gold Mines of Sado Island* (Shokoku meisho), from the series *One Hundred Views of Various Provences,* signed *Hiroshige ga,* published by Uoya Eikichi; good color, impression, and condition; **$700–$900.**

Hiroshige II, oban tate-e, *The Bridge of the Brocade Sash at Suo in Iwa Prefecture* (Shokoku meisho hyakkei), from the series *One Hundred Views of Famous Places,* signed *Hiroshige ga,* published by Uoya Eikichi, good impression and color, some staining, soiled verso, **$900–$1,200.**

Hiroshige II, oban tate-e, *Gankiro Teahouse, Yokohama Bushu,* from the series *One Hundred Views of Various Provences,* signed *Hiroshige ga,* published by Uoya Eikichi, good impression and color, binding holes, some slight staining, **$900–$1,200.**

Hiroshige III, oban tate-e, triptych, a view of Ueno Museum, signed *Hiroshige ga,* good color and impression, **$350–$500.**

Hokkei, kakuban, a surimono triptych, three poets, one on each plate, a fan-shaped cartouche on each plate, Hokkei seal; good color, impression, and condition; **$2,500–$3,500.**

Hokkei, kakuban, surimono of two karako (children) playing, signed *Kien Hokkei,* good condition, **$500–$700.**

Hokkei, kakuban, surimono of a Shinto shrine with poems above, signed *Hokkei,* good impression, some fading, creased, **$400–$600.**

Publishers' Marks

1. Katoya
2. Ezakiya Kichibei
3. Mikawaya Kihei
4. Maruya Kusaemon
5. Mikawaya Rihei
6. Sugiya Kihei
7. Tsuruya Kiemon
8. Tsuruya Kiemon
9. Tsuruya Kiemon
10. Tsuruya Kinsuke
11. Tsutaya Kichizo
12. Tsutaya Juzaburo
13. Maruya Kiyojiro
14. Yamadaya Shojiro
15. Fujiokaya Hikotaro
16. Echigoya Keisuke
17. Iseya Sanjiro
18. Nishimuraya Yohachi
19. Iwatoya Kisaburo
20. Takatsuya Isuke
21. Ningyoya Takichi
22. Kagaya Yasubei
23. Enshuya Hikobei
24. Soshuya Yohei
25. Enshuya Matabei
26. Kagaya Yoshibei
27. Murataya Jirobei
28. Kawachiya Chozo
29. Eirakuya Bunsuke
30. Izumiya Ichibei
31. Kikuya Kozaburo
32. Emiya Kichiemon
33. Izuymiya Ichibei
34. Iwatoya Genpachi
35. Ebiya Rinnosuke
36. Kikuya Ichibei
37. Soneya Ginjiro
38. Kazusaya
39. Ezakiya Tatsuzo
40. Nishimuraya Yohachi
41. Urokogataya
42. Tsujiokaya Bunsuke
43. Nishimuraya Yohachi
44. Moriya Jihei
45. Iseya Magobei
46. Sanoya Kihei
47. Yamamotoya Heikichi
48. Shimizuya
49. Maruya Jinpachi
50. Takeuchi Magohachi
51. Etsuke
52. Itoya Yohei
53. Iseya Tetsukiro
54. Iseya Chubei
55. Ibaya Sensaburo
56. Gusokuya Kahci
57. Daikokuya
58. Wakabayashiya Kiyobei
59. Okuroya Kinnosuke
60. Hiranoya Heisuke
61. Ogawa Heisuke
62. Sumiyoshiya Masagoro
63. Wakasaya Yoichi
64. Moritaya Hanzo
65. Joshuya Shigezo
66. Yamaguchiya Tobei
67. Kawaguchiya Uhei
68. Kagiya Hanjiro
69. Aito
70. Enshuya Yasubei
71. Owariya Kiyoshichi
72. Tamaya Sosuke
73. Mokuya Sojiro
74. Tsujiya Yasubei
75. Uwoya Eikichi
76. Sagamiya
77. Hirookaya Kosuke
78. Tenki
79. Minatoya Kohei
80. Morimoto Junzaburo

Hokusai, oban yoko-e, Fuji from Kanaya on the Tokaido *(Tokaido Kanaya no Fuji), from the series* Thirty-Six Views of Mt. Fuji, *signed* Zen Hokusai Iitsu hitsu *and published by Eijudo, good impression (black outline), slight center fold and slightly faded. Realized price (including the 10-percent buyer's premium), Christie's, New York City,* **$3,520.**

Hokusai, oban yoko-e, *Snowy Morning at Koishikawa,* from the series *Thirty-Six Views of Mt. Fuji,* signed *Zen Hokusai Iitsu hitsu,* published by *Eijudo,* fair impression, center crease, worn edges, minor stains, repaired tear on right edge, **$900–$1,200.**

Hokusai, oban yoko-e, *Fuji from the Umezawa Manor in Sagami Province,* signed *Zen Hokusai Iitsu hitsu,* blue outline, fair impression, soiled and backed, **$1,200–$1,500.**

Hokusai, oban yoko-e, *Fuji in the Well of the Great Wave off Kanagawa,* signed *Hokusai aratame Iitsu hitsu,* fair impression, damaged, stained, faded, **$3,000–$4,000.**

Hokusai, oban yoko-e, *In the Well of the Great Wave off Kanagawa,* signed *Hokusai aratame Iitsu hitsu,* moderate impression, faded, creased, **$7,000–$9,000.**

Hokusai, oban yoko-e, the poem of Gonchernagon Sasaie (Teika), from the series *One Hundred Poems As Told by the Nurse,* published by Eijudo, good impression and color, center crease, **$6,000–$7,000.**

Hokusai, kakuban, a surimono depicting a puppeteer with female puppet, poems in cartouche, signed *Hokusai aratame Katsushika Iitsu hitsu;* good color, impression, and condition; **$1,750–$2,200.**

Jacoulet; *dai oban tate-e*; Femme de Falalap et Coquillages *from the* Série Mollusque; *signed* Paul Jacoulet (*in pencil*); *Mandarin Duck seal; numbered 92/150; good impression, color, and condition. Realized price (including the 10-percent buyer's premium), Christie's, New York City,* **$2,200.**

Date and Censor Seals

1. 1790–1842
2. 1790–1842
3. 1805 (8th month)
4. 1805 (10th month)
5. 1805 (12th month)
6. 1806 (1st month)

15. 1842
16. 1842
17. 1843-5
18. 1843-5
19. 1843-5
20. 1843-5

27. 1847-8
28. 1847-8
29. 1847-50
30. 1849
31. 1849-50
32. 1849-53

36. 1852 (Rat 8)
37. 1852 (Rat 8)
38. 1852 (Rat 8)
39. 1852 (Rat 8)
40. 1853 (Ox)
41. 1853 (Ox)

48. 1858 (Horse)
49. 1859 (Goat)
50. 1860 (Monkey)
51. 1861 (Cock)
52. 1862 (Dog 1)
53. 1863 (Boar 4)

60. 1870 (Horse)
61. 1871 (Goat)
62. 1872 (Monkey)
63. 1873 (Cock)
64. 1874 (Dog)
65. 1875 (Boar)

7. 1806 (2nd month)	8. 1806 (4th month)	9. 1806 (Tiger)	10. 1807 (Hare)	11. 1808 (Dragon)	12. 1809 (Snake)	13. 1810 (Horse)	14. 1811 (Goat)

21. 1843-5	22. 1843-6	23. 1843-6	24. 1843-6	25. 1845-6	26. 1846

33. 1849-53	34. 1851-3	35. 1851-3

42. 1853 (Ox)	43. 1853 (Ox)	44. 1854 (Tiger)	45. 1855 (Hare)	46. 1856 (Dragon)	47. 1857 (Snake)

54. 1864 (Rat)	55. 1865 (Ox)	56. 1866 (Tiger)	57. 1867 (Hare)	58. 1868 (Dragon)	59. 1869 (Snake)

明治　　大正　　昭和

66. 1868-1912 Meiji	67. 1912-26 Taisho	68. 1926 onwards Showa

Jacoulet, *Korean Baby in Ceremonial Costume* (Bébé Coréen en Costume de Cérémonie), Fan seal, published 12 September 1934, good condition, **$600–$750.**

Jacoulet, oban tate-e, *The Jade Ladies* (Les Jades Chinoises), Boat seal, framed, glazed, laid down, good color and impression, **$800–$1,200.**

Jacoulet, oban yoko-e, *Sandalwood Smoke* (Fumée de Sandal), Mitsutomoe seal (the only print with this seal), good condition, **$1,200–$1,500.**

Jacoulet, *The Mandarin with Glasses* (Le Mandarin aux Lunettes), published 22 May 1950, Mandarin Duck seal, good condition, **$900–$1,200.**

Jacoulet, *The Porcelain Garden Seat* (Le Tabouret de Porcelaine), published 25 June 1936, Good Luck Hammer seal, excellent condition, **$1,000–$1,200.**

Jacoulet, *The Old Man in the Chapel: Mr. Kawada*, published 25 July 1940, Butterfly seal, excellent condition, **$700–$900.**

Jacoulet, *Cactus, South Seas* (Cactus, Mers du Sud), published 20 November 1941, Sparrow seal, fair condition, some foxing, **$400–$600.**

Jacoulet, *Longevity* (Longévité), published 28 November 1948, Peach seal, good condition, **$600–$800.**

Jacoulet, *The Chinese Writer* (L'Homme Qui Ecrit, Chinois), Peony seal, published March 1953, good condition, **$600–$900.**

Kiyoshi, large oban tate-e, half-length of a beauty adjusting her hair, signed *Kiyoshi*, Kobayakawa seal; good impression, color, and condition; **$1,500–$2,000.**

Kiyoshi, oban tate-e, a beauty making up, signed *Kobayakawa Kiyoshi*, one artist's seal, dated Showa 5 (1930), good impression and condition, **$1,500–$2,000.**

Kotondo, large oban tate-e, a beauty applying lipstick before a mirror, signed *Genjin ga*, one artist's seal, fine impression and color, soiled margin, **$800–$1,200.**

Kotondo, large oban tate-e, *A Beauty in Summer* (Natsu musume), signed *Genjin ga*, one artist's seal, fine impression and color, soiled upper margin verso, **$2,000–$3,000.**

Kotondo, large oban tate-e, a beauty at the bath, signed *Genjin ga*, one artist's seal, dated Showa 4 (1929), numbered 148; good impression, color, and condition; **$800–$1,200.**

Kunichika, oban tate-e, triptych, women bathers (interior of a bathhouse), signed *Kunichika hitsu*, good color and impression, worn edges, minor staining on upper part of right-hand plate, **$2,000–$3,000.**

Kunisada, oban tate-e, the actor Nakamura Utaemon IV as Kumagae Naozane, from the play *Genpei sakewae tsutsuji* (performed May 1845), signed *Toyokuni ga*, published by Ebisuya Shoshichi, good color and impression, trimmed margins, **$600–$800.**

Kunisada, kakuban, surimono of an okubi-e portrait of an actor of the Sawamura family wearing informal attire, signed *Gototei Kunisada*; good color, impression, and condition; **$1,000–$1,500.**

Kunisada, oban, a geisha leaning on a brazier stirring the charcoal, dated Tempo 2 (1831), signed *Kochoro Kunisada ga*, censor seal (Kiwame), published by Ezaki-ya, good impression, creased, soiled, **$700–$900.**

Munakata, dai oban tate-e, a sumizurie with hand-applied color entitled Yamazakura no tana, *from the series* Shokeisho, *signed Shiko Munakata and sealed, dated 3 December 1951, good impression, paper slightly toned, framed and glazed. Realized price (including the 10-percent buyer's premium), Christie's, New York City,* **$7,150.**

337

Kunisada, oban, the actor Shikan IV as Iga no Kotaro, published in 1852 by Minato-ya Kohei, signed *Toyokuni ga*, censor seals (Fuku and Muramastsu), good impression and color, binding holes, crease, **$350–$450.**

Kunisada, oban tate-e, a young girl set against fabric patterns, signed *Kunisada ga*, published by Dansendo; faded, but overall good condition; **$800–$1,200.**

Kunisada II, oban, twenty-four prints from *Genji's Cards*, by *Lady Murasaki* (parody based on *Tales of Genji*), signed *Baichoro Kunisada ga*, censor seal (Aratame), date seal—Year of the Snake (1857), Tsutaya Kichizo publisher's mark, fair condition, **$1,000–$1,500.**

Kuniyoshi, tanzaku, an elephant and Tengu entitled *Don't Be Conceited*, signed *Kuniyoshi ga*, good impression, soiled, **$400–$500.**

Kuniyoshi, oban yoko-e, *Sukahara on Sado Island*, from the series *Scenes from the Life of the Priest Nichiren*, signed *Ichiyasai Kuniyoshi hitsu*, published by Iseya Rihei, creased, trimmed borders, good color and impression, **$1,500–$2,500.**

Kuniyoshi, oban yoko-e, *Sunrise at New Year in Suzaki*, signed *Ichiyasai Kuniyoshi ga*, published by Kagayu Kichibei, good impression, restoration (but an early work), **$1,500–$2,000.**

Kuniyoshi, oban yoko-e, *Dokaku*, from *Twenty-Four Paragons of Filial Piety*, signed *Ichiyusai Kuniyoshi ga*, published by Izumiya Ichibei, moderate condition (a later series), **$500–$700.**

Kuniyoshi, oban tate-e, triptych, Raiko and retainers confronting the demon Shutendoji, signed *Ichiyusai Kuniyoshi*, fair condition, restoration, **$800–$1,200.**

Shinsui, oban tate-e, a beauty looking at a clock, signed *Shinsui ga*, Ito seal; good color, impression, and condition; **$800–$1,200.**

Shinsui, oban tate-e, a beauty holding a teacup, signed *Shinsui ga*; good color, impression, and condition; **$800–$1,200.**

Shinsui, oban tate-e, a bijin huddled beneath a kotatsu, signed *Shinsui ga*, Ito seal, dated Taisho 4 (1925); good impression, color, and condition; **$700–$900.**

Shinsui, large oban tate-e, a beauty clipping her toenails, signed *Shinsui ga*, Ito seal, dated Showa 4 (1929), published by Watanabe, numbered 300/350, fine impression and color, slightly soiled verso, **$1,500–$2,000.**

Shinsui, oban tate-e, an okubi-e of a beauty holding a fan, signed *Shinsui*, dated Taisho 13 (1924), good impression and color, the verso soiled, **$600–$800.**

Shinsui, oban tate-e, a half-length portrait of a geisha resting against a balustrade in moonlight, signed *Shinsui ga*, dated Showa 6 (1931), numbered 26/300, good impression, slightly faded and soiled, **$1,200–$1,500.**

Shunsho, oban tate-e, the actors Nakamura Nakazo and Nakamura Matsue in the green room with a servant behind, signed *Shunsho ga*, good impression and color, worm holes, slight staining, **$5,000–$7,000.**

Shunsho, hosoban, portrait of the actor Nakajima Meyoemon II, signed *Shunsho ga*, moderate condition, **$800–$1,200.**

Shunsho, hosoban, full-length portrait of the actor Ichikawa Monnoskue, signed *Shunsho ga*, soiled, stained, fair condition, **$1,200–$1,500.**

Shinsui; large oban tate-e; a beauty at the mirror; signed Shinsui ga; Ito seal; published by Watanabe; dated Showa 2 (1927); numbered 12/300; good impression, color, and condition. Realized price (including the 10-percent buyer's premium), Christie's, New York City, **$1,100.**

Toyokuni, square surimono, the actor Ichikawa Danjuro seated beside a sunken tub, signed *Toyokuni ga*, good impression, metallic dust applied, rubbed, **$800–$900.**

Toyokuni, oban tate-e, an okubi-e portrait of an actor holding a pipe, signed *Toyokuni ga*, published by Murataya, good impression, fair condition, **$1,000–$1,500.**

Toyokuni, oban tate-e, the actors Bando Mitsuyoro and Ichikawa Omezo in a scene, signed *Toyokuni ga*, published by Eijudo; good condition, color, and impression; **$1,500–$2,000.**

Toyokuni II, kakemono-e, a hawk perched on a branch at New Year, signed *gosotei Toyokuni hitsu*, published by Yamamotoya Heikichi; good impression; soiled, faded, and creased; **$600–$700.**

Toyokuni II, oban yoko-e, the temple at Kamakura, signed *Toyokuni hitsu*, Utagawa seal, good impression and color, trimmed margins, **$800–$1,200.**

Utamaro, aiban tate-e, the Joruri lovers Oshin and Dembi beneath an umbrella, signed *Utamaro hitsu*, fair condition, **$1,500–$1,800.**

Utamaro, oban tate-e, portrait of a courtesan imitating Jurojin, signed *Utamaro hitsu*, published by Matsumuraya Yahei, fair condition, **$1,500–$2,000.**

Utamaro, oban tate-e, triptych (one sheet), a maid arriving with a kimono for a beauty, signed *Utamaro hitsu*, published by Tsuruya Kiemon, good impression, moderate condition, **$2,000–$3,000.**

Utamaro, oban, a bijin and wakashu as puppeteers, the puppets performing in front of a low screen, fair impression, worm holes, repair on upper left, **$700–$900.**

Utamaro, oban tate-e, a beauty and maid playing with a baby, signed *Utamaro hitsu*, published by Takatsuya Isuke, faded, rimmed, center crease, **$2,000–$2,500.**

Utamaro, oban, seated figure of the Courtesan Ooi pulling her uchikake over her shoulder, signed *Utamaro hitsu*, Oomiya publisher's seal; good impression; faded, soiled, and trimmed; **$2,250–$2,850.**

Utamaro, oban, a bust portrait of Takshima Ohisa, her head turned toward the right, her hand on the collar of her kimono, signed *Utamaro hitsu*, good impression, soiled, trimmed margins, repairs, **$2,200–$2,800.**

Utamaro; oban (left and center sheets of a triptych); a princess alighting from a black, lacquered sedan chair, attended by ladies in waiting; signed *Utamaro hitsu*; Izumiya Ichibei publisher's seal; good color and impression; worm holes; rubbed and soiled; **$2,500–$3,500.**

Utamaro, oban, bust portrait of a beauty (in ceremonial kimono with mon) holding up a battledore, from the series *The Five Faces of Beauties* (Bijin Gomenso), signed *Utamaro hitsu*, published by Tsuruken; good impression; faded, rubbed, and soiled; **$4,000–$5,000.**

Yoshida, oban tate-e, *Camping at Washiba*, signed *Hiroshi Yoshida* (with pencil) and *Yoshida* (with brush), Jizuri seal, dated Taisho 15 (1926), **$1,000–$1,500.**

Yoshida, oban yoko-e, Otengo, signed *Hiroshi Yoshida* (with pencil) and *Yoshida* (with brush), Juzuri seal, dated Taisho 15 (1926); good impression, color, and condition, **$1,000–$1,500.**

Yoshitoshi, oban tate-e, triptych, beauties in a bathhouse, *Summer Women Bathing at Daishoro*, signed *Oju Yoshitoshi ga*, Taiso seal, published by Akiyama Buemon, dated Meiji 16 (1883), good impression and color, trimmed margins, **$3,000–$5,000.**

Yoshitoshi, oban tate-e, triptych, *The Fever of Taira no Kyomori*, signed *Yoshitoshi ga*, Taiso seal, published by Okiyama Buemon, dated Meiji 16 (1883), fair condition, damages to corners of each plate, **$1,000–$1,500.**

Yoshitoshi, oban tate-e, triptych, warriors at a temple in the snow, signed *Yoshitoshi ga*, Yoshitoshi seal, good condition, **$600–$800.**

Yoshitoshi, kakemono-e, *Watanabe no Tsuna and the Demon of Rashomon Gate*, signed *Oju Yoshitoshi ga*, sealed Taiso, dated Meiji 21 (1885), faded, soiled, good impression, **$500–$700.**

Yoshitoshi, kakemono-e, *The Lonely House at Adachigahara*, signed *Oju Yoshitoshi ga*, published by Matsui Eikichi, good condition, **$1,500–$2,000.**

Illustrated Books and Albums

Hiroshige III, *Pictures of Products of Japan* (fold-out album), 42 pages, dated Meiji 10 (1877), fair-to-moderate condition, **$600–$700.**

Hokusai, *One Hundred Views of Mt. Fuji*, three volumes, dated Meiji 8 (1875), fair-to-good condition, **$1,000–$1,500.**

Hokusai, *Ten Thousand Sketches* (Managa), vols. 1–14 (out of 15), fair-to-moderate condition, **$2,500–$3,500.**

Ooka Shunkoku, *A Garden of Famous Japanese and Chinese Paintings*, four of six volumes, good-to-fair condition, **$500–$600.**

Katsukawa Shunsho, *Hyakunin ishu*, one volume complete, dated 1775, brocade covers, good impression and color, wormage, soiled, **$1,200–$1,500.**

Wood block carved as the printing block for book illustrations, warriors in a riverscape (after an illustration by Keisai Eisen), **$800–$1,200.**

Part II

Canton Enamel (Chinese Enamel on Copper)

Ashtray with green jade handle, hexagonal bowl with floral panels on a white ground, green interior, marked China, c1930, **$100–$150.**

Bottle/vase painted with the dragon and cloud pattern, late 19th century, 16½" high, **$600–$800.**

Box and cover, circular, the lid painted with three dignitaries on a pavilion terrace, the sides with fruiting vines, star cracks, 18th century, 3" diameter, **$700–$900.**

Boxes and covers, boats and a mountainscape, both forming a continuous pattern, light and dark blue, light blue interiors, the bases with a four-character Ch'ien Lung mark (and of the period), 3" diameter, **pair, $1,500–$2,500.**

Censer and cover; tripod; painted with panels of European scenes including landscapes and seascapes; famille rose; flaking and star cracks; Ch'ien Lung (Qianlong) four-character mark, but early 19th century; 5½" high, **$1,500–$2,500.**

Figure of a rabbit, pink eyes, blue and white fur, c1900, 3" long, **$600–$800.**

Jardinières, famille jaune, rectangular, canted corners, painted with two panels of flowers on a busy floral ground, filled with trees and branches having hard-stone leaves and berries, old damages, c1900, 14" high, **pair, $600–$800.**

Napkin rings, white ground with floral motifs, early 20th century, **set of 4, $80–$100.**

Saucer dish, famille rose, painted with European gentlemen and attendants near a riverbank, the border with dragons and foliage, the reverse with flower heads on a blue cracked-ice ground, surface chips restored, 18th century, 5" diameter, **$1,200–$1,800.**

Saucer dishes, famille rose, yellow ground painted with five dragons, lotus borders, restored, 18th century, 8½" diameter, **pair, $1,800–$2,500.**

Smoking set: cylindrical cigarette container, round ashtray, and matchbox holder; each with a scenic reserve; pale green interiors; marked Made in China; c1930, **$100–$125.**

Snuff box, famille rose, the cover painted with two European gentlemen and a lady in a picnic scene, the sides and bottom covered with puce floral sprays, restored, 18th century, 3" wide, **$2,000–$3,000.**

Sweetmeat set, eight fan-shaped trays radiating from a central dish, each painted with romantic scenes based on Chinese legends, famille rose with black and turquoise borders, early 19th century, 18" diameter, **set, $200–$300.**

Tray (circular) with six sections around a circular dish, each with motif of figures in landscapes, scratched and chipped, early 20th century, 16" diameter, **$200–$300.**

Vase, famille rose, baluster form, a panel on each side painted with birds perched on peony branches, lime green ground with pink lotus and scrolls, early 19th century, 9" high, **$800–$1,200.**

Vase, 1000 Flowers pattern overall, early 20th century, 6" high, **$100–$125.**

Vase, a panel on each side painted with sages in a landscape, overall yellow floral ground, minor restoration, 19th century, 10" high, **$2,500–$3,500.**

Champlevé

Candleholders, each with 15 upturned branches terminating in a pricket sconce, the bases round and flat, some enamel losses, Chinese, c1900, 28" high, **pair, $1,500–$2,000.**

Censer, Shishi finial, loose ring handles, large peony motif in primary colors, Japanese, early 20th century, 6½" high, **$100–$200.**

Censer and cover; two looped handles; three masked feet; Buddhistic lion finial; the reticulated cover with lappets; the body with alternating panels of longevity characters; Chinese; impressed Ming mark, but late 19th century; 16" high, **$900–$1,200.**

Censer in the form of a Buddhistic lion, squat body, standing four square, the head forming the lid, Chinese, late 19th century, 13" high, **$500–$700.**

Censers modeled as standing geese, detachable wings forming the covers, yellow ground with polychrome feathers, Chinese, early 20th century, 15½" high, **pair, $900–$1,200.**

Figure of Kuan Yin, flowing robes with a lotus scroll pattern, Chinese, 19th century, 6½" high, **$300–$400.**

Figure of a seated Lohan; his green robes decorated with flowers, birds, and dragons; Chinese, late 19th/early 20th century, 18" high, **$800–$1,200.**

Figure of a phoenix with colorful feathers, primary hues, Chinese, early 20th century, 11¾" high, **$600–$800.**

Figure of a Samurai (on horseback) wearing a suit of armor, his pole arm missing, losses to the enamel, c1915, 15" high, **$600–$850.**

Figure of a water buffalo standing four square, Chinese, late 19th century, 6½" long, **$350–$475.**

Lamp, archaic motif, the enamels in primary colors, losses to the enamels, c1905, 5' high, **$1,500–$1,800.**

Lamp (floor), bronze body with archaic motifs, electrified, no shape, losses to the enamels, Japanese, c1900, 63" high, **$1,000–$1,500.**

Lantern, globular, entirely pierced with chrysanthemums and leaves, the top with a loose ring, Japanese, c1885, 16" high, **$700–$900.**

Lantern, open-barrel form with flowers and vines, Japanese, late 19th century, 12½" high, **$285–$400.**

Ruyi sceptre, the center and ends with gilt bats around Shou characters, Chinese, late 19th/early 20th century, 17½" long, **$500–$700.**

Vase, gourd form, peony motif in primary hues, marked *Made in Japan*, c1930, 8" high, **$100–$150.**

Vase, pear-shaped, two elephant-head handles, a peony band around the center in primary hues, early Showa period, 7" high, **$100–$125.**

Vase, baluster form, bronze body with a peony motif, Japanese, early 20th century, 8" high, **$85–$125.**

Weight, Shishi with brocade ball, Japanese, early 20th century, 6½" long, **$100–$125.**

Dolls, Games, and Toys

Dolls

Bijin (Japanese beauty), cloth face and hands, red silk kimono, flowers in her hair, wood base, post World War II, 18" high, **$75–$100.**

Boy on horseback, dressed in suit of armor, encased in glass, Japanese, early Showa period, 16¾" high, **$185–$275.**

Boy and girl, silk garments, used as needle cases, Chinese, c1925, 2½" high, **$125–$185.**

Boy and girl, porcelain heads, movable arms and legs, Japanese, c1925, 6" high, **$125–$175.**

Elderly man and woman; silk garments; movable arms, legs, and heads; garments removable; Chinese, c1930, 11½" high, **$200–$300.**

Eight Immortals, silk padded with cotton and mounted on a strip of paper, Chinese, c1920, 9" high, **$100–$200.**

Eight Immortals, silk padded with cotton and mounted on a strip of paper, Chinese, c1920, 11½" high, **$125–$225.**

Eight Immortals, silk padded with cotton and mounted on a strip of paper, Chinese, c1920, 13" high, **$140–$240.**

Eight Immortals, silk padded with cotton and mounted on a strip of paper, Chinese, c1920, 15⅜" high, **$250–$350.**

Eight Immortals, silk padded with cotton and mounted on a strip of paper, Chinese, c1920, 18" high, **$350–$500.**

Eight Immortals, silk padded with cotton and mounted on a strip of paper, Chinese, c1920, 22" high, **$500–$700.**

Emperor and Empress, both seated on tatami mats, lacquer and oyster-shell faces, elaborate red and gold silk brocade attire, Japanese, late Meiji/early Taisho period, 12" high, **$400–$600.**

Geisha wearing a silk kimono and holding an umbrella, lacquer and oyster-shell face, Japanese, early Showa period, 18½" high, **$125–$200.**

Hakata, geisha with black and gold kimono, Japanese, 20th century, 8⅜" high, **$125–$175.**

Hakata, girl holding fan, marked Made in Japan, 20th century, 10" high, **$65–$96.**

Lama (priest), flexible body, movable arms and legs, silk attire, Chinese, c1900, 10" high, **$200–$300.**

Pin-cushion doll, silk crêpe with floral motif, Japanese, c1915, **$75–$125.**

Left: *Hakata doll of the lion dancer, the costume in red and gilt,* **$150–$250.** Right: *Hakata doll of the wisteria maiden, removable hat, red and lavender robes with gilt trim, 8" high,* **$175–$275.**

Samurai, lacquer face and hands, Japanese, Showa period, 16" high, **$150–$175.**

Samurai seated on a folding chair and wearing helmet, armor, and sword; Japanese, Meiji period, **$400–$650.**

Young girl wearing flowered silk kimono, Japanese, early Showa period, 14½" high, **$200–$275.**

Woman holding a flowering branch, lacquer and silk, Japanese, Showa period, 14¼" high, **$100–$175.**

Woman with four interchangeable wigs, original box, Japanese, c1930, 6" high, **$75–$125.**

Games

Battledore, court lady in brightly colored silk brocade attire, Japanese, early Showa period, 12½" high, **$200–$300.**

Bank, wood inlaid with various colored woods forming a motif of Hotei, Japanese, c1925, 2½" × 4" × 4¾", **$50–$85.**

Battledore (hagoita) with silk brocade karako (children) on one side, painted plum blossoms on the reverse, Japanese, c1925, 17" long, **$300–$400.**

Chess set, ivory, carved as officials and warriors upon puzzle balls and lotus bases, Chinese, c1900, **$500–$700.**

Chess set, emperor and empress and attendants, stained in red and white, Chinese, early 20th century, **$600–$800.**

Chess set; ivory, red, and white; carved as officials and warriors; oval bases; Chinese, early 20th century, **$400–$600.**

Chess set painted in colors and gilt; warriors riding horses, camels, and elephants; each piece with lotus bases, Indian, 20th century, **$1,800–$2,500.**

Child's tea set: tray, cups and saucers, covered creamer and sugar, and teapot; yellow Awaji ware; Japanese, c1925, **$100–$125.**

Child's tea set: tray, cups and saucers, covered creamer and sugar, and teapot; green Awaji ware; Japanese, c1925, **$100–$125.**

Game box containing five small covered boxes, black and gilt lacquer, rectangular with rounded corners, overall decoration of floral sprigs, Chinese, 19th century, 11½" × 10" × 3", **$900–$1,200.**

Game box, octagonal, painted with panels of figures on terraces, elaborate foliate borders, the interior with boxes and small trays with card counters, some missing, Chinese, 19th century, 15" long, **$400–$600.**

Game box, red and black lacquer, octagonal, containing six covered boxes and 12 trays, exterior decorated with fruit and flower borders, the details in red, the interior with garden scenes, Chinese, early 19th century, 11¾" × 13¼" × 4½", **$1,000–$1,500.**

Cribbage board, inlaid wood, Japanese, early Showa period, 10½" × 3" × 2½", **$50–$75.**

Battledore (or hagoita, similar to the paddle used in badminton) showing a Samurai in appliquéd silk brocade; orange, purple, gold, and colors; the reverse with painted flowering branches; Japanese, c1935, 24" high, **$300–$500.**

Furniture (toy); inlaid wood; two benches, two chairs, and a table; Japanese, c1920, 4½" high, **$150–$250.**

Household set (living room with three folding sections) furnished in Japanese style: toy dresser and mirror, wood tea set, and boy and girl dolls; Japanese, c1925, largest piece 5½" high, **$300–$500.**

Mah-jongg set, wood container, rectangular, two drawers, ivory counters, Chinese, c1920, **$150–$200.**

Rare clockwork Kobe toy, wound by rotating the head in front, Japanese, early 20th century, **$4,000–$5,000.** Courtesy of Stephen Leonard.

Mah-jongg set, bamboo and bone tiles, bone counters and dice, flat wooden box with gold Shou character on lid, Chinese, c1925, **$125–$175.**

Pin box, ivory, hinged lid, overall relief carving of floral medallions flanked by leaves, the border with a foliate chain and saw-edge banding, silver hinges, the interior divided into two compartments, Indian, 19th century, 9½" × 2¾" × 2", **$400–$600.**

Toilet set: comb, brush, mirror, and clothes brush; antimony embossed with a scenic motif; Japanese, c1920, 3" × 1", **$100–$125.**

Toys

Battery-operated artist (draws nine different pictures), c1965, Japanese, **$450–$650.**

Equestrian, hand-painted celluloid, Japanese, c1930, **$275–$400.**

Fred Astaire tap dancer, Japanese, **$400–$500.**

Kobe, a boat with two animated figures, Japanese, **$700–$900.**

An early Japanese toy (c1920), double-clockwork biplanes with the original box (right), **$3,000–$4,000.** Courtesy of Stephen Leonard.

Kobe; double figures depicting a thief running with a sake bottle, the other figure beating him upon the head; Japanese, **$800–$1,200.**

Kobe toys
Left: *Watermelon eater with head, mouth, and both arms in animation,* **$200–$300.** Right: *Meatball eater with head, mouth, and right arm in animation,* **$400–$500.** Courtesy of Stephen Leonard.

A *Japanese Kobe toy, largest known, with 12 animations, early 20th century, 6½" long,* **$2,500–$3,000.** Courtesy of Stephen Leonard.

Kobe, a figure reading, Japanese, **$350–$500.**

Kobe, a figure eating, Japanese, **$300–$400.**

Kobe, a figure plucking a musical instrument, Japanese, **$350–$475.**

Kobe, a rabbit and a monkey with musical instruments, Japanese, **$700–$900.**

Kobe, the Three Wise Monkeys, Japanese, **$3,000–$3,700.**

Louie Armstrong (Satchmo), Japanese, **$400–$550.**

Popeye with lantern, Japanese, **$265–$300.**

Sparky, all-tin robot, Japanese, **$225–$300.**

Windup clown on stilts, Japanese, **$300–$450.**

Windup duck, hand-painted, c1935, Japanese, **$125–$200.**

Windup roadster with handpainted figure, Occupied Japan, **$150–$225.**

Erotica

An album of 12 erotic paintings in ink and color on paper, including various domestic scenes such as a lady embracing a scholar drinking wine; a scholar at his window approaching a lady on her bed; a lady with a gentleman seated in a bath; a lady and gentleman and her servant; a lady and gentleman on a broad chair; a lady and gentleman on a yellow carpet; each painting 5¾" × 7¾", Chinese, late Ch'ing (Qing) Dynasty, **$3,500–$4,500.**

Chest tied with tasseled rope, the lid removable to reveal two lovers lying on a tatami mat, boxwood and ivory, c1900, **$1,000–$1,500.**

Hand warmer, porcelain, the top and sides pierced, the front and back with scenes featuring groups of men and women engaged in amorous pursuits, Chinese, early 19th century, 8¼" long, **$1,800–$2,200.**

Illustrated book of wood-block prints, a parody of erotic sumo wrestling scenes, Meiji period, **$350–$550.**

Illustrated book of wood-block prints, a manual attributed to Kunichika, late 19th century, **$500–$700.**

Ivory carving of a pair of lovers, Japanese, late 19th century, **$2,000–$3,000.**

Ivory carving of a reclining nude, two loose bracelets on her left hand, her hair stained black; she wears shoes for bound feet; Chinese, c1930, 10" long, **$500–$700.**

Ivory figure of a reclining nude, her left arm across her waist, her hair painted black; surface cracks, c1900, 11" long, **$250–$400.**

Ivory reclining nude, Chinese, c1920, 9" long, **$600–$800.**

(Note: Although traditionally known as *doctors' dolls* or *medicine ladies*, reclining nudes were never intended as a medical tool, but rather, to have a titillating effect on the owner.)

Netsuke, Okame, the base unscrewing to reveal her innermost secrets, Japanese, late 19th century, **$600–$900.**

Netsuke, a couple lying upon a brocade kimono, Japanese, early Showa period, **$200–$300.**

Netsuke, manju, kagamibuta, Okame laughing as she realizes the erotic significance of the long-nosed Tengu mask on the reverse; ivory with red and black tints; Japanese, late 19th century, **$600–$900.**

Netsuke, walrus ivory, Okame carrying a large mushroom (which has erotic significance), signed Shugetsu, **$1,000–$1,500.**

Painting, gouache with gold on paper, a prince and a lady on a canopied couch set on a veranda, Indian, Guler, c1820, 10" × 8", **$2,500–$3,500.**

Painting; hand scroll with 12 erotic scenes in sumi, color, and gofun on silk; Japanese, early Showa period, **$1,500–$2,000.**

Painting, hand scroll, ink and color on paper, a series of erotic scenes, Chinese, c1900, 5½" × 78", **$800–$1,200.**

Pipe, bamboo with silver terminals, a sliding saya hiding an engraved shunga design of two lovers, Japanese, Meiji period, **$900–$1,200.**

Marble sculpture of Okame: a phallic symbol which, when inverted, reveals Okame engaged in erotic pursuits; 19th century, 5" high, **$1000–$1500.** Courtesy of the Virginia Keresey Collection.

Japanese wood-block print; a young man and a beauty seated on a bench; Utamaro; oban tate-e; good impression and condition, slightly faded. Realized price (including the 10-percent buyer's premium), Christie's, New York City, **$1980.**

Punch bowl (Rose Mandarin); two panels: one with a young woman in the arms of an older man, the other with a lady in converse with a young man; the base with a couple engaged in amorous embrace, mirrored by dogs in a doorway; early 19th century, restored, 9½" diameter, **$1,800–$2,500.**

Screen, ink and colors on paper, *Maidens Bathing in a Mountain Stream*; the right panel opens to reveal an erotic scene of two lovers; panel size 55½" × 30½", **$5,500–$7,500.**

Snuff bottle, famille rose, a nude beauty bathing before her lover, Chinese, early 20th century, **$300–$500.**

Snuff bottle, famille rose, molded in relief with a ménage à trois on one side and a couple on the reverse, early 19th century, **$1,875–$2,500.**

Snuff bottle, a reclining nude on both sides, the stopper in the form of a shoe for bound feet, Chinese, c1925, **$300–$550.**

Wood-block print, a young man and a housemaid; Koryusai; chuban yoko-e, good impression, color, slightly soiled, **$900–$1,200.**

Wood-block print, a couple regarded by a cat, two mice beside them; from *Ehon Tsuhi no Hinagata* (Models for Loving Couples); Hokusai; good color and impression, center fold, soiled and slightly rubbed, nicked edges, oban yoko-e, 1812, **$1,800–$2,200.**

Fans

Ivory/Shibayama; a motif of cranes and flowers in mother-of-pearl, coral, aogai, and lacquer; Japanese, Meiji period, 12" long, **$4,000–$6,000.**

Ivory/Shibayama with a motif of leaves, grasses, insects, and butterflies; the reverse with cranes; Japanese, Meiji period, 10" long, **$2,500–$3,500.**

Black and gilt lacquer, spatulating blades connected by interlaced white ribbon, painted on both sides with gardens and figures, Chinese, c1850, 14¾" wide, **$700–$900.**

Painted gouache landscape, the figures with silk bodies and painted ivory heads, carved sandalwood sticks, Chinese, c1875, 11½" high, **$600–$800.**

Bright colors on paper, the front with three oval panels depicting the harbor of Hong Kong, the reverse with birds perched in a bouquet of flowering peony, mounted in a gold and black lacquered wood frame, Chinese, late 19th century, 25" wide, **$1,000–$1,500.**

Gilt and colors on paper, both sides with audience scenes and court figures within pavilions, their faces in applied painted ivory, Chinese, 19th century, 20" wide, **$500–$750.**

Painted paper, a landscape scene on both sides, ivory mounts, Chinese, late 19th century, **$300–$425.**

Paper painted with a landscape scene, ivory mounts, Chinese, late 19th century, **$275–$400.**

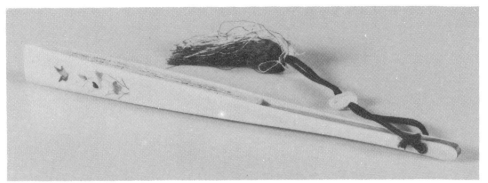

Japanese fan; ivory with Shibayama inlay in designs of flowers, foliage, and insects; the fan with painted scenes of courtesans; ivory ojime in the form of a rabbit with inlaid coral eyes; silk tassle acts as the netsuke; Meiji period, late 19th century, **$1,000–$1,500.**

Chinese fan, bone and feathers, the feathers painted with Chinese beauties and flowers, early 20th century, **$200–$300.**

Peacock feathers, sand-carved-bone sticks, silk tassels, Chinese, c1900, 13½" long, **$175–$200.**

Carved sandalwood with repetitive geometric motifs, silk cord and tassel, Chinese, c1915, 7½" long, **$125–$175.**

Cut silk and painted ivory on paper leaf, one side with a continuous landscape, the other with figures in a courtyard, carved ivory sticks, fitted lacquer box, Chinese, c1830, 10" high, **$500–$700.**

Silk painted with maple leaves, lacquer sticks, silk cord with ivory ojime and tassel, Japanese, late Meiji period, c1900, **$800–$1,200.**

Watercolors and cut silk on paper, ivory details, carved sandalwood sticks, silk tassels and feathers, Chinese, mid-19th century, 11½" high, **$400–$600.**

White feathers, bone handle, silk tassels, the feathers painted with flowers near the top, Chinese, c1910, 9" × 13¼", **$125–$250.**

Glass

Peking (Beijing) Glass

Bottle, blue, translucent, pear-shaped, rim chips, Chinese, 19th century, 5" high, **$200–$400.**

Bottle, yellow, opaque, rim chips; incised Ch'ien Lung (Qianlong) mark, but 19th century; 4¾" high, **$300–$400.**

Bottle/vase, red, the body and neck joined with a molded ring; Ch'ien Lung (Qianlong) mark, but 19th century; 10" high, **$700–$1,000.**

Bowl, amber yellow, relief motif of flowers and figures, Chinese, 19th century, 6½" diameter, **$600–$900.**

Bowl, deep blue, Chinese, 18th century, 8" diameter, **$700–$1,100.**

Bowl, green overlay carved through to the milk glass on the exterior with birds perched on blossoming branches, Chinese, c1910, 6¾" diameter, **$200–$325.**

Bowl, green overlay carved through to the milk glass on the exterior with four panels of foliage, Chinese, c1922, 7" diameter, **$200–$300.**

Bowl, red, four panels featuring carved Buddhistic lions, Chinese, 19th century, 5½" diameter, **$700–$1,000.**

Glass, ruby red, lotus form, Chinese, 19th century, 6½" diameter, **$325–$450.**

Bowl, white with cobalt blue overlay carved with birds on flowering branches, Chinese, 19th century, 6" diameter, **$700–$1,000.**

Bowls; circular; each with short foot and everted rim; carved with a lake, lotus, and carp through red overlay to a milk white ground; Chinese, 19th century, 10½" diameter, **pair, $1,800–$2,500.**

Candlesticks, green clouded glass, square base, Chinese, c1920, 4" diameter, 2½" high, **pair, $125–$285.**

Dish, oval, snowflake glass with etched leaf pattern in blue overlay, Chinese, c1925, 5¾" diameter, **$300–$475.**

Ice cream dish and underplate, hexagonal, clear blue, Chinese, c1930, the dish 4¾" diameter, the plate 6½" diameter, **$100–$175.**

Finger bowl, purple with fluted edge, marked *China*, c1930, 2" high, 4¾" diameter, **$100–$150.**

Jar and cover, magenta-red overlay carved through to the snowflake glass with a large dragon, Chinese, 19th century, 4¾" high, **$900–$1,500.**

Chinese vase; milk glass with green-overlay motifs of birds, flowers, and foliage; early 20th century, 10" high, $300–$500. Courtesy of Richard A. Bowser.

Jars and covers, blue overlay carved through to a milk-glass ground with prunus sprays and birds, each marked *China*, c1930, 6¾" high, **pair, $575–$685.**

Plates, blue glass recessed at the center, minute rim chips on three, each marked *China*, c1950, 7" diameter, **set of 6, $300–$400.**

Saucers, opaque white with fluted sides, each marked *China*, c1935, 5" diameter, **set of 6, $150–$225.**

Vase, baluster form, green overlay carved through to a white ground with flowering branches, marked *China*, c1930, 6" high, **$150–$250.**

Vase, globular form, milk glass with red overlay in a continuous pattern of prunus and rock-work, Chinese, 19th century, 8½" high, **$1,500–$2,500.**

Vase, globular form, milk glass with red overlay in a continuous pattern of prunus and rock-work, Chinese, 19th century, 8½" high, **$1,500–$2,500.**

Vase, yellow, baluster form with waisted neck, carved around the sides with meanders and stiff leaves above a band of lappets, Chinese, 19th century, 8½" high, **$800–$1,200.**

Vase, three-color overlay carved through to the milk white body with two blue dragons, a smaller green dragon on the neck, red foot rim, Chinese, 19th century, 6" high, **$600–$800.**

Vases, baluster form, red overlay carved with a lotus, milky white ground, marked *China*, c1920, 8" high, **pair, $525–$725.**

Vases, oviform, blue overlay carved with phoenix and peony blossoms to a milk white ground, marked *China*, c1935, 8" high, **pair, $300–$400.**

Vases, ovoid, yellow, carved with bird and floral reserves, stiff-leaf border, rim nicks, Chinese, 19th century, 8" high, **pair, $1,500–$2,000.**

Reverse Paintings on Glass

A beautiful lady seated beside a desk and holding a fan, an open book lying on the desk, gilt wood frame, Chinese, early 20th century, framed size 14½" × 18½", **$500–$700.**

A beautiful mandarin lady lavishly dressed and seated on a bench, gilt wood frame, Chinese, early 19th century, framed size 7¾" × 7¼", **$700–$900.**

A beautifully dressed mandarin lady holding a fan and seated beside a table, a vase full of flowers on the desk, gilt wood frame, Chinese, late 19th/early 20th century, framed size, 14" × 18", **$500–$700.**

A Chinese beauty seated beside a table, scattered fruit and lotus blossoms on the table, Chinese, early 20th century, 12" × 15", **$300–$500.**

A Chinese beauty seated at a table, fixing her hair; through the open window beside her, a lake scene; black and gilt lacquer frame; Chinese, late 18th century, framed size 12" × 17", **$1,000–$1,500.**

A court lady sitting beside a table, reading, her robe lavishly detailed, wood frame, Chinese, early 20th century, 18" × 24", **$550–$750.**

A courtesan smoking a hugga, wood frame, Indian, 19th century, framed size 8¼" × 19½", **$200–$300.**

A family gathered around the patriarch, who is seated on a high-back chair, wood frame, Chinese, early 20th century, 23½" × 17", **$400–$600.**

A European shepherdess and a young boy watching a lamb by a river bank, gilt wood frame, Chinese, late 18th century, framed size 6½" × 8¾", **$900–$1,200.**

A lady holding a hand mirror and seated by a table piled high with books, hardwood frame, Chinese, early 20th century, framed size 12¾" × 18", **$350–$550.**

Chinese reverse painting on glass, late Ch'ing dynasty, c1900, hardwood frame, framed size 17" × 21", **$300–$500.**

A lady wearing a vibrant blue robe over pale red trousers, Chinese, early 20th century, 13¾" × 19¼", **$300–$500.**

Five ladies on the terrace of a walled garden, watering flowers and picking blossoms, hardwood frame, Chinese, early 20th century, framed size 26" × 20", **$600–$800.**

Three scholars chatting with attendants beneath a tree, all within a landscape, gilt wood frame, Chinese, early 20th century, framed size 18½" × 14", **$500–$700.**

Pair: Looking to the left, a Chinese beauty holding a fan, her long fingernails characteristic of Chinese ladies of the house, her robes apricot; looking to the right, she holds a book; Chinese, early 20th century, 24" × 37", **$1,300–$1,700.**

Pair: Full-length portraits of a prince and princess, the prince seated on a throne and wearing elaborate gilt-decorated garments and jewelry, the princess leaning against a bolster holding a vina, gilt wood frames, South Indian, late 19th century, framed size 10" × 14¼", **$400–$600.**

Hard Stones

Jade

Note: The type of jade classified as *nephrite* was used by the Chinese until the late eighteenth century, when jadeite was imported from Burma. This type of jade was endowed with rich hues, and it soon surpassed nephrite in popularity, so much so that the emerald green variety became the property of the Emperor.

Archer's ring, green with ochre inclusions, plain, 19th century, **$100–$200.**

Belt buckle, white, the two sections pierced with scrolling ruyi forming a pierced loop, Chinese, 19th century, 2" long, **$600–$900.**

Belt hook, celadon with a dragon in relief, Chinese, early 19th century, 3¾" long, **$250–$400.**

Boulder; celadon with brown mottling; carved with pine trees, mountains, streams, and horses; Chinese, late Ch'ing (Qing) dynasty, 7¼" long, **$700–$900.**

Bowl, green, lobed ovoid ring foot, boat-shaped body carved with three lobed bands, each end with a duck's head finial, Indian, 19th century, 8½" wide, **$1,200–$1,800.**

Bowl, white, lotus-form, the body entwined with pierced lotus and vines, Chinese, 19th century, 3¾" long, **$500–$700.**

Bowl, deep green, thin body, everted rim, mottled black flecks, Chinese, 18th century, 8" diameter, **$3,000–$4,000.**

Bowl, celadon, straight sides, well-hollowed foot, Chinese, 19th century, 4" diameter, **$400–$600.**

Box, apple green, oval with straight sides, Chinese, early 20th century, 3" wide, **$700–$900.**

Brush washer; white; double-gourd form joined by scrolling tendrils; the sides with leafy, gnarled stems; Chinese, 19th century, 4" long, **$1,200–$1,500.**

Brush washer, green and white, the sides carved with gnarled branches and a leaf spray, Chinese, c1900, 3" wide, **$800–$1,200.**

Censer, apple green and white, carved as a kylin standing four square with a bell around its neck, the head as the cover (its mouth open), fitted wood stand, Chinese, late 18th/early 19th century, 9" high, **$8,000–$10,000.**

Censer, green and white, globular, three lion mask feet, lion mask and loose ring handles, Buddhistic lion cub finial, Chinese, 19th century, 6½" high, **$2,500–$3,500.**

Ewer and cover, celadon with brown mottling, loop handle, curved spout, panels of dragons on a floral ground, finial missing, Chinese, late 19th/early 20th century, 10½" high, **$600–$800.**

Left: A green and lavender jade censer and cover, ornately carved, the body supported on four leaf-form carbriole legs with monster mask terminals and dragon head handles, the domed cover with a high pierced finial depicting a dragon pursuing a flaming pearl, the lavender stone with green inclusions carved to highlight details, late Ch'ing (Qing) dynasty, 5¾" high. Realized price (including the 10-percent buyer's premium), Christie's East, New York City, **$3,300.** Right: A jade censer and cover with bands of rough, archaic foliage masks in crisp relief; open-work dragon handles and coiled dragon finial; the stone a mottled putty color with some russet and mustard clouding; carved in K'ang Hsi style; small chips to finial; 8¼" across the handles. Realized price (including the 10-percent buyer's premium), Christie's East, New York City, **$2,090.**

Figure of a recumbent boy carved from a pebble, celadon, Chinese, 18th century, 2½" wide, **$750–$1,000.**

Figure of a Buddhistic lion, recumbent with curly mane, celadon, Chinese, early Ch'ing (Qing) dynasty, 4" long, **$2,500–$3,500.**

Figure of a Buddhistic lion, recumbent, with brocade ball, Chinese, late 19th century, 3" long, **$450–$650.**

Figure of Kuan Yin holding a flowering branch, the stone a pale green with light brown patches, Chinese, 19th century, 5½" high, **$600–$800.**

Figure of a Lohan, white, wearing flowing robes and holding a sceptre, Chinese, late 19th century, 6" high, **$700–$1,000.**

Figure of a water buffalo, gray, its legs tucked beneath its body, Chinese, early 20th century, 5" long, **$500–$600.**

Group, celadon with brown inclusions, a boy riding a carp, Chinese, 18th century, 3" wide, **$1,500–$2,500.**

Group, mutton fat, a monkey climbing on a peach, the leaves forming the base, Chinese, 4½" wide, c1900, **$800–$1,200.**

Hand mirror, white-gray, carved with interlacing flowers below lotus buds, carved foliate borders, mirror replaced with modern glass, Indian, 19th century, 6" long, **$500–$675.**

Inkwell, pale green, silver hinge and mount, fitted wood stand, the lid with Buddhistic lion finial, Chinese, late 19th century, **$600–$800.**

Pebble, celadon and russet, carved as a peach with a leafy stem, Chinese, 18th century, 2½" wide, **$900–$1,200.**

Pi disc, greenish brown, circular and pierced, carved in high relief with two confronting dragons, rim chips, Han dynasty, 3½" diameter, **$900–$1,200.**

Plaque, round, spinach green, carved with pavilions and pines, the reverse with an incised poem, fitted wood stand, Chinese, late 19th century, 5¾" diameter, **$900–$1,200.**

Plaque; white with pale green splashes; one side carved with a sage and waterfall; Ch'ien Lung (Qianlong) mark, but 19th century; 14¾" high, **$3,000–$4,000.**

Plaque; celadon; carved with bats, ruyi heads, flowers, and leaves; Chinese; early 20th century, 2½" wide, **$300–$450.**

Plaques; pale green; oval; applied amethyst, quartz, and agate motif of birds perched on flowering branches; each in a fitted wood stand; Chinese; early 20th century, 16" high, **pair, $800–$1,200.**

Scroll weight, dark green, rectangular, 7½" long, **$300–$500.**

Seal, celadon, square with a dragon handle, Chinese, c1900, 4½" long, **$600–$900.**

Ruyi sceptre, celadon, the handle carved with bosses and chrysanthemums, the underside with bosses, Chinese, 19th century, 10" long, **$1,500–$2,200.**

Ruyi sceptre, pale green, carved with Taoist symbols in low relief, Chinese, 19th century, 8½" long, **$600–$800.**

Sceptre, green, the shaft and head carved with birds, Chinese, 19th century, 15" long, **$900–$1,400.**

Vase, celadon, carved as a carp leaping from breaking waves, its mouth forming the rim, Chinese, 19th century, 7" high, **$800–$1,200.**

Vase, celadon, the stone with brown patches, carved with birds at the base, Chinese, 19th century, 4½" high, **$1,500–$2,000.**

Vase and cover, celadon, flattened baluster form, pierced handles at the waisted neck, both sides carved with phoenix, Chinese, early 20th century, 9¼" high, **$600–$950.**

Assorted Stones

Agate brush washer, the dish with lavender and brown hues, Chinese, early 20th century, 3" wide, **$1,200–$1,500.**

Agate brush washer, brown-gray, carved as a lotus leaf with flower sprays, chipped, Chinese, late 19th century, 2½" wide, **$175–$250.**

Agate brush washer, honey-hued, oval and carved around the body with vines, Chinese, late 19th century, 2" wide, **$200–$300.**

Agate, wine ewer with ribbed body and domed lid, Chinese, early 20th century, 3¼" high, **$300–$450.**

Amber brush washer carved with peony blossoms, reddish yellow, Chinese, 20th century, 4" wide, **$1,000–$1,500.**

Amber figure of a ram, yellowish orange, naturalistically carved, Chinese, 20th century, 4" wide, **$1,000–$1,500.**

Amber group, boulder form, fruit (including peaches and pomegranates), brownish red, Chinese, 19th century, 4" long, **$1,200–$1,500.**

Amber group, yellowish orange, two dragons carved with C-scrolls, Chinese, c1900, 3½" wide, **$600–$800.**

Amethyst quartz, a recumbent Buddhistic lion, Chinese, c1900, 2¼" long, **$200–$300.**

Carnelian agate vase carved as a large fruit with entwined vines, Chinese, 19th century, 6" high, **$900–$1,200.**

Carnelian agate vase carved with fruiting plum branches, Chinese, 19th century, 4" high, **$1,500–$2,500.**

Carnelian box and cover carved in the form of a cicada, Chinese, late 19th century, 3" long, **$250–$400.**

Chalcedony agate vase and cover, flattened baluster form, gray-violet, lion mask handles and Buddhistic lion finial, Chinese, c1900, 9¾" high, **$1,000–$1,500.**

Coral belt plaque with Shou character, Chinese, c1920, 3¾" long, **$225–$325.**

Coral carved in the form of peony blossom arranged in a slender vase, Chinese, 20th century, 4" high, **$900–$1,200.**

Coral group, two female deities, each below a phoenix, one standing on clouds and one leaning on a prunus branch, chipped, hardwood stand, Chinese, 20th century, 9" high, **$1,500–$2,000.**

Lapis lazuli Buddhistic lions, bushy manes, one with a foot on a brocade ball, the other with a foot on its cub, Chinese, early 20th century, 6½" high, **pair, $1,200–$1,800.**

Lapis lazuli elephants, trunks raised, mottled stones with pyrite inclusions, Chinese, 20th century, 10¼" wide, **pair, $700–$1,100.**

Lapis lazuli Lohan holding a fly whisk, the stone with gray and white inclusions, Chinese, early 20th century, 4½" high, **$800–$1,200.**

Malachite brush washer, gourd-shaped, fruit and leaves coiling around the surface, Chinese, early 20th century, 4¾" diameter, **$850–$1,200.**

Malachite dragon, fierce expression, fitted wood stand, Chinese, 20th century, 5" long, **$400–$600.**

Marble carpet weights, white, each on a square block, octagonal upper section with lotus-head finial, Indian, 19th century, 9" high, **pair, $850–$1,200.**

Marble dish; Pietra Dura work; rectangular; scrolling foliate design of carnelian, jade, lapis lazuli, and other inlaid flowering plants; lobed flower-head border; Indian; early 20th century, 10" × 8", **$500–$700.**

Marble figure of a deer, white, standing on an oval base, Indian, 19th century, 17" high, **$750–$1,050.**

Marble vase; baluster form; carved with dragons, bats, and cloud scrolls; Chinese; c1900, 9½" high, **$500–$700.**

Rock crystal, Kuan Yin seated on rockwork base and holding a ruyi sceptre, Chinese, 20th century, 4½" high, **$1,200–$1,600.**

Rock crystal, the Eight Immortals, each with attribute, Chinese, 20th century, 8" high, **set, $800–$1,200.**

Rock crystal vase and cover, baluster form, loose ring handles below Buddhistic lion masks, lappet band at the base, chipped, Chinese, c1900, 11" high, **$700–$950.**

Rose quartz censer, domed cover, globular body, loose ring and lion mask handles, Buddhistic lion finial, Chinese, late 19th century, 5" wide, **$500–$700.**

Chinese soapstone seal surmounted with a recumbent dragon and waves, gray with brown inclusions, 19th century, 4" high, **$150–$225.**

Chinese serpentine censer with tripod feet, the pierced cover surmounted by a recumbent kylin, 19th century, 5" high, **$250–$400.**

Rose quartz figure of Kuan Yin holding a peony spray, mounted as a lamp, Chinese, early 20th century, 12½" high, **$500–$700.**

Rose quartz vase and cover, slender, carved with floral foliate branches, mounted as a lamp, Chinese, early 20th century, 14" high, **$700–$900.**

Rose quartz vase and cover, pierced and carved with flowering branches on each side, floral finial, Chinese, c1910, 7" high, **$400–$600.**

Rose quartz vase and cover, knop finial, Buddhistic lion handles at the shoulders, mounted as a lamp, Chinese, c1900, 6½" high, **$300–$400.**

Slate, panel carved in relief through a buff surface to a darker ground with cliffs and pavilions, Chinese, c1900, 13½" X 11", **$900–$1,200.**

Serpentine ruyi sceptre, the ends carved with Immortals, the stone a yellowish hue, chipped, Chinese, 19th century, 14½" long, **$400–$600.**

Soapstone figure of a guardian, bearded and wearing a layered tunic, Chinese, 19th century, 8" high, **$600–$800.**

Soapstone figure of Kuan Yin, the stone with gray tones, chipped, Chinese, late 19th century, 8½" high, **$300–$500.**

Soapstone figures of the Eight Immortals, each with attribute, several chipped, Chinese, c1925, 7¾" high, **$400–$600.**

Soapstone figure of Pu Tai holding staff and sack, Chinese, late 19th century, 22" high, **$500–$650.**

Soapstone figure of a seated Lohan, Chinese, 19th century, 4" high, **$700–$950.**

Left: *Cylindrical soapstone brush pot; cut and pierced in deep relief on the side with a continuous broad band of pavilions nestling in pine and prunus, plus figures and travelers, all within narrow bands of formal key pattern; Chinese, mid-19th century, 6" high. Realized price (including the 10-percent buyer's premium), Christie's East, New York City,* **$550.** Right: *Cylindrical hardwood brush pot, the sides applied with mother-of-pearl and colored hard stones depicting Immortals, minor losses, Chinese, 6½" high. Realized price (including the 10-percent buyer's premium), Christie's East, New York City,* **$880.**

Soapstone seal, boulder-shaped, amber hue, carved with two Buddhistic lion cubs, Chinese, 7" high, **$800–$1,200.**

Soapstone seal, rectangular, brown, surmounted by a Buddhistic lion cub, Chinese, c1910, 2" high, **$200–$300.**

Soapstone seal carved as a rocky landscape, Chinese, late 19th century, 4" high, **$400–$700.**

Soapstone seal, rectangular with rounded corners, greenish white, Chinese, 20th century, 4½" high, **$200–$300.**

Soapstone seal surmounted by a phoenix, Chinese, c1910, 2¾" high, **$200–$325.**

Soapstone seal, plinth shape, cream color, the top carved with a Buddhistic lion, Chinese, early 19th century, 2¾" high, **$500–$700.**

Soapstone tea caddy and cover carved in relief with pavilions, metal neck, Chinese, late 19th century, 6" high, **$900–$1,200.**

Turquoise group of three children playing, Chinese, late 19th century, 4" high, **$800–$1,200.**

Ink Stones

Rounded rectangular duan ink stone carved with cosmic star patterns around the edges and at the sloping recess, a yi character in archaic script on the base in a recessed panel, Chinese, 17th century, 6¼" wide, **$1,500–$2,000.**

Rounded rectangular duan ink stone carved to one side with a bird on a prunus branch above a hollowed crescent moon, Chinese, 17th century, 6" wide, **$800–$1,200.**

Rounded rectangular duan ink stone mottled with green inclusions, an inscription on the base in a slightly recessed panel, Chinese, 18th century, 5¾" wide, **$875–$1,125.**

Square duan ink stone slightly recessed at one end with a cloud-pattern border, fitted wood box, dated 1936, Chinese, 6¼" wide, **$1,000–$1,500.**

Trapezoidal duan ink stone with a raised border carved on the base (shui yen shen pin—underwater rock of the divine class), Chinese, 18th century, 3¾" wide, **$1,800–$2,400.**

Trapezoidal duan ink stone carved to simulate a rock with a sloping recess to one side, Chinese, 18th century, 7¾" wide, **$2,000–$3,000.**

Jewelry

Left: *Silver pin, the character reading* good fortune, *marked* D'argent *and* Saigon, *made in Saigon for export to France, c*1930, **$100–$150.** Right: *Silver pin with fan below a bamboo-form bar (the character translates* good fortune), *Japanese, c*1920, **$175–$200.**

Matching bracelet and pin, silver and black enamel, marked Siam; pin, **$50–$75,** *bracelet,* **$50–$75.** Courtesy of Roni Simon.

Silver beads, China trade, late 19th century, 3" diameter, **each, $50–$75.**

Bar pin, Komai, scenic design, signed, Japanese, c1900, **$400–$600.**

Bar pin, silver inset with six settings of topaz between filigree leaves, Chinese, c1900, **$200–$250.**

Belt, silver with eight rectangular sections, each section with a repoussé motif of flowers and leaves joined by plain loops, Chinese, late 19th century, extended to 27", **$450–$600.**

Belt buckle, silver, oblong, cherry blossoms in relief, Japanese, **$135–$175.**

365

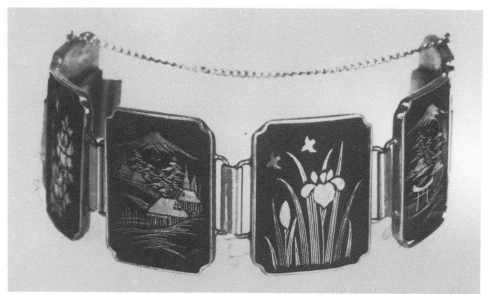

Komai bracelet with inlaid gold and silver floral and scenic plaques, Japanese, c1925, **$500–$700.**

Mother-of-pearl and silver button bracelet, Chinese, late Ch'ing (Qing) dynasty, **$225–$300.**

Silver bracelet with gold wash, the motif including a scenic design with warriors on horseback, mother-of-pearl, and bamboo leaves; hallmarked CW (and Chinese characters), the mark of Cum Woo; Queen's Road, Hong Kong, c1850, **$2,000–$3,000.**

Silver bracelet with green enameled oval reserves containing silver characters for long life *and* good fortune, *marked* Siam, *c*1920, **$150–$225.**

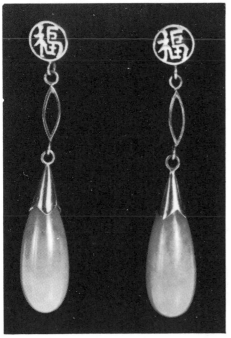

Celadon jade and 14-karat-gold earrings (for pierced ears), Chinese, c1900, **$350–$450.**

Belt buckle, silver set with coral and turquoise in three hinged sections, the stones set amongst filigree scrolls, Nepalese, 19th century, 7½" diameter, **$500–$700.**

Belt hook, celadon jade, tongue-shaped fitting with dragon head pierced across its mouth, the underside with a flower head, button, Chinese, 18th century, 5½" long, **$2,000–$2,500.**

Bracelet, bangle, carved ivory with dragon motif, Chinese, c1925, **$100–$150.**

Bracelet, Komai, seven round medallions with plain links, each of the medallions with a floral motif, Japanese, c1925, **$500–$700.**

Bracelet, Komai, the plaques in silver mounts, plain silver links, each plaque with a varied motif (including a landscape, a lake scene, and a view of Mt. Fuji), Japanese, c1925, **$450–$650.**

Bracelet, gilt, repoussé work, riders on horseback in a landscape, key borders, Chinese, mid-19th century, **$2,550–$3,500.**

Bracelet; gold; eight tiger-eye discs, each set in 14-karat gold with a Fuku character at its center; plain links; Chinese, 20th century, **$200–$275.**

Bracelet, pewter, bangle engraved with birds and flowers, Chinese, c1930, **$25–$50.**

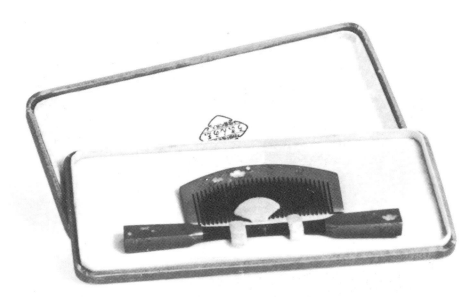

Lacquered tortoiseshell hair ornament set inlaid with mother-of-pearl and coral, Shibayama, gold lacquer, Japanese, c1920, **$600–$900.**

Bracelet, silver, five green jade plaques carved with Shou characters and two rows of plain silver links, Chinese, c1935, **$100–$150.**

Bracelet, silver, hinged form, closed by a pin attached to a chain, three rows of pierced rosettes and two large clusters of plain silver beads attached to the terminals, Indian, **$300–$400.**

Brooch, Komai with design of birds and flowers, marked S. *Komai,* Japanese, c1910, **$550–$750.**

Brooch, Satsuma, dragon and clouds in gilt and colors, mounted in silver, Japanese, c1930, 2½" diameter, **$400–$600.**

Brooch, silver with carved coral rose inset, Chinese, c1935, **$100–$125.**

Brooch, silver with malachite insert carved with three flowers, Chinese, c1930, **$150–$200.**

Cabochon; jade; brilliant, translucent green; 7mm × 5.3mm × 2mm; realized price at an auction conducted by Christie's in Hong Kong (January 1986), **$9,000.**

Cigarette case; Sentoku with gold, silver, and shakudo motifs of bamboo and flowers; Japanese, c1925, **$100–$150.**

Clip, silver with gold wash, round and flat, set with a carved red lacquer plaque in a floral motif, Chinese, c1930, **$20–$30.**

Cuff links, cloisonné, green ground, white peony blossoms, silver rims, dark green backs, Japanese, c1910, **$225–$350.**

Cuff links, Komai, round with paulownia leaves in gold and silver, signed *Komai,* c1910, **$275–$400.**

Cuff links, Satsuma, a motif of bamboo in colors and gold, silver mounts, Japanese, c1935, **$150–$200.**

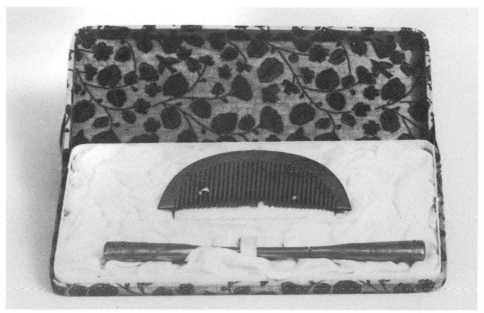

Hair ornament set, gilt lacquer on tortoiseshell with Shibayama inlay, c1910, **$700–$900.**

Cuff links, silver set with a round green jade plaque carved in low relief with a flower and foliage, Chinese, c1925, **$50–$75.**

Earrings, carnelian drops, silver mountings, Chinese, c1920, **$100–$185.**

Earrings, pale green cabochons set in 14-karat gold, pierced backs, Chinese, early 20th century, **$300–$500.**

Earrings, plain carnelian loops, screw backs, Chinese, c1935, **$35–$65.**

Earrings, carved celadon jade with a phoenix motif below seed pearls, screw backs, Chinese, c1925, **$175–$275.**

Earrings, silver with gold wash and carved red lacquer drop bead, screw backs, China, c1930, **$20–$30.**

Fingernails, silver inset with turquoise and coral beads, Chinese, early 20th century, **pair, $250–$325.**

Comb, ivory with Shibayama inlay in a motif of flowers and butterflies, Japanese, late 19th century, 3½" wide, **$900–$1,200.**

Comb, tortoiseshell with seed pearls, Chinese, c1900, **$150–$250.**

Comb, tortoiseshell with seed pearls along the top, two pearls missing, Chinese, c1910, **$150–$250.**

Comb, tortoiseshell decorated with gold hiramakie and hirame and inlaid in aogai on a gold ground, Japanese, late 19th century, 3¾" wide, **$500–$700.**

Hair ornament, kingfisher on a metal sheet forming a phoenix, embellished with semiprecious stones, Chinese, late 19th century, 7" long, **$200–$300.**

Hair ornament, gold, circular, the border pierced with flower heads, a peacock medallion at the center, the whole set with rubies, Indian, 3¼" diameter, **$1,200–$1,500.**

Hairpin, jade and pink tourmaline, Chinese, c1920, **$300–$500.**

Hairpin and comb, roiro ground with large flower heads, Zeshin style, Japanese, Taisho period, **$600–$900.**

Hairpin, kingfisher resembling a phoenix, Chinese, early 20th century, **$100–$150.**

Hat pin, Komai with motif of a willow tree and crane, Japanese, c1900, **$250–$350.**

Headdress; kingfisher feathers with jade, rose quartz, and glass beads; some stones missing; Chinese, 19th century, **$300–$500.**

Necklace, 33 reticulated celadon and brown jade beads, each carved with the character for long life (Shou), restrung, Chinese, 19th century, **$1,500–$2,200.**

Necklace; 73 graduated jade beads, each measuring anywhere from 8mm to 3mm in diameter; the beads a brilliant, translucent emerald green; diamond and gold clip attachment; **$60,000–$70,000.**

Necklace, 24 uniform beads of carved red lacquer, hand-knotted, choker, Chinese, c1930, 16" long, **$50–$85.**

Necklace, carnelian and 14-karat-gold beads, 32" long, **$500–$700.**

Necklace, carved ivory beads (uniform in size), hand-knotted, Chinese, c1925, 18" long, **$250–$350.**

Necklace, jade beads of various colors, hand-knotted, Shou character on clasp (14-karat-gold), 18" long, **$400–$550.**

Necklace, lapis lazuli, 21 round beads alternating with woven silk and metal discs, Indian, 21¼" long, **$250–$350.**

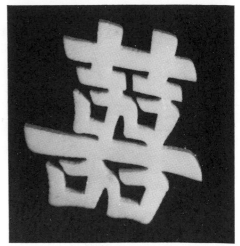

Ivory pin in the double happiness character, Chinese, c1925, **$100–$150.**

Komai pin inlaid with gold, the back reads S. Komai, *3¾" diameter, c1910,* **$400–$650.**

Necklace, pink coral beads, graduated, Chinese, c1920, 18" long, **$150–$225.**

Nose rings, six crescentic rows of small pearls, one row inside with a crystal-inset lozenge at the top, the whole strung on gold wires and fringed with seed pearls and blue glass beads, Indian, 1¾" diameter, **$450–$600.**

Pendant, aquamarine carved with a bat in flight, the stone with natural faults, Chinese, early 20th century, 2" long, **$300–$400.**

Left: *Satsuma pin set in silver, gilt and raised enamels of a flowering tree with full moon above, Japanese, c1910, 3¾" diameter,* **$200–$300.** Right: *Cloisonné pin set in silver, ginbari (foil) with floral motif set against a silver-blue ground, silver wire, Japanese, c1920,* **$275–$375.**

Pendant, aquamarine carved as a peach, Chinese, late Ch'ing (Qing) dynasty, **$300–$500.**

Pendant, carnelian carved as a length of bamboo with a carved centipede, pierced for hanging, Chinese, late 19th century, 2¾" long, **$200–$300.**

Pendant, carnelian, a spider carved from the lighter skin, Chinese, c1920, **$200–$400.**

Pendant, celadon jade carved as the celestial twins, Chinese, late 19th/early 20th century, 2½" wide, **$300–$500.**

Pendant, celadon jade carved as two peaches with foliage, Chinese, late 19th century, 2½" wide, **$200–$300.**

Pendant, gold with a central turquoise surrounded by 11 coral insets, the whole surrounded by 14 turquoise-inset petal forms with open-work sections in between, Indian, 3" diameter, **$300–$425.**

Pendant, 14-karat-gold Shou character, 1" diameter, **$200–$275.**

Pendant, ivory, oval, carved in high relief with flowers and filigree, black silk cord, ivory bead slide, silver clasp, Chinese, c1920, 36" long, **$175–$225.**

Ring, pale green jade cabochon, 14-karat-gold mounting, **$700–$900.**

Ring, silver with a design of a seated Buddha, Chinese, c1900, **$150–$200.**

Ring, silver with gold wash, set with oblong plaque of carved red lacquer, Chinese, c1935, **$50–$75.**

Ring, silver with square turquoise inset and carved with Fuku character, Chinese, c1930, **$75–$100.**

Ring; white gold set with a green jade cabochon measuring 25.2mm × 16.2mm × 6mm; realized price at an auction conducted by Christie's in Hong Kong (January 1986), **$60,000.**

Stick pin, Komai, round medallion with floral pattern, Japanese, c1900, **$250–$350.**

Stick pin, Komai, diamond-shaped, scenic motif, Japanese, c1900, **$250–$350.**

Tiara, kingfisher feathers, semiprecious stones and glass beads, Chinese, c1900, **$200–$300.**

Korean Ceramics

Bottle, blue and white with large peony blossom, Yi Dynasty, 12" high, **$350–$550.**

Bottle/vase, blue and white, faceted pear shape painted with a sparrow perched on a blossoming branch, the long neck ending in a rounded lip, Yi Dynasty, 11" high, **$700–$950.**

Bowl, celadon, inlaid with cranes and clouds, Yi Dynasty, 5" diameter, **$125–$175.**

Bowl, white glaze stopping high above a spreading foot, Yi Dynasty, 5" high, **$50–$100.**

Box and cover, mishima inlay, flying cranes, rim chips, 13th century, 7" diameter, **$750–$1,000.**

Box and cover, mishima inlay, cranes inlaid in black and white slip on a stylized-cloud ground with flower-head medallion, lacquer repair, Koryo Dynasty, 6½" diameter, **$500–$750.**

Brush pot, blue and white with a scenic motif including a fenced terrace, Yi Dynasty, 4¾" high, **$600–$850.**

Brush pot, white glazed, open-work motif including confronting phoenixes and clouds, Yi Dynasty, 5½" high, **$475–$700.**

Dish, short ring foot, flaring sides, pale green glaze, Yi Dynasty, 5" diameter, **$100–$200.**

Jar; short, everted neck painted in underglaze blue with peony; rim chips; Yi Dynasty, 7" high, **$175–$250.**

372

Underglaze blue bottle set on recessed ring foot with cylindrical neck and decorated in underglaze blue over an incised rambling-flower-spray pattern, covered in a clear glaze, Korean, Yi dynasty, 19th century, 8½" high. Realized price (including the 10-percent buyer's premium), Christie's, New York City, $2,200.

Jar, globular, blue and white with a motif of flowering peony branches below a collar of florets and fret pattern, minor rim chips, Yi Dynasty, 4½" high, **$1,500–$2,500.**

Jar, opaque gray glazed stoneware, lacquer repair on rim, Yi Dynasty, 8½" diameter, **$500–$700.**

Left to right: *Blue and white jar with underglaze blue phoenix flying amid clouds, Korean, Yi dynasty, 19th century, 8¼" high. Realized price (including the 10-percent buyer's premium), Christie's, New York City,* **$4,400.** *Blue and white dish, recessed ring foot, decorated in underglaze blue with a crane flying amid clouds, covered in a creamy white overall glaze, Korean, Yi dynasty, 19th century, 6" diameter. Realized price (including the 10-percent buyer's premium), Christie's, New York City,* **$3,080.** *Blue and white bottle, pear-shaped, recessed ring foot, everted rim, underglaze blue hanging-grapevine design, white glaze, Korean, Yi dynasty, 7½" high. Realized price (including the 10-percent buyer's premium), Christie's, New York City,* **$2,640.**

Jar, blue and white, painted with stylized foliage, Yi Dynasty, 8½" high, **$150–$200.**

Spittoon, celadon, flaring neck, globular body, olive green glaze, biscuit foot fired brown, Koryo Dynasty, 13th/14th century, 7½" diameter, **$1,500–$2,200.**

Vase, ovoid, flattened lip covered with a translucent green glaze, Yi Dynasty, 7" high, **$200–$300.**

Vase, pear-shaped, decorated in white mishima on a celadon ground with floral medallions below a lappet band on the shoulder, lacquer repair on lip, Koryo Dynasty, 7" high, **$275–$375.**

Vase; oviform body with short, ribbed neck and deep, cup-shaped lip; celadon glaze; 15th/16th century, 10½" high, **$300–$500.**

Water dropper, blue and white, square form with bamboo motif, Yi Dynasty, 3¼" high, **$100–$200.**

Mud Figures (Chinese)

Elder, white beard and hair, brown and green attire, marked *China,* c1910, 1" high, **$10–$15.**

Elder, green glazed attire, holding a bowl, marked *China,* c1905, 1" high, **$10–$15.**

Elder, green glazed attire, holding a fan, marked *China,* c1925, 3" high, **$25–$35.**

Elder with beard, blue glazed attire, holding a book, marked *China,* c1925, 3½" high, **$20–$30.**

Elder, fisherman, pole missing, marked *China,* c1930, 4½" high, **$15–$20.**

Mud *figure of an elder with coin and peach (long life)*, *marked* China, *c*1925, 5" *high*, **$45–$65.**

Elder, coin carrier, marked *China*, c1935, 6" high, **$30–$45.**

Elder seated on rock-work, yellow and green glazed attire, marked *China*, c1935, 6" high, **$40–$50.**

Elder with yellow and blue attire, large yellow hat at the back, marked *China*, c1930, 7" high, **$50–$75.**

Vase; brown, green, and blue glazes with figures of elders in various poses; marked *China*; c1920, 8" high, **$100–$150.**

Mud *figure of an elder with a fan*, *marked* China, *c*1930, 5" *high*, **$45–$65.**

Wall pocket, blue and green glazing with flowers, marked *China*, c1925, 6" wide, **$75–$100.**

Woman with basket of flowers, marked *China*, c1930, 6" high, **$45–$65.**

Woman holding a bowl, green and yellow attire, her hair with a high topknot, marked *China*, c1920, 4" high, **$40–$55.**

Southeast Asian Ceramics

Annamese jar and cover; the footed jar painted with four iron brown flower-head panels within pale olive surrounds, pooling to a deeper shade in the areas of low relief; crack in cover; 11th / 12th century, 10" high, **$3,000–$5,000.**

Sawankhalok box and cover, ribbed and decorated with iron brown foliage, 15th century, 5½" diameter, **$200–$300.**

Sawankhalok bowl and cover incised and painted with scrolling foliage panels, 15th century, 6½" diameter, **$300–$500.**

Sawankhalok flask painted iron brown with foliage, body with ribs, neck restored, 15th century, 5½" high, **$100–$200.**

Sawankhalok, group, an elephant surmounted by two figures and painted iron brown under a white slip, restored, 14th century, 5" high, **$300–$400.**

Sawankhalok kendi painted iron brown with foliage panels, mammiform spout, restored flange and neck, 15th century, 6½" high, **$200–$300.**

Sawankhalok jar, two handles at rim, ribbed body, celadon glaze, 14th / 15th century, 5" high, **$200–$300.**

Sawankhalok vase, gourd-shaped, two loop handles, lotus bud neck, horizontal ribbing, glazed brown, 16th century, 7" high, **$75–$100.**

Sawankhalok vase, pear-shaped, celadon glaze over a ribbed body, wide rim, restored, 14th / 15th century, 5½" high, **$185–$275.**

Sawankhalok roof tile, a dragon with pierced mane, its scaly body picked out in brown, 19½" high, **$700–$900.**

Wood Carvings, Bamboo, and Basketry

Basket, bamboo, double-gourd form, woven with intricate designs, used for flower arranging (it lies on its side), Japanese, c1900, 9½" long, **$600–$800.**

Basket, splint bamboo with entwined bail handle, Japanese, early 20th century, 12½" high, **$50–$100.**

Basket, splint bamboo, pitcher shape with bail handle, Japanese, early 20th century, 6½" high, **$100–$150.**

Basket, root and wicker, double-gourd form, Japanese, late Meiji period, 12" long, **$175–$250.**

Fish basket, bamboo and wicker, Japanese, Meiji period, 15½" high, **$150–$225.**

Picnic baskets, woven bamboo, each finely pierced with a bracket foot and trimmed in gilt, the three sections having diapers and woven decorations, pierced handle, Chinese, early 20th century, 8" high, **pair, $275–$400.**

Bamboo carving of a phoenix upon an open-work base, Chinese, late Ch'ing dynasty, 11" high, **$900–$1,200.**

Left: *Bamboo cylindrical container*, Chinese, *c*1920, 10" *high*, **$100–$150.** Right: *Woven three-tiered basket with incised bamboo handle, brass mounts*, Chinese, *early 20th century, 9½" × 13½",* **$275–$375.**

Box, three-tiered, rectangular handle on rectangular base, Chinese, late 19th century, 6" × 8", **$400–$600.**

Box, carved wood, joined at one corner, the sides and top inset with carved panels of flowers, the base on short bracket feet, Chinese, c1900, 14" long, **$500–$650.**

Brush pot, cylindrical, the patina a honey-brown, the base with a Ch'ien Lung mark (and of the period), Chinese, 18th century, 6¼" high, **$1,000–$1,500.**

Brush pot, bamboo, cylindrical, a scene of pine trees and figures, Chinese, early 19th century, 6½" high, **$900–$1,200.**

Wood dish with hard-stone motif of a seated Pu Tai, *Chinese, c1900, 8½" diameter,* **$200–$325.**

Brush pot, bamboo, carved with a scholar on a terrace in a landscape, Chinese, 19th century, 6" high, **$250–$375.**

Miniature house (the interior added by the author's husband) with movable doors, floors, and so on; the roof on both sides lifting off as well; movable trees and shrubs; Japanese, late Meiji / early Taisho period, 17" wide, 11" high, **$700–$950.**

Brush rest, bamboo, carved with a mountainscape, Chinese, late 19th century, 5" long, **$150–$225.**

Cosmetic box; mirrored, hinged door; three drawers; Japanese, Meiji period, 12" X 8½" X 9½", **$225–$375.**

Hibachi, keyaki wood, five drawers, copper-lined burner, Japanese, early 20th century, 12" X 26" X 16", **$500–$700.**

Hibachi, kiri wood, the body decorated with bamboo and birds in gold lacquer, copper liner, Japanese, late 19th century, 8½" high, **$200–$300.**

Hibachi, kiri wood, gold lacquer and mother-of-pearl flowers, Japanese, Taisho period, 9" high, 14" wide, **$300–$425.**

Hibachi, root wood with copper liner, Japanese, Meiji period, 34" diameter, **$900–$1,200.**

Hibachi, wood with gold and red lacquer flowers, copper liner, Japanese, late Meiji period, 12¾" diameter, **$200–$300.**

Jewel case, keyaki and kiri wood, three drawers, Japanese, c1910, 10" high, 8" wide, **$225–$325.**

No mask, an old man, chipped, signed *Tetsuya*, Japanese, late 19th century, **$200–$400.**

Panel, carved and pierced wood with motif of birds and flowering prunus, repainted red and gold, Chinese, c1900, 12" X 15", **$50–$85.**

Panel, carved wood with Mandarins in a scenic motif, much open work, repainted red and gold, Chinese, early 20th century, 8¼" × 24½", **$75–$125.**

Panel depicting a female figure standing on a lotus throne supported by two lions and flanked by female attendants amidst open-work; she holds a bow and arrow and is wearing elaborate jewelry (and a quiver on her back); South Indian, 20th century, 76", **$1,800–$2,600.**

Panel carved and pierced with birds and leafy branches, gilt intact, mounted in a black frame, Japanese, late 19th century, 35" × 72", **$1,650–$2,400.**

Panel carved with flower heads surrounded by scrolling foliage, traces of red paint, Indian, late 19th/early 20th century, 56" high, **$500–$650.**

Panels (probably removed from a pavilion) carved with peony and leaves, traces of red and gilt, Chinese, late 19th/early 20th century, 11" square, **pair, $100–$125.**

Root carving of a dragon, Chinese, late 19th century, 9" high, **$600–$900.**

Root carving of an Immortal seated upon a tree stump, Chinese, 19th century, 10½" high, **$300–$500.**

Shop sign in the form of a badger holding a sake bottle, Japanese, early Showa period, 18½" high, **$600–$800.**

Shop sign (doll maker's), two dolls seated under a tree, Japanese, early 20th century, 9½" long, **$125–$225.**

Shop sign (fan maker's), fan form with calligraphy, Japanese, late 19th century, 24" long, **$300–$500.**

Carved wood panel (probably taken from a door— now framed for hanging), Chinese, c1900, frame size 23½" long, **$250–$300.**

Shop sign (pawnbroker's) in the shape of a bat, red and gilt lacquer on wood, iron suspension hook, Chinese, 19th century, 78" high, **$1,000–$1,500.**

Shrine, miniature, kiri wood, Torii gate, Japanese, early Showa period, **$300–$400.**

Shrine, miniature, kiri wood, Torii gate, Japanese, late Meiji period, 4" high, **$300–$400.**

Smoker's box, rosewood, two drawers and copper liner, Japanese, early 20th century, 9" long, **$100–$175.**

Carved wood panel depicting bakemono (the one in the center is called Hitosume Kozo), Japanese, Meiji period, 20" × 13¼", **$1,500–$2,000.**

Carved wood figure of Daikoku with mallet and sack, "Mingei" (folk art), Japanese, Meiji period, 23" high, **$1,000–$1,500.**

Table for playing Go, hardwood, Japanese, 20th century, 9" × 16" × 17", **$75–$125.**

Vase, bamboo, carved mountainscape, Chinese, late 18th/early 19th century, 9¼" long, **$1,200–$1,600.**

Vases, bamboo, carved with birds in relief amidst pine trees, signed Seko, Japanese, late 19th century, 13½" high, **pair, $500–$800.**

Wood carving of Amida wearing loose vestments and raising his hand, his hair in rahotsu style, old wear and damages, wood worm, replacement of hands, possibly late 16th/early 17th century, Japanese, **$2,500–$3,500.**

Wood carving of a bearded elder seated upon rock-work, inlaid ivory eyes and teeth, marked China, c1925, 9" high, **$65–$95.**

Left: *Wood carving of Kuan Yin, Chinese, c1930, 4" high,* **$50–$75.** Right: *Wood carving of the Disappointed Rat Catcher, Japanese, late 19th century,* **$500–$700.**

Wood carving of Bodiharma wearing a cowled robe, Chinese, late 19th century, 9" high, **$450–$600.**

Wood carving of Buddha seated on a waisted throne, his hands in bhumi-sparasa and dhyana mudra, traces of gilt on the figure, Burmese, 20th century, 24" high, **$700–$900.**

Wood carving of Daikoku, a sack over one shoulder, a mallet over the other, one leg raised, some damage, Japanese, c1900, 6½" high, **$600–$800.**

Wood carving of an elder wearing a large, round hat; inlaid ivory eyes and teeth; marked *China*; c1925, 7" high, **$50–$75.**

Wood carving of a falcon perched on a gnarled tree stump, Japanese, late 19th century, 14" high, **$300–$500.**

Wood carving of Gama Sennin standing on a rock-work base and holding a basket of flowers, toads clambering about, Japanese, late 19th century, 7½" high, **$600–$800.**

Carved wood group of three Immortals depicted as hermits in tattered clothing, one standing with a gnarled staff, another seated with a fly whisk, their female companion holding a branch of lingzhi, crack, Chinese, Ch'ing dynasty, 10" high. Realized price (including the 10-percent buyer's premium), Christie's East, New York City, **$1,540.**

Wood carvings of gong bearers, each standing with articulated arms poised on a mound base, elaborate robes carved with zigzag motifs, Burmese, 19th century, 28½" high, **pair, $800–$1,200.**

Wood carving of Handaka Sonja holding a bowl aloft in one hand and a tobacco pouch in the other, Japanese, late 19th century, 5¼" high, **$500–$600.**

Wood carving of Shoki, his robes with phoenix mon in red and black lacquer, Japanese, late Edo / early Meiji period, 9" high, **$900–$1,200.**

Wood carving of Hotei, treasure bag over his shoulder, slight damage, signed Masanao, Japanese, late 19th century, 5" high, **$600–$750.**

Wood carving of smiling Hotei with inlaid-ivory teeth and eyes, accompanied by children, marked China, early 20th century, 10" high, **$125–$150.**

Wood carving of Kuan Yin, the patina a yellowish brown, Chinese, late 19th century, 7" high, **$400–$600.**

Wood carvings of Kuan Yin, each seated on a rocky base, each having traces of gilt, Chinese, late 19th century, **pair, $2,500–$3,500.**

Wood carvings of Lohan, each having inlaid-ivory eyes, the ivory teeth missing from one, marked China, c1920, 7½" high, **pair, $100–$125.**

Wood carving of two bakemono masks, each grotesque face inlaid with ivory teeth and horn eyes, Japanese, c1900, 4" diameter, **$900–$1,200.**

Wood-carved mask of a demon with fanged teeth and sunken eyes, some gilt remaining, Japanese, 19th century, 30" high, **$700–$900.**

Wood carving of a No performer holding a sceptre, the kimono painted in colors, Japanese, late 19th century, 11" high, **$800–$900.**

Wood carving of a priest (in sitting position) holding a lotus pod surmounted by a sacred pearl, glass-inlaid eyes, some gilt remaining, old wear and damages, Japanese, 18th century, **$3,000–$4,000.**

Wood carving of a recumbent water buffalo looking to the right, signed Kiromitsu, Japanese, 19th century, **$500–$600.**

Wood carving of Sennin Kiku Jido upon a mountain overlooking a stream, chrysanthemums covering the entire sculpture, Japanese, late Edo period, 18" diameter, **$3,500–$4,500.**

Wood carving of Shoki and Oni, the demon killer struggling to hold Oni, some damage, signed Kogetsu, Japanese, c1900, 7" high, **$750–$950.**

Wood carving of a seated tiger looking to the right, ittobori style, Japanese, c1900, 9" long, **$400–$600.**

Wood carving of a warrior riding on a rampant horse supported by a kneeling attendant, Indian, 20th century, 29" high, **$300–$600.**

Wood carving of a water buffalo, inlaid ivory eyes, marked *China*, early 20th century, 5½" long, **$50–$65.**

Wood carving of a woman holding a basket of fruit, signed *Kogetsu*, Japanese, early 20th century, 6" high, **$400–$600.**

Wood carvings of the Eight Immortals, each with attribute, some damage, Chinese, early 20th century, 8" high, **$1,800–$,2400.**

Wood sake container, kiri wood, well-bucket form, the exterior with three bamboo bands, Japanese, early 20th century, 13½" diameter, **$175–$300.**

Wrist rest, bamboo carved with a riverscape, Chinese, early 20th century, 9" long, **$200–$275.**

Appendices

Appendix A

Appraisers

Sandra Andacht
Japanese and Chinese pottery, porcelain, cloisonné, metalwares, lacquer, furniture, and all other decorative arts

Lee Chinalai
Southeast Asian tribal rugs and related arts

Leonard Davenport
Japanese paintings and screens

Harold Jaffe
European Chinoiserie and Japonaiserie

Michael Krassner
Chinese paintings, hard stones, Southeast Asian bronzes, and related arts

Stephen Leonard
Toys and games
Mr. Leonard also repairs toys and games.

David Migden
Japanese swords, tsuba, and other sword accoutrements

Dr. Bernard Rosett
Netsuke and related arts

Dr. Sam Sokolov
Japanese wood-block prints

Appendix B

Chinese Cycles and Japanese Year Periods

Five Complete Chinese Cycles, or 300 Years, from A.D. 1744–2043

No. of year in Cycle	Name of year in Cycle (combined Stems and Branches)		Corresponding Elements			Symbolic Animals			Five Cycles of Sixty				
									74th	75th	76th	77th	78th
1	Chia Tzŭ	甲子	Mu	木	Wood	Shu	鼠	Rat	1744	1804	1864	1924	1984
2	I Chou	乙丑	,,	,,	,,	Niu	牛	Ox	1745	1805	1865	1925	1985
3	Ping Yin	丙寅	Ho	火	Fire	Hu	虎	Tiger	1746	1806	1866	1926	1986
4	Ting Mao	丁卯	,,	,,	,,	T'u	兎	Hare	1747	1807	1867	1927	1987
5	Wu Ch'ên	戊辰	T'u	土	Earth	Lung	龍	Dragon	1748	1808	1868	1928	1988
6	Chi Ssŭ	己巳	,,	,,	,,	Shê	蛇	Snake	1749	1809	1869	1929	1989
7	Kêng Wu	庚午	Chin	金	Metal	Ma	馬	Horse	1750	1810	1870	1930	1990
8	Hsin Wei	辛未	,,	,,	,,	Yang	羊	Ram	1751	1811	1871	1931	1991
9	Jên Shên	壬申	Shui	水	Water	Hou	猴	Monkey	1752	1812	1872	1932	1992
10	Kuei Yu	癸酉	,,	,,	,,	Chi	雞	Cock	1753	1813	1873	1933	1993
11	Chia Hsü	甲戌	Mu	木	Wood	Ch'üan	犬	Dog	1754	1814	1874	1934	1994
12	I Hai	乙亥	,,	,,	,,	Chu	猪	Boar	1755	1815	1875	1935	1995
13	Ping Tzŭ	丙子	Ho	火	Fire	Shu	鼠	Rat	1756	1816	1876	1936	1996
14	Ting Chou	丁丑	,,	,,	,,	Niu	牛	Ox	1757	1817	1877	1937	1997
15	Wu Yin	戊寅	T'u	土	Earth	Hu	虎	Tiger	1758	1818	1878	1938	1998
16	Chi Mao	己卯	,,	,,	,,	T'u	兎	Hare	1759	1819	1879	1939	1999
17	Kêng Ch'ên	庚辰	Chin	金	Metal	Lung	龍	Dragon	1760	1820	1880	1940	2000
18	Hsin Ssŭ	辛巳	,,	,,	,,	Shê	蛇	Snake	1761	1821	1881	1941	2001
19	Jên Wu	壬午	Shui	水	Water	Ma	馬	Horse	1762	1822	1882	1942	2002
20	Kuei Wei	癸未	,,	,,	,,	Yang	羊	Ram	1763	1823	1883	1943	2003
21	Chia Shên	甲申	Mu	木	Wood	Hou	猴	Monkey	1764	1824	1884	1944	2004
22	I Yu	乙酉	,,	,,	,,	Chi	雞	Cock	1765	1825	1885	1945	2005
23	Ping Hsü	丙戌	Ho	火	Fire	Ch'üan	犬	Dog	1766	1826	1886	1946	2006
24	Ting Hai	丁亥	,,	,,	,,	Chu	猪	Boar	1767	1827	1887	1947	2007
25	Wu Tzŭ	戊子	T'u	土	Earth	Shu	鼠	Rat	1768	1828	1888	1948	2008
26	Chi Chou	己丑	,,	,,	,,	Niu	牛	Ox	1769	1829	1889	1949	2009
27	Kêng Yin	庚寅	Chin	金	Metal	Hu	虎	Tiger	1770	1830	1890	1950	2010
28	Hsin Mao	辛卯	,,	,,	,,	T'u	兎	Hare	1771	1831	1891	1951	2011
29	Jên Shên	壬辰	Shui	水	Water	Lung	龍	Dragon	1772	1832	1892	1952	2012
30	Kuei Ssŭ	癸巳	,,	,,	,,	Shê	蛇	Snake	1773	1833	1893	1953	2013
31	Chia Wu	甲午	Mu	木	Wood	Ma	馬	Horse	1774	1834	1894	1954	2014
32	I Wei	乙未	,,	,,	,,	Yang	羊	Ram	1775	1835	1895	1955	2015
33	Ping Shên	丙申	Ho	火	Fire	Hou	猴	Monkey	1776	1836	1896	1956	2016
34	Ting Yu	丁酉	,,	,,	,,	Chi	雞	Cock	1777	1837	1897	1957	2017
35	Wu Hsü	戊戌	T'u	土	Earth	Ch'üan	犬	Dog	1778	1838	1898	1958	2018
36	Chi Hai	己亥	,,	,,	,,	Chu	猪	Boar	1779	1839	1899	1959	2019
37	Kêng Tzŭ	庚子	Chin	金	Metal	Shu	鼠	Rat	1780	1840	1900	1960	2020
38	Hsin Chou	辛丑	,,	,,	,,	Niu	牛	Ox	1781	1841	1901	1961	2021
39	Jên Yin	壬寅	Shui	水	Water	Hu	虎	Tiger	1782	1842	1902	1962	2022
40	Kuei Mao	癸卯	,,	,,	,,	T'u	兎	Hare	1783	1843	1903	1963	2023
41	Chia Ch'ên	甲辰	Mu	木	Wood	Lung	龍	Dragon	1784	1844	1904	1964	2024
42	I Ssŭ	乙巳	,,	,,	,,	Shê	蛇	Snake	1785	1845	1905	1965	2025
43	Ping Wu	丙午	Ho	火	Fire	Ma	馬	Horse	1786	1846	1906	1966	2026
44	Ting Wei	丁未	,,	,,	,,	Yang	羊	Ram	1787	1847	1907	1967	2027
45	Wu Shên	戊申	T'u	土	Earth	Hou	猴	Monkey	1788	1848	1908	1968	2028
46	Chi Yu	己酉	,,	,,	,,	Chi	雞	Cock	1789	1849	1909	1969	2029
47	Kêng Hsü	庚戌	Chin	金	Metal	Ch'üan	犬	Dog	1790	1850	1910	1970	2030
48	Hsin Hai	辛亥	,,	,,	,,	Chu	猪	Boar	1791	1851	1911	1971	2031
49	Jên Tzŭ	壬子	Shui	水	Water	Shu	鼠	Rat	1792	1852	1912	1972	2032
50	Kuei Chou	癸丑	,,	,,	,,	Niu	牛	Ox	1793	1853	1913	1973	2033
51	Chia Yin	甲寅	Mu	木	Wood	Hu	虎	Tiger	1794	1854	1914	1974	2034
52	I Mao	乙卯	,,	,,	,,	T'u	兎	Hare	1795	1855	1915	1975	2035
53	Ping Ch'ên	丙辰	Ho	火	Fire	Lung	龍	Dragon	1796	1856	1916	1976	2036
54	Ting Ssŭ	丁巳	,,	,,	,,	Shê	蛇	Snake	1697	1857	1917	1977	2037
55	Wu Wu	戊午	T'u	土	Earth	Ma	馬	Horse	1798	1858	1918	1978	2038
56	Chi Wei	己未	,,	,,	,,	Yang	羊	Ram	1799	1859	1919	1979	2039
57	Kêng Shên	庚申	Chin	金	Metal	Hou	猴	Monkey	1800	1860	1920	1980	2040
58	Hsin Yu	辛酉	,,	,,	,,	Chi	雞	Cock	1801	1861	1921	1981	2041
59	Jên Hsü	壬戌	Shui	水	Water	Ch'üan	犬	Dog	1802	1862	1922	1982	2042
60	Kuei Hai	癸亥	,,	,,	,,	Chu	猪	Boar	1803	1863	1923	1983	2043

FIVE COMPLETE CYCLES, OR 300 YEARS, FROM A.D. 1744-2043.

Japanese Year Periods
(Nengo)

Characters	Name of period	Commenced A.D.
永應	O-ei	1394
長正	Shocho	1428
享永	Eikio	1429
吉嘉	Kakitsu	1441
安文	Bun-an	1444
德宝	Hotoku	1449
德享	Kotoku	1452
正康	Kosho	1455
禄長	Choroku	1457

正	寛	Kwansho	1460
正	文	Bunsho	1466
仁	應	Onin	1467
明	文	Bunmei	1469
享	長	Choko	1487
德	延	Entoku	1489
應	明	Meio	1492
亀	文	Bunki	1501
正	永	Eisho	1504
永	大	Daiei	1521
禄	享	Koroku	1528

天文	Tembun	1532
弘治	Koji	1555
永禄	Eirko	1558
元亀	Genki	1570
天正	Tensho	1573
文禄	Bunroku	1592
慶長	Keicho	1596
元和	Genna	1615
寛永	Kwanei	1624
正保	Shoho	1644
慶安	Keian	1648

承應	Jo-o	1652
明曆	Meireki	1655
萬治	Manji	1658
寬文	Kwambun	1661
延宝	Empo	1673
天和	Tenna	1681
貞享	Jokio	1684
元禄	Genroku	1688
宝永	Hoei	1704
正德	Shotoku	1711
享保	Kioho	1716

文	元	Gembun	1736
保	寛	Kwanpo	1741
享	延	Enkio	1744
延	寛	Kwanen	1748
暦	宝	Horeki	1751
和	明	Meiwa	1764
永	安	Anei	1772
明	天	Temmei	1781
政	寛	Kwansei	1789
和	享	Kiowa	1801
化	文	Bunkwa	1804

文政	Bunsei	1818
天保	Tempo	1830
弘化	Kokwa	1844
嘉永	Kaei	1848
安政	Ansei	1854
萬延	Manen	1860
文久	Bunkiu	1861
元治	Genji	1864
慶應	Keio	1865
明治	Meiji	1868
大正	Taisho	1912

 Showa

1926
to the present

Appendix C

Chronology

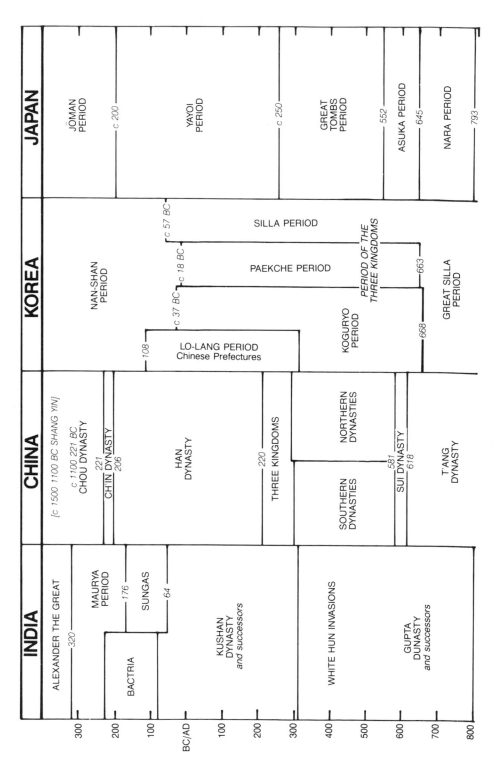

INDIA	CHINA	KOREA	JAPAN

INDIA

ALEXANDER THE GREAT
— *320*

MAURYA PERIOD
— *176*

SUNGAS
— *64*

BACTRIA

KUSHAN DYNASTY
and successors

WHITE HUN INVASIONS

GUPTA DYNASTY
and successors

CHINA

[*c 1500 1100 BC SHANG YIN*]

c 1100 221 BC
CHOU DYNASTY

221
CH'IN DYNASTY
206

HAN DYNASTY

220

THREE KINGDOMS

SOUTHERN DYNASTIES

NORTHERN DYNASTIES

581
SUI DYNASTY
618

T'ANG DYNASTY

KOREA

NAN-SHAN PERIOD

c 37 BC

108

LO-LANG PERIOD
Chinese Prefectures

c 57 BC

c 18 BC

SILLA PERIOD

PAEKCHE PERIOD

KOGURYO PERIOD

PERIOD OF THE THREE KINGDOMS

663

668

GREAT SILLA PERIOD

JAPAN

JŌMON PERIOD

c 200

YAYOI PERIOD

c 250

GREAT TOMBS PERIOD

552

ASUKA PERIOD

645

NARA PERIOD

793

300 · 200 · 100 · BC/AD · 100 · 200 · 300 · 400 · 500 · 600 · 700 · 800

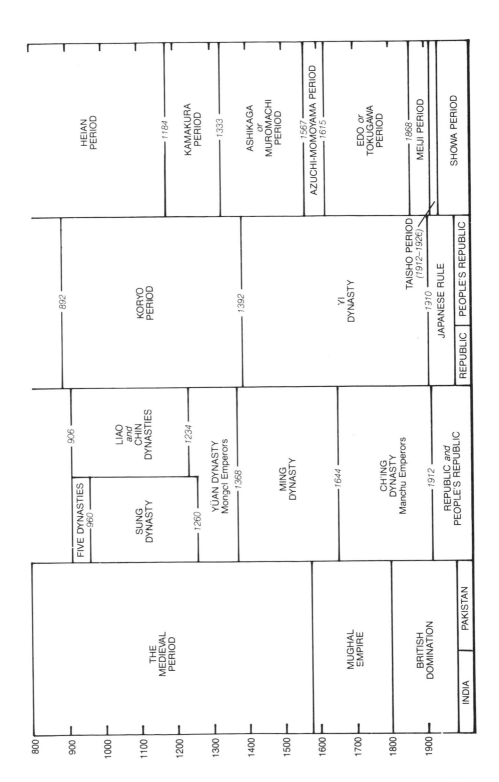

Appendix D

Guidelines for Care of Oriental Antiques and Art

Ceramics

Under no circumstances should you use the dishwasher to clean ceramic objects. Fine antiques and collectibles are not dishwasher-safe; in fact, pottery and terracotta objects should not even be immersed in water. Instead, pottery should be cleaned with a damp cloth, and terracotta should be cleaned with a minimal amount of water and dried immediately. Gentle dusting may be the best way to keep terracotta clean.

Porcelain, on the other hand, is safely cleaned with mild soap and tepid water. Always be sure, though, to place a thick towel in the bottom of the sink or wash area to prevent damaging the object by bringing it into direct contact with the surface of the wash area.

Never hang cups from cup hooks. Handles are not strong and can easily break.

Furniture

Never use liquid wax on Oriental furniture. To clean kiri wood and other blonde woods, first mix a solution that is one-third turpentine, one-third vinegar, and one-third warm water, and test it on an inconspicuous part of the object. If the solution cleans that portion safely, apply it overall. Then use the finest grade of steel wool to take off old wax and dirt. Hard wax or shoe polish, the same color as the finish, may be used after cleaning—approximately 12 to 15 layers for a hard surface. Buff the last layer with a soft cloth for the perfect finish.

Always check the interior of a tansu: Its condition should be as good as that of the exterior. Sometimes, however, you'll find that fine-quality wood has been used on the doors and/or drawers, and that cheaper, thinner, or otherwise inferior wood has been used on the interior. Beware of objects in this category, as the inferior wood may crack from the weight of the objects in the drawers.

Also check the back panel, which is often cracked. If damaged, it should be replaced. The replacement will not diminish value.

Ivory

A brush is the best tool to use for cleaning ivory, although you can use mild soap and tepid water to remove surface dirt, provided the object is in excellent condition. Ivory should be dried immediately in order to prevent warping and cracking.

Jade

Jade can also be washed with mild soap and tepid water, but be sure to rinse it thoroughly, and use a soft cloth for drying the object.

Lacquer

Clean lacquer wares by wiping them with a lint-free cloth. Applying a very small amount of lemon with the cloth is permissible, but never use wax or strong detergents on lacquered objects.

Any room in which lacquered furniture is stored should contain a humidifier. In addition, lacquered objects should be rotated, especially in the winter, when they are generally subjected to a great deal of dry heat.

Finally, lacquer should be kept out of direct sunlight.

Metalwares

Silver should be cleaned with a fine-quality polish according to the directions on the label of the polish container. Never clean other metalwares. Their natural patina (finish), which changes over the years, is highly prized by collectors. Metalwares which have been cleaned either with polishes or abrasive cleansers are less valuable.

Paintings, Screens, and Scrolls

Silk or paper paintings, screens, and hanging scrolls should be displayed for only short periods of time. Remember to avoid displaying them in direct sunlight, which will cause fading.

Otherwise, store paintings, screens, and scrolls away from heat, light, and dampness, with tissue layers between panels. Periodically unroll scrolls (every three to six months) to allow them to "breathe." Keep the atmosphere in which they are displayed or stored temperate by using a humidifier in the winter and air conditioning in the summer.

Always check the backs of screens for mildew.

Prints

A print should be sharp and clear, and made from the first or original strike. Trimming, fading, holes, dirt, and foxing (brown spots) will reduce its value, so it is wise to protect the print from these problems by framing it. If you prefer not to frame a print, store it between sheets of paper (or of cardboard with rag content). Chemically treated paper will damage a print.

Like scrolls, prints should never be hung in direct sunlight. Occasionally rotate the prints you wish to display prominently with those which have been put in darker places.

Appendix E

Marks

For the most part, collectors cannot rely solely upon marks as a gauge for authenticity. The McKinley Tariff Act of 1891—requiring that all articles of foreign manufacture be plainly marked, stamped, branded, or labeled in legible English words so as to indicate the country of origin—was instituted in order to provide consumers with a more complete knowledge of what they were buying. Still, many wares which are unmarked, or which are marked in Japanese or Chinese characters without the country of origin written in English, are not necessarily objects produced prior to 1891.

From 1891 to March 21, 1921, the word *Nippon* was acceptable as proper marking of country of origin for goods manufactured in Japan and exported to the U.S. Later, Treasury Decision #26989 used the words *gummed label* and *rubber stamp* for the first time in defining identification requirements, many collectors have assumed that the use of an affixed sticker on Japanese export wares (and on Chinese exports, to a lesser degree) was not initiated until this 1917 decision. However, the word *labeled* in the McKinley Tariff Act also indicated an affixed sticker, whereby the use of labels to indicate country of origin has been acceptable since March 1, 1891.

Chinese Marks

Chinese six-character reign marks are written in three vertical rows. Other Chinese marks include hallmarks, maker's marks, place marks, commendation marks, and symbols. Some of these take the form of six characters written in two horizontal rows.

Written in standard script, Chinese marks were most often done in underglaze blue. However, marks can be found in pink, red, gold, orange, and so on. Seal marks were written with a brush and seldom were stamped. Incised and stamped marks are most commonly found on monochromatic wares.

The periods whose reign marks which were most often copied in later periods include Yung Lo, 1402–1423; Hsüan Te, 1426–1435; Cheng Hua, 1465–1487; Wan Li, 1573–1619; K'ang Hsi, 1662–1723; Yung Cheng, 1723–1736; and Ch'ien Lung, 1736–1796. Some of these periods became significant because of their shortness (and the resulting rarity of objects produced during those periods), and some were important because of the innovations that occurred within them.

Authentic period pieces, of course, have always brought the highest prices. Pieces with *Imperial* marks are also especially valuable.

Japanese Marks

Japanese marks and seals include maker's names, date marks, and place marks. Like their Chinese counterparts, significant Japanese marks were copied, forged, and bartered: One potter in awe of another had no difficulty copying the other's mark or seal. To further complicate matters, Chinese reign marks were copied and are frequently found on Japanese Imari (Arita). If the Japanese characters for *Dai Ni Hon* (or *Dai Nippon*—see the list of marks in Chapter 9) appear in a mark, the object was produced no earlier than 1868.

Assessing Quality

The quality of any object *should* correspond to the quality of the mark. The surest way to obtain quality pieces, however, is to buy from reputable sources. In addition, take every opportunity to acquaint yourself thoroughly with the kinds of objects that interest you most: Handle them, ask questions about them, and read as much as you can about them, subscribing to relevant periodicals and building your own reference library. If courses or seminars dealing with the topic are offered locally, enroll in them. It is better to buy one piece of high quality than to buy several pieces of lesser quality.

Appendix F

North American Museums with Permanent Exhibitions of Orientalia

Mailing Addresses

Albright-Knox Art Gallery
1285 Elmwood Ave.
Buffalo, NY 14202

The Art Gallery of Greater Victoria
1040 Moss St.
Victoria, British Columbia
Canada V8V4P1

The Art Institute of Chicago
Michigan Ave. and Adams St.
Chicago, IL 60603

The Boston Museum of Fine Arts
465 Hunt Ave.
Boston, MA 02115

The Brooklyn Museum
188 Eastern Pkwy.
Brooklyn, NY 11238

The Cincinnati Art Museum
Eden Park
Cincinnati, OH 45202

The City Art Museum of St. Louis
St. Louis, MO 63110

Cleveland Museum of Art
11150 East Blvd.
Cleveland, OH 44106

E. B. Crocker Art Gallery
216 O St.
Sacramento, CA 95814

The Denver Art Museum
100 W. 14 Pkwy.
Denver, CO 80204

The Detroit Institute of Arts
Detroit, MI 48202

The M. H. De Young Memorial Museum
Golden Gate Park
San Francisco, CA 94118

The Freer Gallery of Art
Washington, D.C.

Herron Museum of Art
Purdue University
Indianapolis, IN 46205

Honolulu Academy of Arts
900 S. Beretania St.
Honolulu, HI 98614

Los Angeles County Museum of Art
5905 Wilshire Blvd.
Los Angeles, CA 90036

The Jacques Marchais Center of Tibetan Art
338 Lighthouse Ave.
Staten Island, NY 10306

The Metropolitan Museum of Art
5th Ave. and 82nd St.
New York, NY 10028

The Minneapolis Institute of Arts
2400 3rd Ave.
Minneapolis, MN 55404

The Montclair Art Museum
Montclair, NJ 07042

Museum of Art
Providence, RI

William Rockhill Nelson Gallery of Art
Mary Atkins Museum of Fine Art
4525 Oak St.
Kansas City, MO 64111

The Newark Museum
Newark, NJ 07101

The Portland Art Museum
Portland, OR

The Ringling Museum of Art
Sarasota, FL 33580

Riverside Museum
Riverside, CA 94305

Royal Ontario Museum
100 Queen's Park
Toronto, Ontario
Canada M5S2C6

Seattle Art Museum
Volunteer Park
Seattle, WA 98112

The Stanford University Museum
Stanford, CA 94305

The Toledo Museum of Art
Toledo, OH 43697

The University Museum
Philadelphia, PA 19104

The Wadsworth Atheneum
600 Main St.
Hartford, CT 06103

Walker Art Center
Vineland Pl.
Minneapolis, MN 55403

The Walters Art Gallery
222 State St.
Springfield, MA 01103

Worcester Art Museum
55 Salisbury St.
Worcester, MA 01608

Yale University Art Gallery
New Haven, CT 06520

Appendix G

Organizations and Publications Dealing with Orientalia

Clubs/Organizations

Included among the following are several groups which may appeal to readers interested in specific aspects of Orientalia. Write to the address listed to request information about a group's focus, activities, dues, and so on.

Asia Society
725 Park Ave.
New York, NY 10021

The Bead Society
Box 2513
Culver City, CA 90231

The International Chinese Snuff Bottle Society
2601 North Charles St.
Baltimore, MD 21218

Society for Japanese Arts and Crafts
Secretariat
Witte de Withlaan 4
2341 SR Oegstgeest
The Netherlands

Japan House
33 E. 47th St.
New York, NY 10017

Netsuke Kenkyukai Society
Box 11248
Torrance, CA 90510

The Ukyio-e Society of America
Box 665 F.D.R. Station
New York, NY 10150

Auction Houses

Christie's
502 Park Ave.
New York, NY 10022

Christie's East
219 E. 67th St.
New York, NY 10021

Christie's (London)
8 King St.
St. James, London
England SW1Y6QY

Publications

Edited and published by Sandra Andacht, the *Orientalia Journal* is issued bimonthly for collectors, dealers, interior designers, and investors. Each issue contains special features and illustrations on such topics as cloisonné, prints, hard stones, porcelain, pottery, rugs, and all other aspects of Orientalia. Plus, a question-and-answer column provides active reader responses. The *Orientalia Journal* costs $15 for one year and $28 for two (in the U.S. and Canada). Its foreign rate is $24 per year (payable in U.S. funds), and the single-copy price is $5. Payment should be directed to *The Orientalia Journal*, P.O. Box 94, *Little Neck*, NY 11363.

In addition, check your local listings for various regional and national publications on antiques and collectibles; some of them carry regular features or columns dealing with Orientalia.

Appendix H

Restoration

Antiques lovers cannot always expect special finds to be in perfect condition. With regard to Orientalia, one must consider the material from which an object was created, and the use and abuse an object has sustained over the years. The smart shopper who spots an early, rare, or unusual object does not hesitate to purchase it as is. The object can be professionally restored—either with hidden repairs, or in the case of Japanese ceramics, with gold lacquer repairs in Japanese style.

Rosine Green, as illustrated in the following accounts of her work, is highly accomplished in the art of restoring Oriental antiques. If you have a purchase which could benefit from restoration, the author recommends that you send good-quality photos and a brief description of the object to Rosine Green Associates, 45 Bartlett Cres., Brookline, MA 02146. *Please enclose a self-addressed, stamped envelope.*

Two Approaches to Restoring Oriental Antiques

Rosine Green

One of the most beautiful pieces on display at Boston's Old State House is the Peacock Bowl. This punch bowl, produced as Chinese export porcelain, is in the famille rose palette, Mandarin style. Among its lavishly decorative paintings of flowers and scenes are depictions of the hongs (warehouses) at Canton—a most unusual subject for this kind of piece. On the outside wall, a shield encloses the inscription *From the Commander and the Ward Room Officers of the* U.S. Ship Peacock *to* Dwight Boyden, Tremont House, Boston, 1832. (The Peacock was a three-masted naval sloop used for diplomatic and mercantile missions. Her officers, when in Boston, were accommodated at the Tremont House, a fine hotel whose proprietor at the time was Dwight Boyden.)

Peacock Bowl Before Assembly

Peacock Bowl Before Painting, with Missing Pieces Recast

412

Peacock Bowl Completely Restored

The Peacock Bowl is a rather large piece, measuring 20 inches in diameter at its upper rim, and 9 inches deep. It is also quite heavy. By the time the bowl came to our studio, the seams of its previous repairs had discolored with age and two large pieces were missing. To begin our work, we removed the unsightly metal clips which, prior to World War II, were customarily used in the restoration of porcelain. When we soaked the bowl to free the original pieces, the bowl came apart into more than a dozen fragments. After joining together the available fragments, we cast the missing pieces, filled in the chips, and repainted and reglazed the repairs.

Western Restoration Techniques

Our restoration of the Peacock Bowl was executed so that, once the repair had been made, the closely matched repainting made it impossible to discern. Porcelains made for the Western market—such as Rose Medallion, Canton blue and white, Fitzhugh, and Imari—are best repaired in this Western manner: using modern technology and Oriental painting techniques to render the restored portions stylistically indistinguishable from the original decorations. The Oriental manner of positioning a brush perpendicular to the surface is especially important, since it creates an effect quite different from that of the Western technique of holding a brush at a slant.

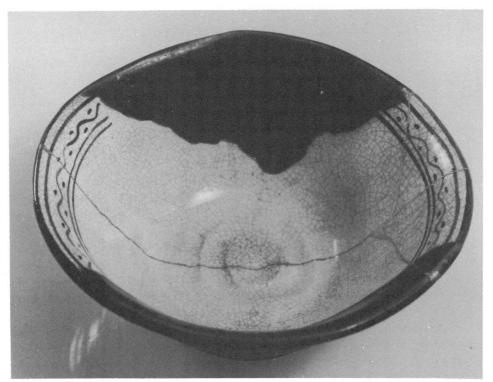

An Example of Oriental Gold Lacquer Repair

The Oriental Approach

There is, however, a special Oriental style of mending porcelain which is seldom practiced in the United States, but which should be an option available to all serious collectors. About ten years ago, one of my clients, a dealer from San Francisco who had a great feeling for Oriental art as well as an impressive collection of his own, asked me if I would undertake a gold repair on a Sanda Seiji porcelain piece. Although I had seen such repairs in museums, I had no notion of how to go about creating this marvelous rivulet of gold that fills the seam of the repair and embellishes it instead of concealing the course of damage.

Shortly thereafter, I went to Japan to study the art of lacquer restoration. I was fortunate to meet and have a pri-

vate lesson with the eminent lacquer artist, Professor Fuyuki of Kyoto University. In his studio, I noticed many pieces of fine porcelain and earthenware whose repairs had been done in gold, whose fineness cannot be matched by anything available in this country. I discovered that the basis and adhesive for Oriental gold repairs is none other than Urushi lacquer. When I returned to Boston, I was able to meet the request of my client, to our mutual delight.

At first I found that most of my clients were less than eager to commission this type of repair, preferring, instead, the Western style of repair, which conceals the damage. Yet gradually, with Oriental gold repairs being done for a number of museums and connoisseurs, gold repairs have become an increasingly accepted way to proceed.

The White House Chigai-Dana

Rosine Green Associates has completed restoration of a historic *chigai-dana* for the White House. The chigai-dana, a traditional Japanese shelving system, was presented to President James Buchanan in 1860 by the first Japanese delegation to the United States.

In the main room of a traditionally designed Japanese home, the chigai-dana occupied one of two alcoves, while the other was typically adorned with a hanging scroll and perhaps an arrangement of flowers. Characterized by shelves asymmetrically arranged—*chigai* meaning *different*, and *dana*, *shelves*—and partially enclosed by sliding doors to resemble a cupboard, the chigai-dana was often elaborately decorated with lacquer and gold. As Edward Morse explains in his 1886 classic, *Japanese Homes and Their Surroundings* (the Dover reprint of which is available at your local bookstores), the chigai-dana is sometimes called *usu-kasumi-dana*, or *thin-mist shelf*, because the alternating positions of the shelves evokes the conventional manner of drawing mist or clouds. The chigai-dana represents an example of the Japanese approach to asymmetry in furniture design; as such, it was one of the early influences on American design of the nineteenth century.

Other restorers had worked with the White House chigai-dana earlier in the century, but the lack of understanding of Japanese joinery made their attempts unsatisfactory. Consequently, the chigai-dana was in very poor condition when it arrived from the White House.

Mrs. Green and her staff of skilled artisans from all over the world devoted their collective expertise and two years of meticulous care to the superb restoration of the chigai-dana. They fabricated the missing parts, reassembled the pieces, hand-painted the 24-karat-gold decoration, cast the missing silver hardware and chased their ornamentation, straightened the warps, secured the blisters, and relacquered the entire piece, restoring its original luster. Rosine Green Associates also restored a lacquer writing table which was part of the same gift presented to President Buchanan. It is currently on display in the guest sitting room of the White House.

Choosing Appropriately

In an evaluation for restoration, one should consider carefully the principles behind the creation of a piece. In export wares, for instance, the decoration has been designed to satisfy the tastes of Western collectors. Some pieces, in fact, are so closely identified with their owners that family initials or coats-of-arms, or even homes, were integrated into their design. However, in pieces made in the Orient for the domestic market, the point of view is different. To the Japanese, especially, every piece is alive: The signature of the artist does not signal the end of the creative process. There, moreover, one does not *own* a piece. Rather, one has the privilege of caring for it. Should a piece be damaged, the Japanese do not undertake in its repair to create the illusion that the damage never occurred. This would be a violation of the spirit—the essence of the maker. Instead, they strive to integrate the mending itself into the unique character of the piece. This is the philosophy behind the Oriental gold repair.

In any case, respect for the integrity of the piece itself, as well as for the artistic tradition in which it was created, is as essential in the art of restoration as the technical skill involved.

The White House Chigai-Dana

Before

After

Appendix I

Spelling and Pronunciation of Terms

Chinese

The letters in the left-hand columns below are from the Pinyin system currently being used to romanize the Chinese language. The letters in the right-hand columns are from the standard Wade-Giles system. For a summary of common terms as they appear in each system, see the more extensive table which follows the spelling key.

Note that collectors tend to use whichever system suits them best. Both are acceptable; both have been used in this guide.

Spelling Key

Initial		Termination	
Pinyin	**Wade-Giles**	**Pinyin**	**Wade-Giles**
b	p	an	en
p	p'	e	o
d	t'	i	ih
g	k	i (si)	u (ssu)
k	k'	ie	ieh
zh	ch	ong	ung
j	ch	uo	o
ch	ch'	ui	uei
c	ts', tz'	yi	i
r	j	you	yu
x	hs		

Wade-Giles/Pinyin Comparison Chart

Dynasties

Pinyin	Wade-Giles	
Shangyin	Shang Yin	B.C. 1600–1027
Zhou	Chou	1027–475
Qin	Ch'in	221–206
Han	Han	206–220 A.D.
Sui	Sui	581–618
Tang	T'ang	618–906
Liao	Liao	916–1125
Song	Sung	960–1279
Jin	Chin	1115–1234
Yuan	Yuan	1279–1368

Reigns

Pinyin	Wade-Giles	
Ming		
Hongwu	Hung Wu	1368–1398
Yongle	Yung Lo	1402–1423
Xuande	Hsüan Te	1426–1435
Chenghua	Ch'eng Hua	1465–1487
Hongzhi	Hung Chih	1488–1505
Zhengde	Cheng Te	1506–1521
Jaijing	Chia Ching	1522–1566
Longqing	Lung Ch'ing	1567–1572
Wandi	Wan Li	1573–1619
Tianqi	T'ien Ch'i	1621–1627
Chongzheng	Ch'ung Cheng	1628–1643
Qing	**Ch'ing**	
Shunzhi	Shun Chih	1644–1661
Kangxi	K'ang Hsi	1662–1723
Yongzheng	Yung Cheng	1723–1736
Qianlong	Ch'ien Lung	1736–1796
Jiaqing	Chia Ch'ing	1796–1820
Daoguang	Tao Kuang	1821–1850
Xianfeng	Hsien Feng	1851–1861
Tongzhi	T'ung Chih	1862–1874
Guangxu	Kuang Hsü	1875–1908
Xuantong	Hsüan T'ung	1909–1912
Hongxian	Hung Hsien	1916

Bronzes

	Pinyin	Wade-Giles
Vessels:	Ding	Ting
	Li	Li
	Gui	Kuei
	Dou	Tou
	Jue	Chüeh
	Jiao	Chiao
	Jia	Chia
	Gu	Ku
	Zun	Tsun
	Fangyi	Fang-i
	Hu	Hu
	Lei	Lei
Dagger axe:	Ge	Ko
Thunder pattern:	Leiwen	Lei-wen
Dragon:	Kui	K'uei
Monster mask:	Taotie	T'ao-t'ieh

Jade

	Pinyin	Wade-Giles
Jade:	Yu	Yü
Kingfisher:	Feicuiyu	Fei-ts'ui-yü
Disc:	Bi	Pi
Disc:	Huan	Huan
Disc:	Yuan	Yüan
Tube:	Cong	Ts'ung
Sceptre:	Gui	Kuei
Disc:	Xuanji	Hsüan-chi
Grain pattern:	Guwen	Ku-wen
Belt hook:	Daigou	Tai-kou
Sceptre:	Ruyi	Ji-i

Ceramics

Pinyin	Wade-Giles
Yue	Yüeh
Xing	Hsing
Ding	Ting
Ru	Ju
Guan	Kuan
Longchuan	Lung-ch'uan
Ge	Ko
Cizhou	Tz'u-chou
Jian	Chien
Jizhou	Chi-chou
Jingdezhen	Ching-te-chen
Dehua	Te-hua
Yixing	I-hsing
Yingqing	Ying-ch'ing
Qingbai	Ch'ing-pai
Jihong	Chihung
Sancai	San-ts'ai
Wucai	Wu-ts'ai
Doucai	Tou-ts'ai
Anhua	An-hua
Fahua	Fa-hua
Nianzhi	Nien-chih
Nianzao	Nien-tsao
Yuzhi	Yu-chih
Guyeuxuan	Ku Yüen Hsüan
Guangdong	Kuang-tung

Japanese Pronunciation

a as in *far*
e as in *hay*
i as in *meet*
o as in *no*
u as in *flue*
g as in *go*
j as in *gin*

Example: *netsuke* sounds like *net skay* (When *u* precedes *k* or *g*, it becomes practically silent.)

About the Author

Sandra Andacht is the editor and publisher of the *Orientalia Journal*. Her column, "East Meets West: Exploring Orientalia," is a regular feature of the *Antique Trader Weekly*. Her "Orientalia Journal" column appears in a number of antiques publications throughout the U.S. She has written articles on various aspects of Oriental antiques and art for a number of other publications, including *Andon, Interior Design, Antiques and Collecting (Hobbies), Arts of Asia,* and *Antique Monthly.* Mrs. Andacht also contributes to the newsletter of the New England Appraisers' Association, and is a member of NEAA, Netsuke Kenkyukai, the International Chinese Snuff Bottle Society, Vereniging voor Japanese Kunst (Society for Japanese Arts and Crafts), and the Louis Comfort Tiffany Society (with regard to Tiffany's collection of Orientalia).

Mrs. Andacht's books include *Treasury of Satsuma* and *Satsuma: An Illustrated Guide;* she coauthored the *Wallace-Homestead Price Guide to Oriental Antiques* (first and second editions). In addition to her work with Orientalia, she is the resident antiques expert for "The Joe Franklin Show," as well as the author of *Joe Franklin's Show Biz Memorabilia.*

Mrs. Andacht is a dealer, lecturer, research consultant, and appraiser, and is called upon for her assessments by agencies such as the U.S. Customs Service. As a faculty member at both New York University and C. W. Post, she teaches Oriental Decorative Arts in the Appraisal Studies Programs. She also participates in various seminars conducted by New York University and C. W. Post.

Bibliography

Alcock, Sir Rutherford. *Art and Art Industries in Japan*. London, 1878.

Andacht, Sandra. *The Orientalia Journal Annual of Articles*. Little Neck, New York: Sandra Andacht Publishing, 1982.

——————. *Treasury of Satsuma*. Des Moines, Iowa: Wallace-Homestead Book Company, 1981.

Andacht, Sandra, Nancy Garthe, and Robert Mascarelli. *Wallace-Homestead Price Guide to Oriental Antiques*. 2d ed. Des Moines, Iowa: Wallace-Homestead Book Company, 1984.

Audsley, George. *Notes on Japanese Art*. London: H. Sotheran & Co., 1882.

Beurdeley, M. *Chinese Furniture*. New York: Kodansha International U.S.A., Ltd., 1979.

Bing, S. *Artistic Japan*. London: Marston, Searle, and Rivington, Ltd., 1889.

Blacker, J. F. *Chats On Oriental China*. London: T. Fisher Unwin, 1919.

Bowes, James L. *Notes on Shippo*. London: H. Sotheran & Co., 1885.

Brinkley, Capt. F. *Japan: Its History, Arts, and Literature*. 9 vols. Boston: J. P. Millet, 1901.

——————. *China: Its History, Arts, and Literature*. vols. 10–12. Boston: J. P. Millet, 1899.

Bushell, Raymond. *Collectors' Netsuke*. Salem, Massachusetts: John Weatherhill, Inc.

——————. *Netsuke: Familiar and Unfamiliar*. Salem, Massachusetts: John Weatherhill, Inc.

——————. *The Inro Handbook*. Salem, Massachusetts: John Weatherhill, Inc.

Ceramic Art Series. New York: Kodansha International U.S.A., Ltd.

Chu, Grace. *The Collector's Book of Jade*. New York: Crown Publishers, Inc., 1978.

——————. *Oriental Antiques and Collectibles*. New York: Crown Publishers, Inc., 1973.

——————. *Oriental Cloisonné and Other Enamels*. New York: Crown Publishers, Inc., 1975.

Chung, Young. *Art of Oriental Embroidery*. New York: Charles Scribner's Sons, 1979.

Coben and Ferster. *Cloisonné*. Salem, Massachusetts: John Weatherhill, Inc.

De Vasselot, J. J. Marquet, and M. J. Ballot. *La Céramique Chinoise*. Paris: Albert Morouce, 1922.

Dick, Stewart. *Arts and Crafts of Old Japan*. Chicago, 1905.

Eastham, B. C. *Chinese Art Ivory*. Ann Arbor: Ars Ceramica, 1976.

Feddersen, Martin. *Japanese Decorative Art*. London, 1962.

Frasche, D. F. *Southeast Asian Ceramics*. Greenwich, Connecticut: Asia House Gallery, 1976.

Fukui, Kikusaburo. *Japanese Ceramic Art*. Tokyo, 1926.

Garner, Harry. *Chinese and Japanese Enamels*. Rutland, Vermont: Charles E. Tuttle Co., Inc., 1962.

Heinken, Ty. *Tansu*. Salem, Massachusetts: John Weatherhill, Inc., 1981.

Hobson, R. L. *Chinese Pottery and Porcelain*. New York: Dover Publications, Inc., 1976.

Jenyns, S. *Later Chinese Porcelain*. New York, 1965.

Kates. *Chinese Household Furniture*. New York: Dover Publications, Inc., 1962.

Laufer, B. *Ivory in China*. Chicago: Westwood Press, 1925.

—————. *Jade: A Study in Chinese Archaeology and Religion*. Chicago, 1912.

Macintosh, Duncan. *Chinese Blue and White*. North Pomfret, Vermont: David and Charles, Inc., 1977.

Michener, James. *The Floating World*. New York, 1954.

—————. *The Modern Japanese Print*. Rutland, Vermont: Charles E. Tuttle Co., Inc., 1968.

Miller, Roy. *Japanese Ceramics*. Rutland, Vermont: Charles E. Tuttle Co., Inc., 1960.

Morse, Edward. *Japanese Homes and Their Surroundings*. New York: Dover Publications, Inc., 1961.

Munsterberg, Hugo. *The Ceramic Art of Japan*. Rutland, Vermont: Charles E. Tuttle Co., Inc., 1964.

—————. *A Short History of Chinese Art*. East Lansing, Michigan: Michigan State University Press, 1949.

National Palace Museum. *Chinese Cultural Art Treasures*. National Palace Museum Series. Taipei, 1969.

Pirazzoli-Serstevens, M. *The Han Dynasty*. New York: Rizzoli International Publications, Inc., 1982.

Rowland, Benjamin. *The Art of Central Asia*. New York: Crown Publishers, Inc., 1974.

Sato, Masahiko. *Chinese Ceramics*. Salem, Massachusetts: John Weatherhill, Inc., 1981.

Silcock, A. *Introduction to Chinese Art*. London, 1936.

Scott, Hugh. *The Golden Age of Chinese Art*. Rutland, Vermont: Charles E. Tuttle Co., Inc., 1966.

Stevens, Bob. *Collector's Book of Snuff Bottles*. Salem, Massachusetts: John Weatherhill, Inc., 1976.

Thiel, Albert William R. *Chinese Pottery and Stoneware*. New York, 1953.

Ueda, Reikichi. *The Netsuke Handbook*. Rutland, Vermont: Charles E. Tuttle Co., Inc., 1979.

Watson, William. *Tang and Liao Ceramics*. New York: Rizzoli International Publications, Inc., 1984.

Waley, Arthur. *An Introduction to the Study of Chinese Painting*. New York, 1923.

Glossary

Note: For the most part, this list consists of Japanese terms used frequently in the text; the other types of Oriental objects mentioned are usually given English descriptions.

Bakemono. A monster, goblin, or other such creature, in human form.

Baku. A mythological beast with an elephant's trunk. Baku devours bad dreams.

Bijin. Beautiful girl.

Biscuit. Clay which was fired, but not glazed.

Biwa. A stringed musical instrument.

Cha no yu. The tea ceremony.

Cha wan. Traditional tea bowl.

Conventional. Traditional-style motif.

Diaper. A repetitive design.

Enamel. Usually an opaque composition applied to the surface of an object, and which is fused to the object by firing.

Fundame. A matte gold background produced in lacquer by using fine gold powder.

Gama Sennin. A Sennin associated with a toad.

Go. An intricate board game.

Gofun. Powdered oyster shell.

Guri. A lacquer technique using colored lacquers and carving at an angle to reveal the various hues.

Hibachi. A wooden, metal or ceramic charcoal brazier.

Hiramakie. Designs in low relief on lacquer.

Ishime. A lacquer technique imitating the texture of stone.

Ittobori. Carving style employing single knife-cuts to create angular effects.

Kakemono. A hanging scroll.

Kakihan. A distinctive mark that identifies a specific artist.

Kannon/Kuan Yin. The deity of mercy.

Karako. Chinese children depicted in Japanese art.

Kiku. Chrysanthemum. Note that the Imperial Kiku has 16 petals.

Kinji. A densely sprinkled gold ground on lacquer, characterized by a shiny finish.

Kinmakie. Gold-decorated lacquer.

Kogo. A box in which incense is stored.

Koro. An incense burner (censer).

Mingei. Folk art.

Minogame. A turtle with a long tail.

Namban. Describes an object which shows European influence.

Nashiji. A pear-finish ground.

Oni. A creature with an impish face, two horns, and usually dressed in a loin cloth.

Rakan (*or* Lohan). The disciples of Buddha.

Ruyi. A sceptre or staff.

Sennin. Taoist mountain hermit or ascetic.

Shibayama. A very decorative form of inlay work featuring mother-of-pearl in some combination with ivory, coral, and/or jade.

Shishi. Lion dogs of Chinese origin.

Somada. A lacquer technique employing inlays of shell.

Takamakie. Raised lacquer and sprinkled metallic powder design in high relief.

Index

Super LOTTO PLUS

WED.'S 2/14 SUPERLOTTO PLUS
JACKPOT IS WORTH $20 MILLION

QUICK PICK

						MEGA
A	03	23	25	39	47	13
B	14	20	36	37	46	21
C	20	21	30	32	45	17
D	15	22	31	34	43	14
E	03	04	18	21	25	26
F	03	05	11	24	41	05
G	15	27	29	33	40	19
H	01	05	09	26	40	16
I	01	09	14	42	45	15
J	11	25	30	31	42	20

CASH VALUE
WED FEB14 01

Xtra Reward

26001053
26001054
26001055

WED FEB14 01

015477 $ 10.00
R135822 045-05073183-13362